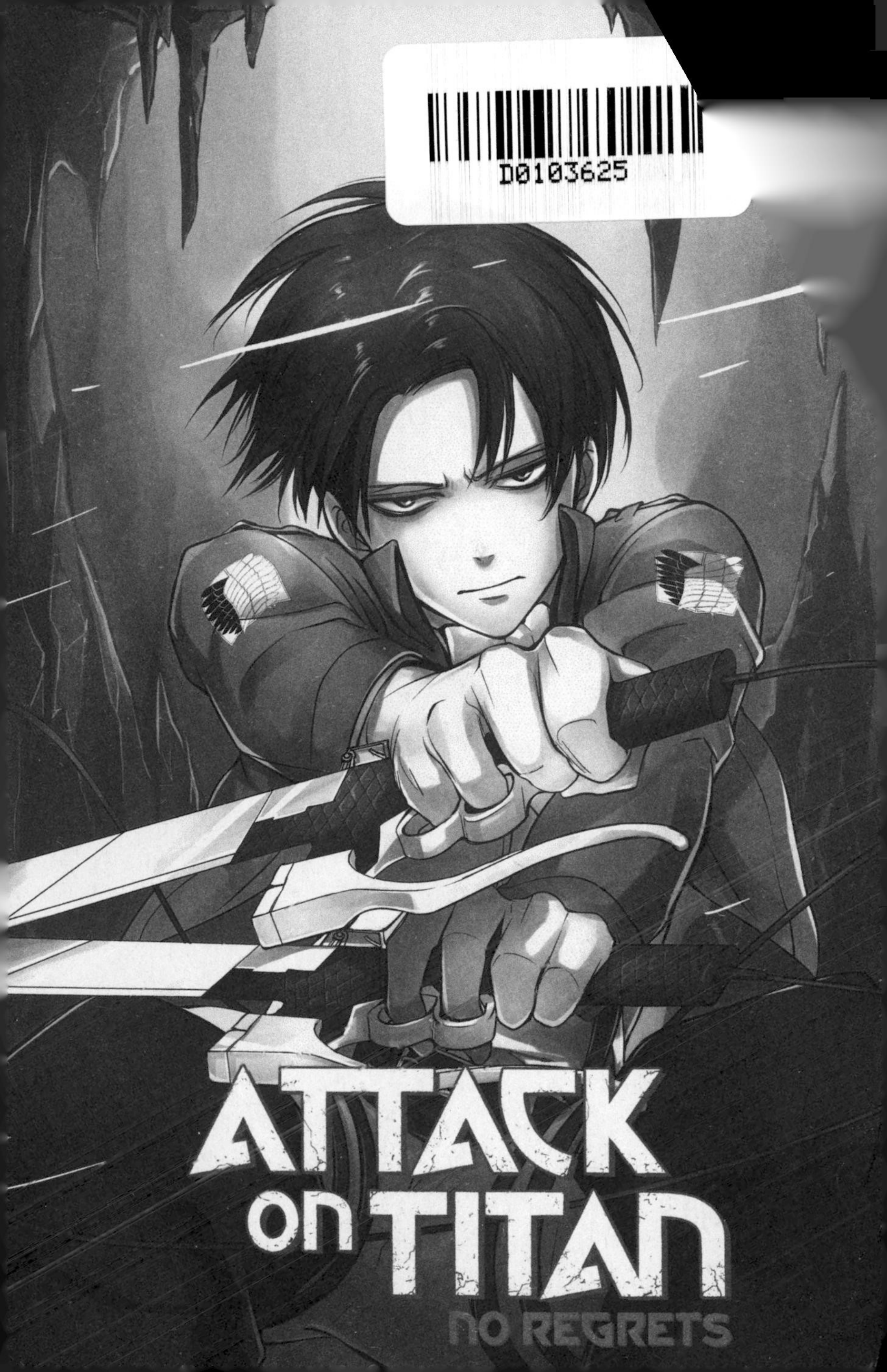
ATTACK
on TITAN
NO REGRETS

Table of Contents

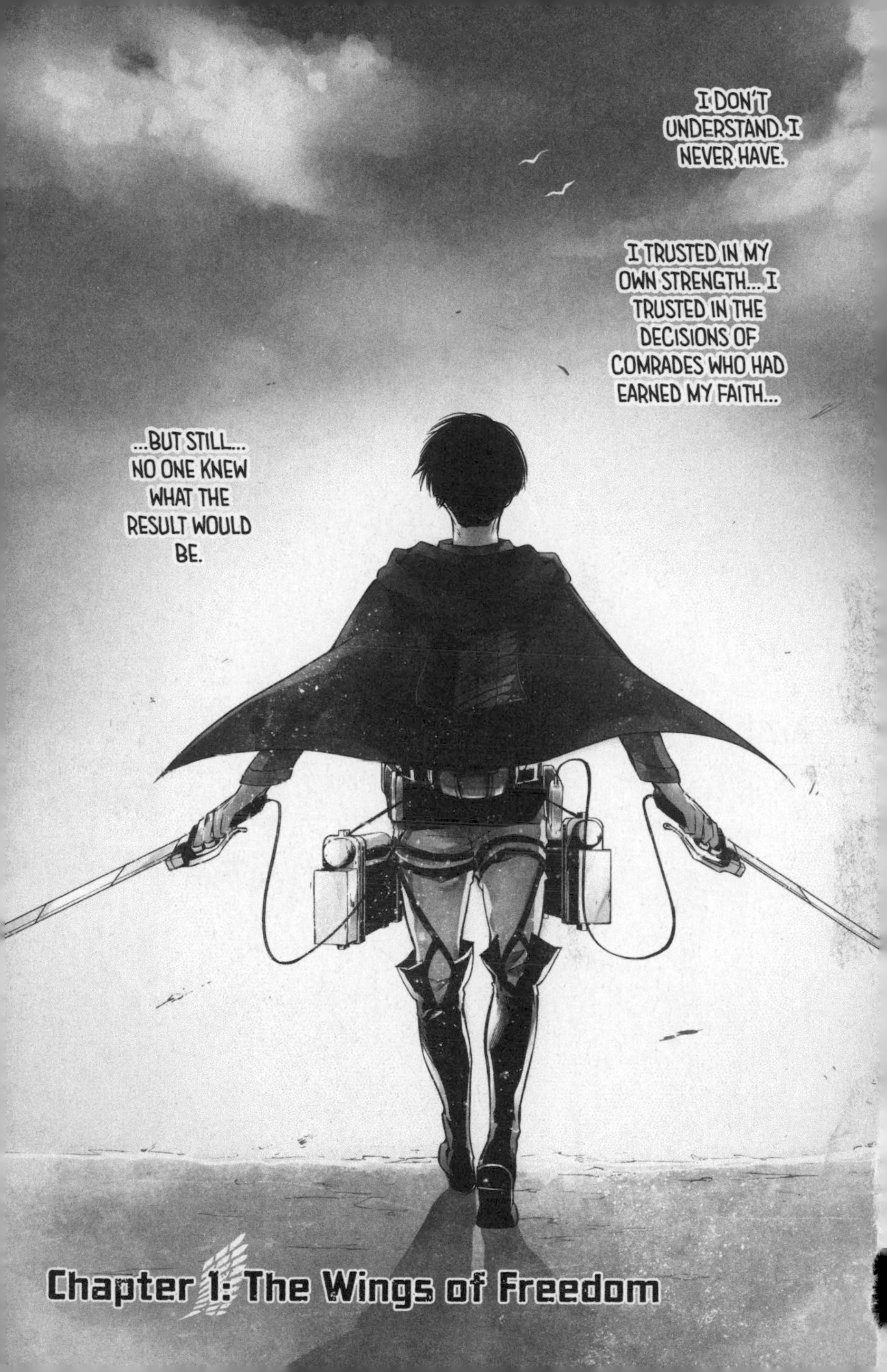
I DON'T UNDERSTAND. I NEVER HAVE.
I TRUSTED IN MY OWN STRENGTH... I TRUSTED IN THE DECISIONS OF COMRADES WHO HAD EARNED MY FAITH...
...BUT STILL... NO ONE KNEW WHAT THE RESULT WOULD BE.

Chapter 1: The Wings of Freedom

Chapter 1: The Wings of Freedom

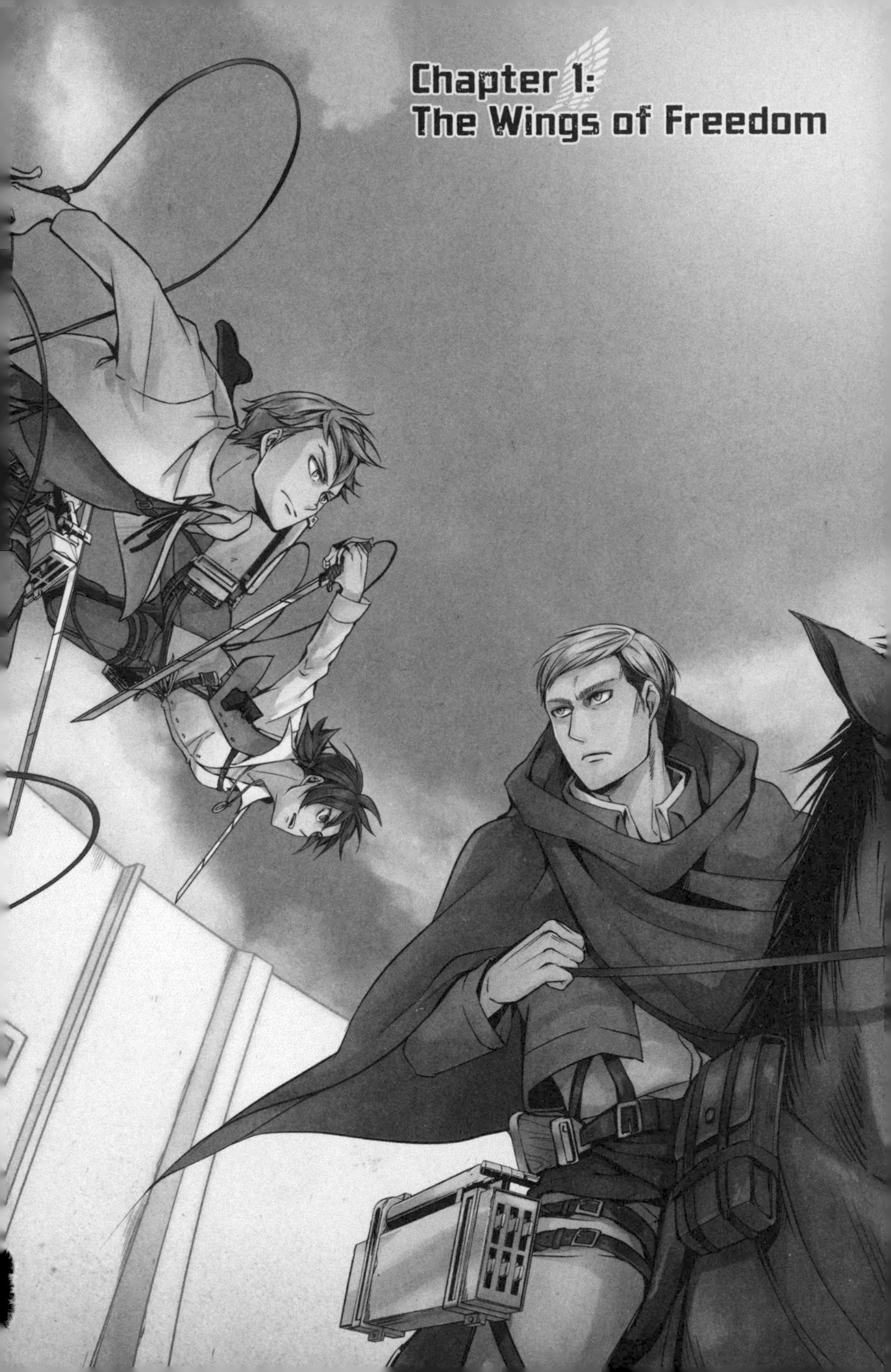

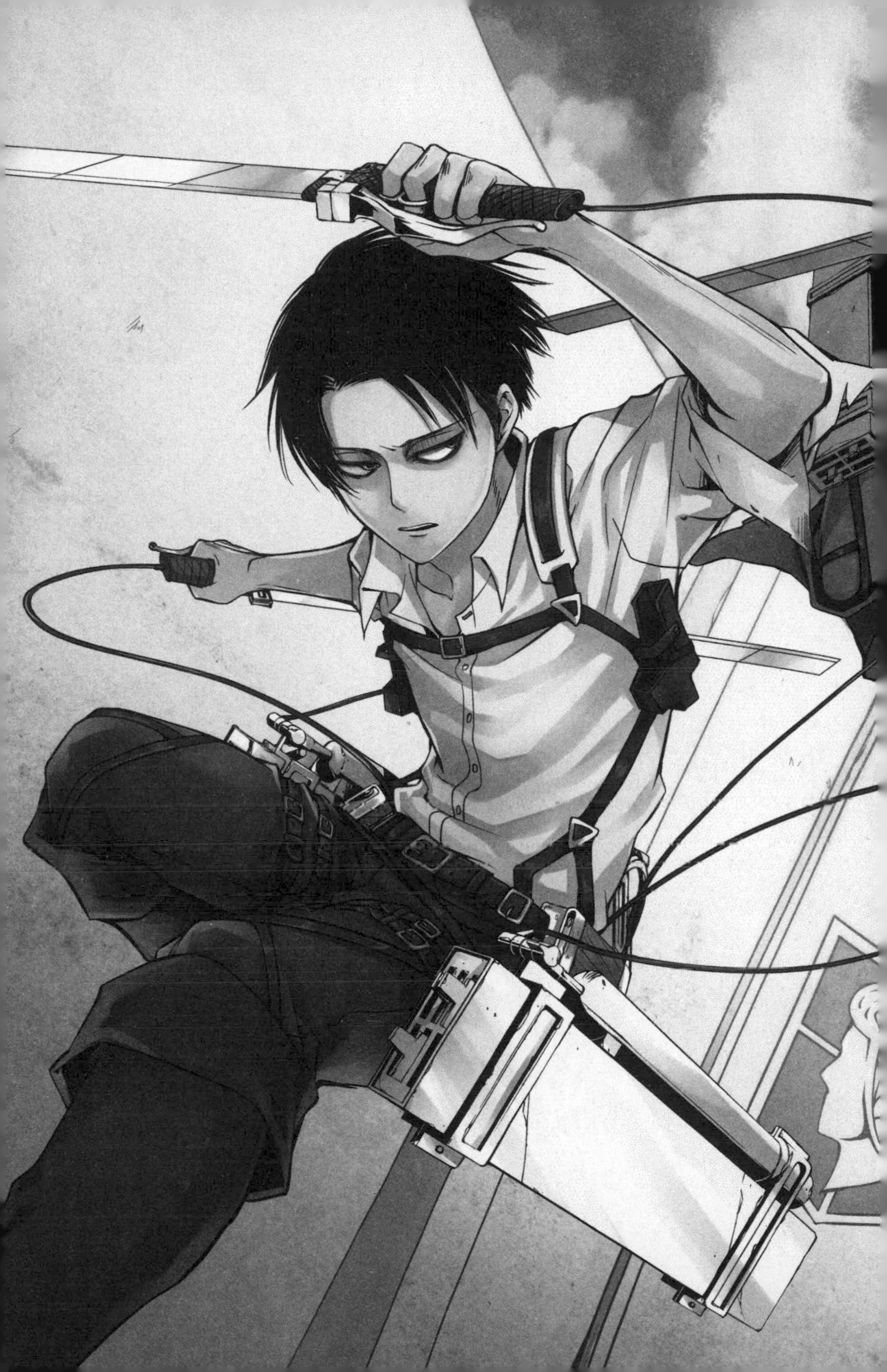

ATTACK on TITAN
NO REGRETS

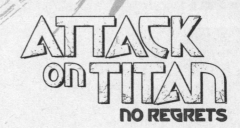

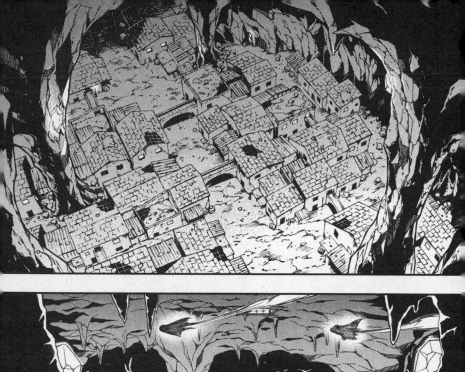

HEY! WE'RE BEING FOLLOWED!!

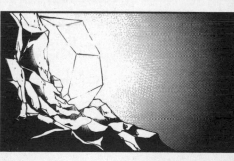

TAK

WHUK!!

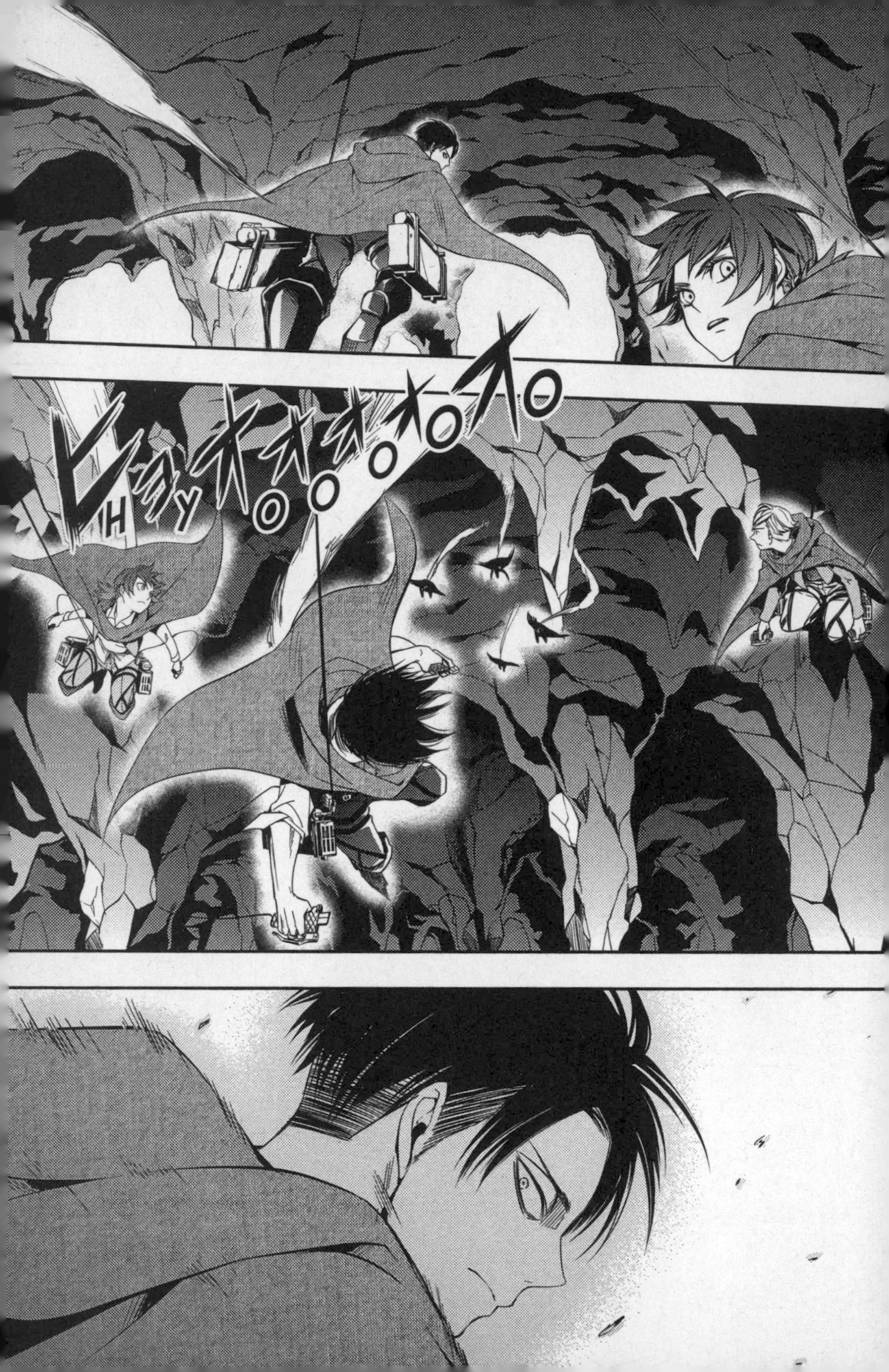
ヒョオオオオオ
HYOOOOO

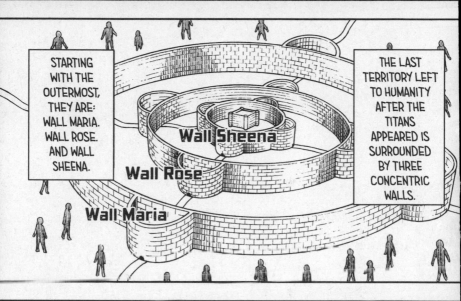

844
THE LAST TERRITORY LEFT TO HUMANITY AFTER THE TITANS APPEARED IS SURROUNDED BY THREE CONCENTRIC WALLS.
STARTING WITH THE OUTERMOST, THEY ARE: WALL MARIA. WALL ROSE. AND WALL SHEENA.
Wall Sheena
Wall Rose
Wall Maria
IN THE MOST PROTECTED LOCATION AT THE CENTER OF THE THREE WALLS IS THE ROYAL CAPITAL.
THIS IS THE CENTER OF ALL HUMAN ACTIVITY, INCLUDING THE GOVERNMENT AND THE ECONOMY.

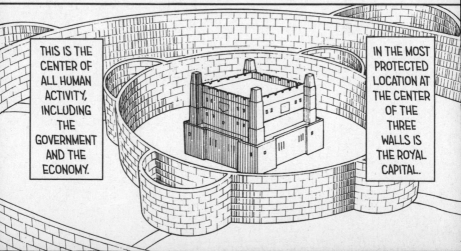

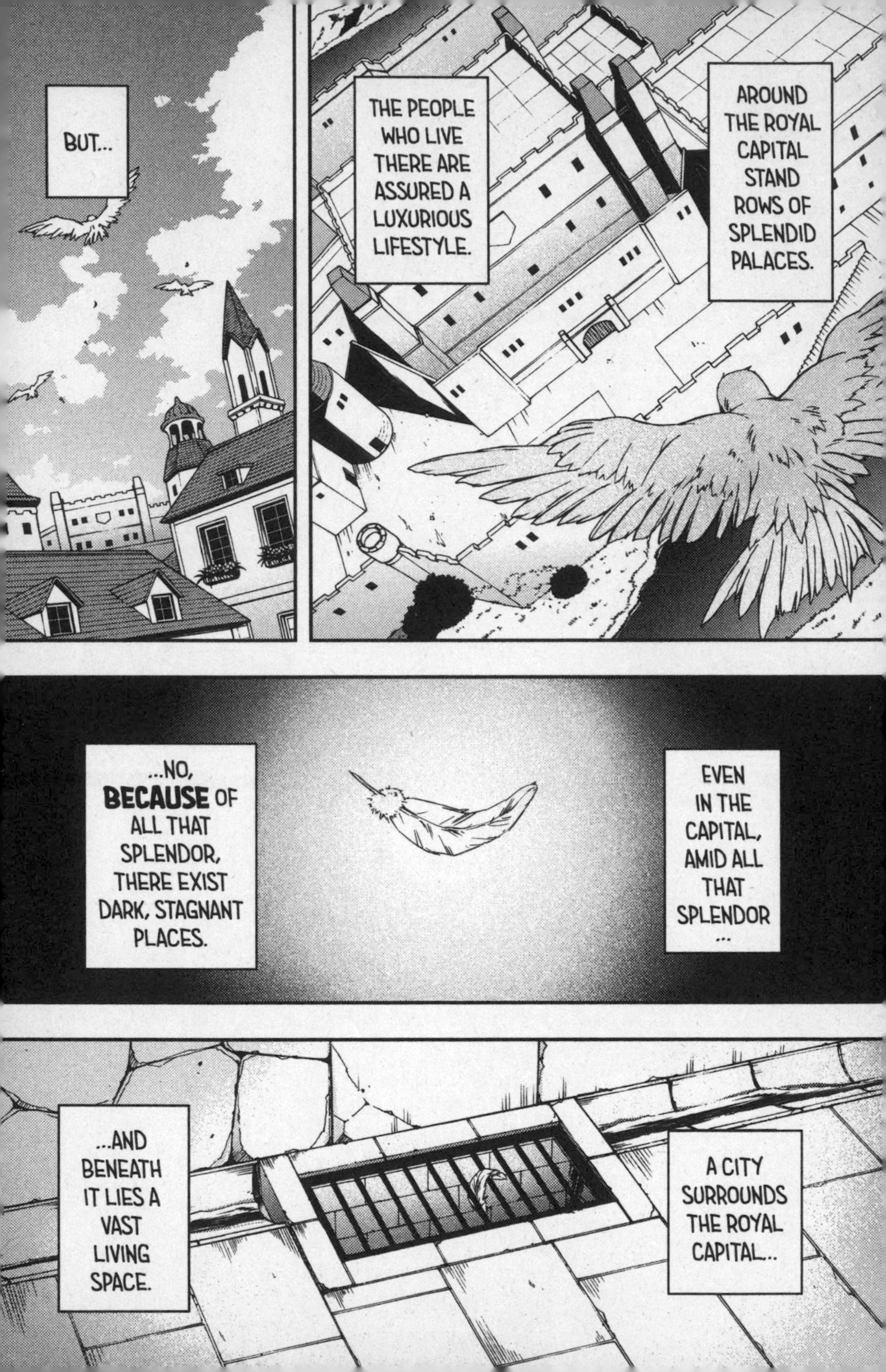
AROUND THE ROYAL CAPITAL STAND ROWS OF SPLENDID PALACES.
THE PEOPLE WHO LIVE THERE ARE ASSURED A LUXURIOUS LIFESTYLE.
BUT...
EVEN IN THE CAPITAL, AMID ALL THAT SPLENDOR...
...NO, **BECAUSE** OF ALL THAT SPLENDOR, THERE EXIST DARK, STAGNANT PLACES.
A CITY SURROUNDS THE ROYAL CAPITAL...
...AND BENEATH IT LIES A VAST LIVING SPACE.

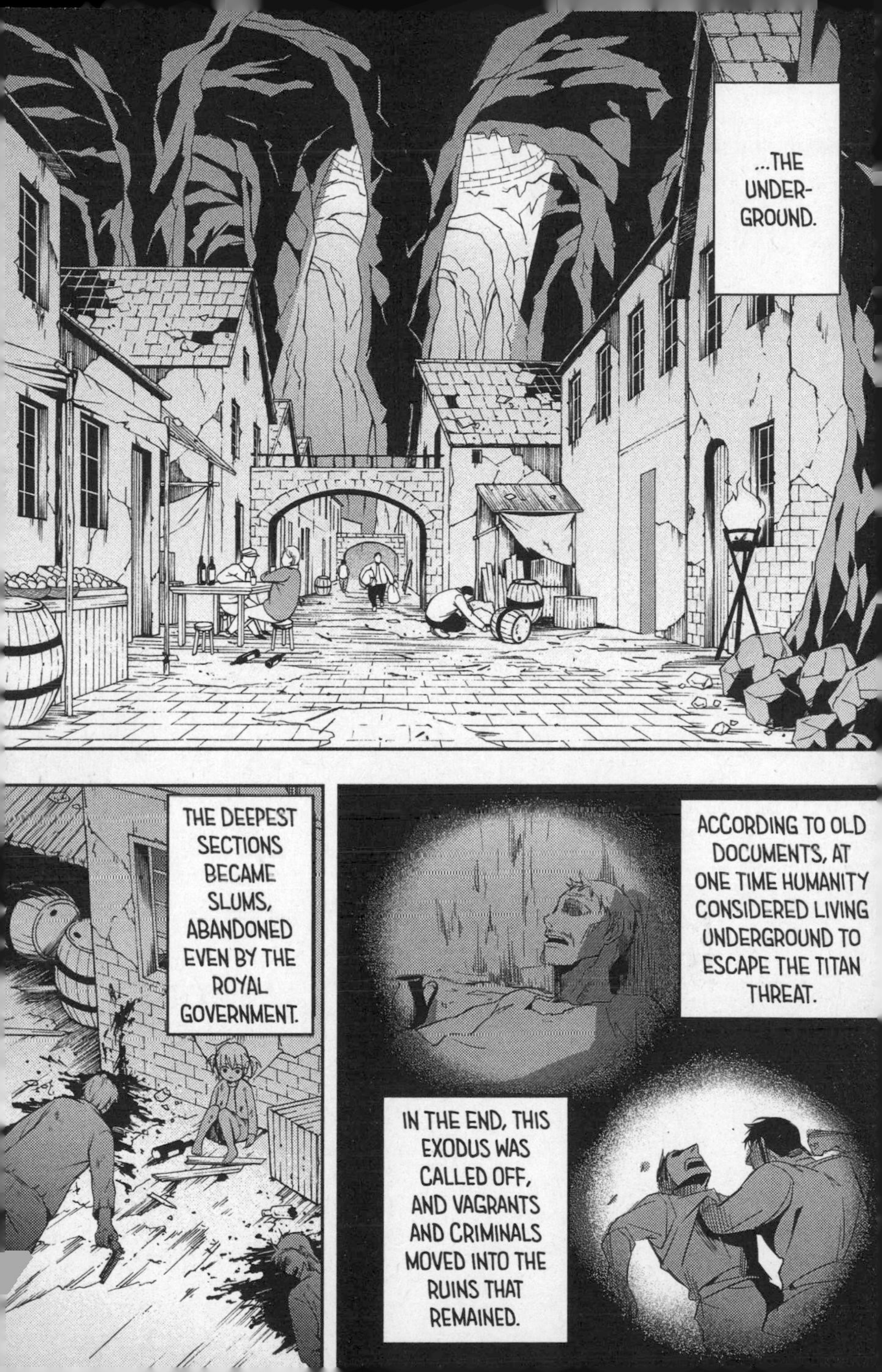
...THE UNDER-GROUND.
ACCORDING TO OLD DOCUMENTS, AT ONE TIME HUMANITY CONSIDERED LIVING UNDERGROUND TO ESCAPE THE TITAN THREAT.
IN THE END, THIS EXODUS WAS CALLED OFF, AND VAGRANTS AND CRIMINALS MOVED INTO THE RUINS THAT REMAINED.
THE DEEPEST SECTIONS BECAME SLUMS, ABANDONED EVEN BY THE ROYAL GOVERNMENT.

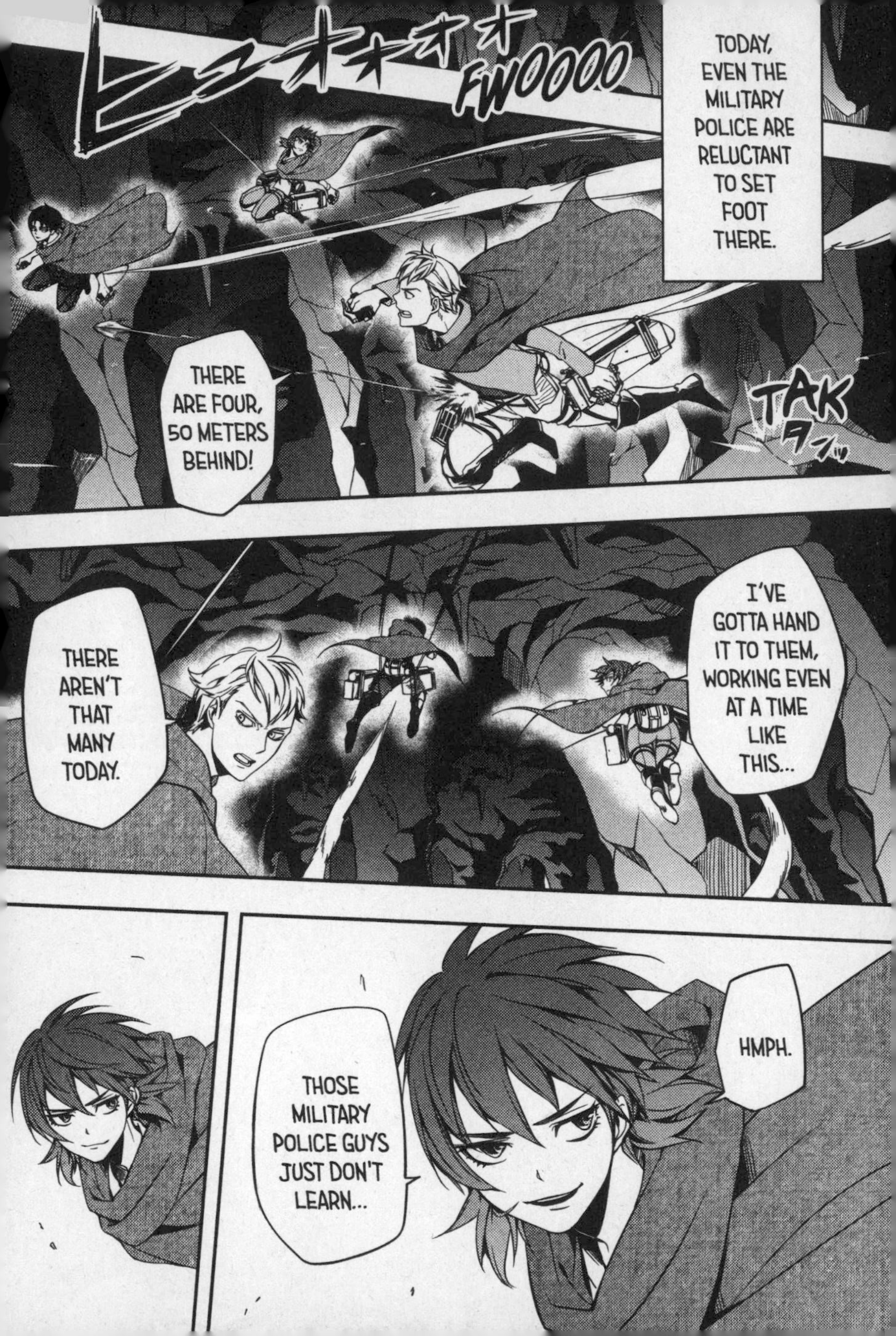
TODAY, EVEN THE MILITARY POLICE ARE RELUCTANT TO SET FOOT THERE.
ヒュオオオオ FWOOOO
TAK タッ
THERE ARE FOUR, 50 METERS BEHIND!
I'VE GOTTA HAND IT TO THEM, WORKING EVEN AT A TIME LIKE THIS...
THERE AREN'T THAT MANY TODAY.
HMPH.
THOSE MILITARY POLICE GUYS JUST DON'T LEARN...

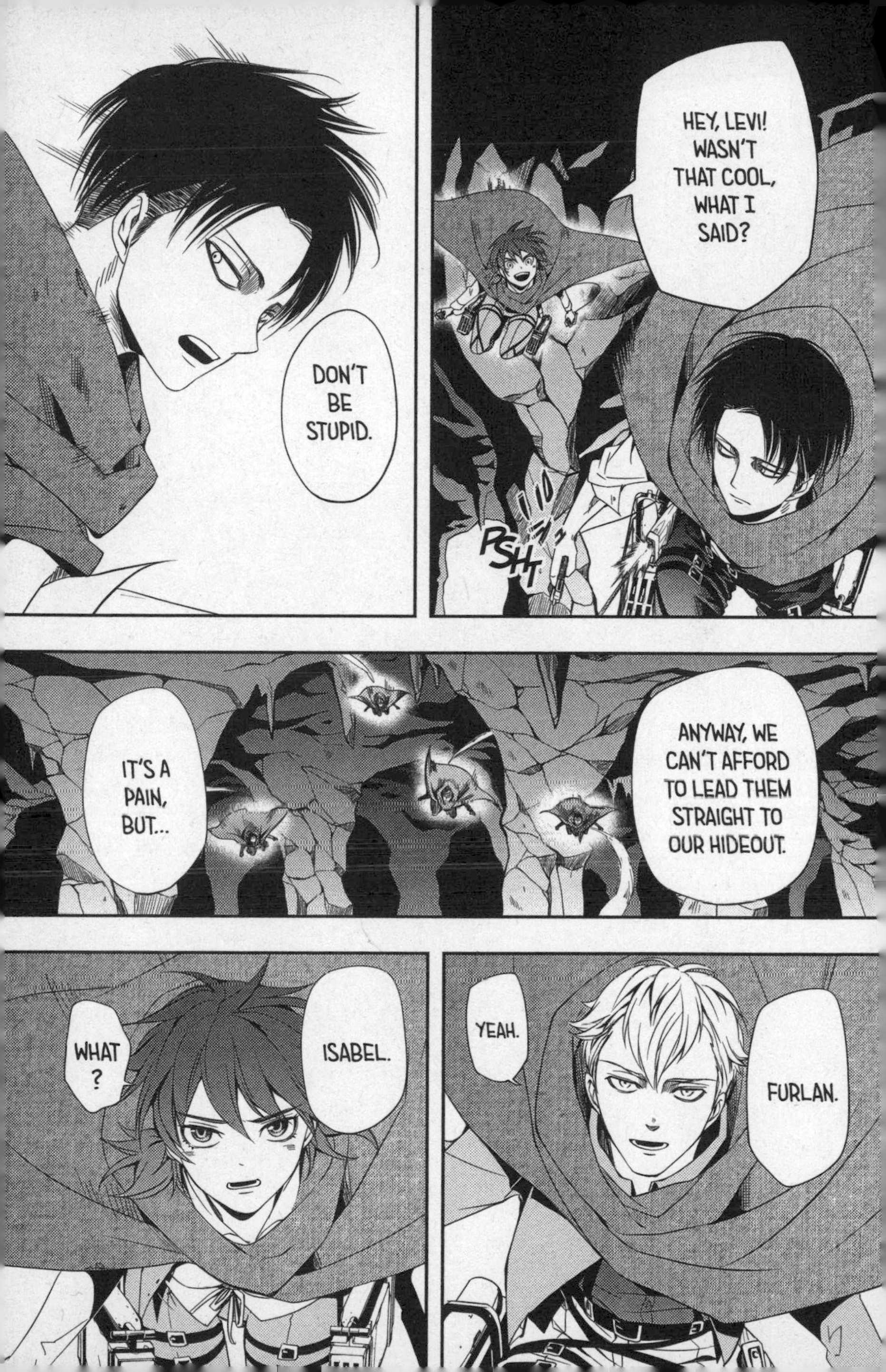
HEY, LEVI! WASN'T THAT COOL, WHAT I SAID?
PSHT
DON'T BE STUPID.
ANYWAY, WE CAN'T AFFORD TO LEAD THEM STRAIGHT TO OUR HIDEOUT.
IT'S A PAIN, BUT...
FURLAN.
YEAH.
ISABEL.
WHAT?

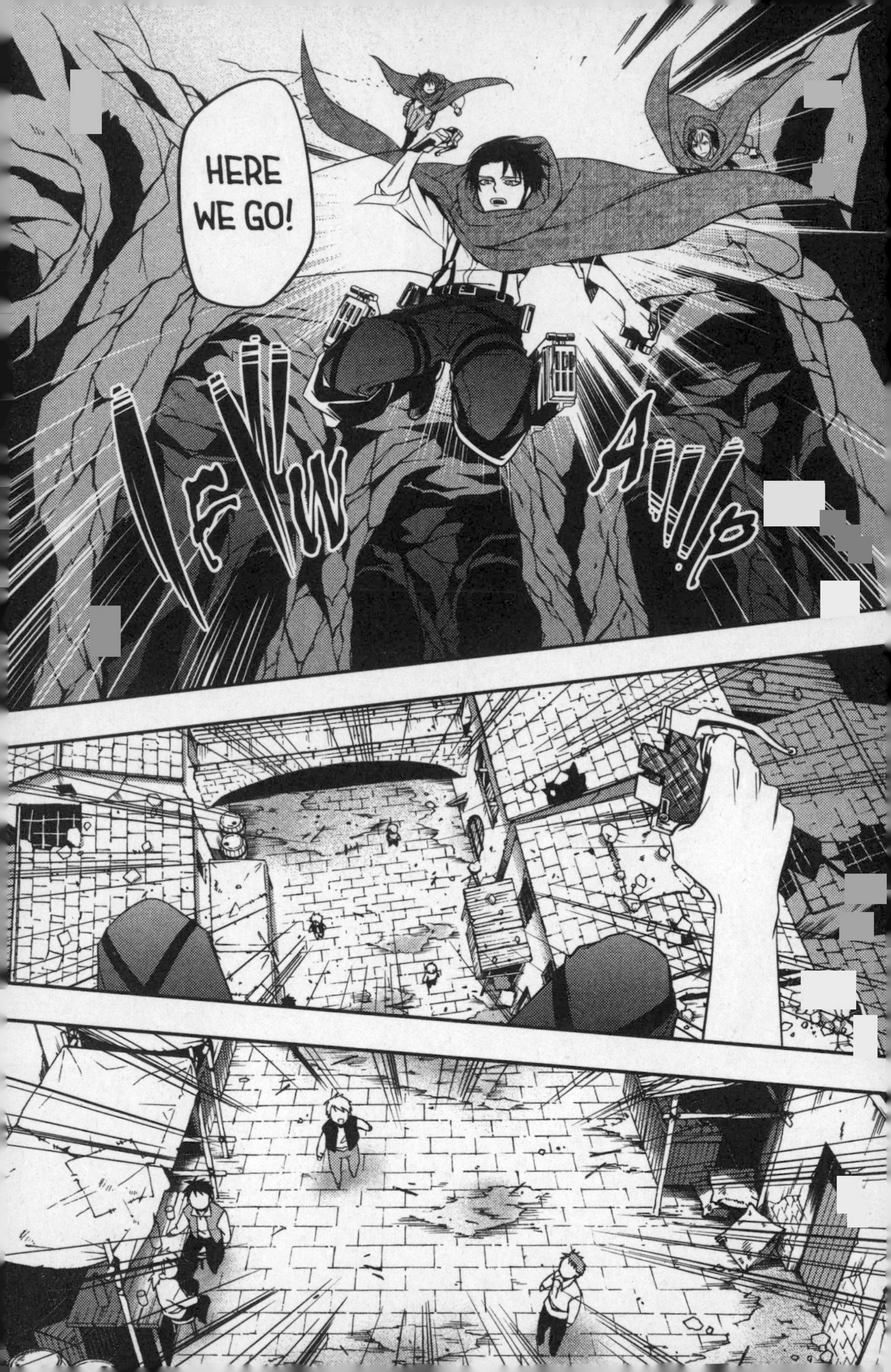
HERE WE GO!

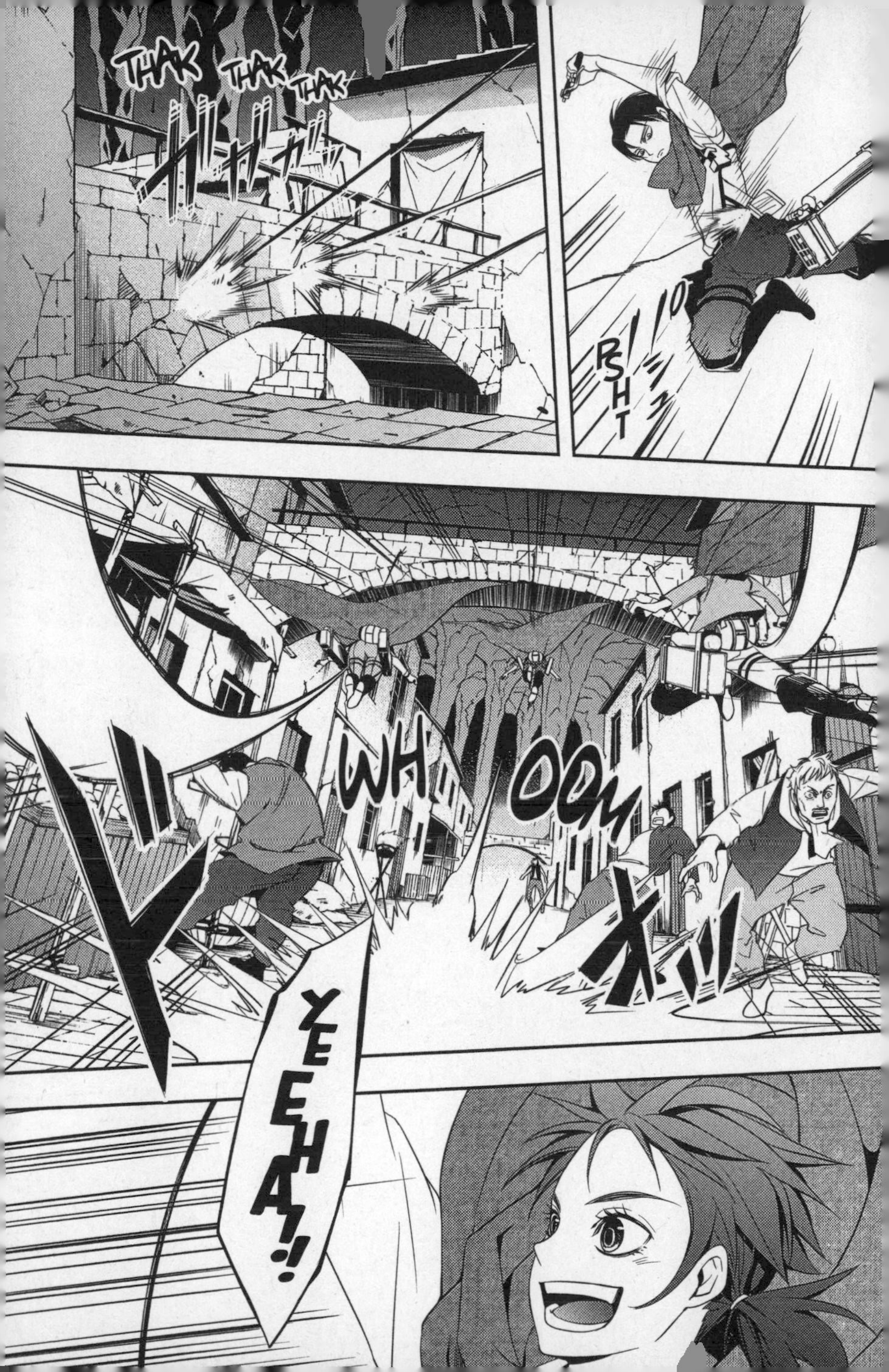
PSHT
THAK THAK THAK
WHOOOM
YEEHA!!

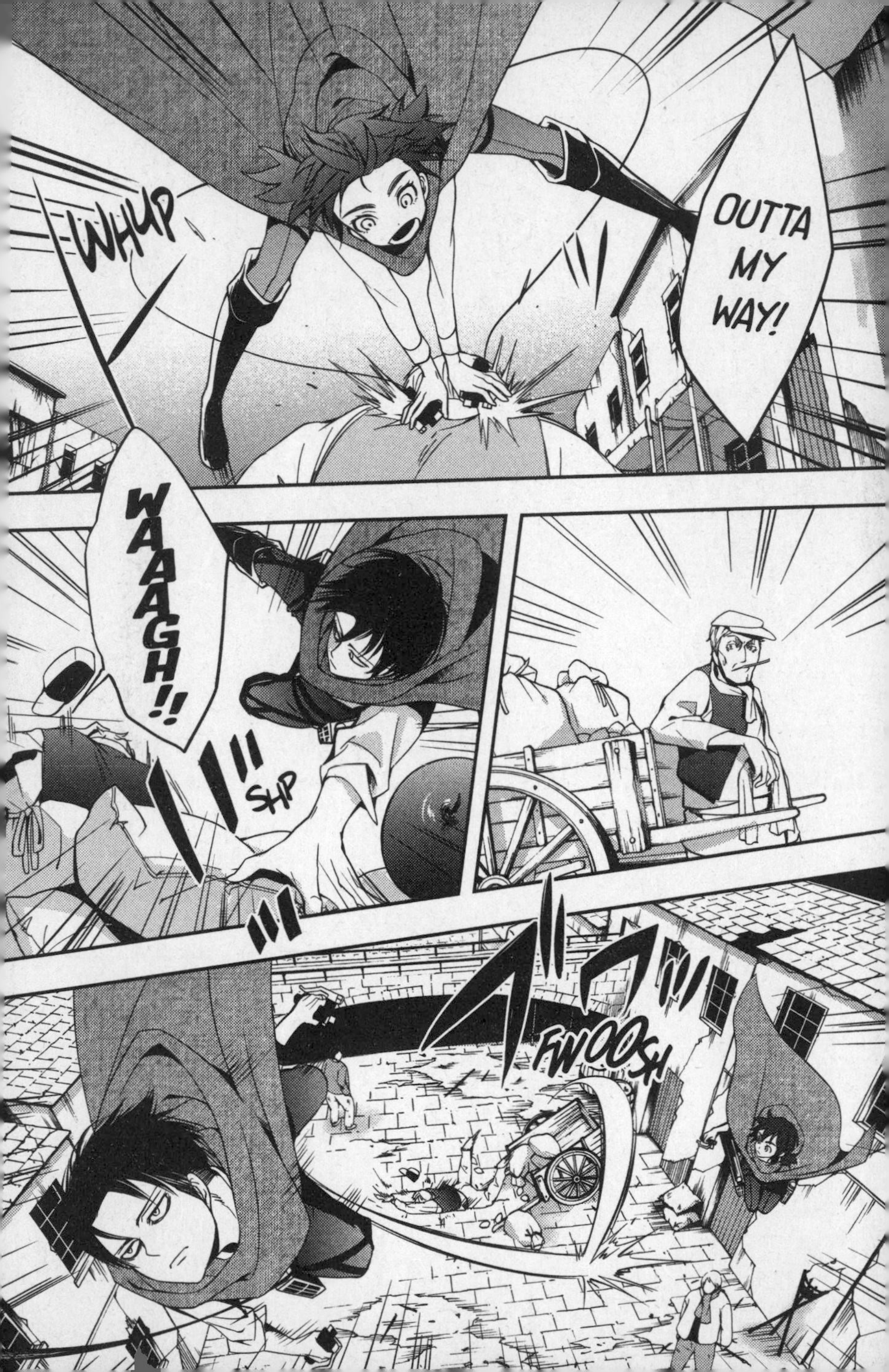
OUTTA MY WAY!
WHUP
WAAAGH!!
SHP
FWOOSH

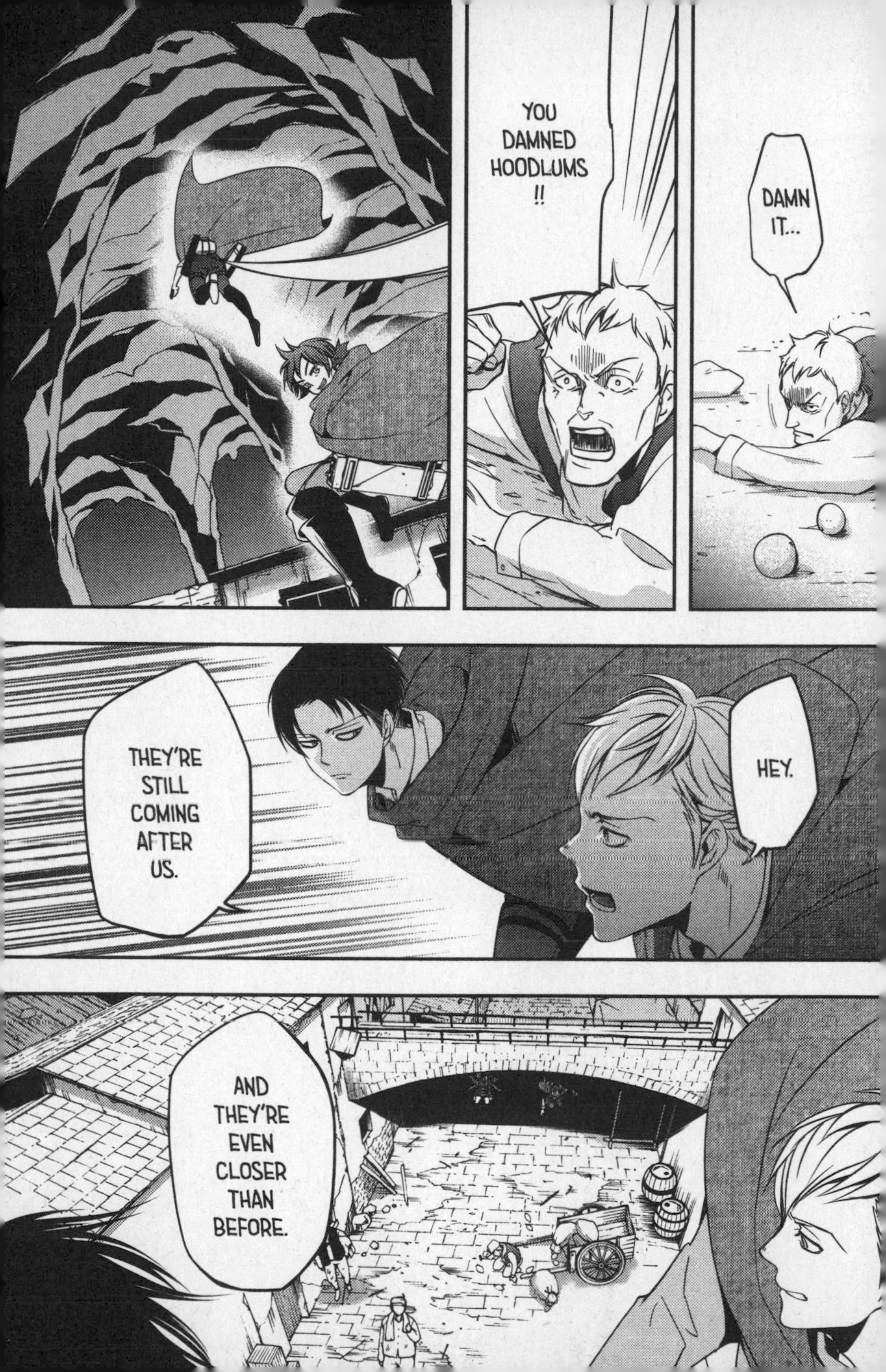
DAMN IT...
YOU DAMNED HOODLUMS !!
HEY.
THEY'RE STILL COMING AFTER US.
AND THEY'RE EVEN CLOSER THAN BEFORE.

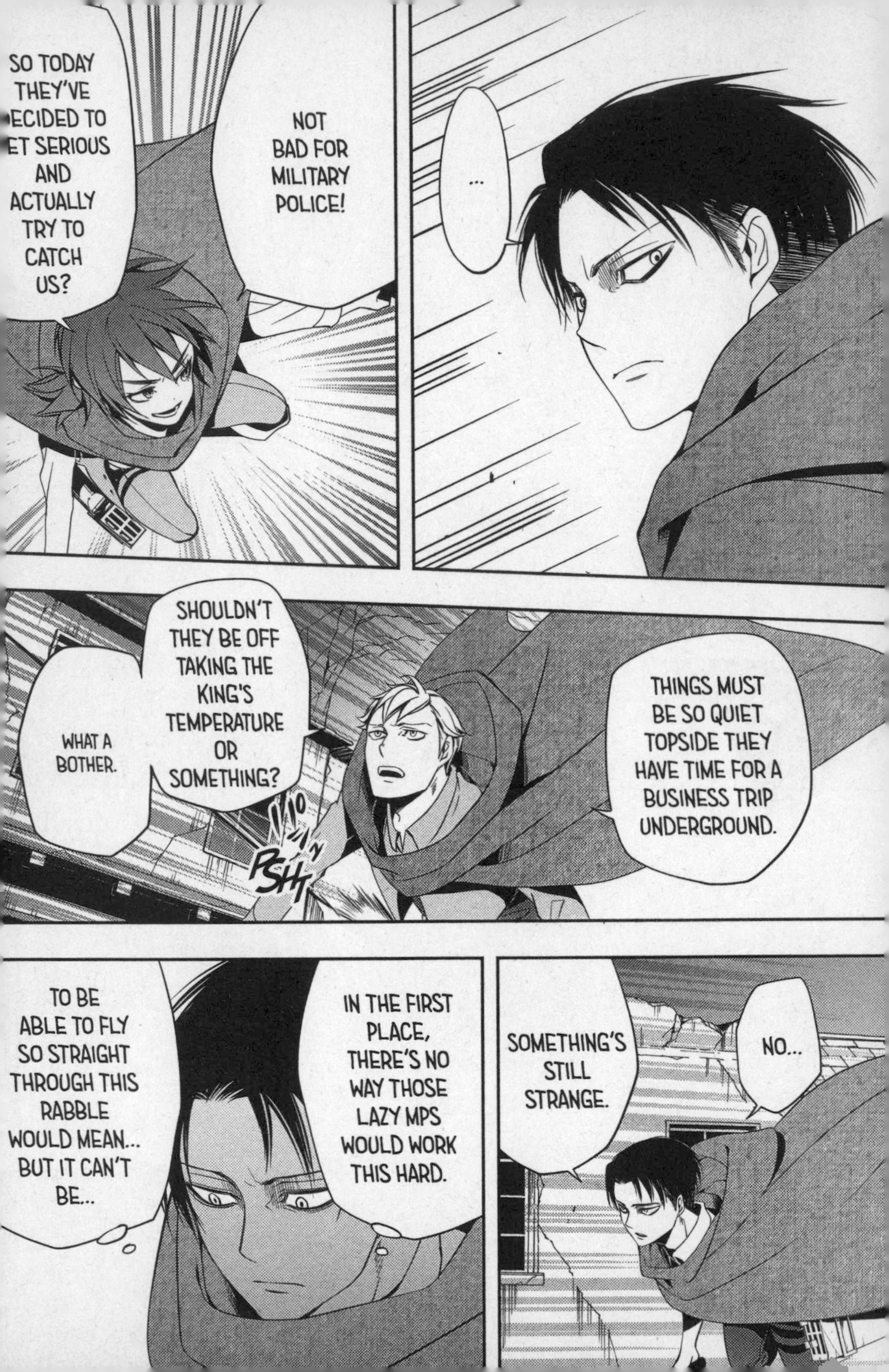
...
NOT BAD FOR MILITARY POLICE!
SO TODAY THEY'VE ECIDED TO ET SERIOUS AND ACTUALLY TRY TO CATCH US?
THINGS MUST BE SO QUIET TOPSIDE THEY HAVE TIME FOR A BUSINESS TRIP UNDERGROUND.
SHOULDN'T THEY BE OFF TAKING THE KING'S TEMPERATURE OR SOMETHING?
WHAT A BOTHER.
PSHH
NO...
SOMETHING'S STILL STRANGE.
IN THE FIRST PLACE, THERE'S NO WAY THOSE LAZY MPS WOULD WORK THIS HARD.
TO BE ABLE TO FLY SO STRAIGHT THROUGH THIS RABBLE WOULD MEAN... BUT IT CAN'T BE...

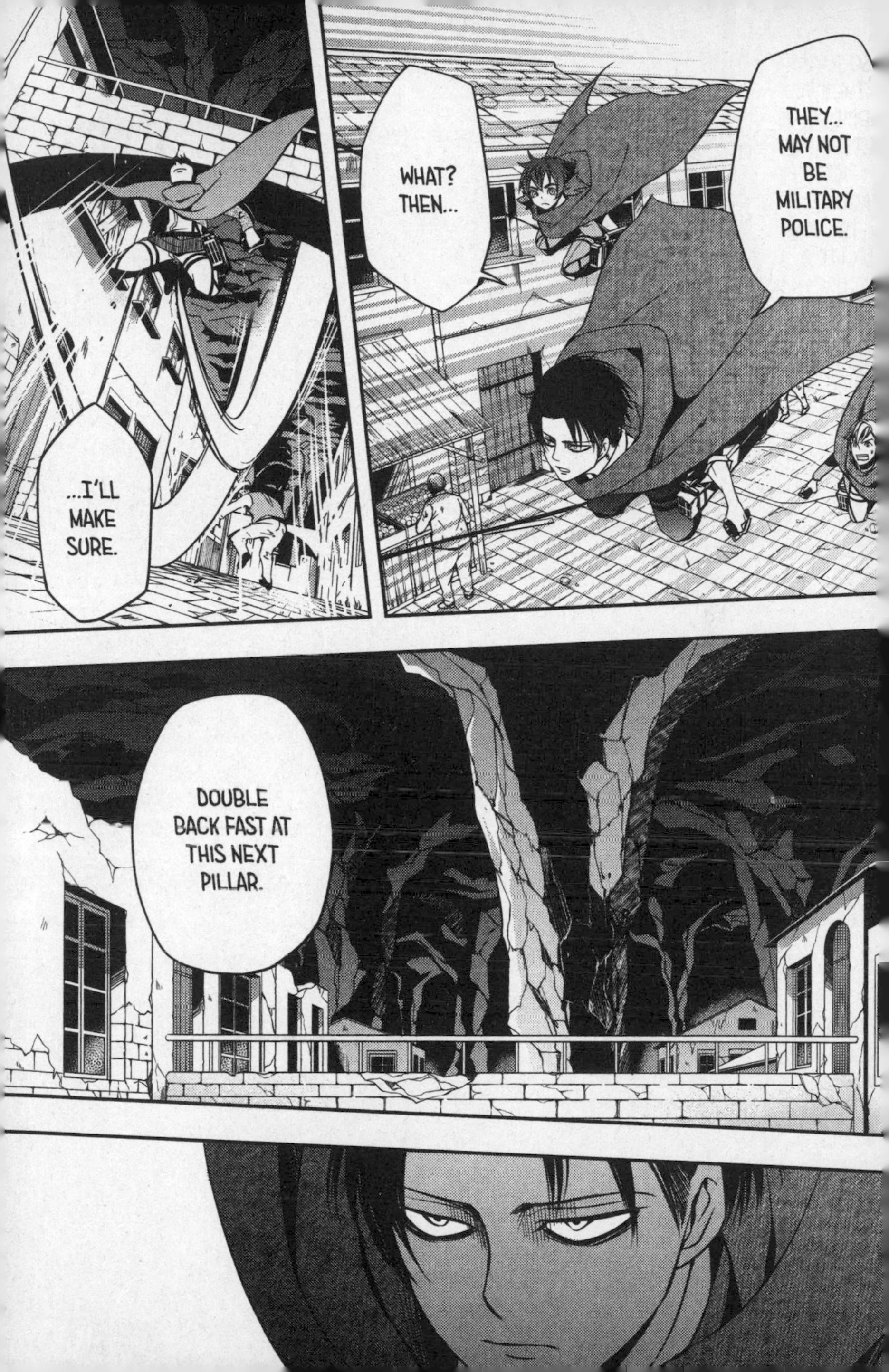
THEY... MAY NOT BE MILITARY POLICE.
WHAT? THEN...
...I'LL MAKE SURE.
DOUBLE BACK FAST AT THIS NEXT PILLAR.

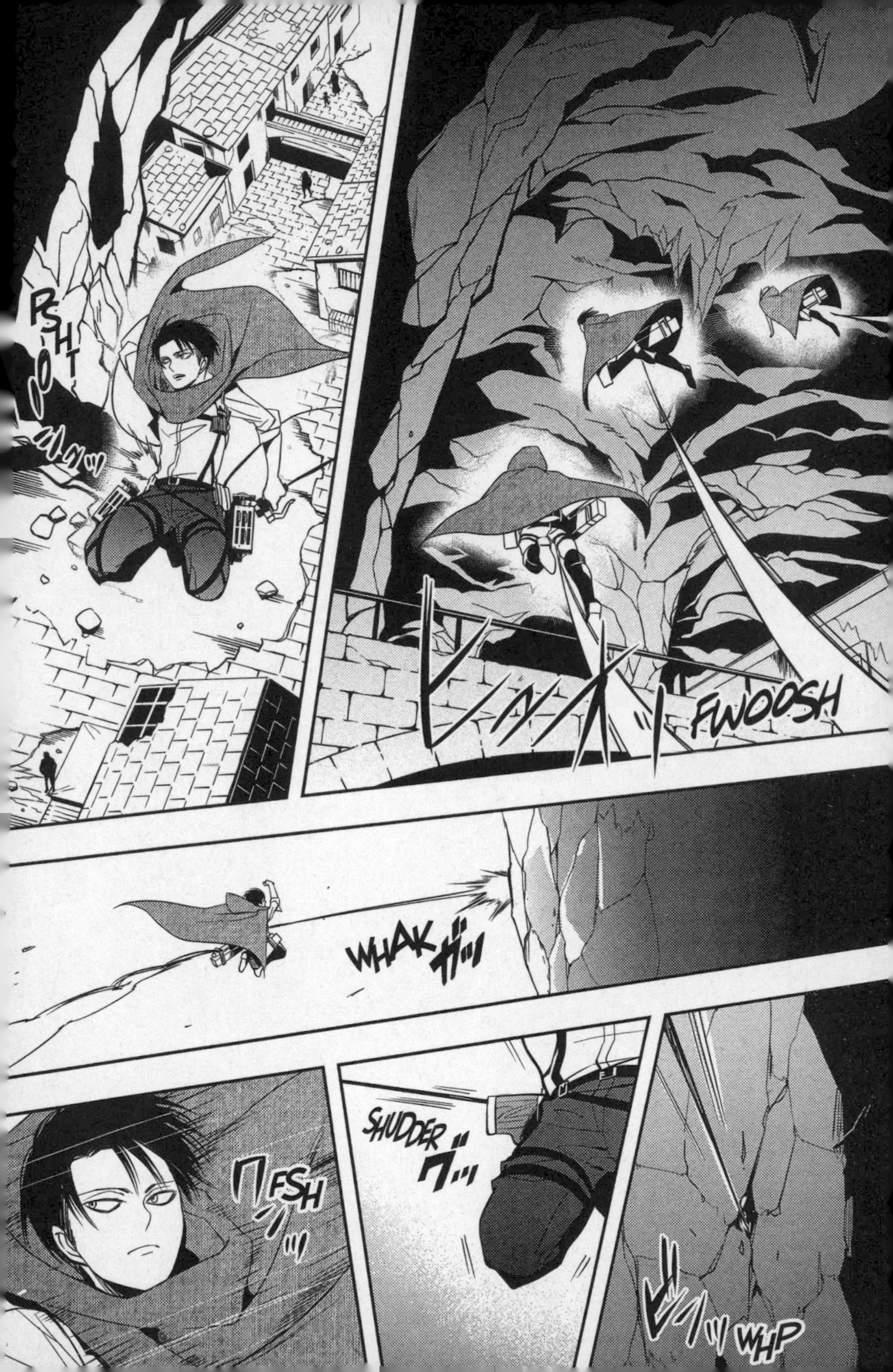
FWOOSH
PSHT
WHAK
WHP
SHUDDER
FSH

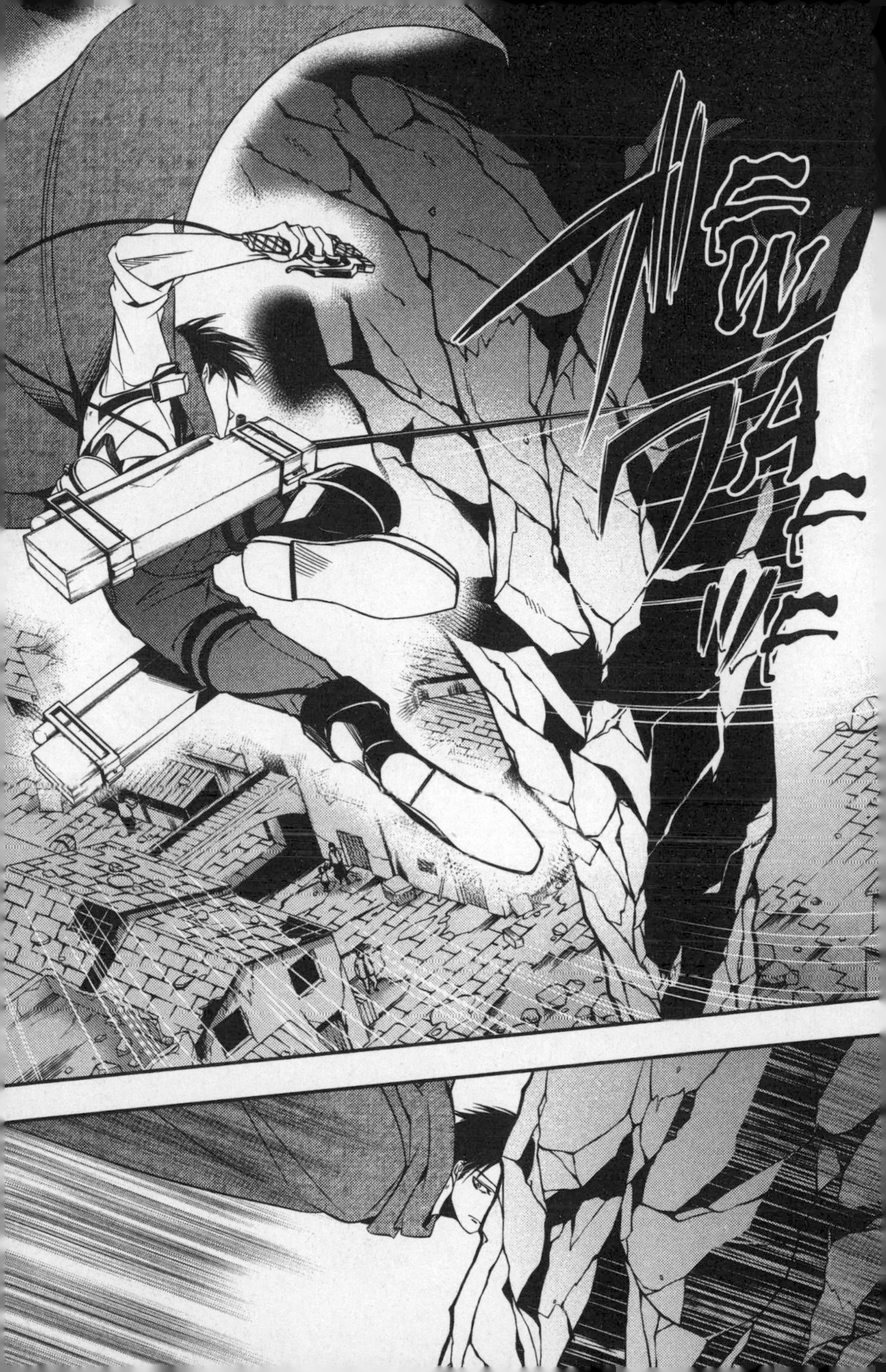
FWA
EWE

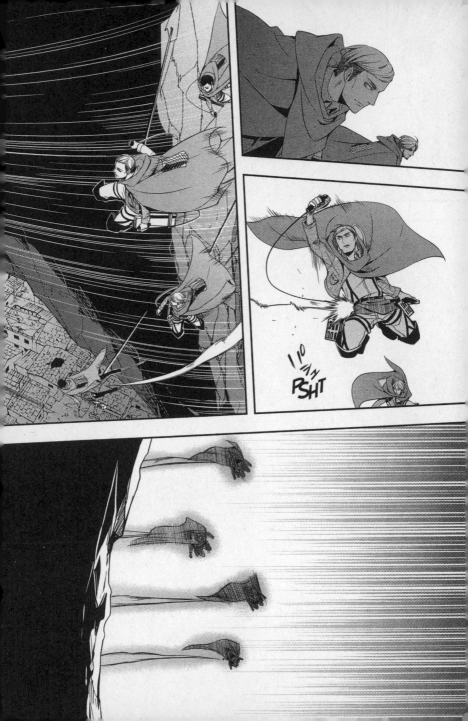

PSHT

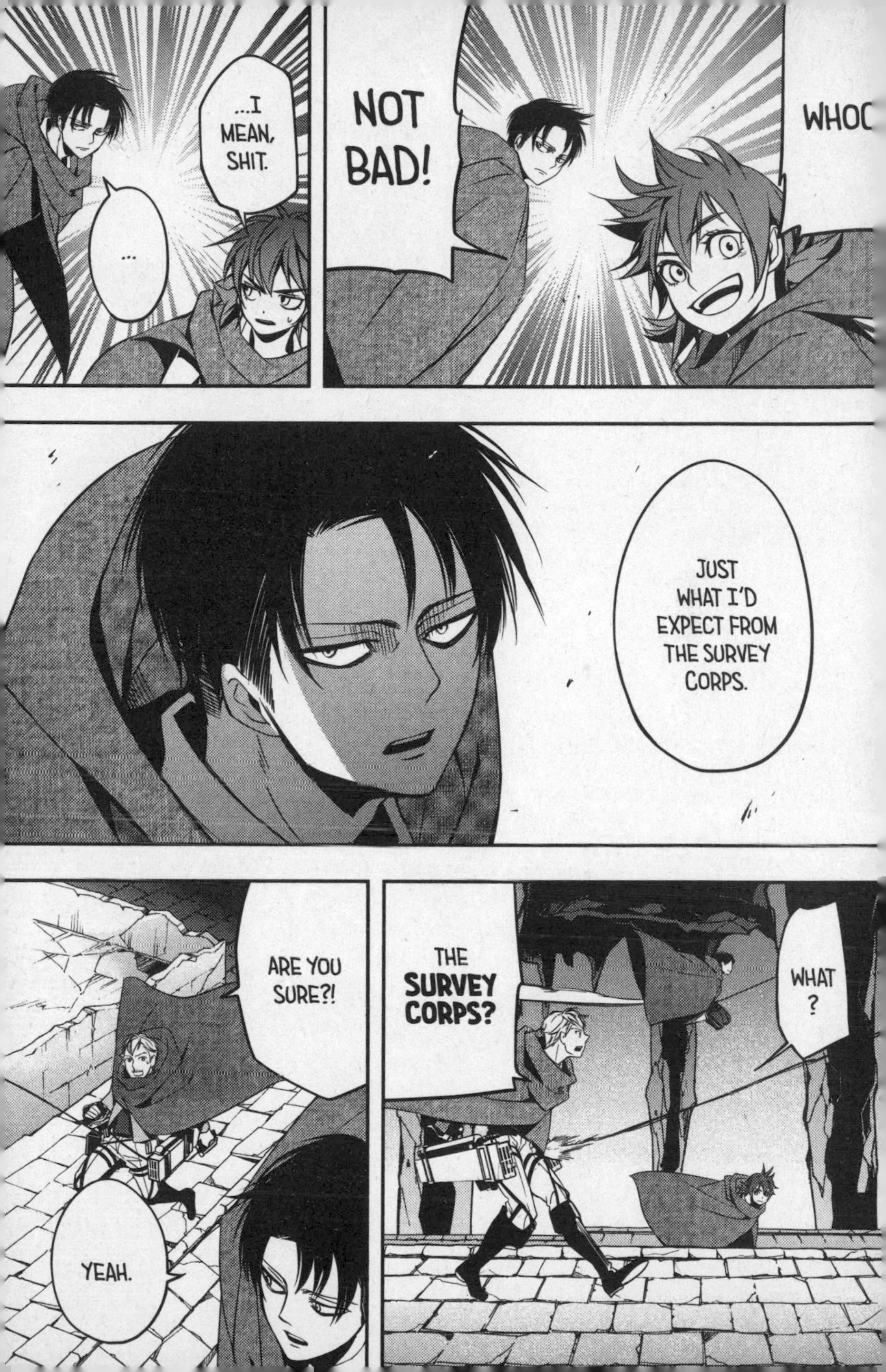
WHOO
NOT BAD!
...I MEAN, SHIT.
...
JUST WHAT I'D EXPECT FROM THE SURVEY CORPS.
WHAT?
THE SURVEY CORPS?
ARE YOU SURE?!
YEAH.

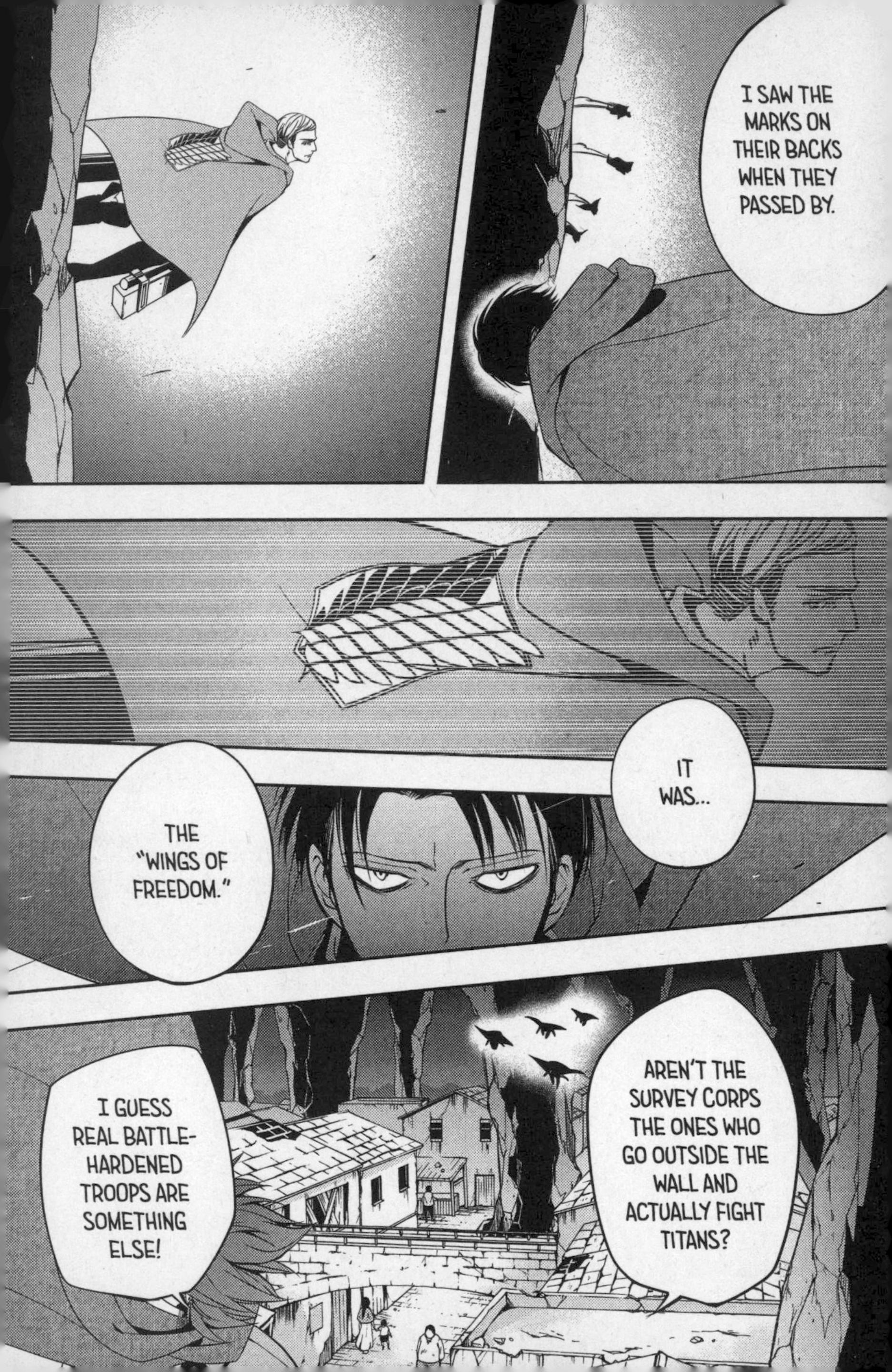
I SAW THE MARKS ON THEIR BACKS WHEN THEY PASSED BY.
IT WAS...
THE "WINGS OF FREEDOM."
AREN'T THE SURVEY CORPS THE ONES WHO GO OUTSIDE THE WALL AND ACTUALLY FIGHT TITANS?
I GUESS REAL BATTLE-HARDENED TROOPS ARE SOMETHING ELSE!

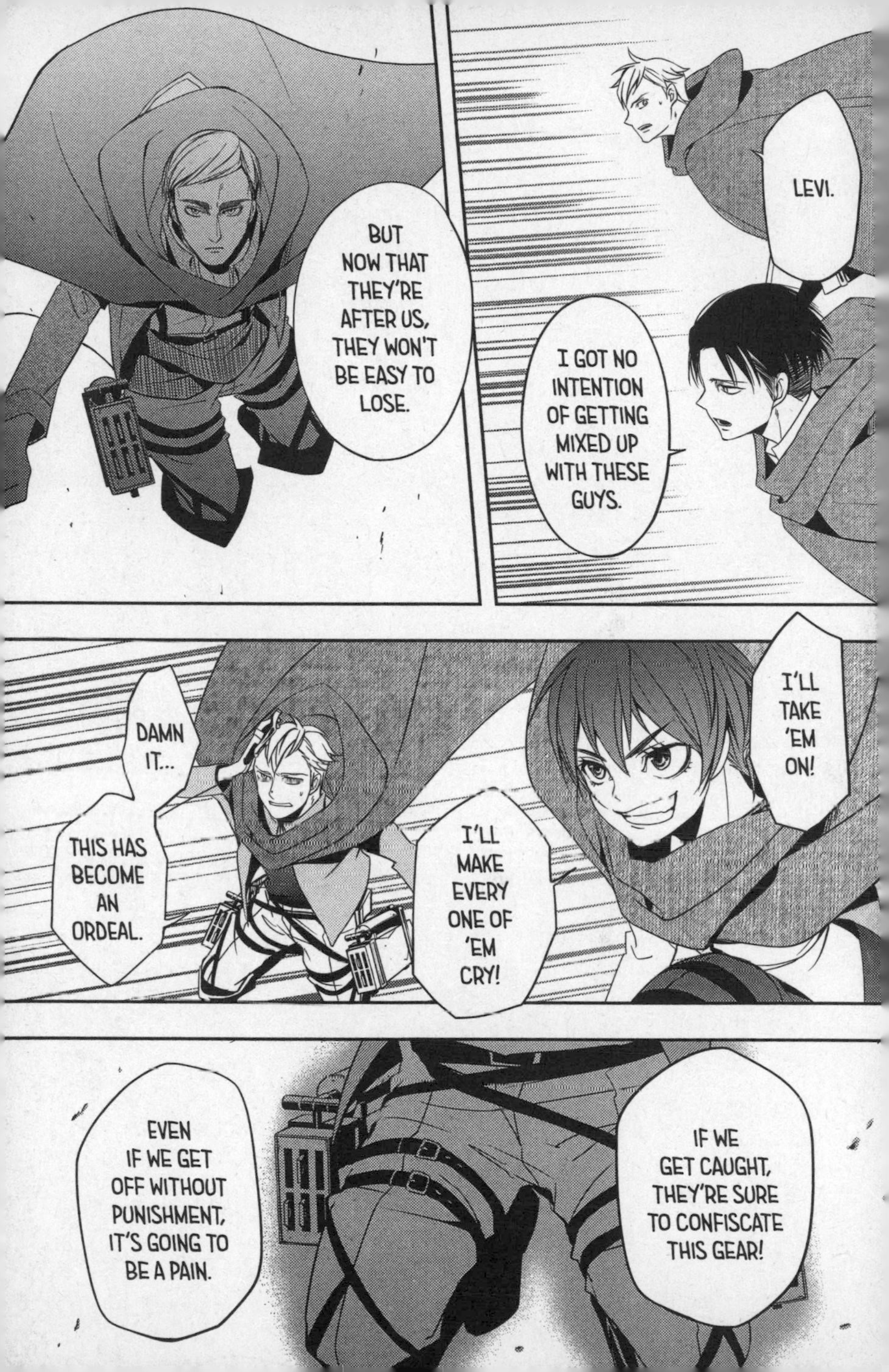
LEVI.
I GOT NO INTENTION OF GETTING MIXED UP WITH THESE GUYS.
BUT NOW THAT THEY'RE AFTER US, THEY WON'T BE EASY TO LOSE.
I'LL TAKE 'EM ON!
I'LL MAKE EVERY ONE OF 'EM CRY!
DAMN IT...
THIS HAS BECOME AN ORDEAL.
IF WE GET CAUGHT, THEY'RE SURE TO CONFISCATE THIS GEAR!
EVEN IF WE GET OFF WITHOUT PUNISHMENT, IT'S GOING TO BE A PAIN.

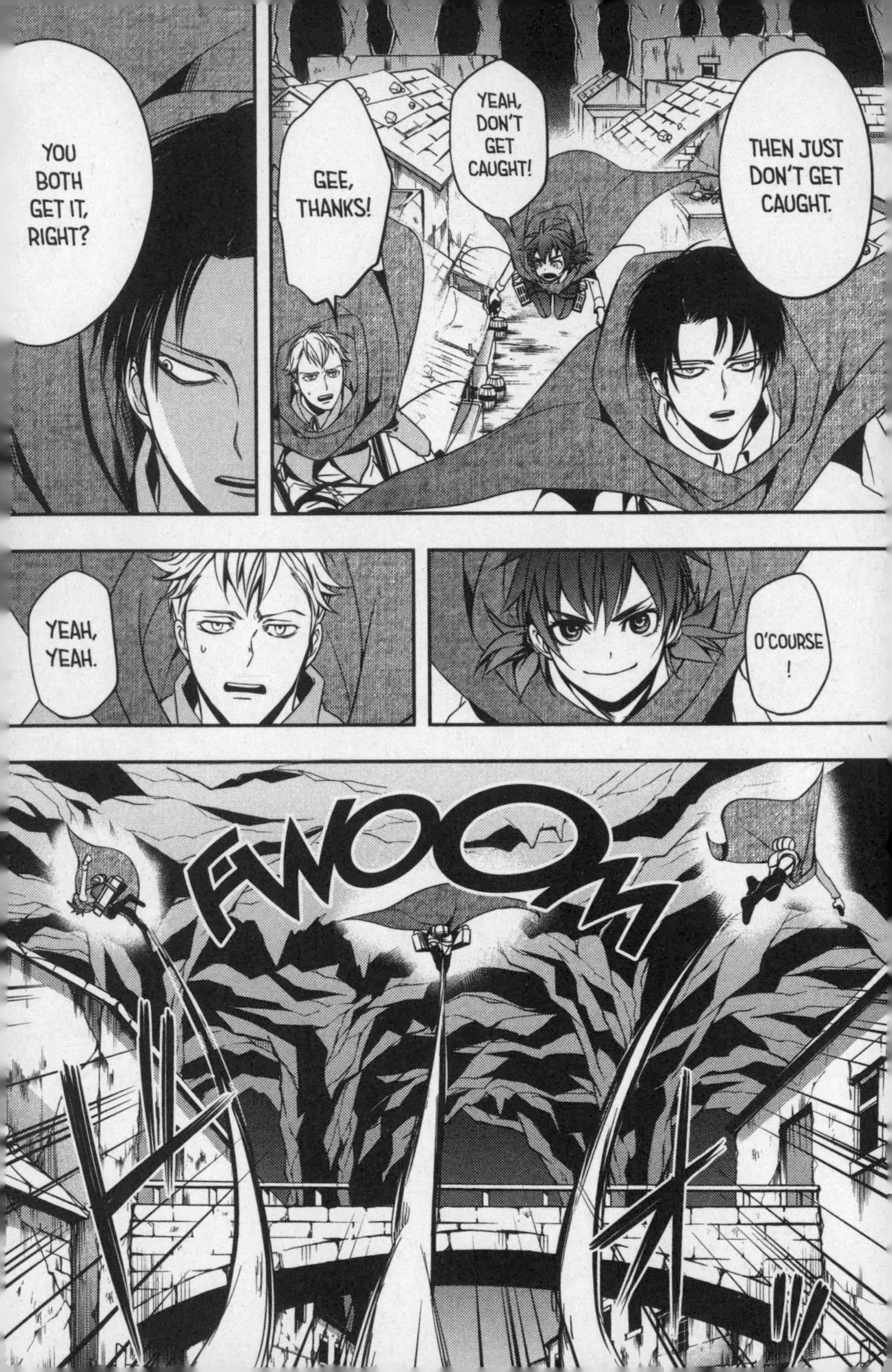
THEN JUST DON'T GET CAUGHT.
YEAH, DON'T GET CAUGHT!
GEE, THANKS!
YOU BOTH GET IT, RIGHT?
O'COURSE !
YEAH, YEAH.
FWOOM

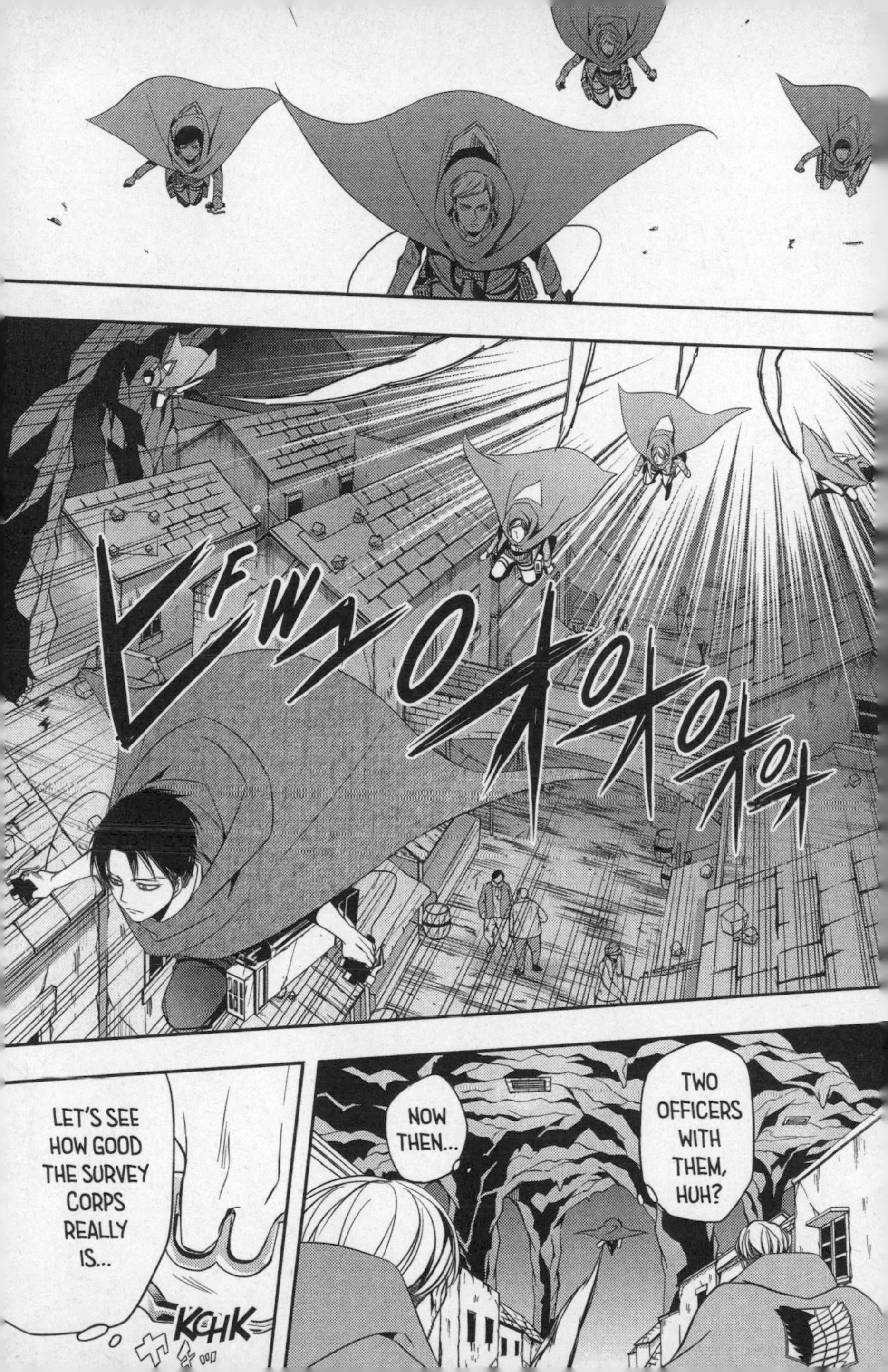
TWO OFFICERS WITH THEM, HUH?
NOW THEN...
LET'S SEE HOW GOOD THE SURVEY CORPS REALLY IS...
KCHK

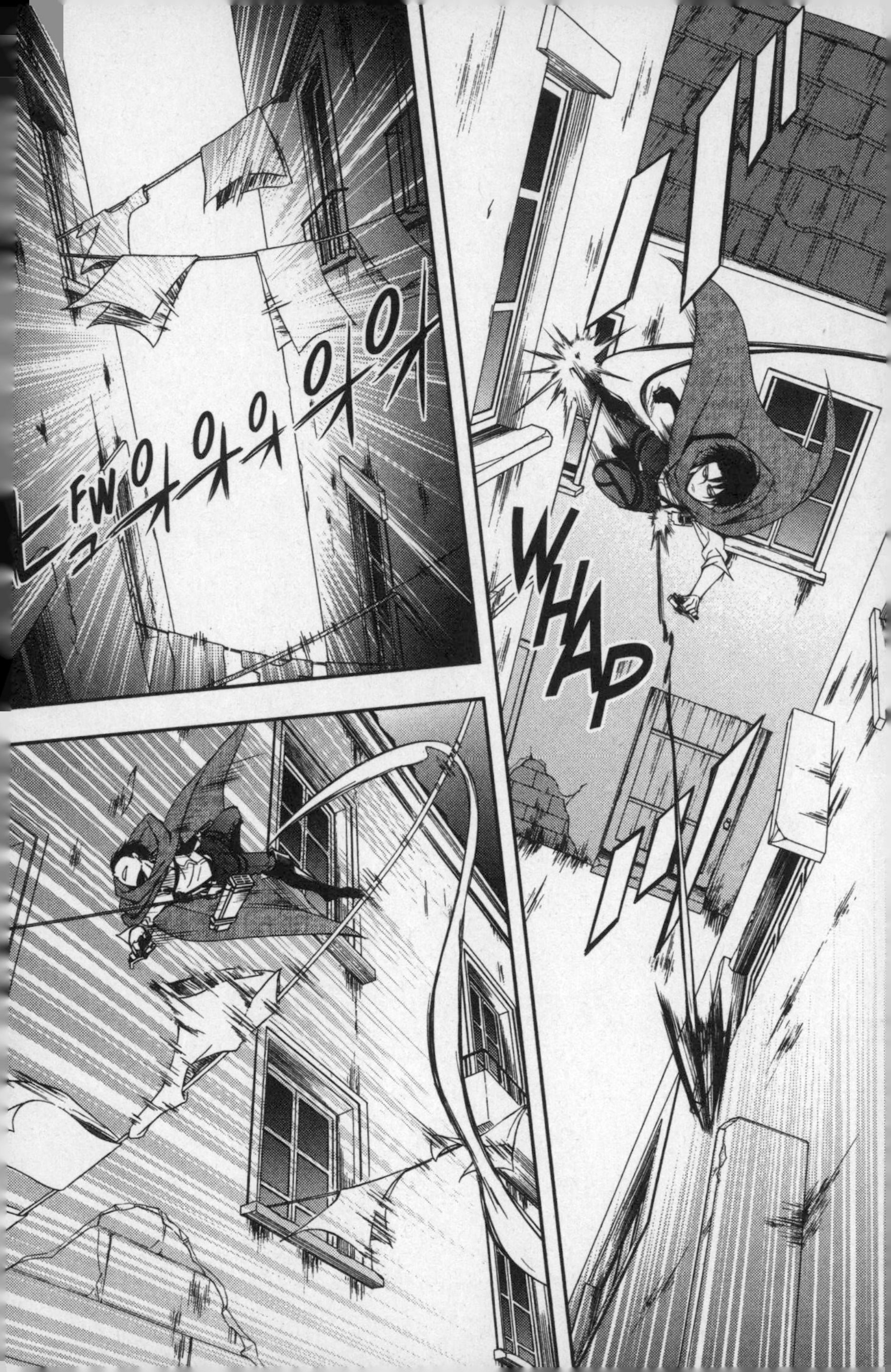
WHAP
FWOOOOO

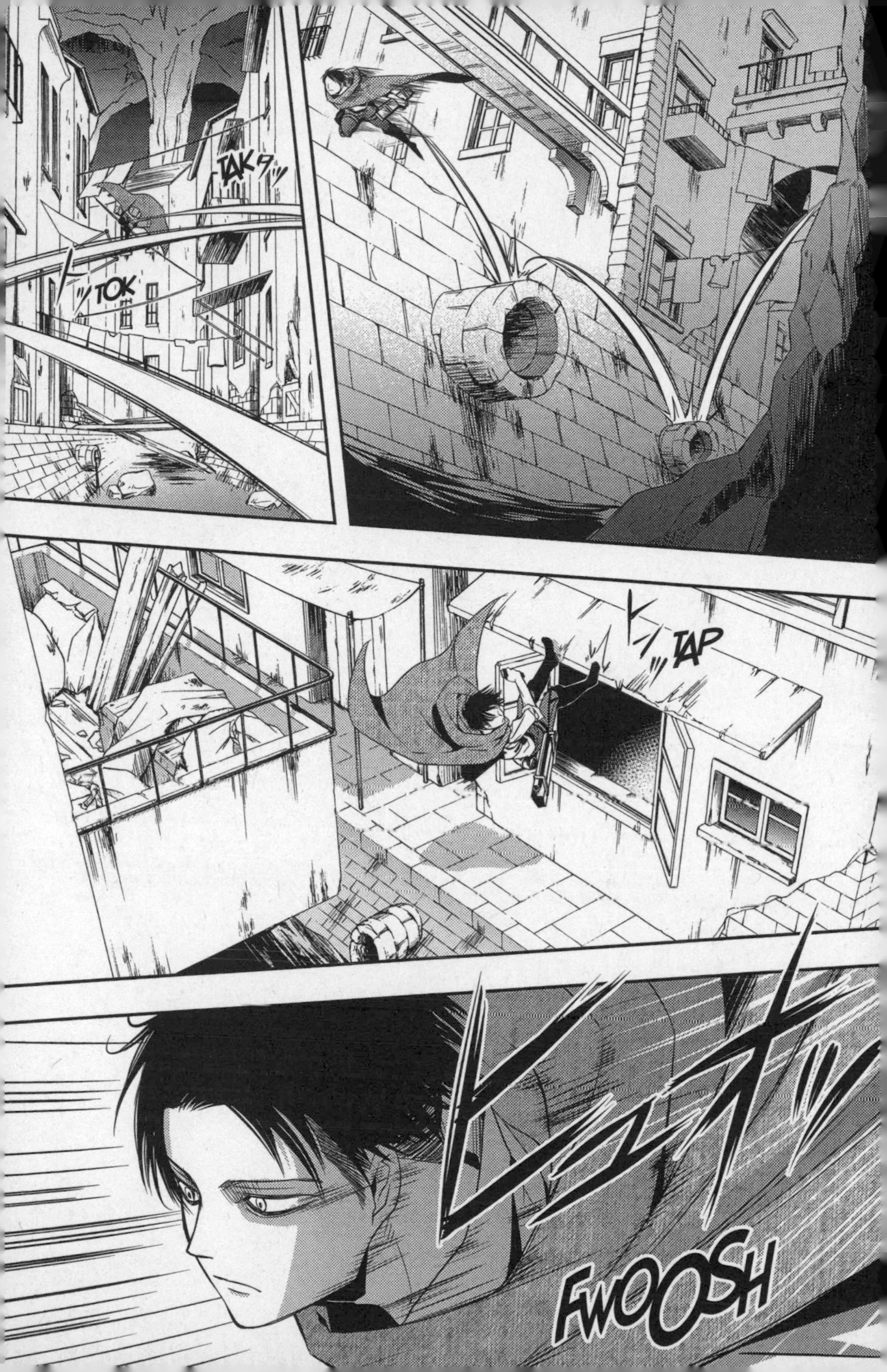
TAK
TOK
TAP
FWOOSH

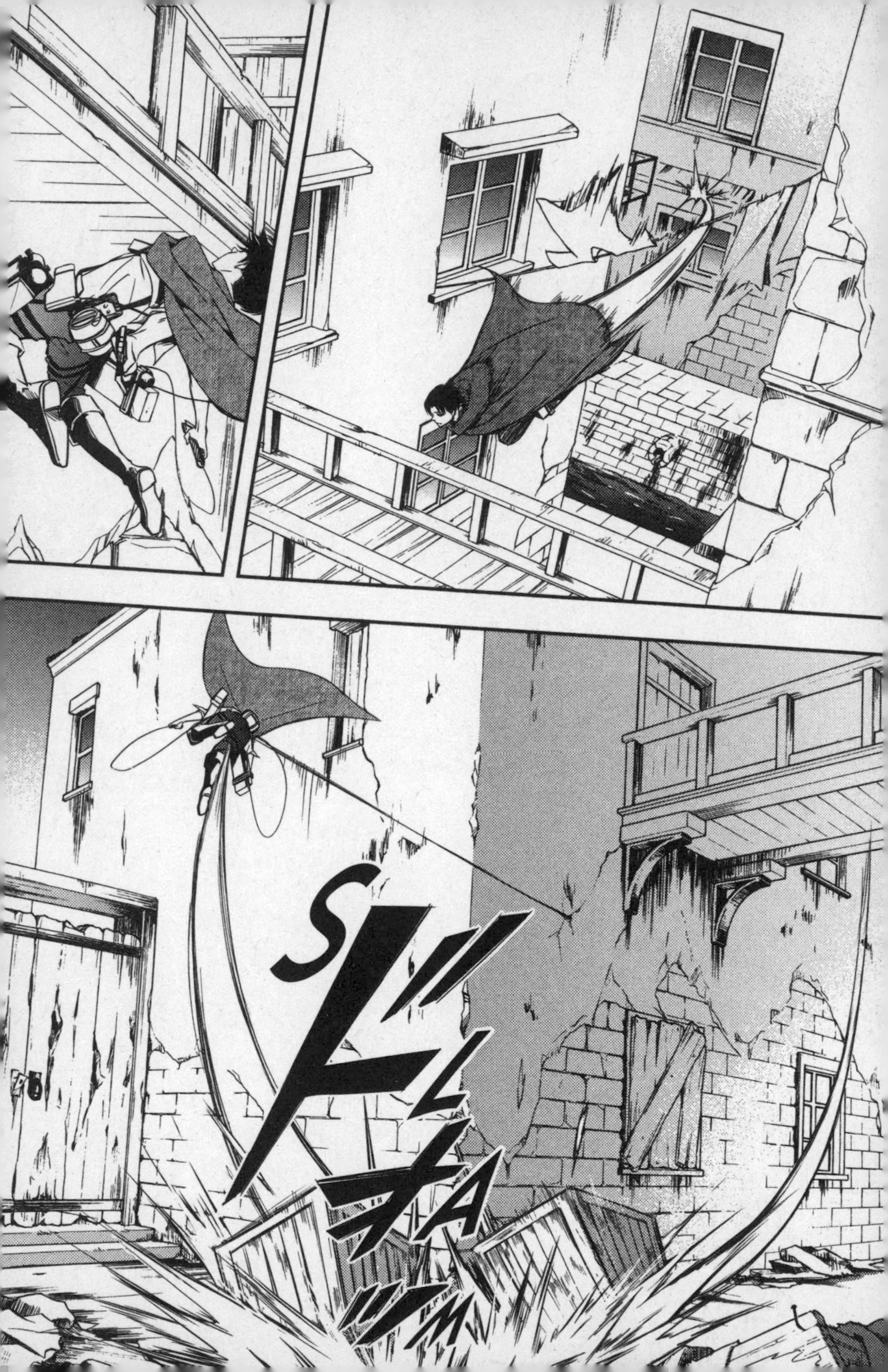
SHHHAAA

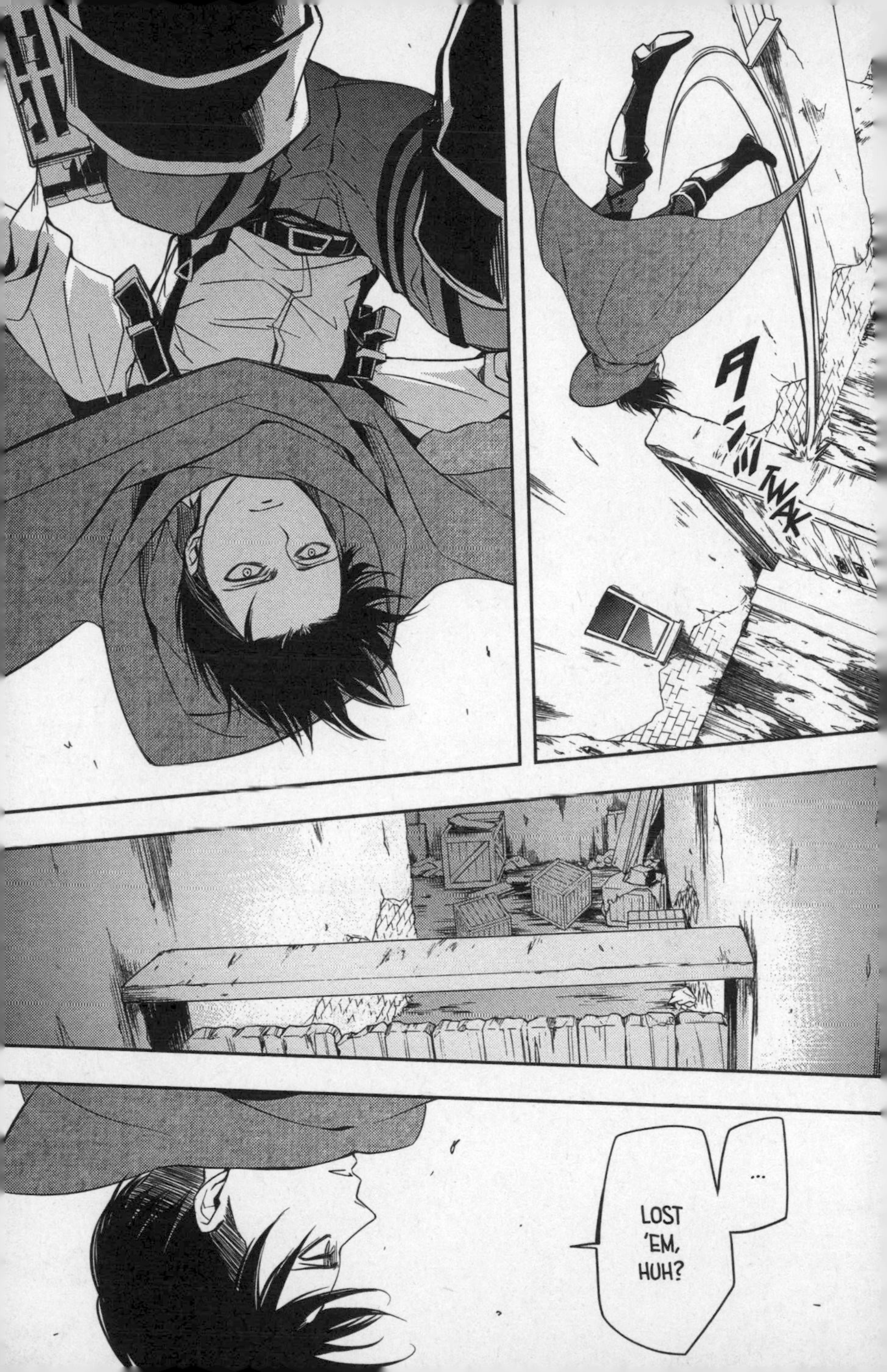
TWAK
... LOST 'EM, HUH?

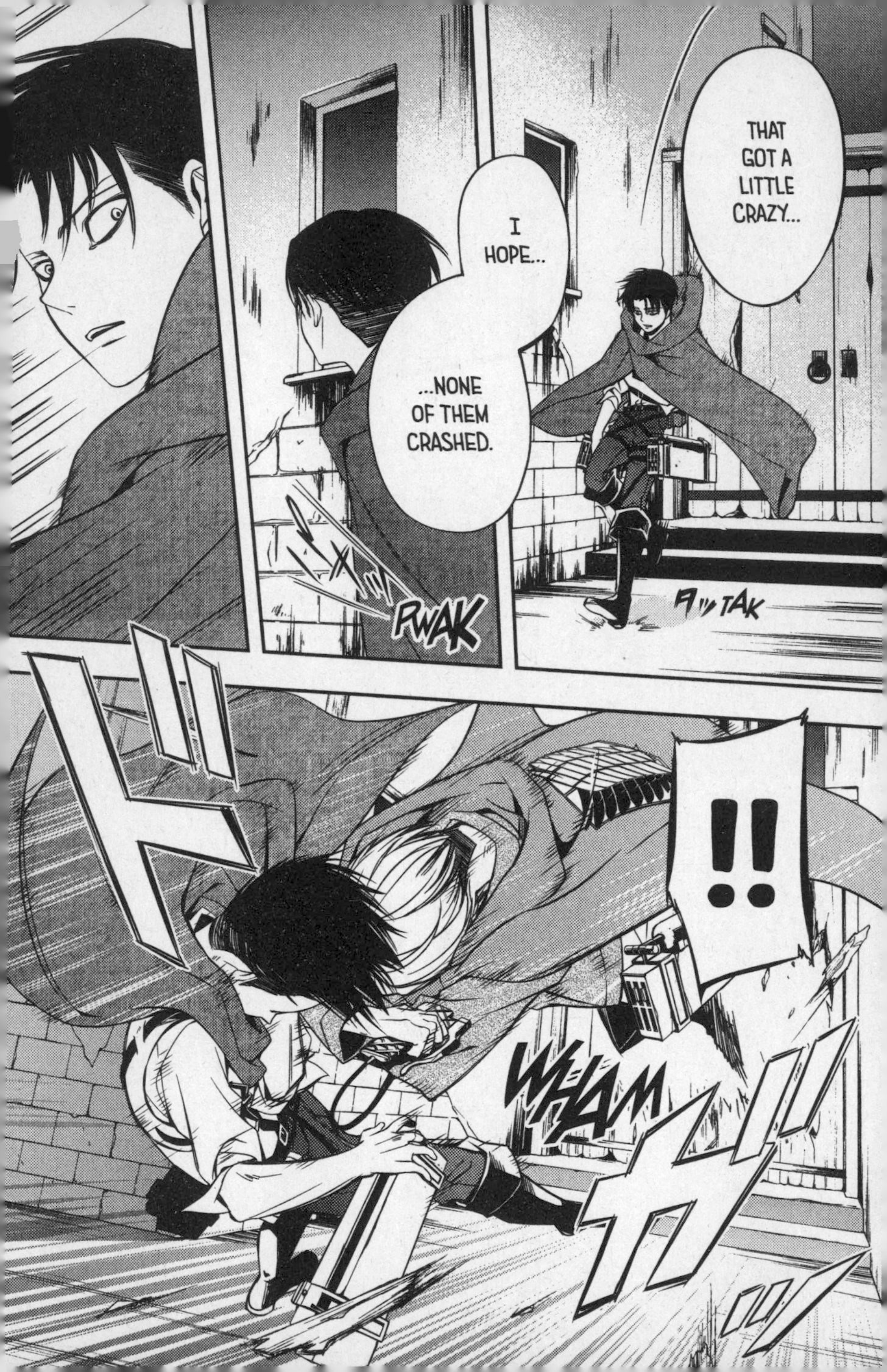
THAT GOT A LITTLE CRAZY...
TAK
I HOPE...
...NONE OF THEM CRASHED.
PWAK
!!
WHAM

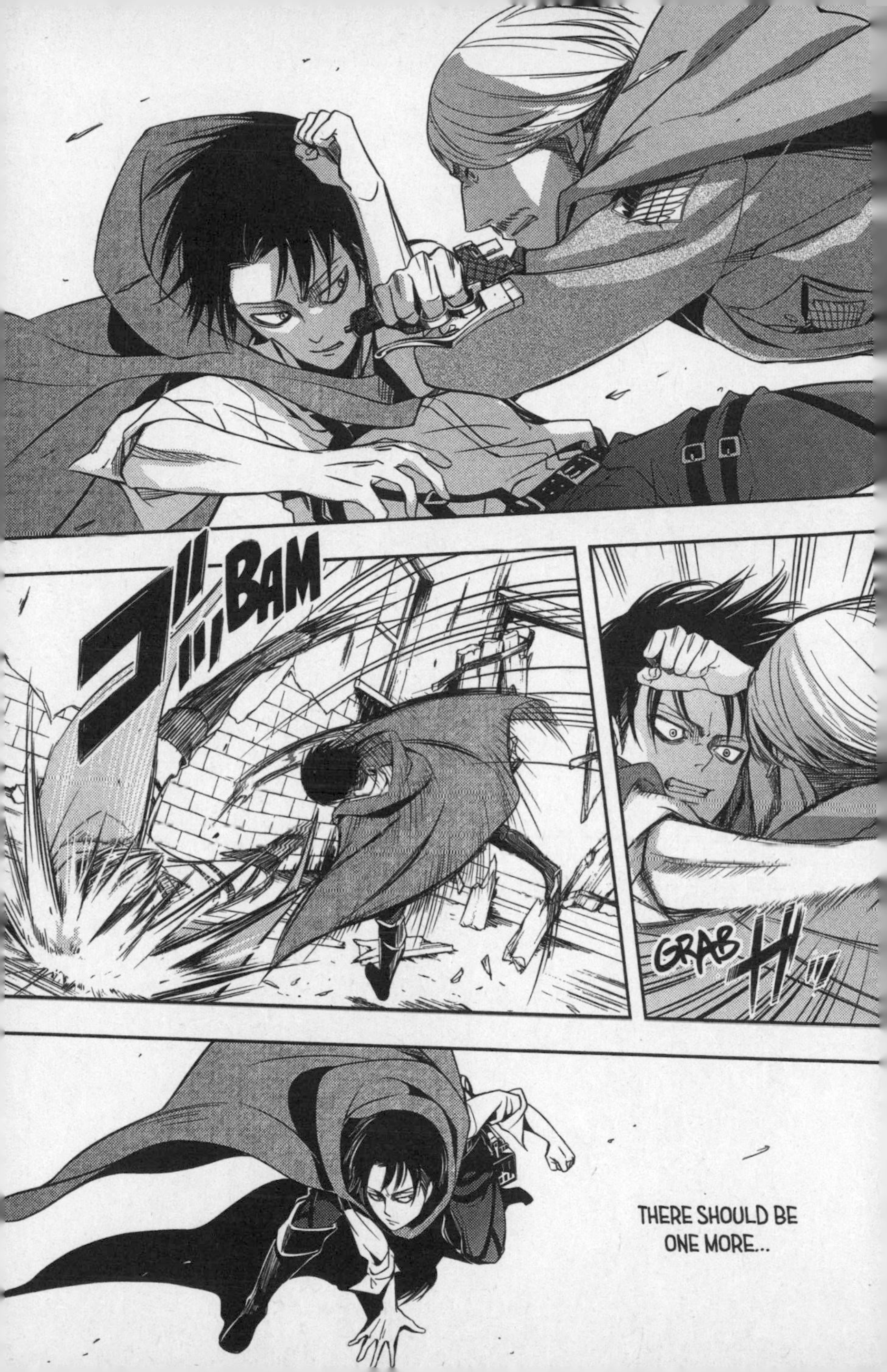
GRAB
BAM
THERE SHOULD BE ONE MORE...

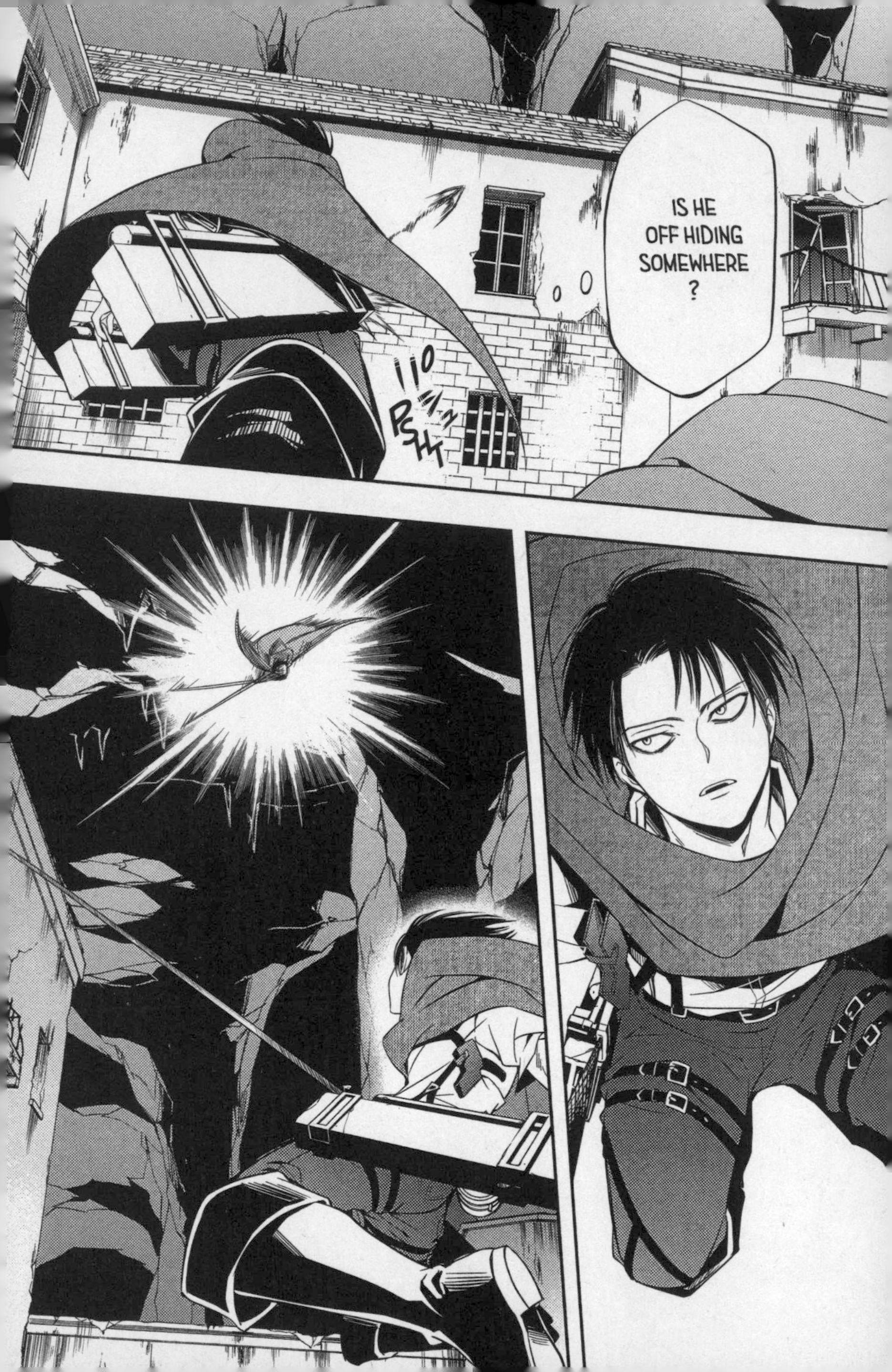
IS HE OFF HIDING SOMEWHERE?
PSHHT

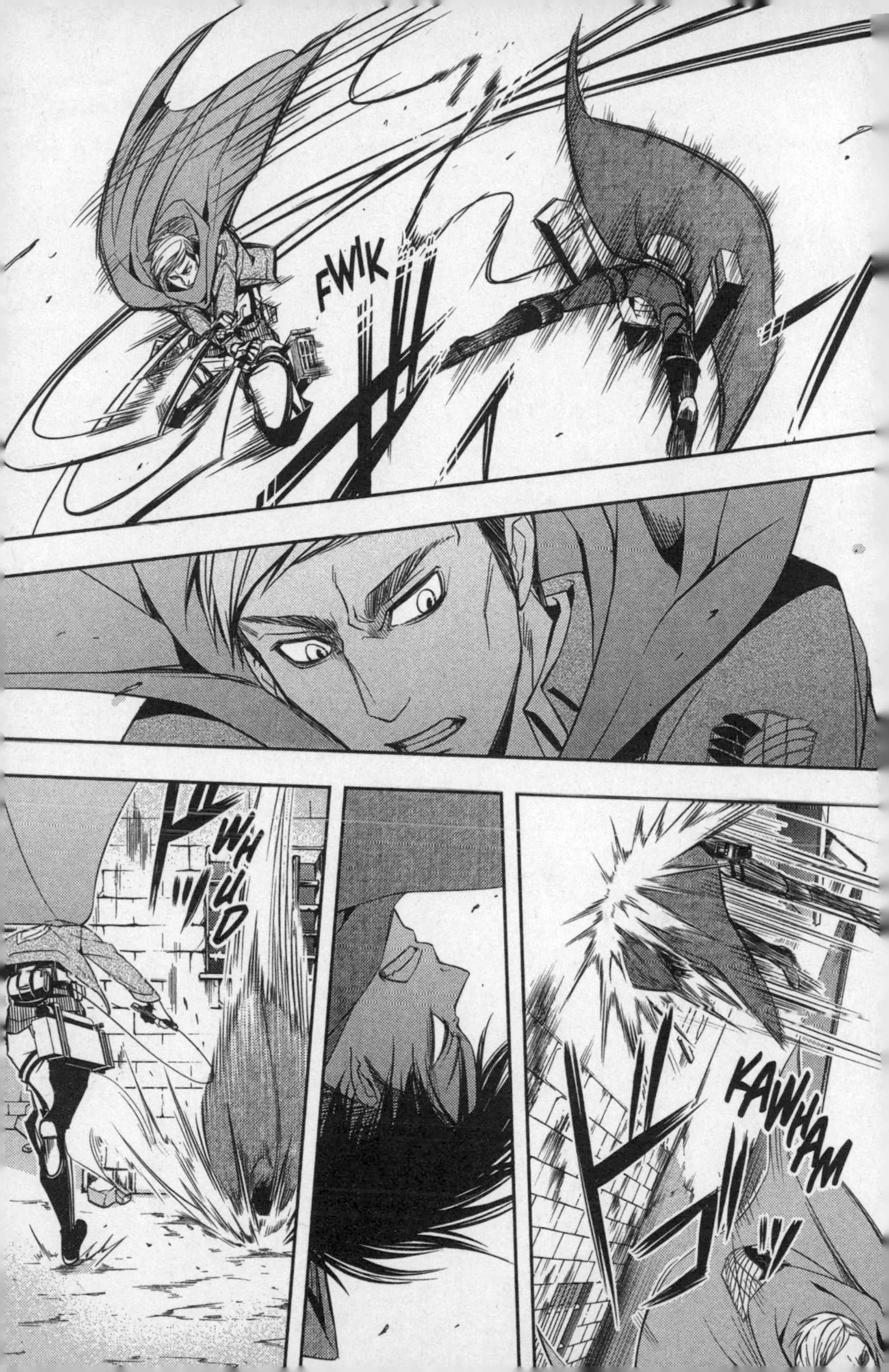
FWIK
KAWHAM
WHUD

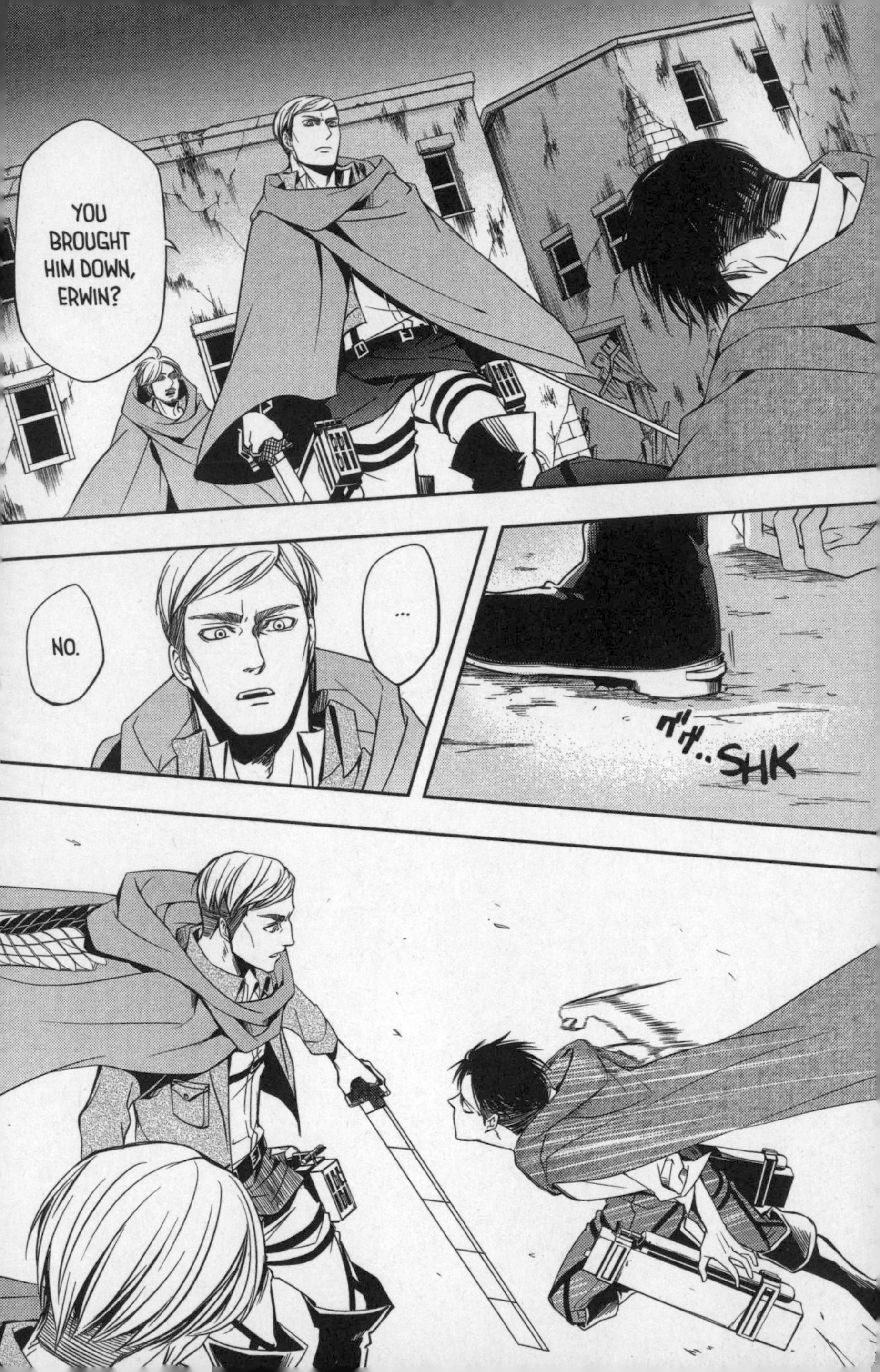
YOU BROUGHT HIM DOWN, ERWIN?
ザッ..SHK
...
NO.

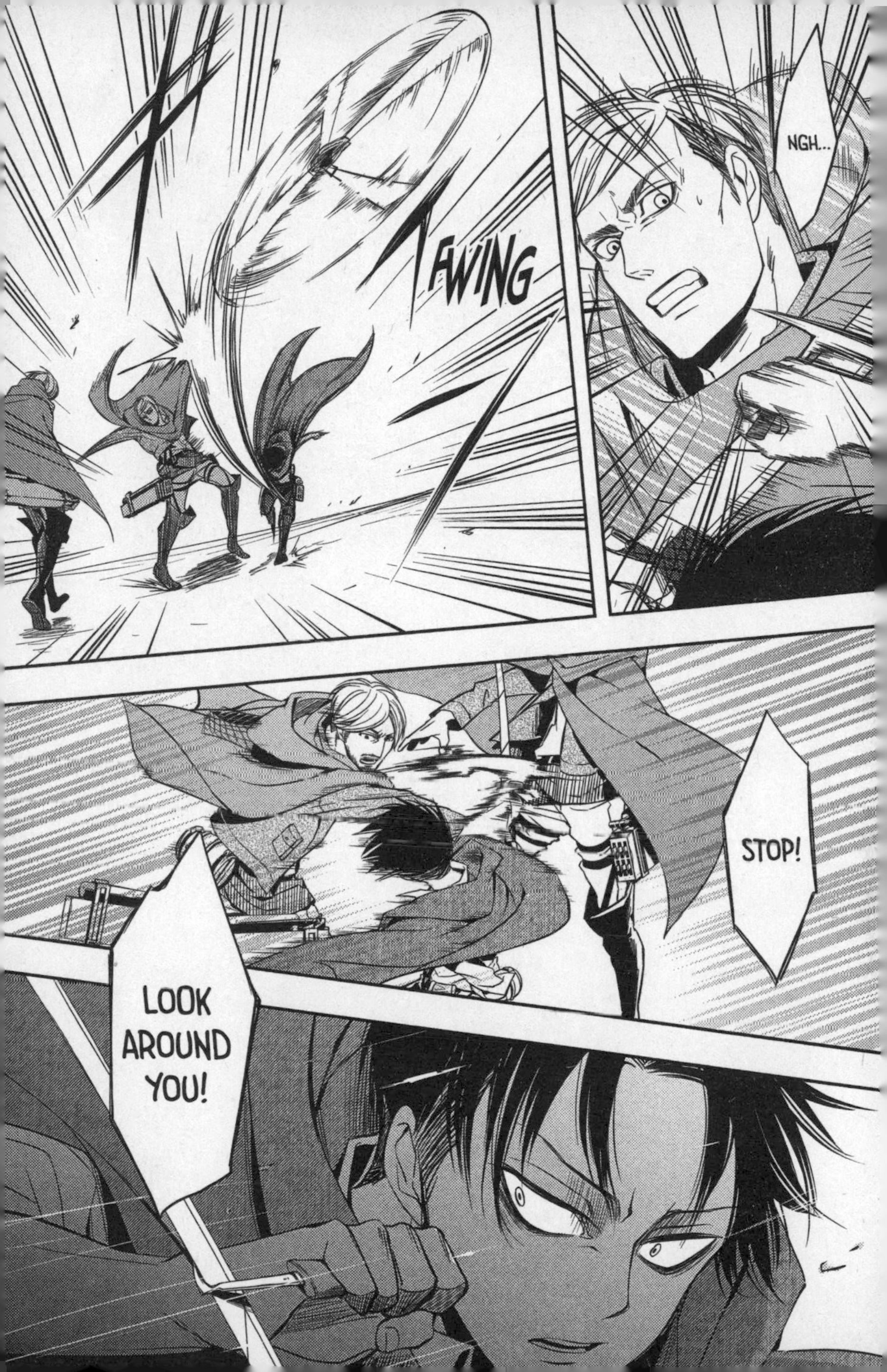
NGH...
FWING
STOP!
LOOK AROUND YOU!

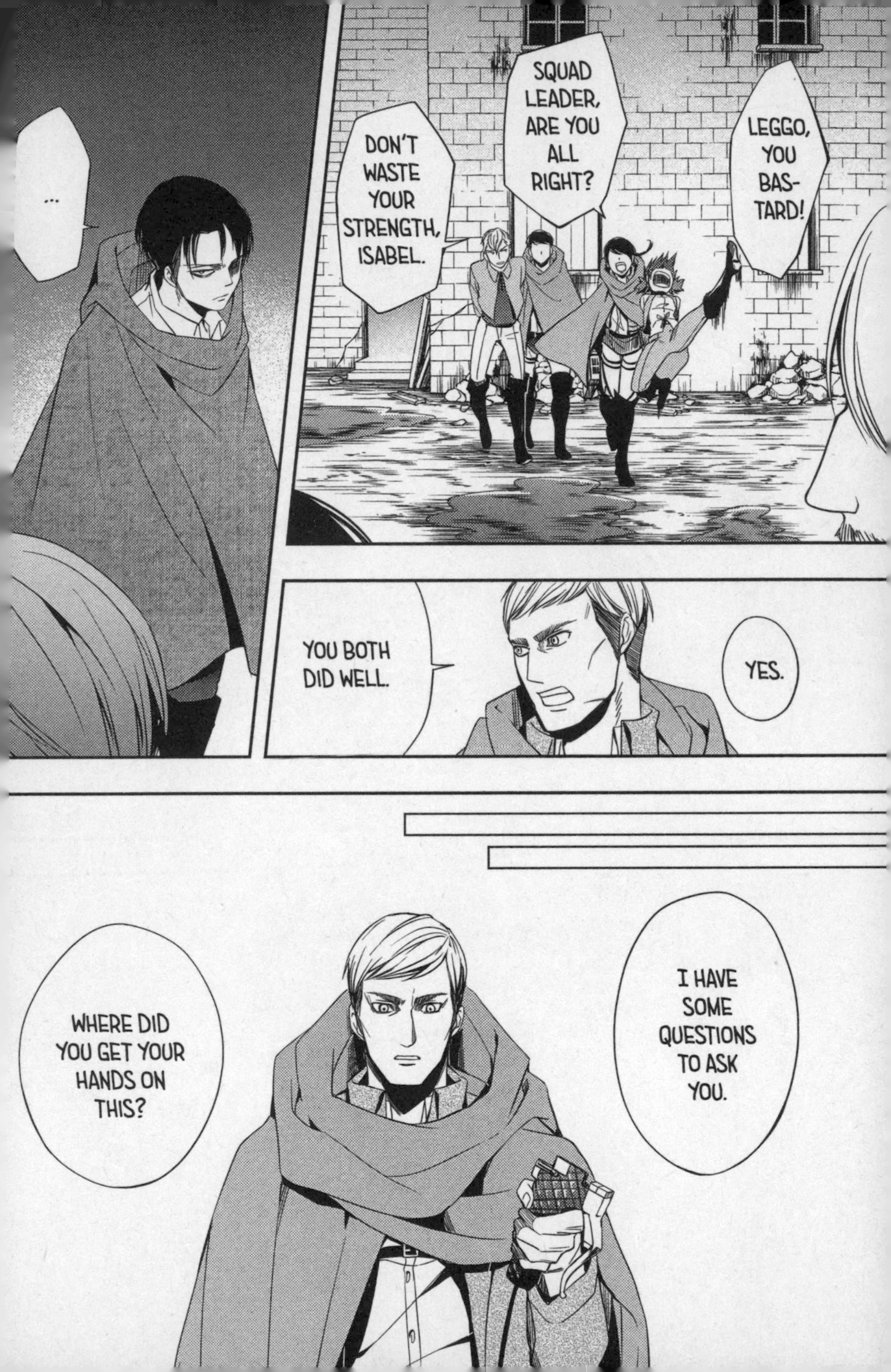
LEGGO, YOU BAS-TARD!
SQUAD LEADER, ARE YOU ALL RIGHT?
DON'T WASTE YOUR STRENGTH, ISABEL.
YES.
YOU BOTH DID WELL.
...
I HAVE SOME QUESTIONS TO ASK YOU.
WHERE DID YOU GET YOUR HANDS ON THIS?

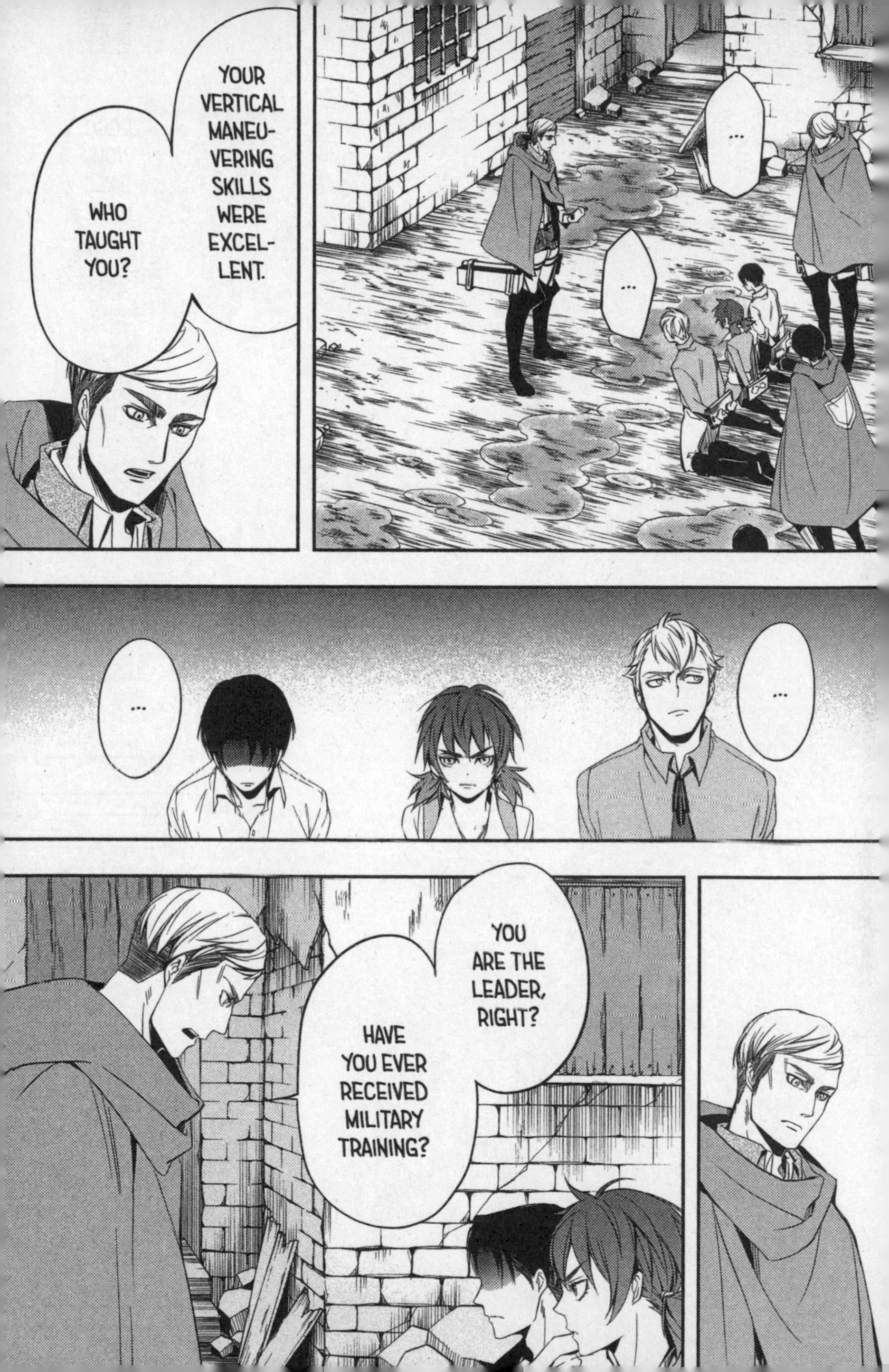
...
...
YOUR VERTICAL MANEU-VERING SKILLS WERE EXCEL-LENT.
WHO TAUGHT YOU?
...
...
YOU ARE THE LEADER, RIGHT?
HAVE YOU EVER RECEIVED MILITARY TRAINING?

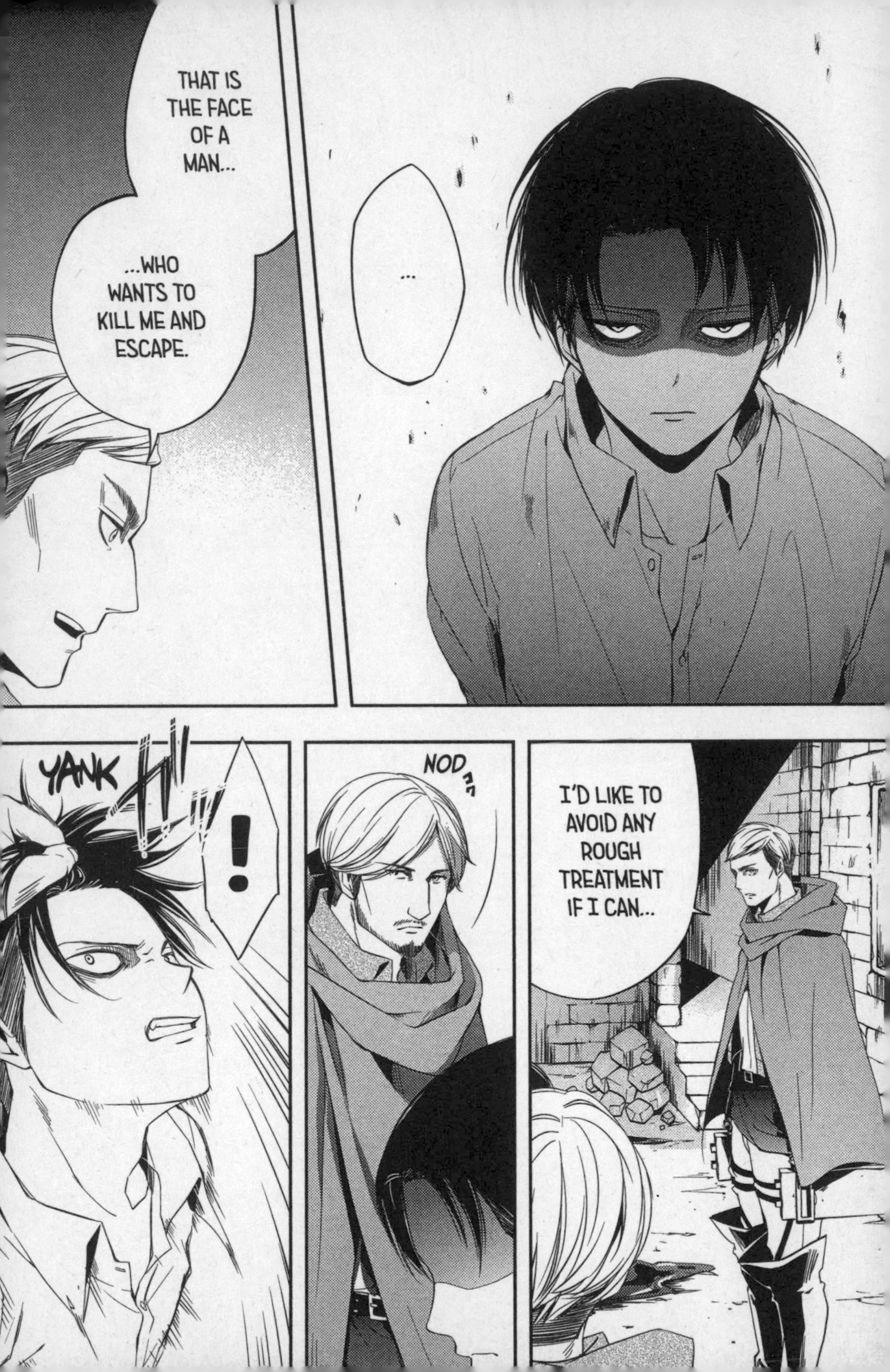
...
THAT IS THE FACE OF A MAN...
...WHO WANTS TO KILL ME AND ESCAPE.
I'D LIKE TO AVOID ANY ROUGH TREATMENT IF I CAN...
NOD
YANK
!

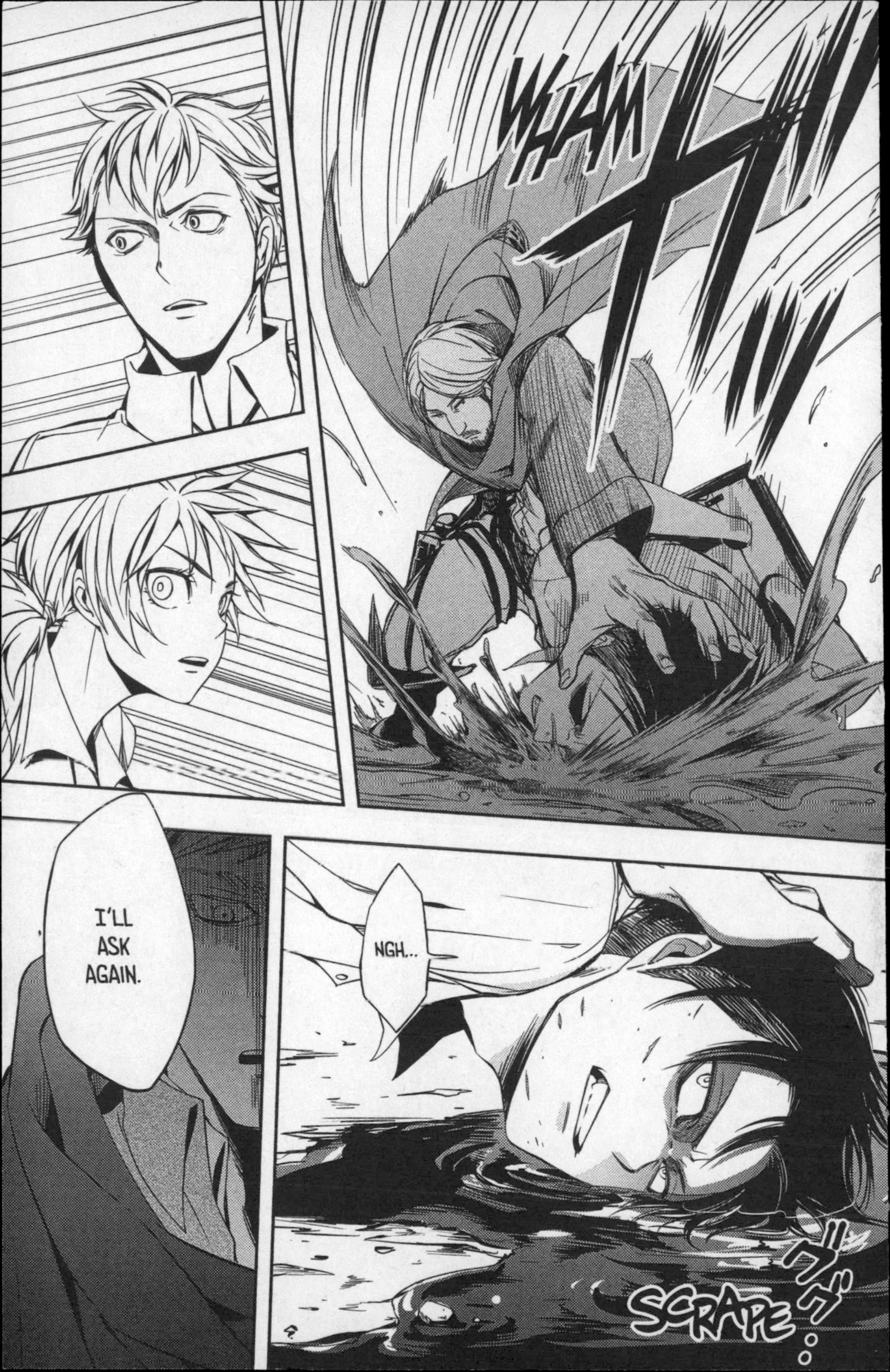
WHAM
NGH...
SCRAPE
I'LL ASK AGAIN.

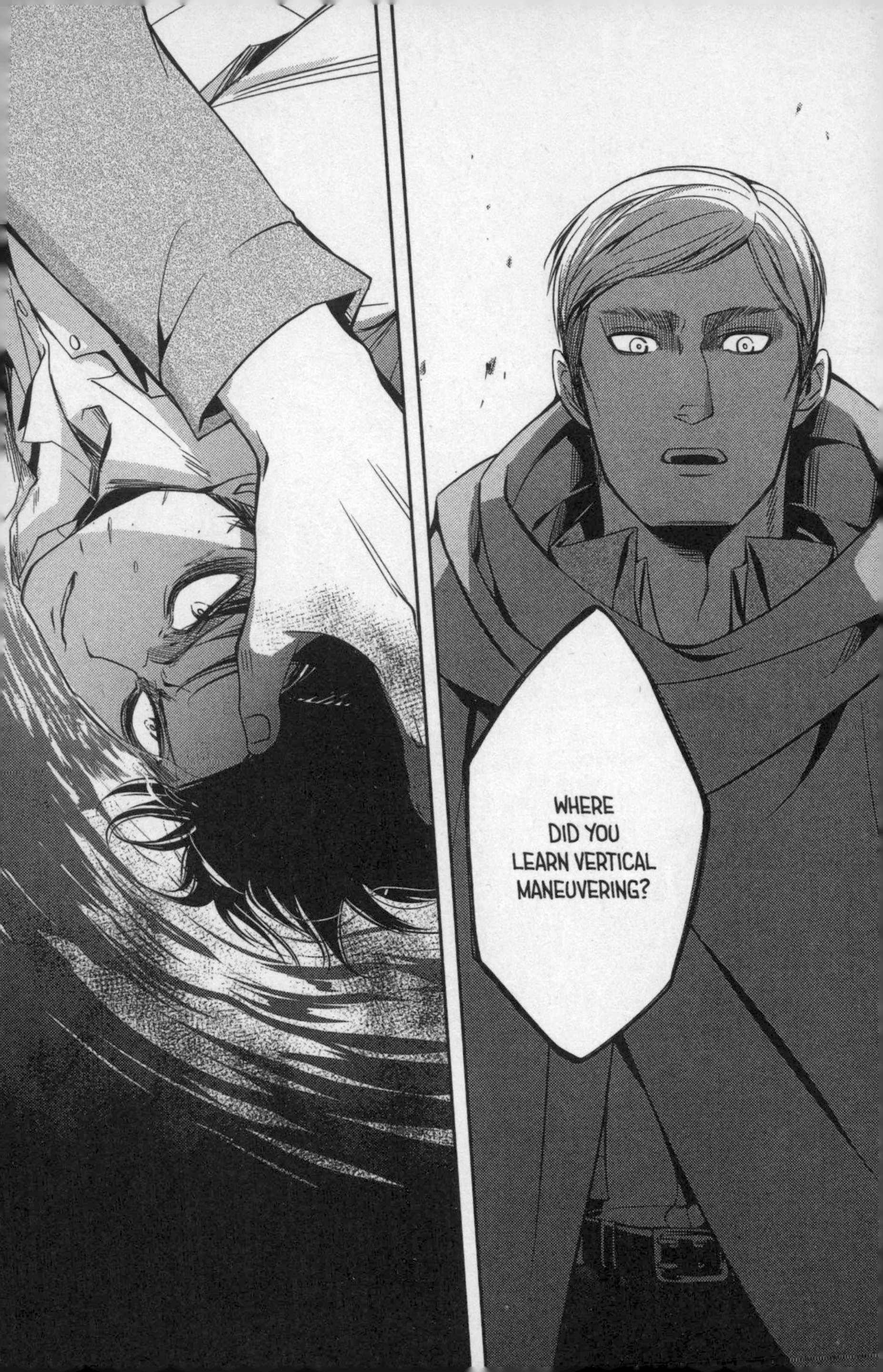
WHERE DID YOU LEARN VERTICAL MANEUVERING?

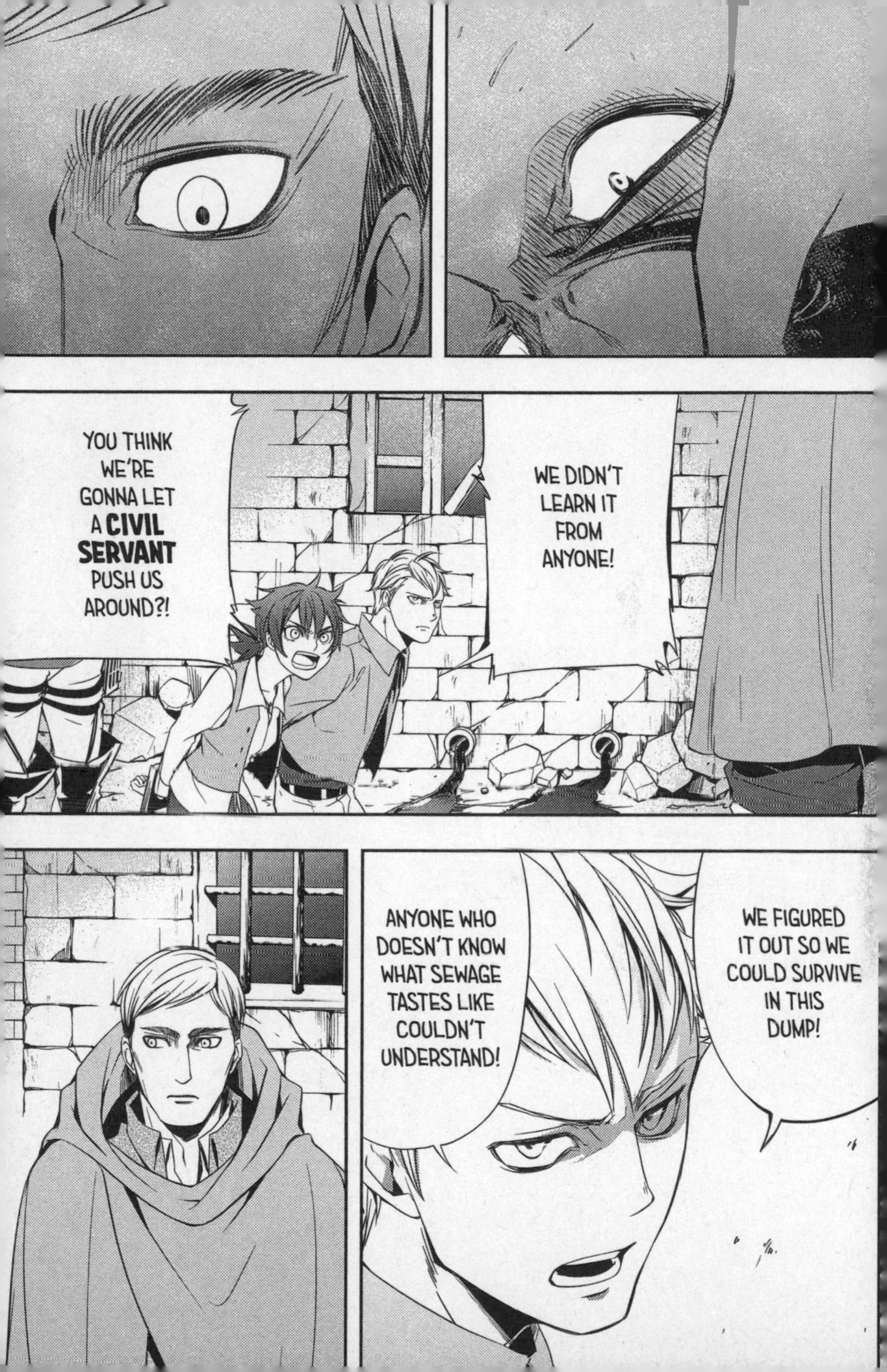
WE DIDN'T LEARN IT FROM ANYONE!
YOU THINK WE'RE GONNA LET A **CIVIL SERVANT** PUSH US AROUND?!
WE FIGURED IT OUT SO WE COULD SURVIVE IN THIS DUMP!
ANYONE WHO DOESN'T KNOW WHAT SEWAGE TASTES LIKE COULDN'T UNDERSTAND!

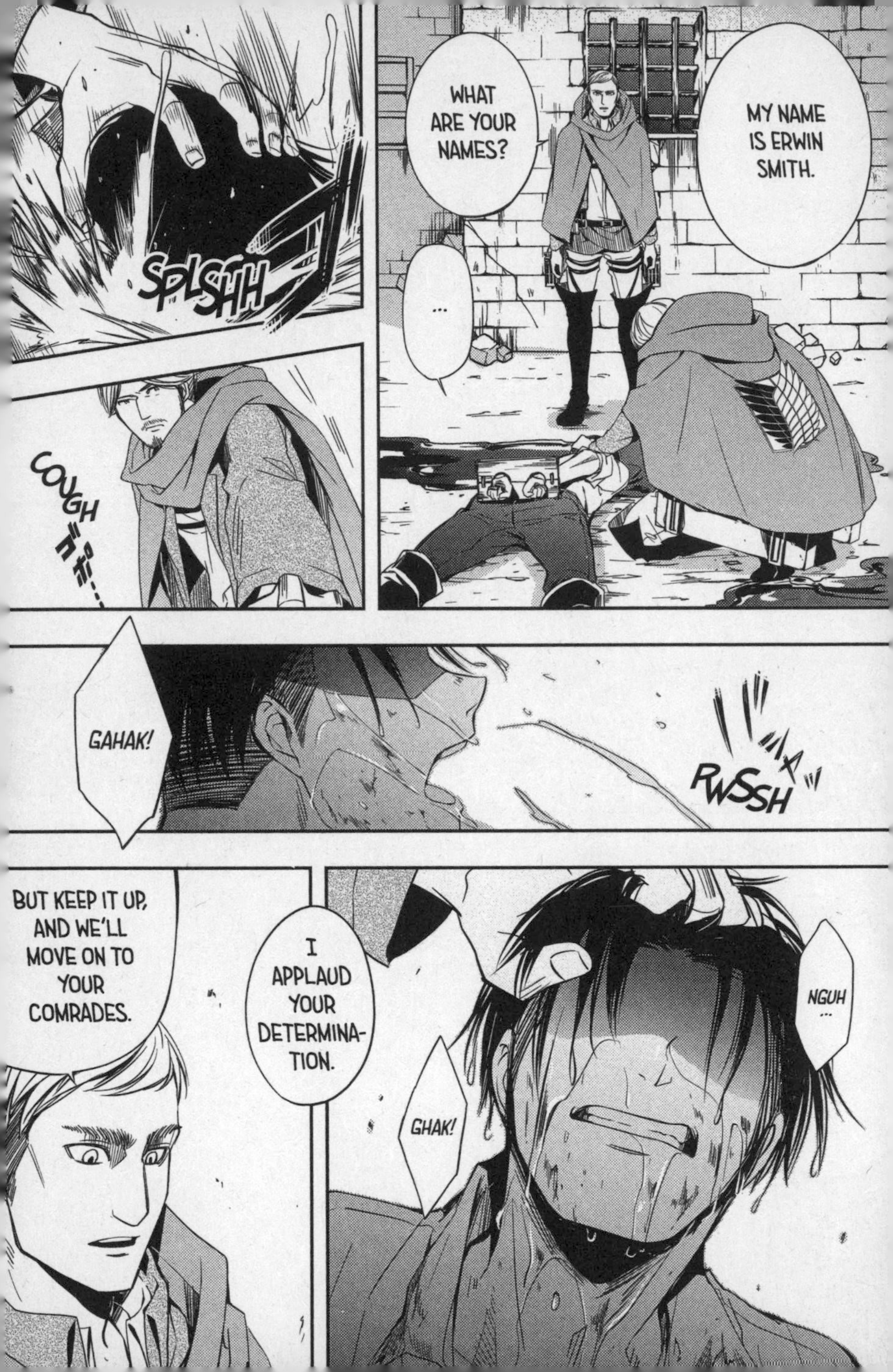
MY NAME IS ERWIN SMITH.
WHAT ARE YOUR NAMES?
...
SPLSHH
COUGH
RWSSH
GAHAK!
NGUH ...
GHAK!
I APPLAUD YOUR DETERMINATION.
BUT KEEP IT UP, AND WE'LL MOVE ON TO YOUR COMRADES.

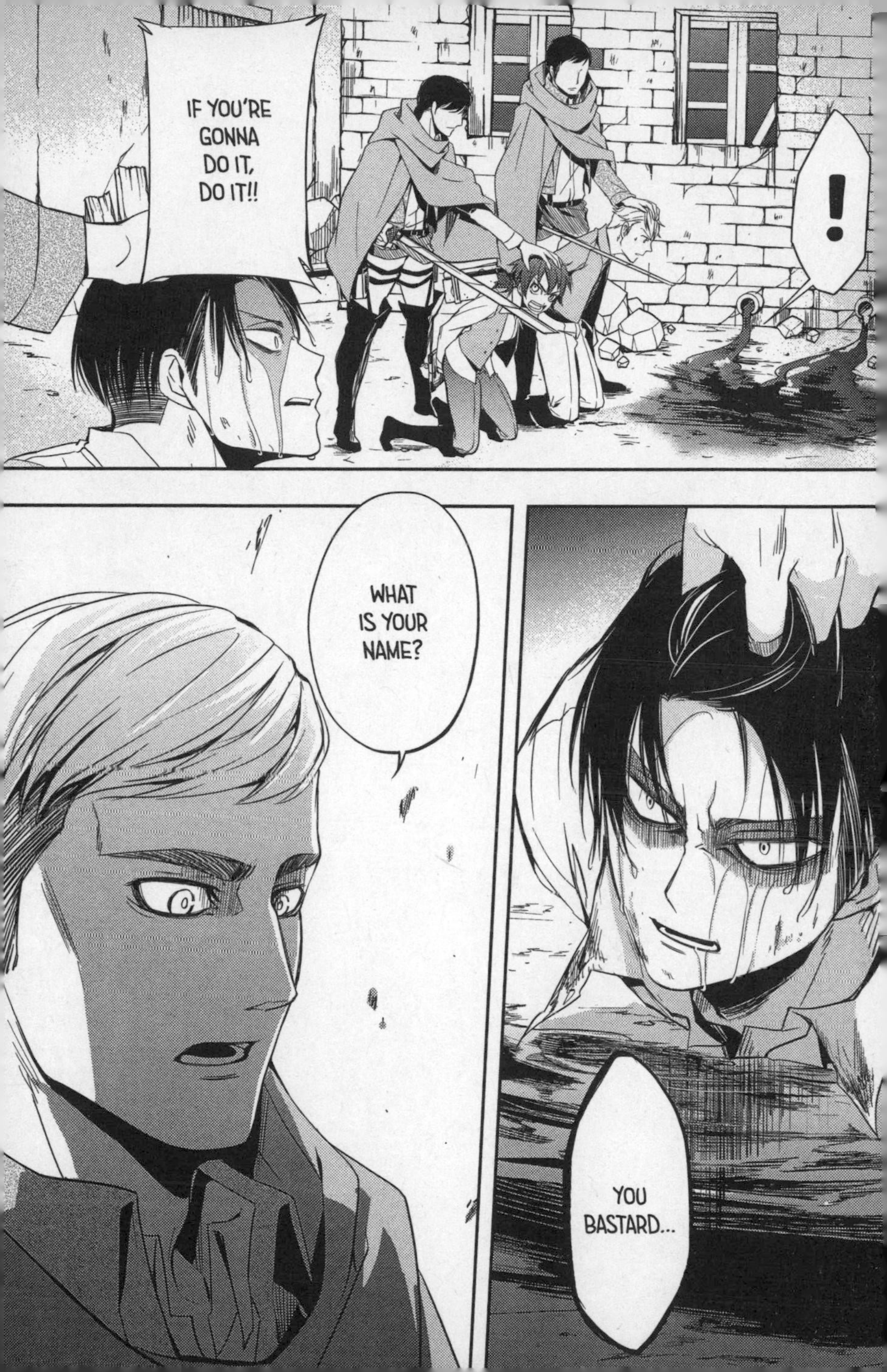
!
IF YOU'RE GONNA DO IT, DO IT!!
YOU BASTARD...
WHAT IS YOUR NAME?

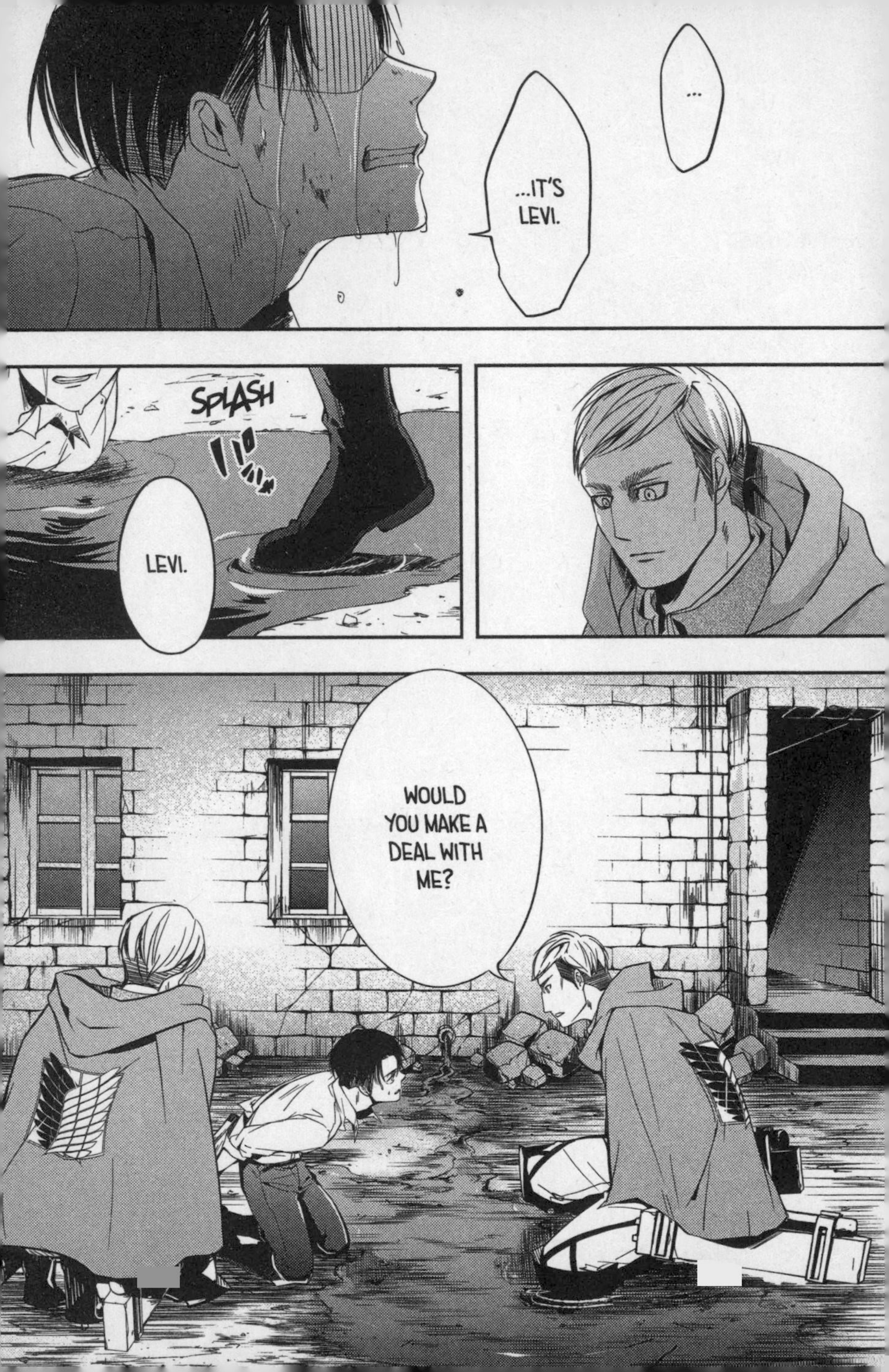
...
...IT'S LEVI.
SPLASH
LEVI.
WOULD YOU MAKE A DEAL WITH ME?

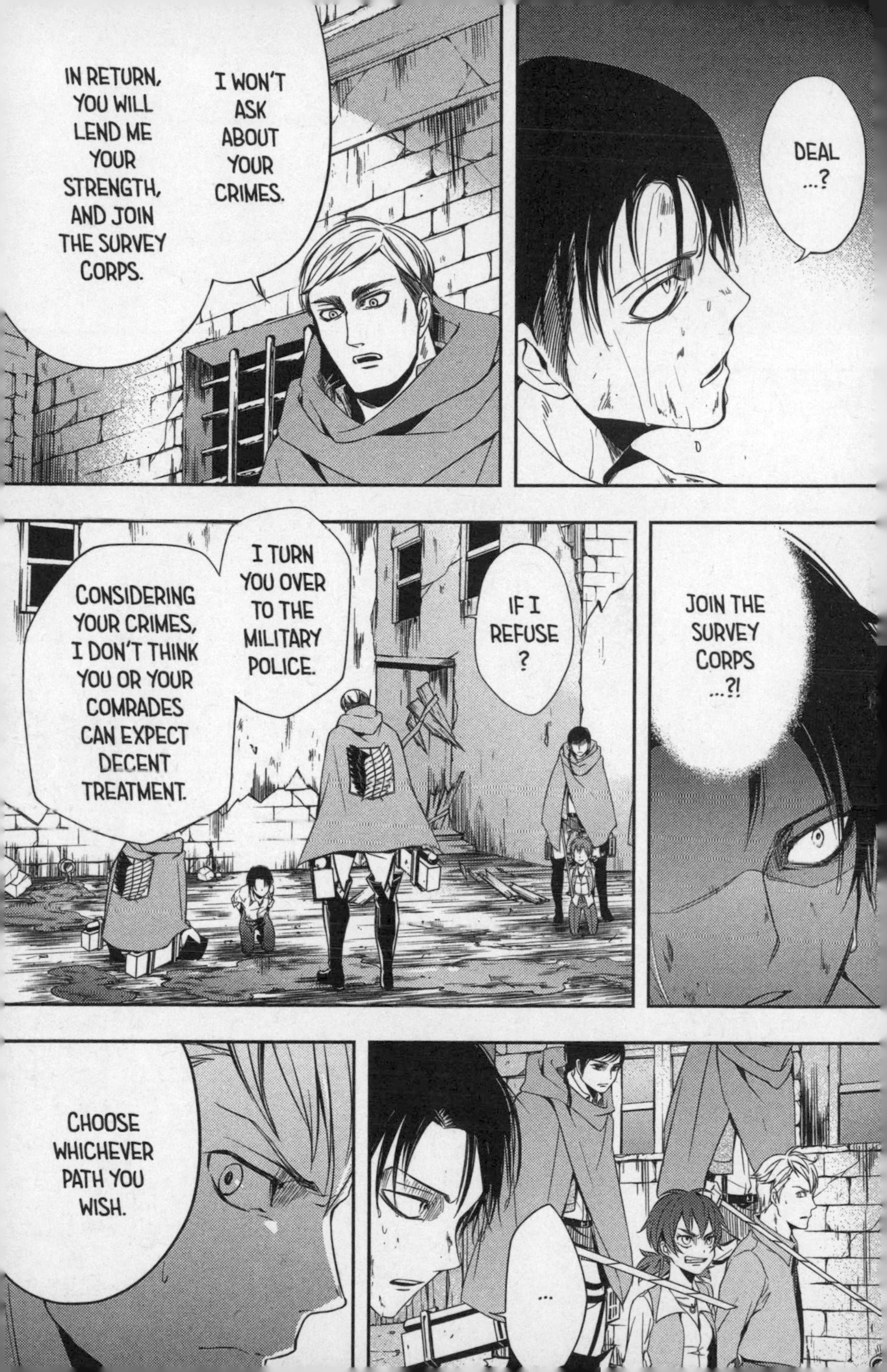
DEAL ...?
I WON'T ASK ABOUT YOUR CRIMES.
IN RETURN, YOU WILL LEND ME YOUR STRENGTH, AND JOIN THE SURVEY CORPS.
JOIN THE SURVEY CORPS ...?!
IF I REFUSE ?
I TURN YOU OVER TO THE MILITARY POLICE.
CONSIDERING YOUR CRIMES, I DON'T THINK YOU OR YOUR COMRADES CAN EXPECT DECENT TREATMENT.
...
CHOOSE WHICHEVER PATH YOU WISH.

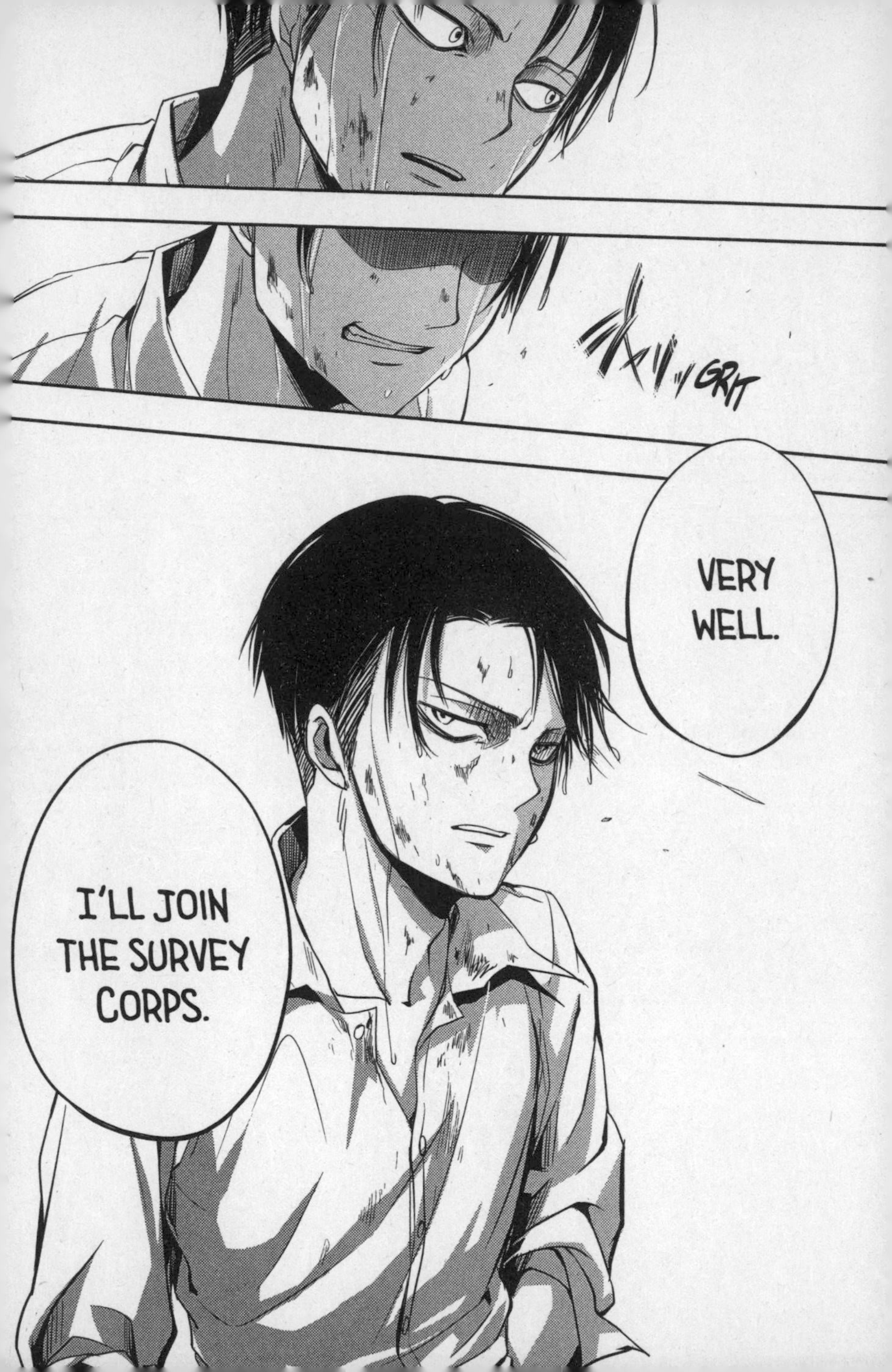
GRIT
VERY WELL.
I'LL JOIN THE SURVEY CORPS.

ATTACK on TITAN

NO REGRETS

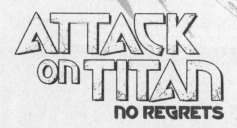

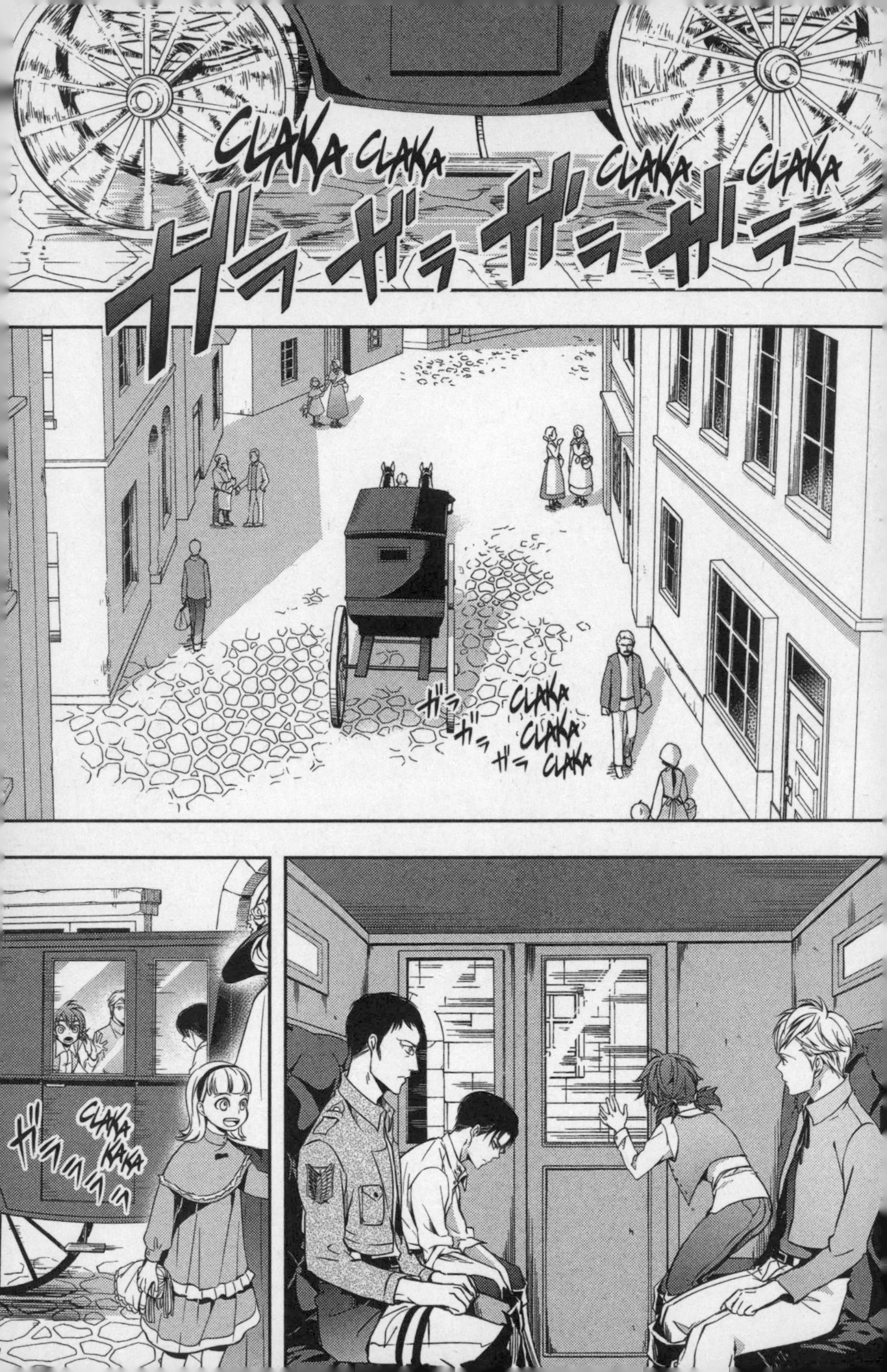
CLAKA CLAKA CLAKA CLAKA
ガラガラガラガラ
ガラ ガラ ガラ
CLAKA CLAKA CLAKA
CLAKA KAKA
ガラララララ

Chapter 2: One Arrow

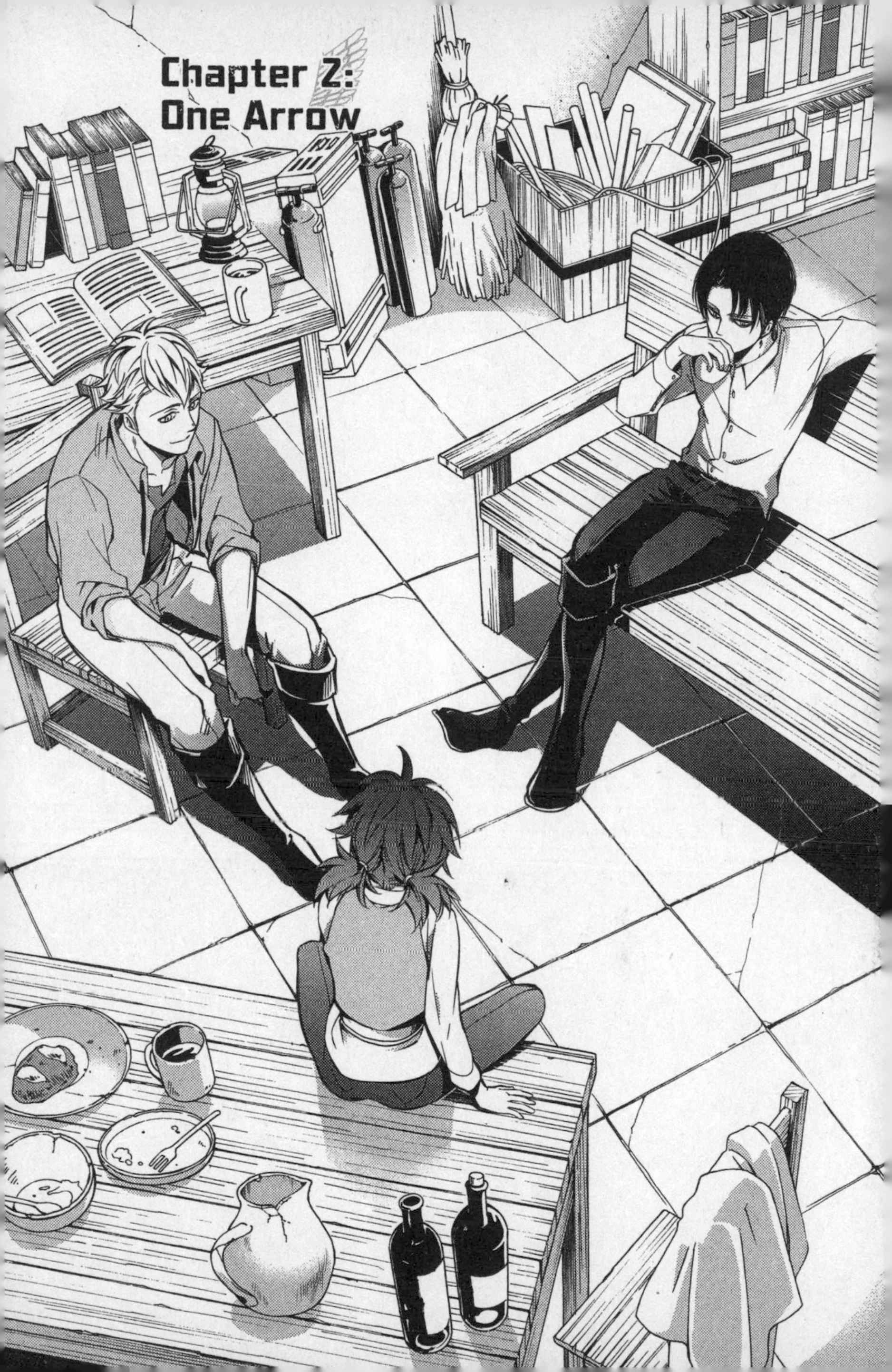

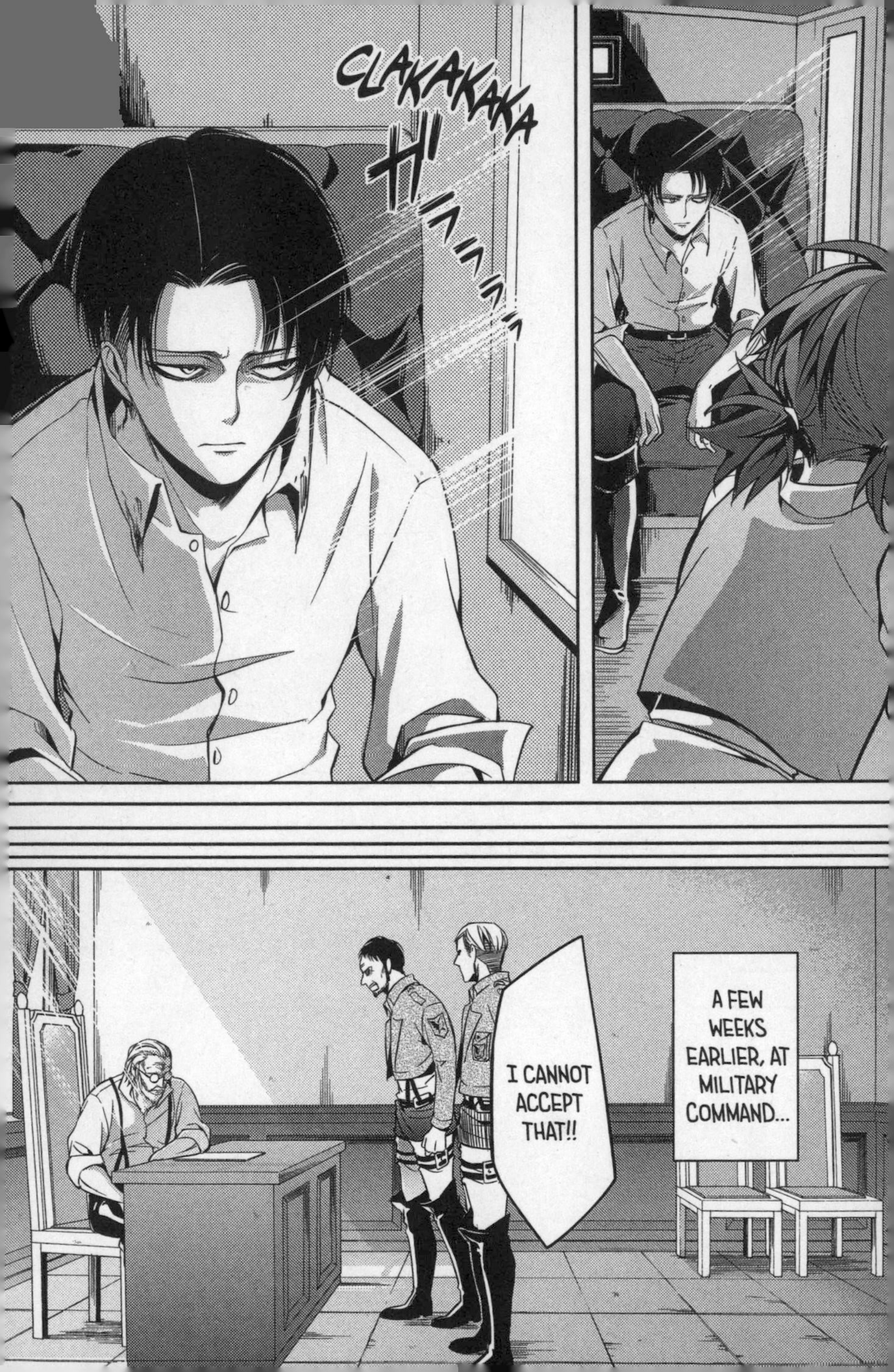
CLAKAKAKA
HI
A FEW WEEKS EARLIER, AT MILITARY COMMAND...
I CANNOT ACCEPT THAT!!

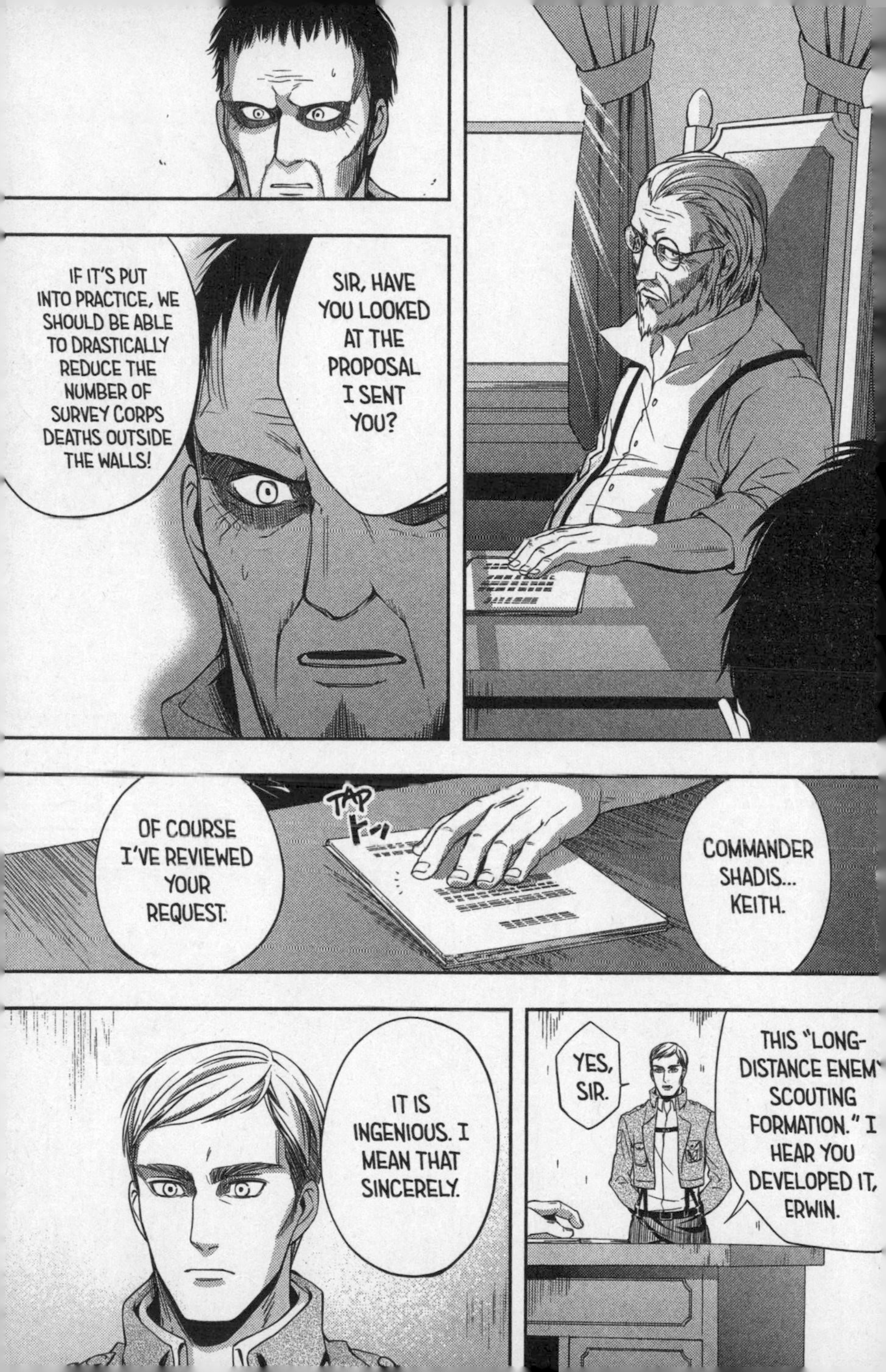
SIR, HAVE YOU LOOKED AT THE PROPOSAL I SENT YOU?
IF IT'S PUT INTO PRACTICE, WE SHOULD BE ABLE TO DRASTICALLY REDUCE THE NUMBER OF SURVEY CORPS DEATHS OUTSIDE THE WALLS!
COMMANDER SHADIS... KEITH.
TAP
OF COURSE I'VE REVIEWED YOUR REQUEST.
THIS "LONG-DISTANCE ENEM SCOUTING FORMATION." I HEAR YOU DEVELOPED IT, ERWIN.
YES, SIR.
IT IS INGENIOUS. I MEAN THAT SINCERELY.

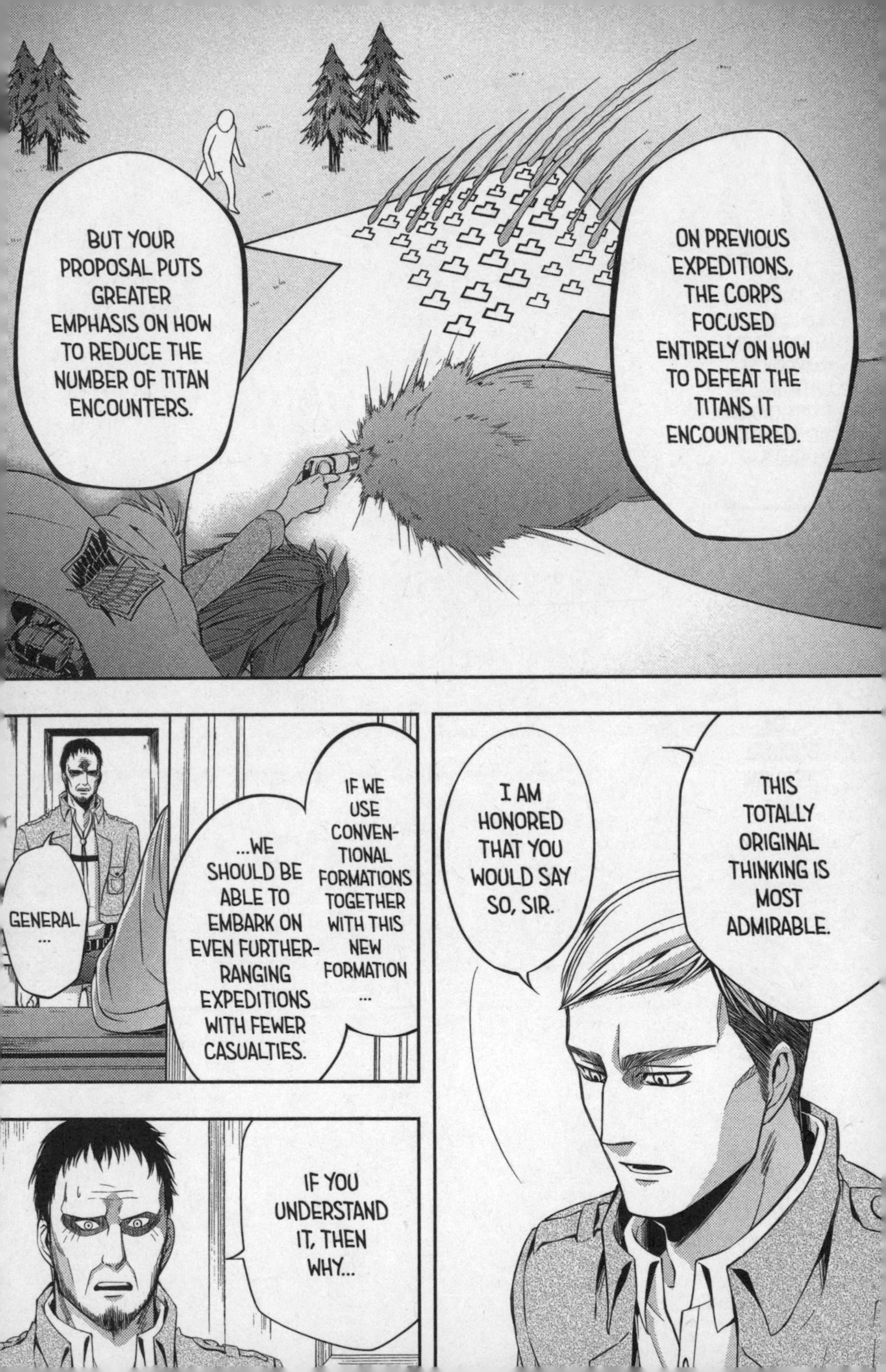
ON PREVIOUS EXPEDITIONS, THE CORPS FOCUSED ENTIRELY ON HOW TO DEFEAT THE TITANS IT ENCOUNTERED.
BUT YOUR PROPOSAL PUTS GREATER EMPHASIS ON HOW TO REDUCE THE NUMBER OF TITAN ENCOUNTERS.
THIS TOTALLY ORIGINAL THINKING IS MOST ADMIRABLE.
I AM HONORED THAT YOU WOULD SAY SO, SIR.
IF WE USE CONVEN-TIONAL FORMATIONS TOGETHER WITH THIS NEW FORMATION ...
...WE SHOULD BE ABLE TO EMBARK ON EVEN FURTHER-RANGING EXPEDITIONS WITH FEWER CASUALTIES.
GENERAL ...
IF YOU UNDERSTAND IT, THEN WHY...

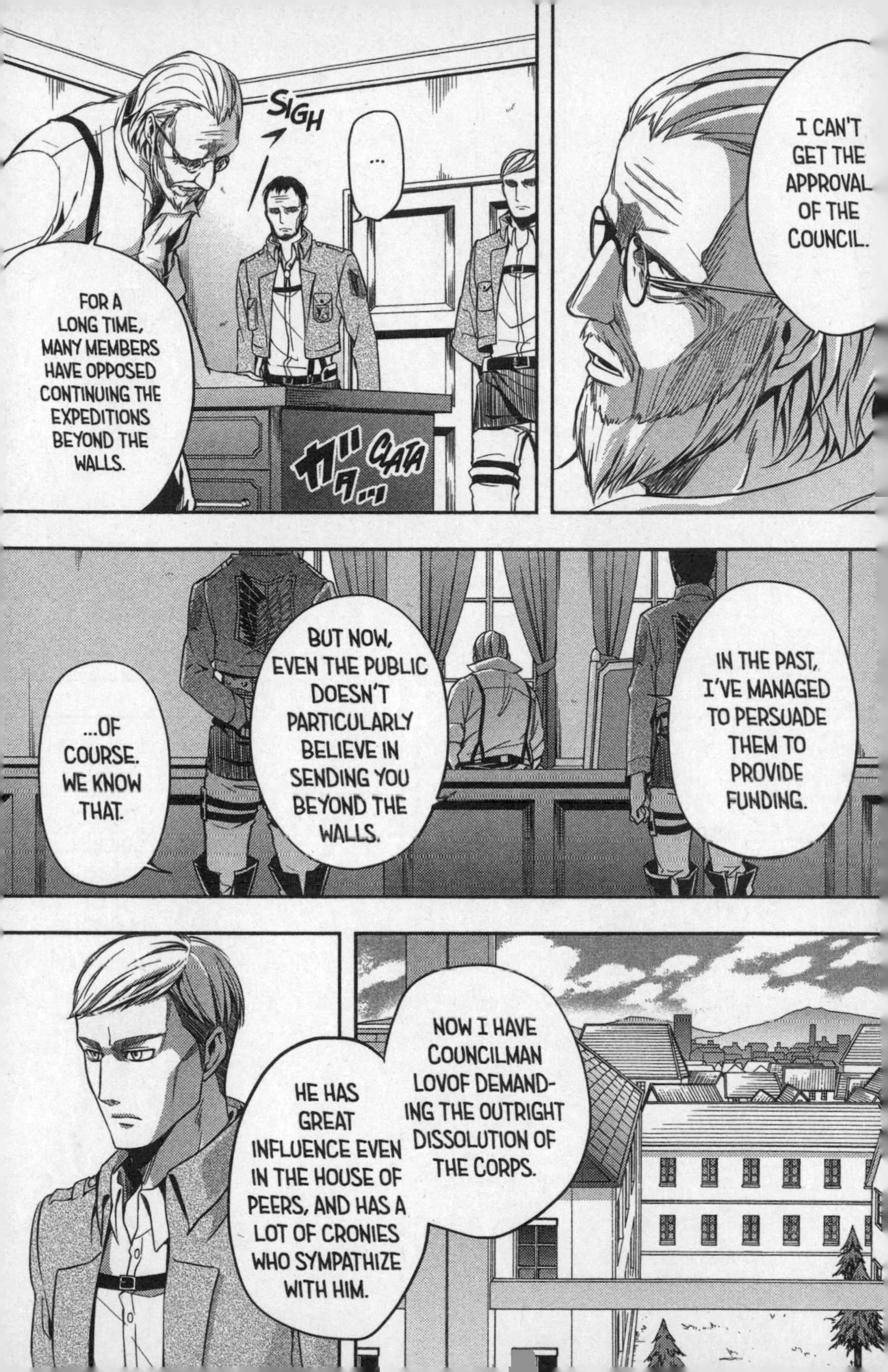
I CAN'T GET THE APPROVAL OF THE COUNCIL.
SIGH
...
FOR A LONG TIME, MANY MEMBERS HAVE OPPOSED CONTINUING THE EXPEDITIONS BEYOND THE WALLS.
CLATA
IN THE PAST, I'VE MANAGED TO PERSUADE THEM TO PROVIDE FUNDING.
BUT NOW, EVEN THE PUBLIC DOESN'T PARTICULARLY BELIEVE IN SENDING YOU BEYOND THE WALLS.
...OF COURSE. WE KNOW THAT.
NOW I HAVE COUNCILMAN LOVOF DEMANDING THE OUTRIGHT DISSOLUTION OF THE CORPS.
HE HAS GREAT INFLUENCE EVEN IN THE HOUSE OF PEERS, AND HAS A LOT OF CRONIES WHO SYMPATHIZE WITH HIM.

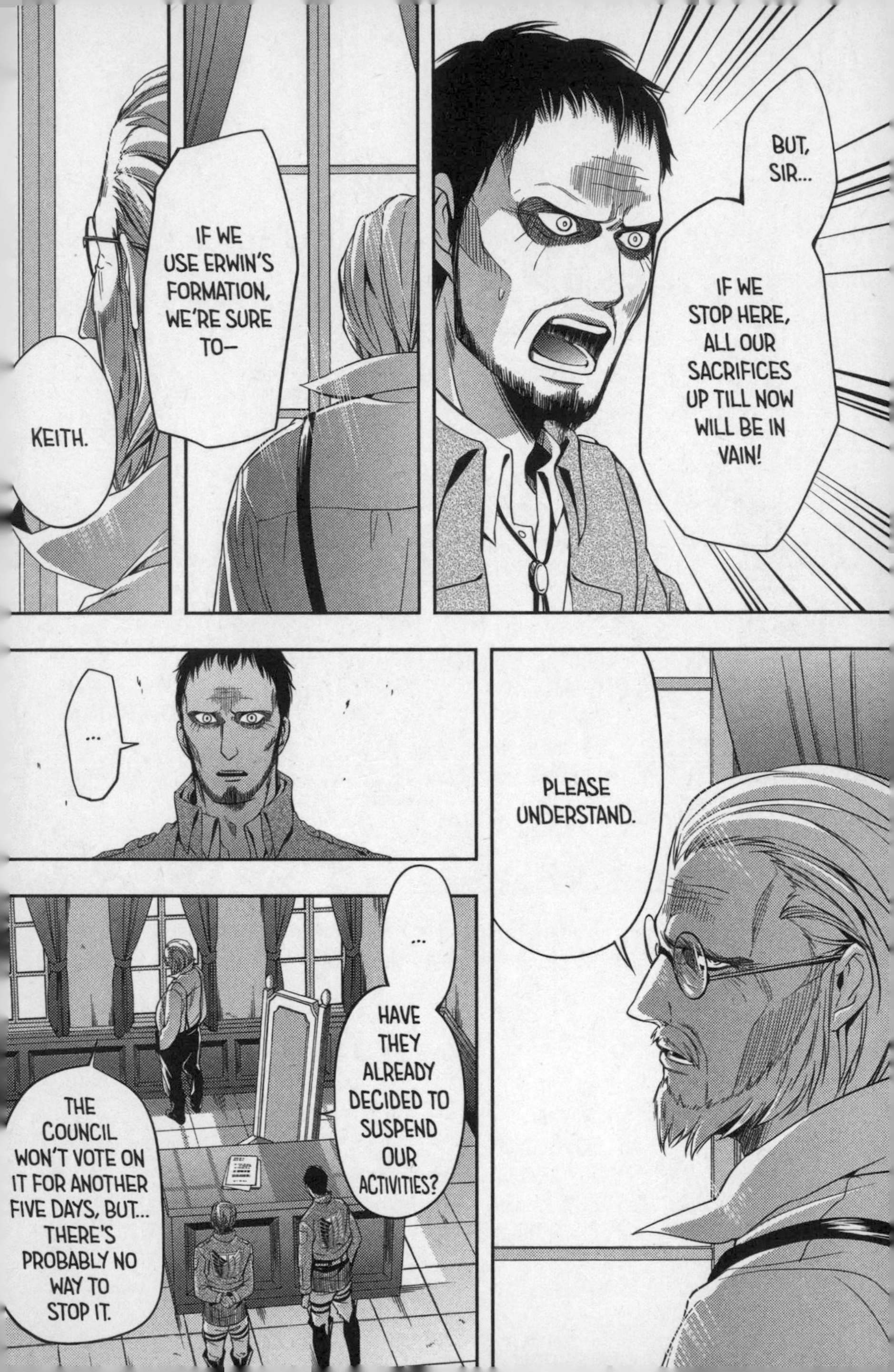
BUT, SIR...
IF WE STOP HERE, ALL OUR SACRIFICES UP TILL NOW WILL BE IN VAIN!
IF WE USE ERWIN'S FORMATION, WE'RE SURE TO—
KEITH.
PLEASE UNDERSTAND.
...
...
HAVE THEY ALREADY DECIDED TO SUSPEND OUR ACTIVITIES?
THE COUNCIL WON'T VOTE ON IT FOR ANOTHER FIVE DAYS, BUT... THERE'S PROBABLY NO WAY TO STOP IT.

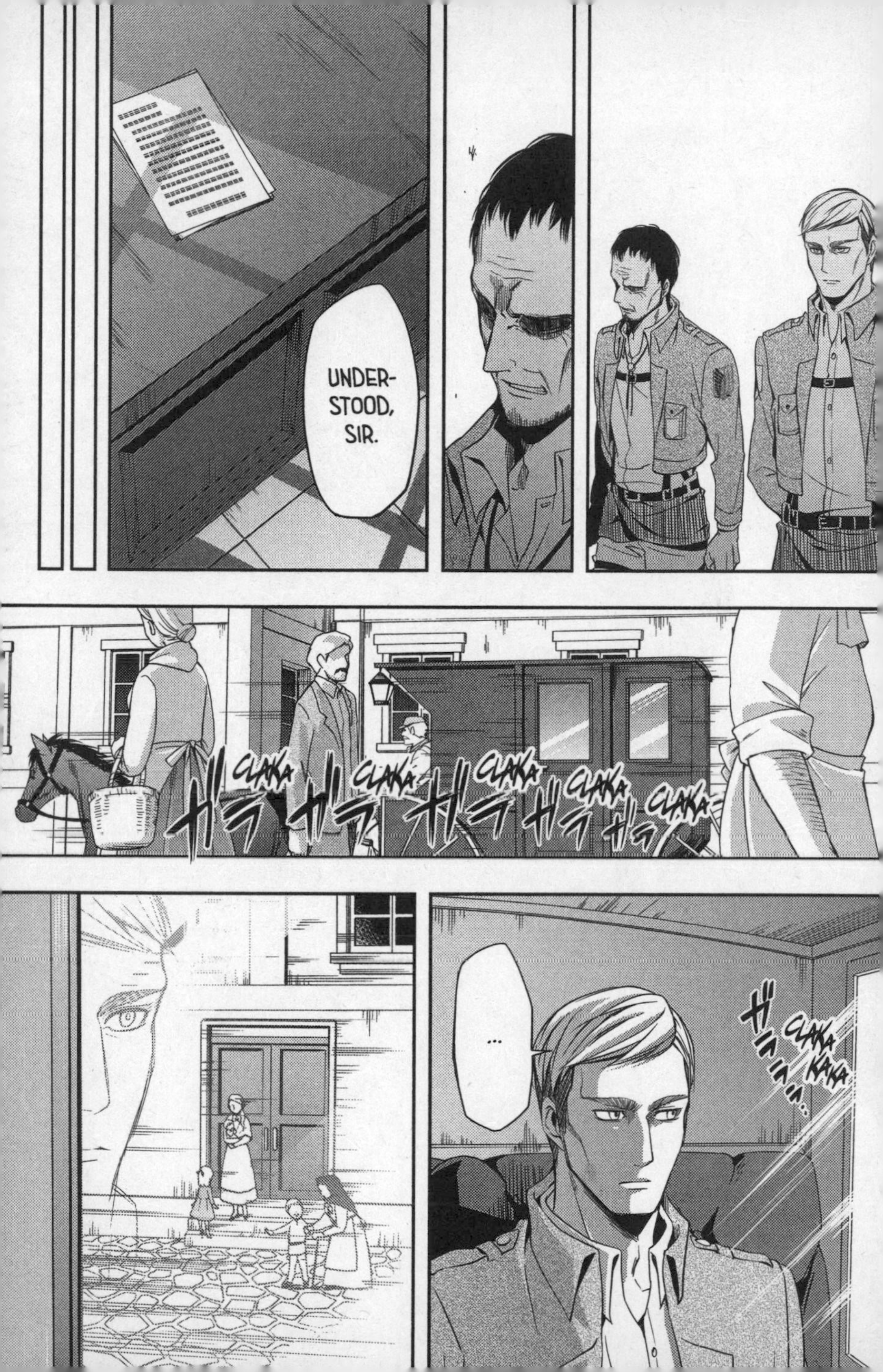
UNDER-STOOD, SIR.
CLAKA
CLAKA
CLAKA
CLAKA
CLAKA
...
CLAKA KAKA

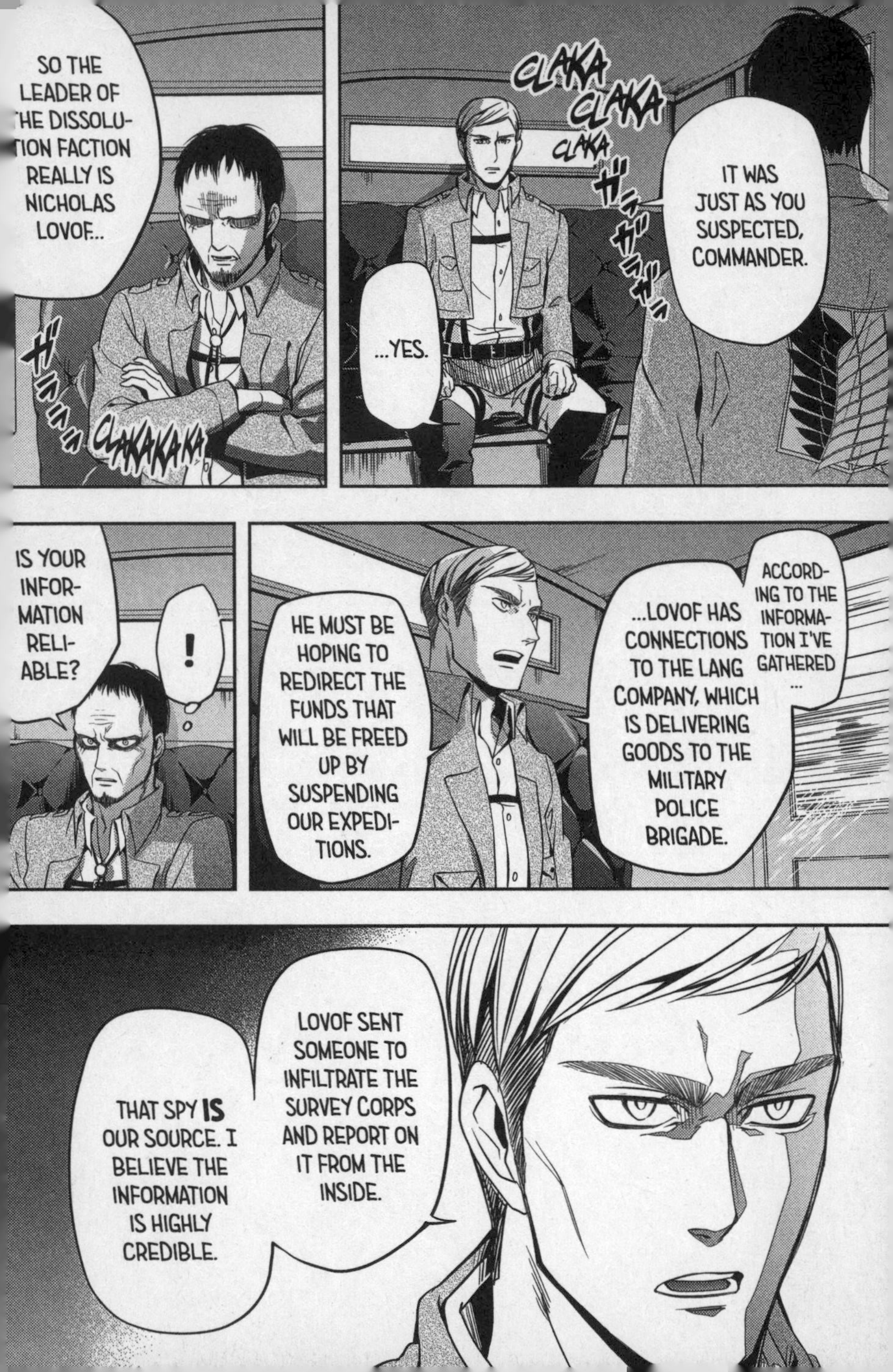
CLAKA CLAKA CLAKA
IT WAS JUST AS YOU SUSPECTED, COMMANDER.
...YES.
SO THE LEADER OF THE DISSOLUTION FACTION REALLY IS NICHOLAS LOVOF...
CLAKAKAKAKA
ACCORDING TO THE INFORMATION I'VE GATHERED...
...LOVOF HAS CONNECTIONS TO THE LANG COMPANY, WHICH IS DELIVERING GOODS TO THE MILITARY POLICE BRIGADE.
HE MUST BE HOPING TO REDIRECT THE FUNDS THAT WILL BE FREED UP BY SUSPENDING OUR EXPEDITIONS.
IS YOUR INFORMATION RELIABLE?
!
LOVOF SENT SOMEONE TO INFILTRATE THE SURVEY CORPS AND REPORT ON IT FROM THE INSIDE.
THAT SPY **IS** OUR SOURCE. I BELIEVE THE INFORMATION IS HIGHLY CREDIBLE.

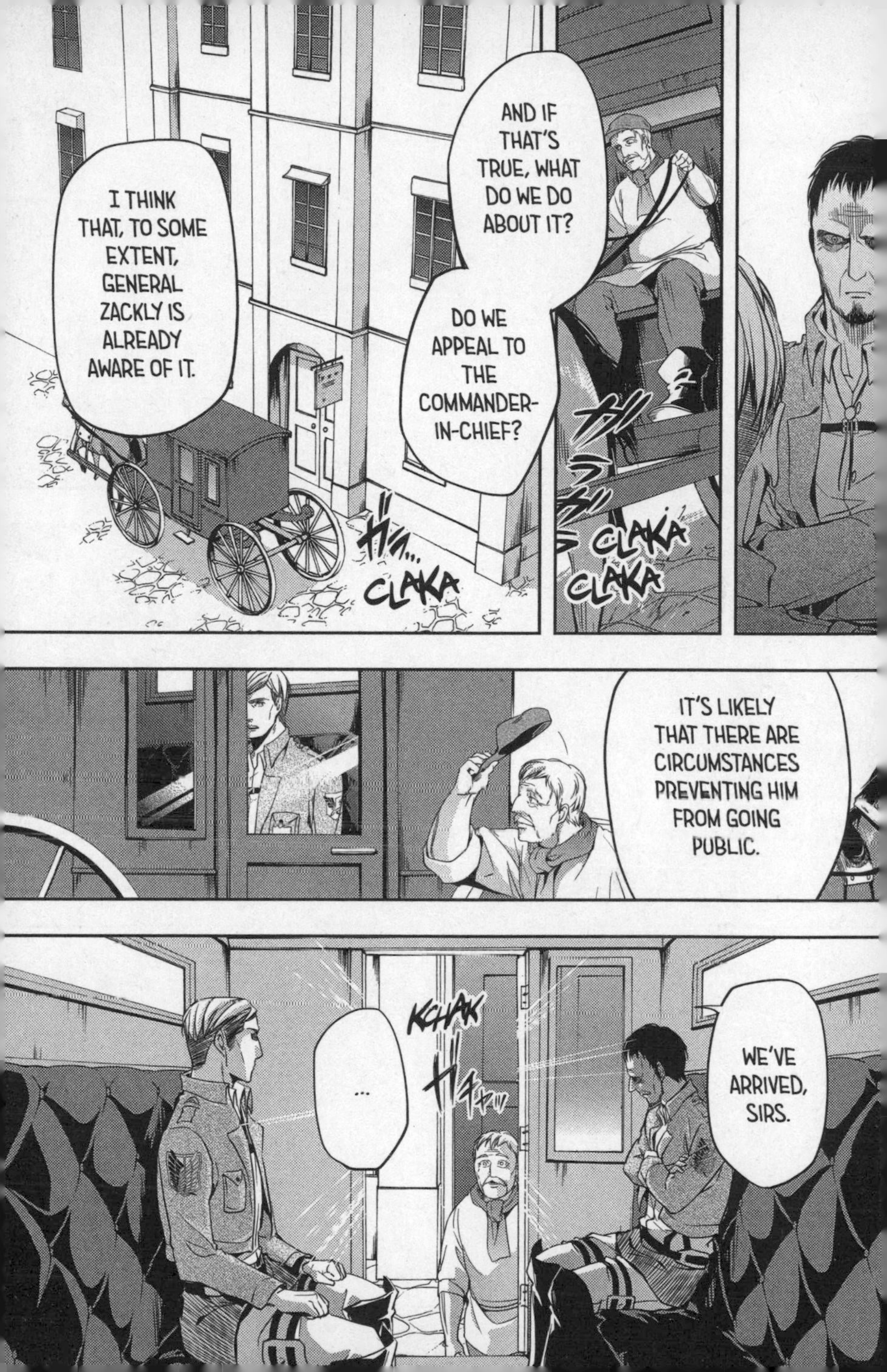
AND IF THAT'S TRUE, WHAT DO WE DO ABOUT IT?
DO WE APPEAL TO THE COMMANDER-IN-CHIEF?
CLAKA CLAKA
I THINK THAT, TO SOME EXTENT, GENERAL ZACKLY IS ALREADY AWARE OF IT.
CLAKA
IT'S LIKELY THAT THERE ARE CIRCUMSTANCES PREVENTING HIM FROM GOING PUBLIC.
WE'VE ARRIVED, SIRS.
KCHAK
...

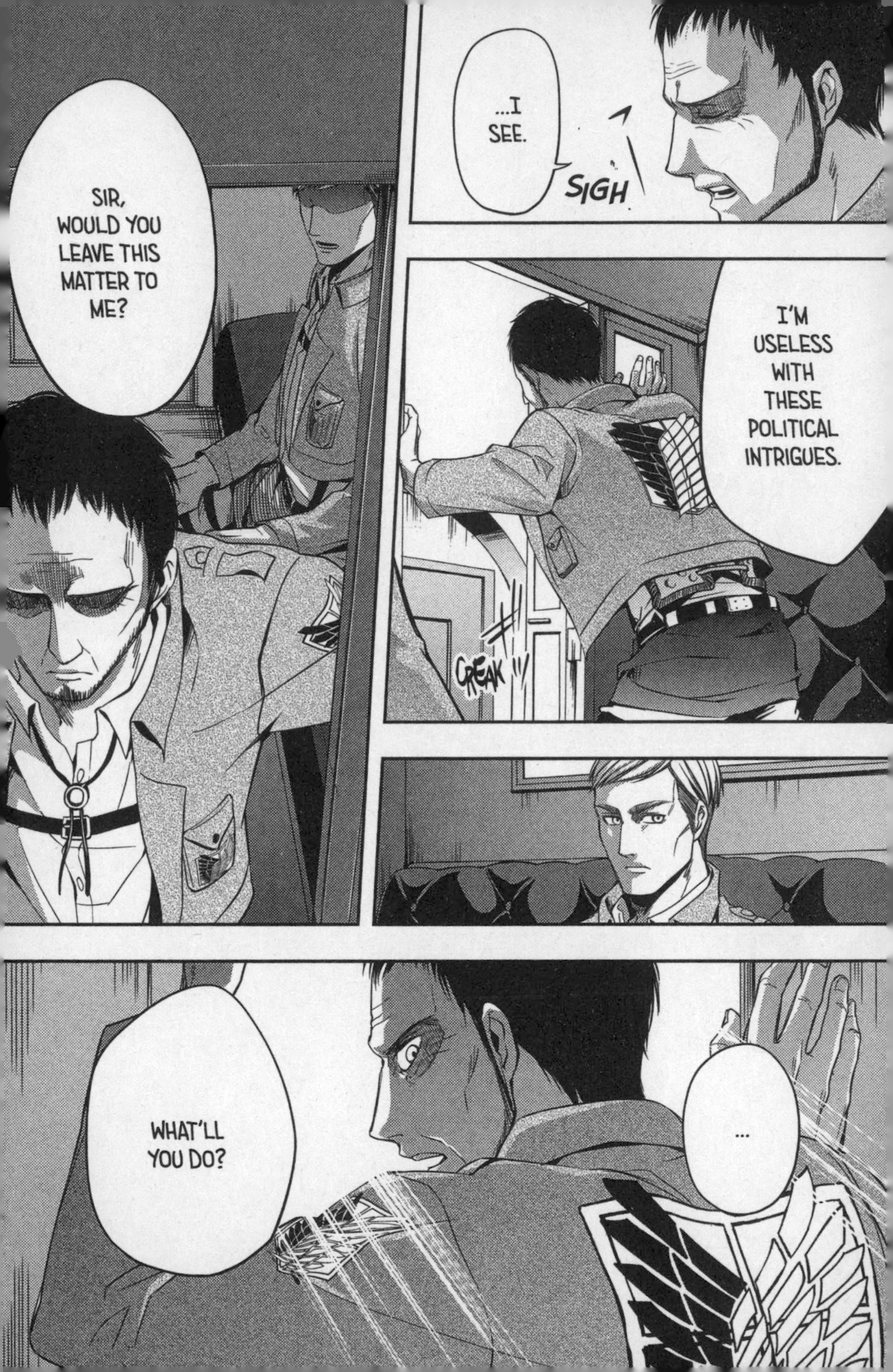
...I SEE.
SIGH
I'M USELESS WITH THESE POLITICAL INTRIGUES.
CREAK
SIR, WOULD YOU LEAVE THIS MATTER TO ME?
...
WHAT'LL YOU DO?

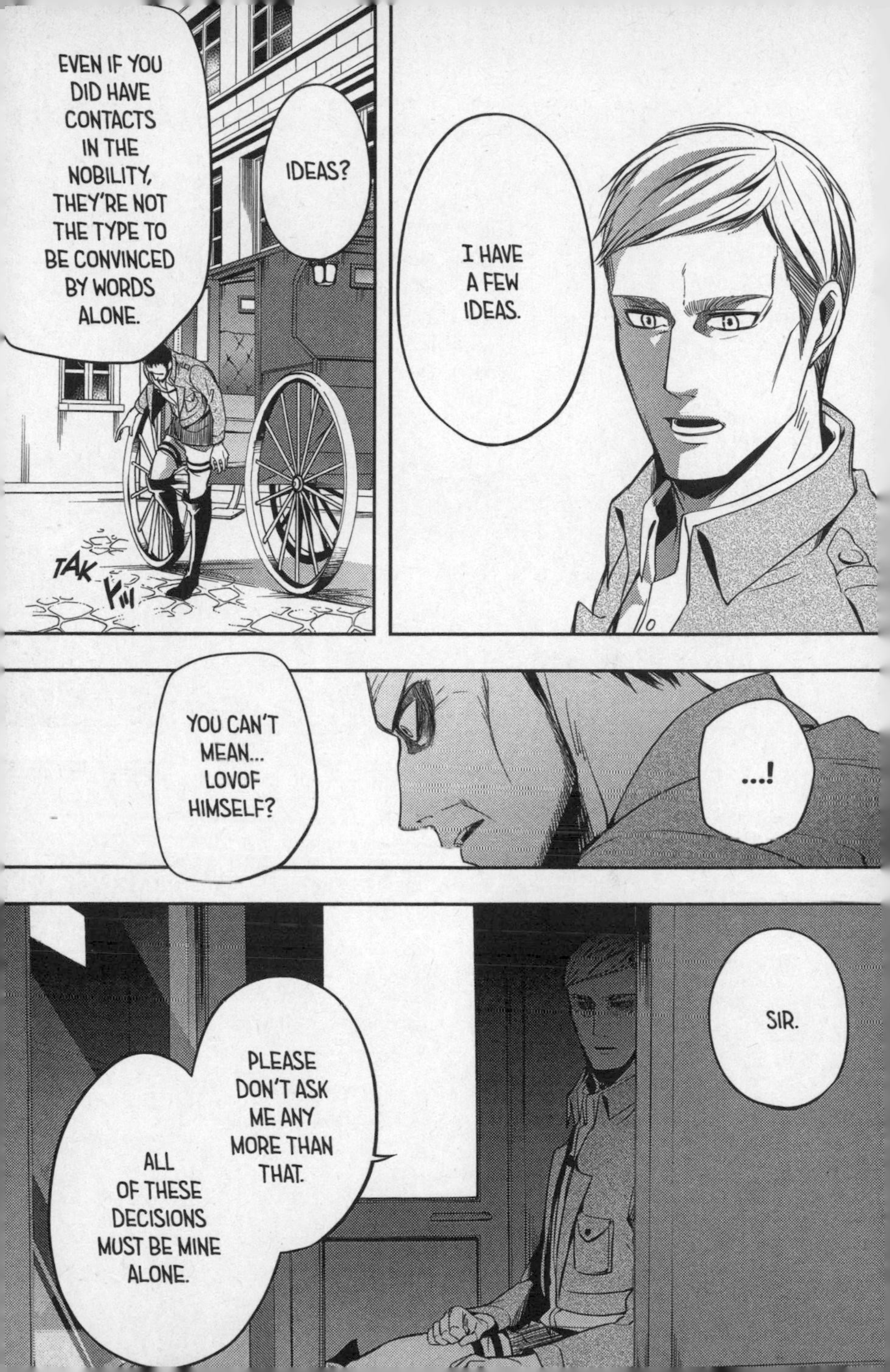
I HAVE A FEW IDEAS.
IDEAS?
EVEN IF YOU DID HAVE CONTACTS IN THE NOBILITY, THEY'RE NOT THE TYPE TO BE CONVINCED BY WORDS ALONE.
TAK
...!
YOU CAN'T MEAN... LOVOF HIMSELF?
SIR.
PLEASE DON'T ASK ME ANY MORE THAN THAT.
ALL OF THESE DECISIONS MUST BE MINE ALONE.

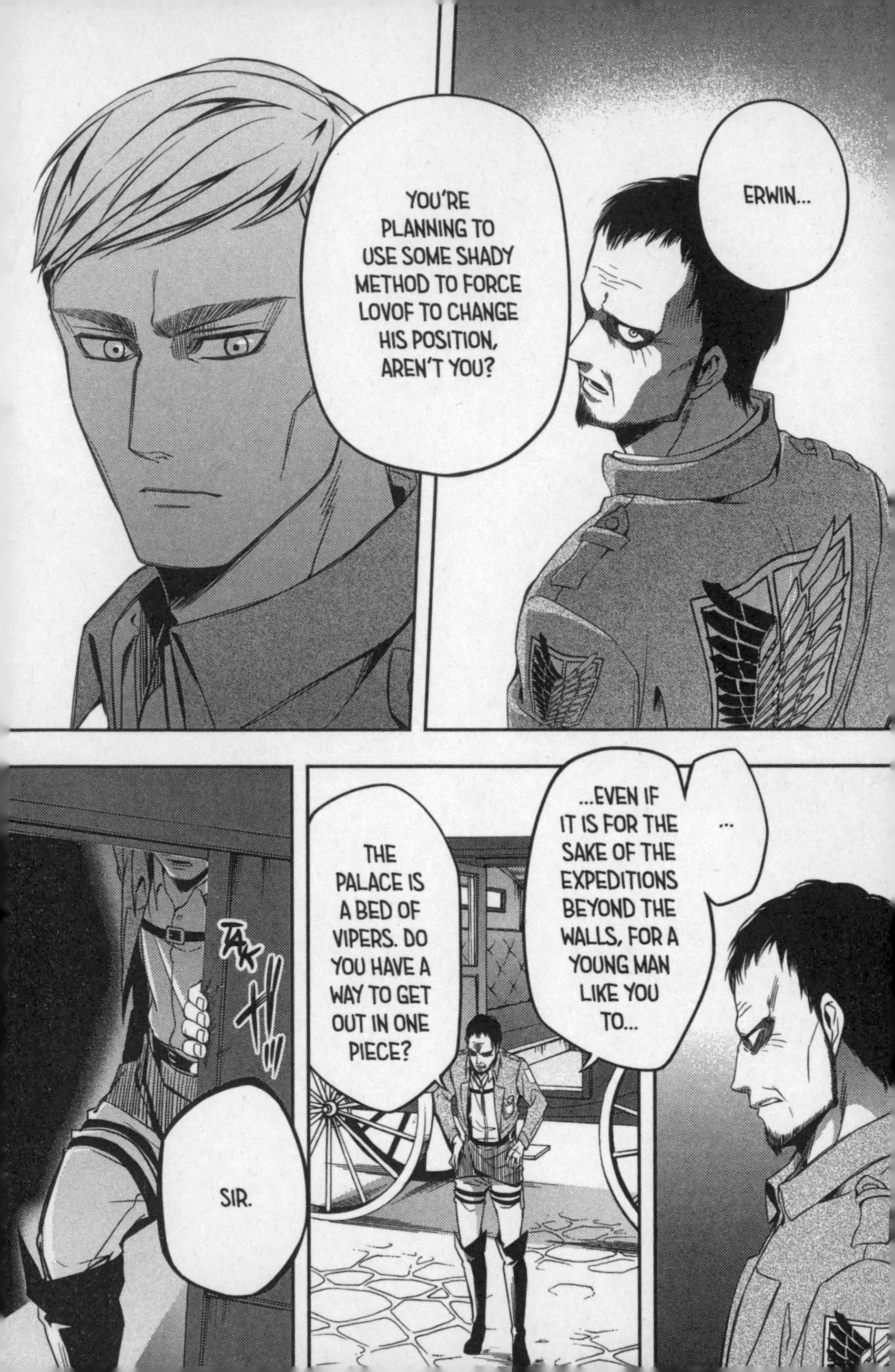
ERWIN...
YOU'RE PLANNING TO USE SOME SHADY METHOD TO FORCE LOVOF TO CHANGE HIS POSITION, AREN'T YOU?
...
...EVEN IF IT IS FOR THE SAKE OF THE EXPEDITIONS BEYOND THE WALLS, FOR A YOUNG MAN LIKE YOU TO...
THE PALACE IS A BED OF VIPERS. DO YOU HAVE A WAY TO GET OUT IN ONE PIECE?
TAK
SIR.

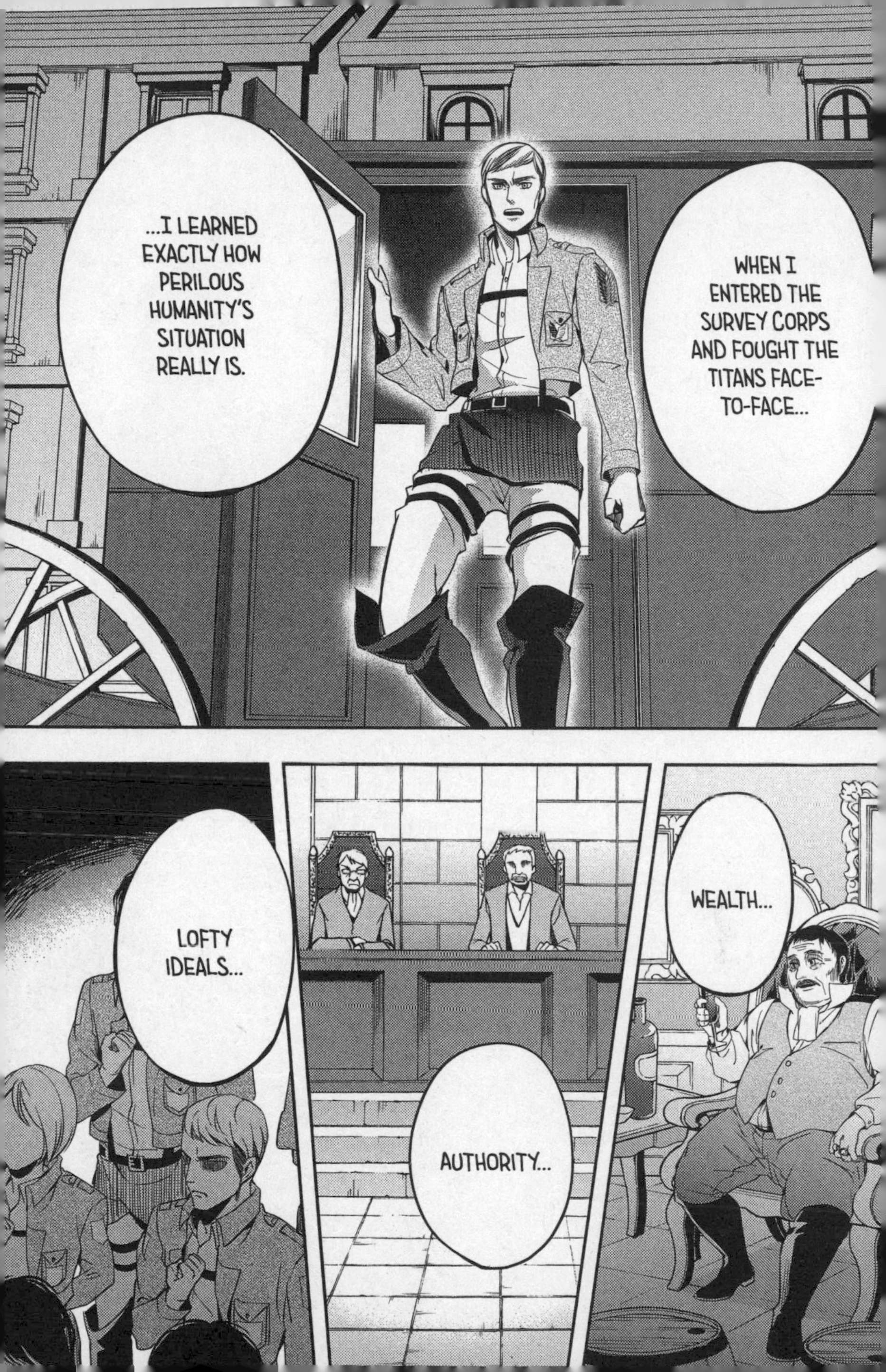
WHEN I ENTERED THE SURVEY CORPS AND FOUGHT THE TITANS FACE-TO-FACE...
...I LEARNED EXACTLY HOW PERILOUS HUMANITY'S SITUATION REALLY IS.
WEALTH...
AUTHORITY...
LOFTY IDEALS...

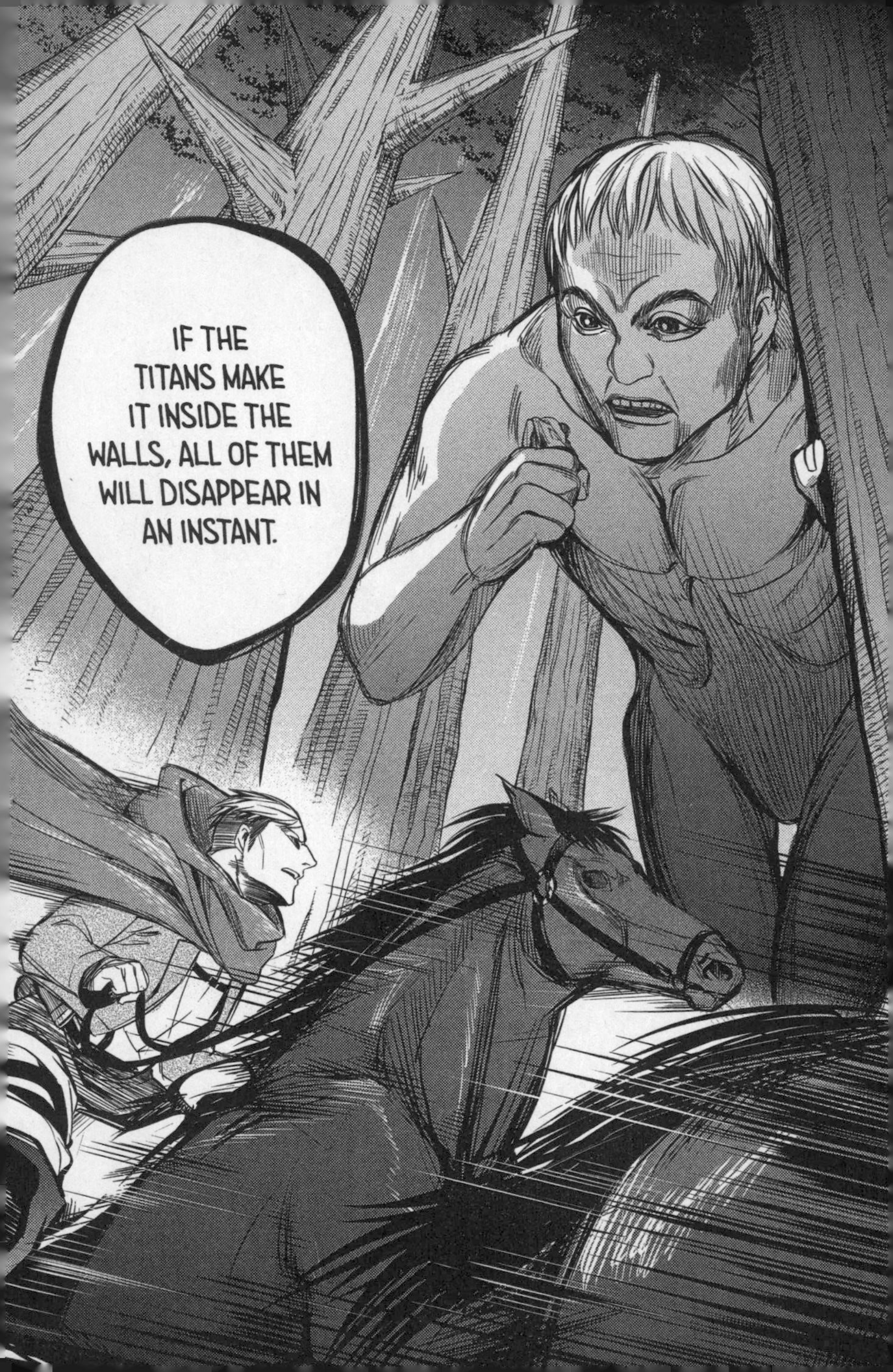
IF THE TITANS MAKE IT INSIDE THE WALLS, ALL OF THEM WILL DISAPPEAR IN AN INSTANT.

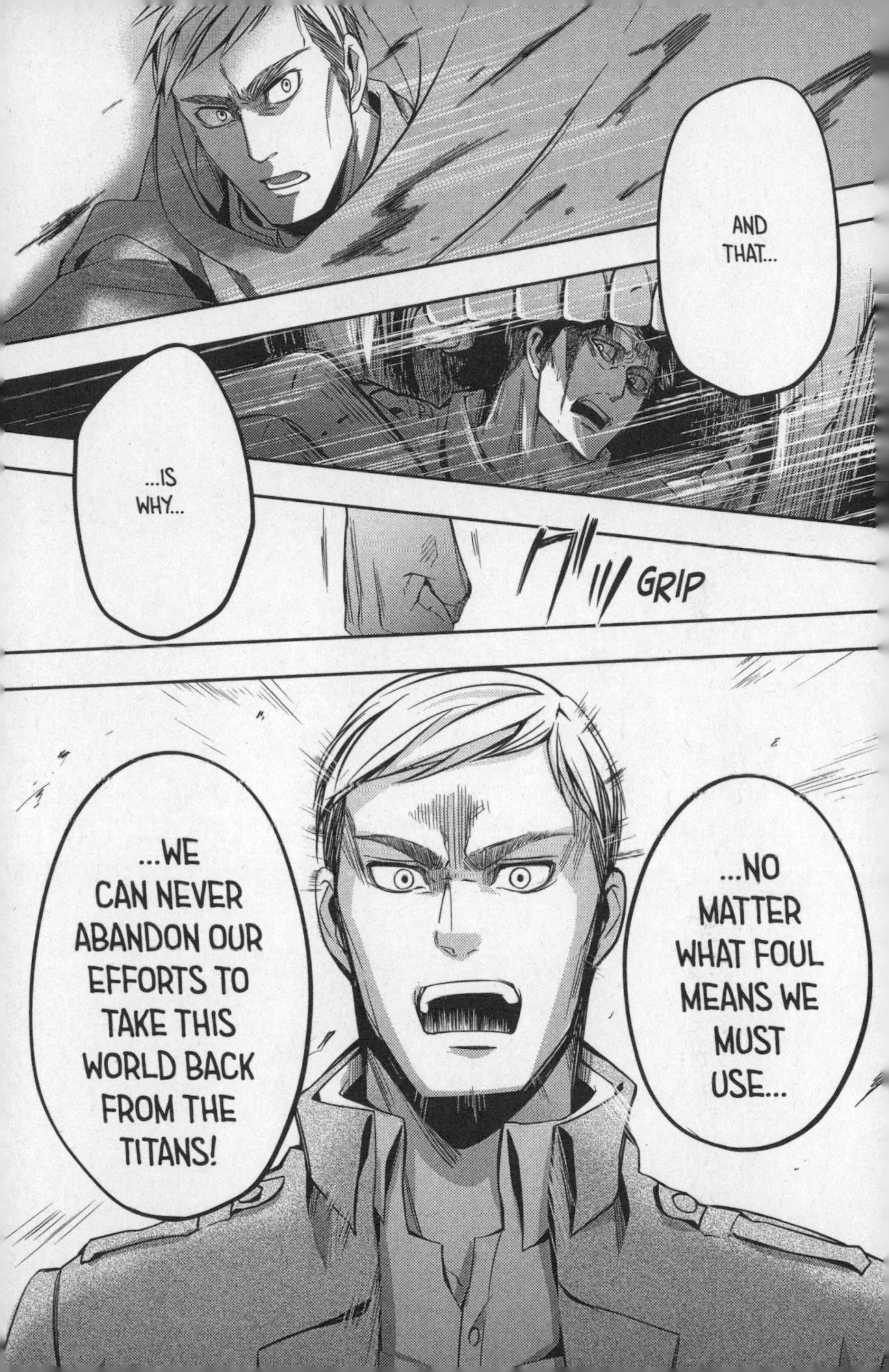
AND THAT...
...IS WHY...
GRIP
...NO MATTER WHAT FOUL MEANS WE MUST USE...
...WE CAN NEVER ABANDON OUR EFFORTS TO TAKE THIS WORLD BACK FROM THE TITANS!

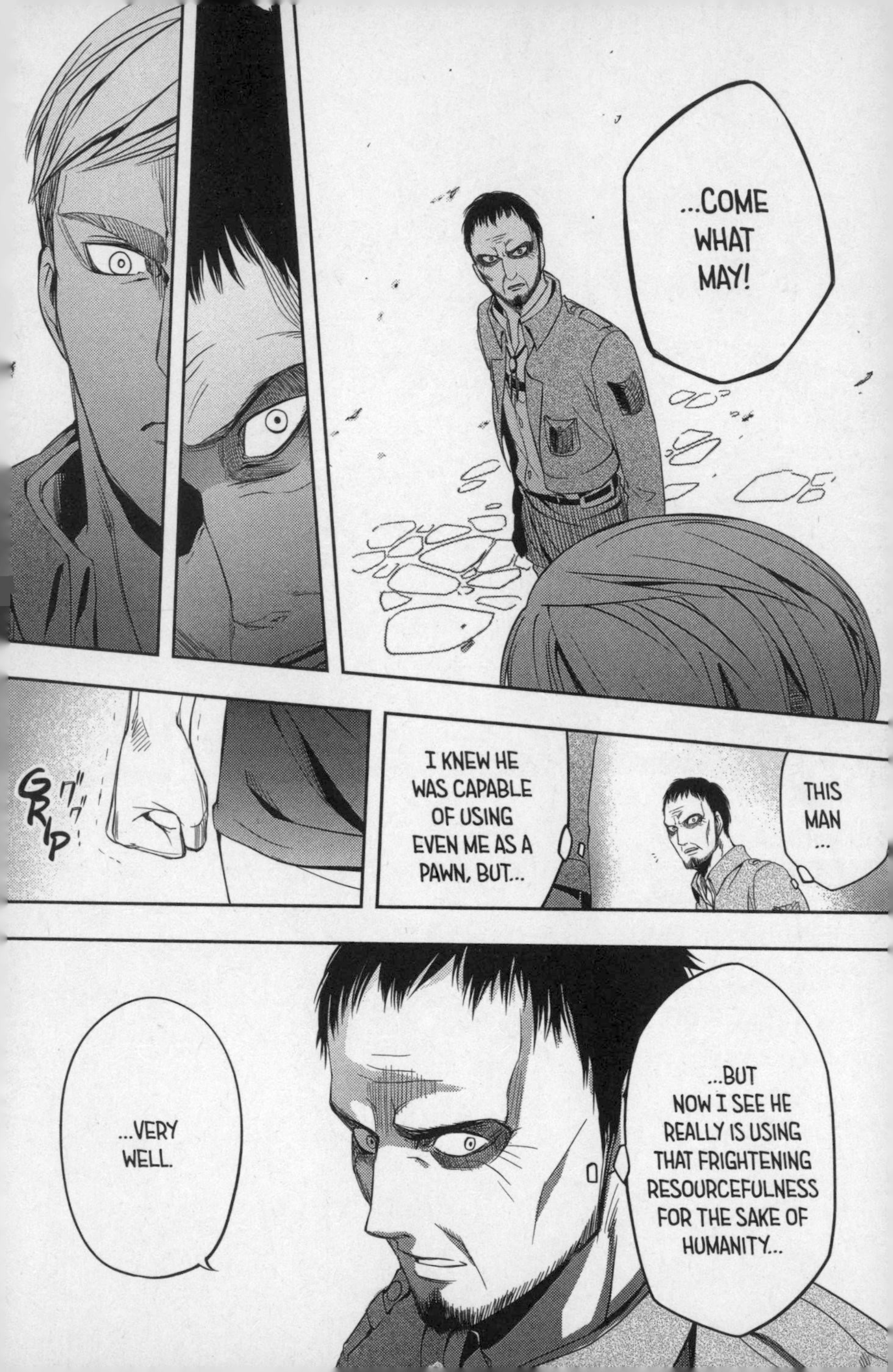
...COME WHAT MAY!
THIS MAN ...
I KNEW HE WAS CAPABLE OF USING EVEN ME AS A PAWN, BUT...
GRIP
...BUT NOW I SEE HE REALLY IS USING THAT FRIGHTENING RESOURCEFULNESS FOR THE SAKE OF HUMANITY...
...VERY WELL.

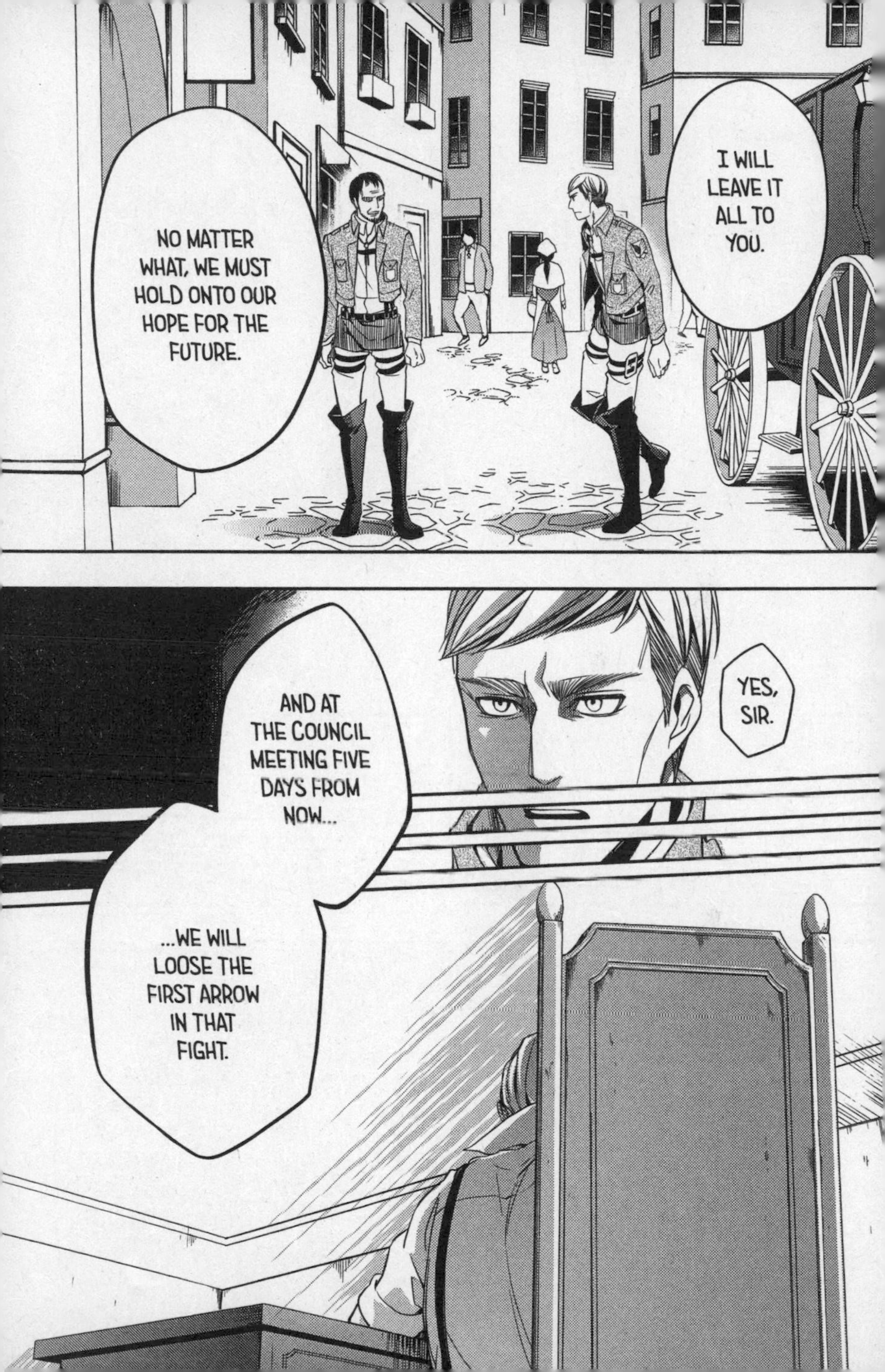
I WILL LEAVE IT ALL TO YOU.
NO MATTER WHAT, WE MUST HOLD ONTO OUR HOPE FOR THE FUTURE.
YES, SIR.
AND AT THE COUNCIL MEETING FIVE DAYS FROM NOW...
...WE WILL LOOSE THE FIRST ARROW IN THAT FIGHT.

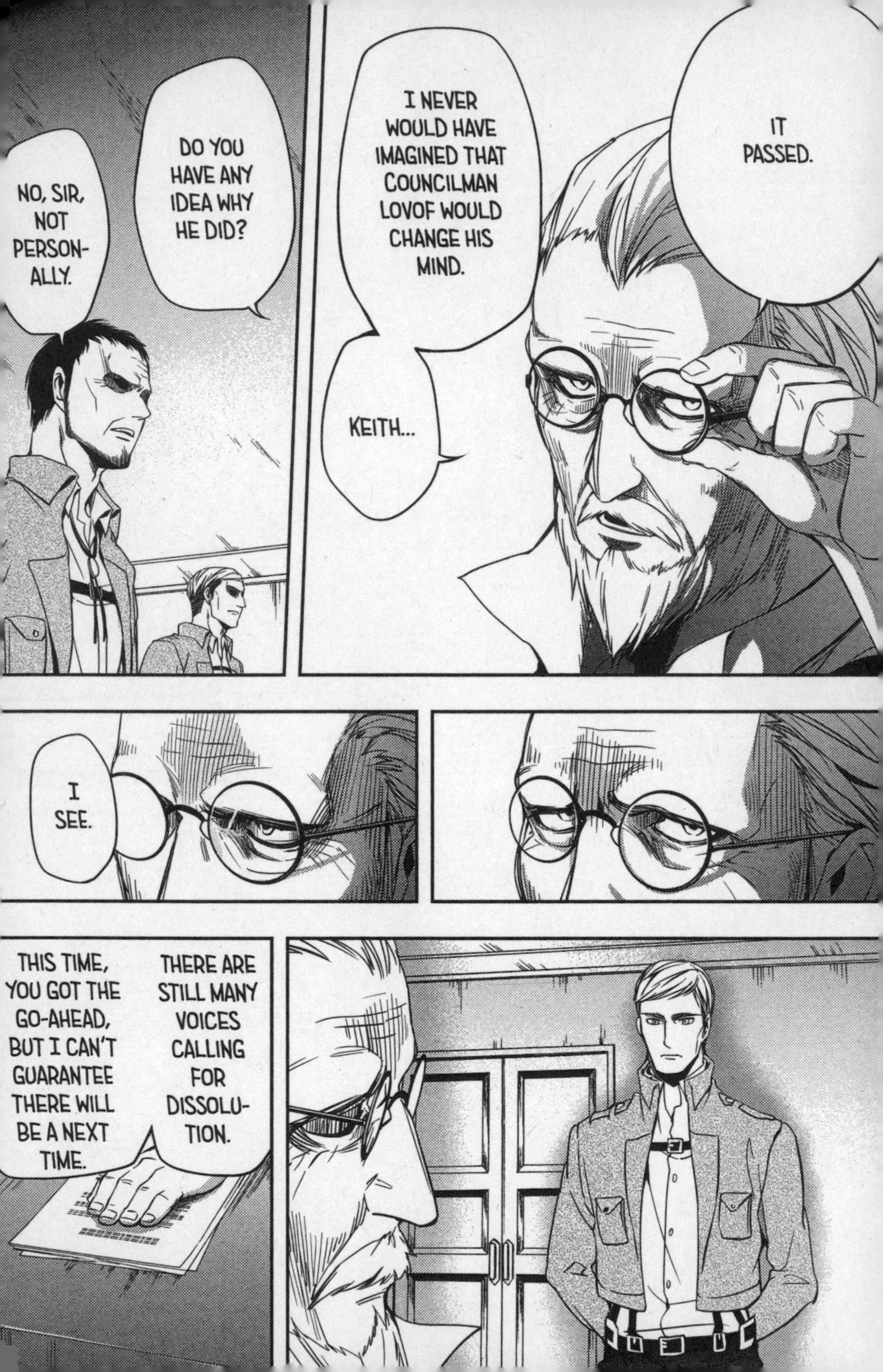
IT PASSED.
I NEVER WOULD HAVE IMAGINED THAT COUNCILMAN LOVOF WOULD CHANGE HIS MIND.
KEITH...
DO YOU HAVE ANY IDEA WHY HE DID?
NO, SIR, NOT PERSON-ALLY.
I SEE.
THERE ARE STILL MANY VOICES CALLING FOR DISSOLU-TION.
THIS TIME, YOU GOT THE GO-AHEAD, BUT I CAN'T GUARANTEE THERE WILL BE A NEXT TIME.

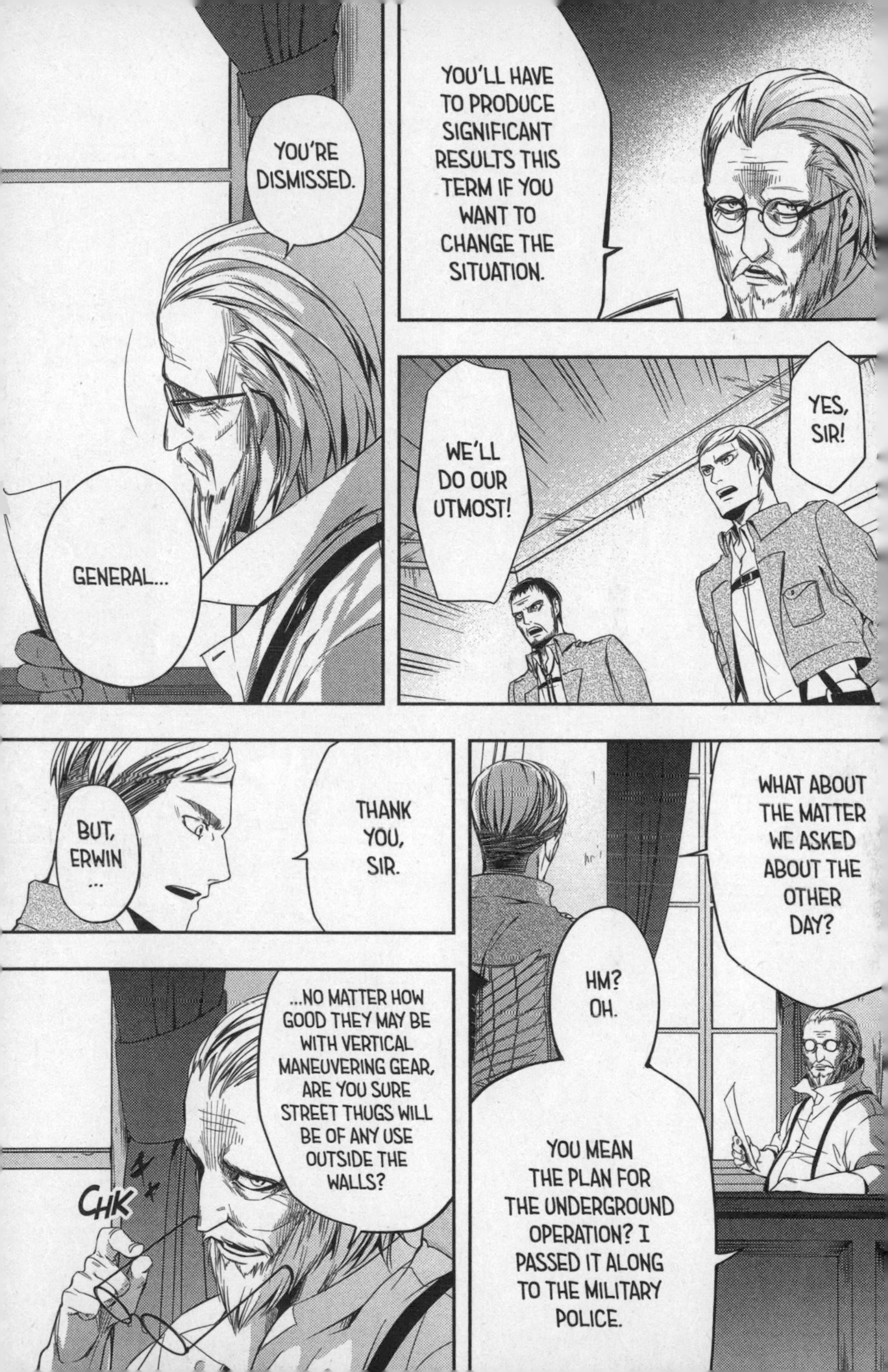

YOU'LL HAVE TO PRODUCE SIGNIFICANT RESULTS THIS TERM IF YOU WANT TO CHANGE THE SITUATION.
YES, SIR!
WE'LL DO OUR UTMOST!
YOU'RE DISMISSED.
GENERAL...
WHAT ABOUT THE MATTER WE ASKED ABOUT THE OTHER DAY?
HM? OH.
YOU MEAN THE PLAN FOR THE UNDERGROUND OPERATION? I PASSED IT ALONG TO THE MILITARY POLICE.
THANK YOU, SIR.
BUT, ERWIN ...
...NO MATTER HOW GOOD THEY MAY BE WITH VERTICAL MANEUVERING GEAR, ARE YOU SURE STREET THUGS WILL BE OF ANY USE OUTSIDE THE WALLS?
CHK

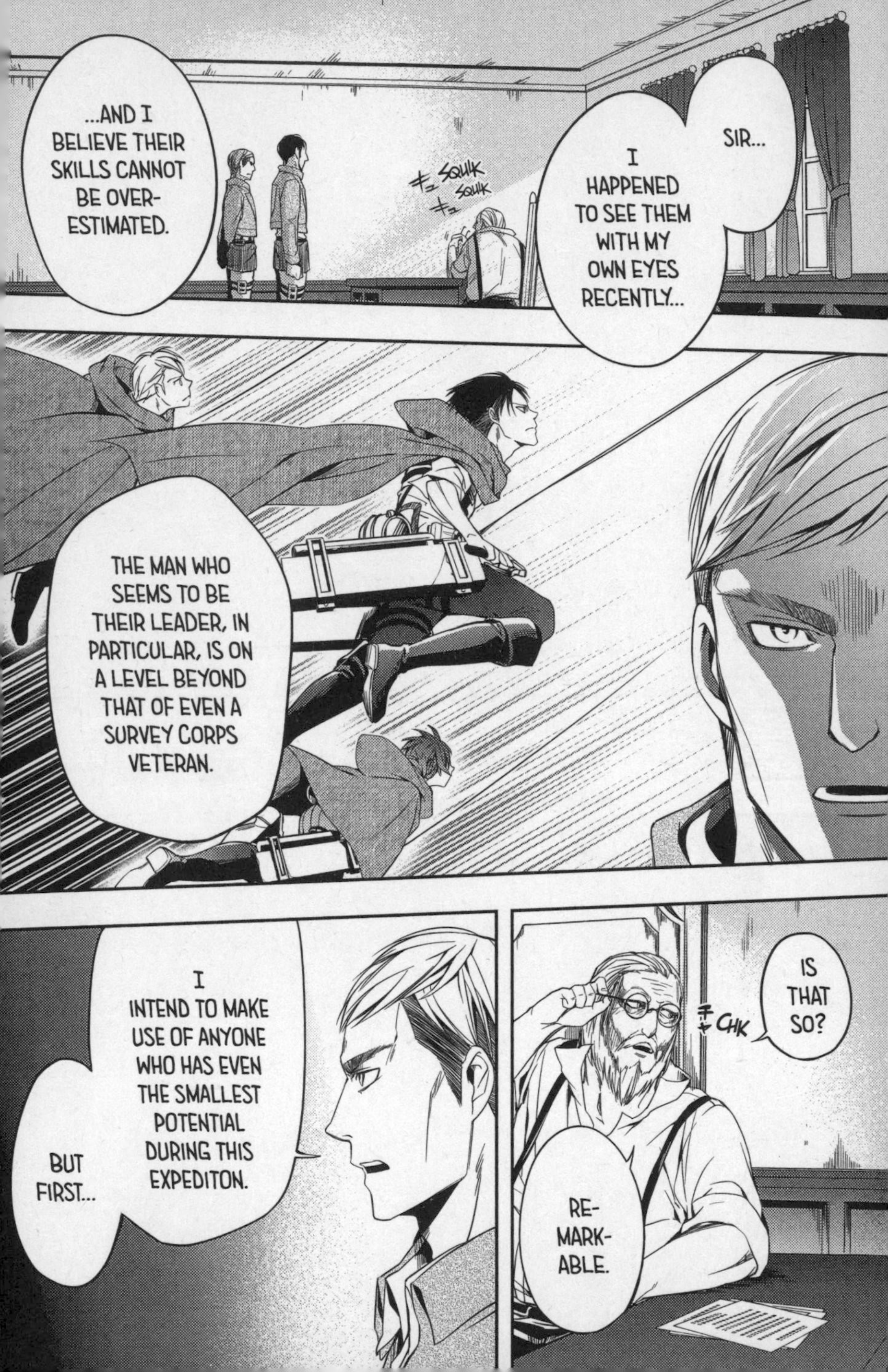
SIR...
I HAPPENED TO SEE THEM WITH MY OWN EYES RECENTLY...
SQUIK SQUIK
...AND I BELIEVE THEIR SKILLS CANNOT BE OVER-ESTIMATED.
THE MAN WHO SEEMS TO BE THEIR LEADER, IN PARTICULAR, IS ON A LEVEL BEYOND THAT OF EVEN A SURVEY CORPS VETERAN.
IS THAT SO?
CHK
RE-MARKABLE.
I INTEND TO MAKE USE OF ANYONE WHO HAS EVEN THE SMALLEST POTENTIAL DURING THIS EXPEDITON.
BUT FIRST...

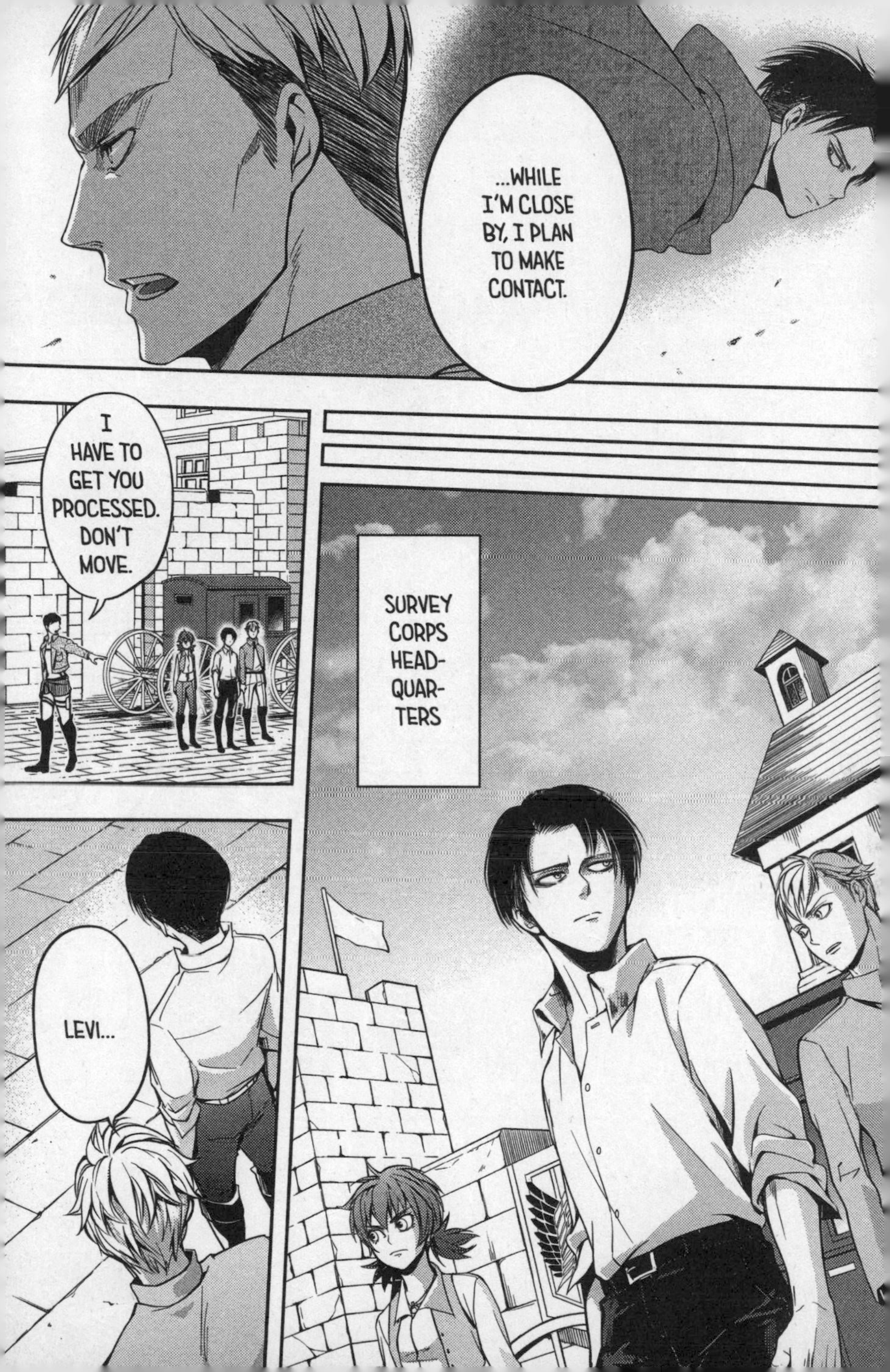
...WHILE I'M CLOSE BY, I PLAN TO MAKE CONTACT.
SURVEY CORPS HEAD-QUARTERS
I HAVE TO GET YOU PROCESSED. DON'T MOVE.
LEVI...

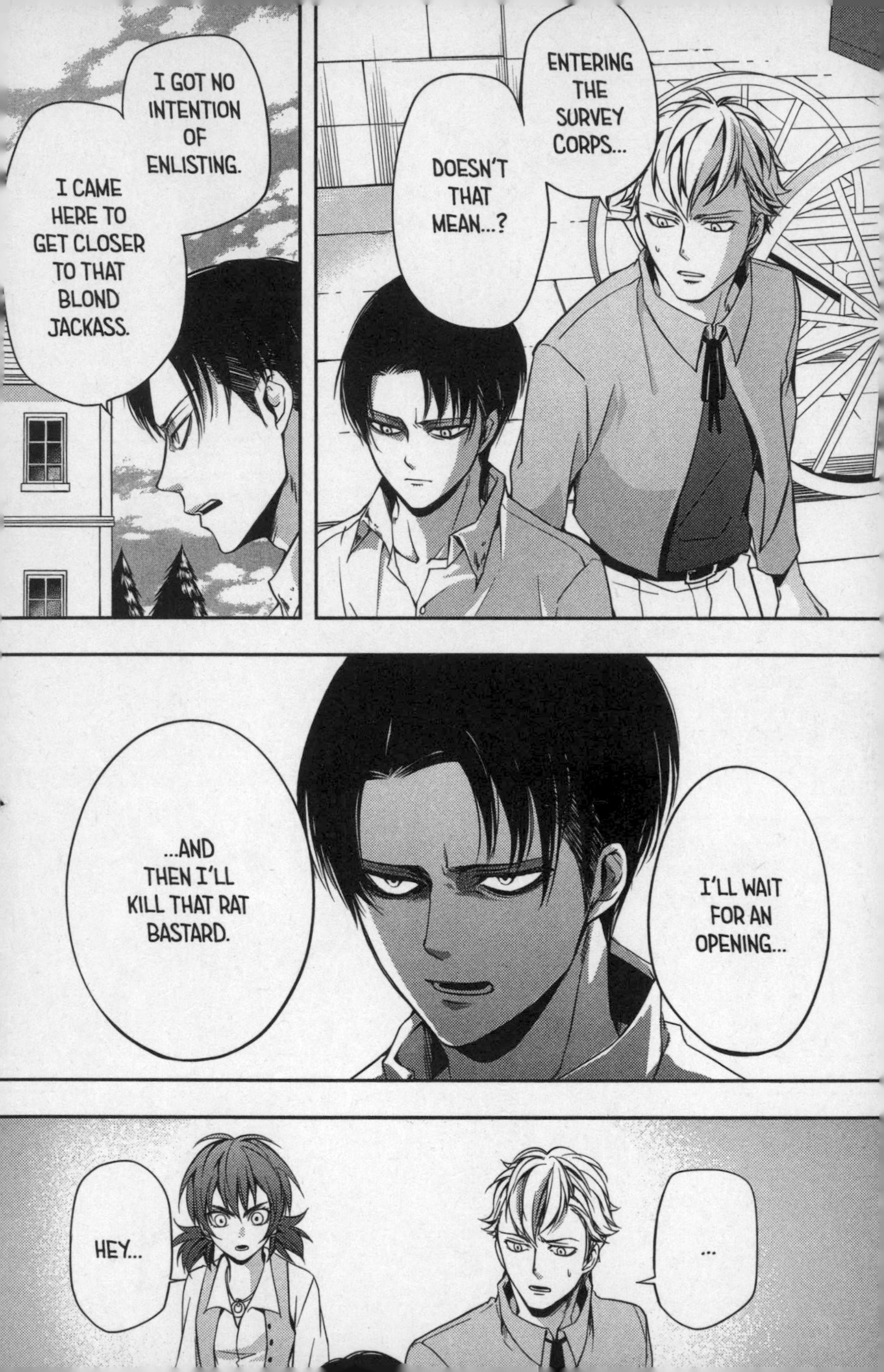
ENTERING THE SURVEY CORPS...
DOESN'T THAT MEAN...?
I GOT NO INTENTION OF ENLISTING.
I CAME HERE TO GET CLOSER TO THAT BLOND JACKASS.
I'LL WAIT FOR AN OPENING...
...AND THEN I'LL KILL THAT RAT BASTARD.
...
HEY...

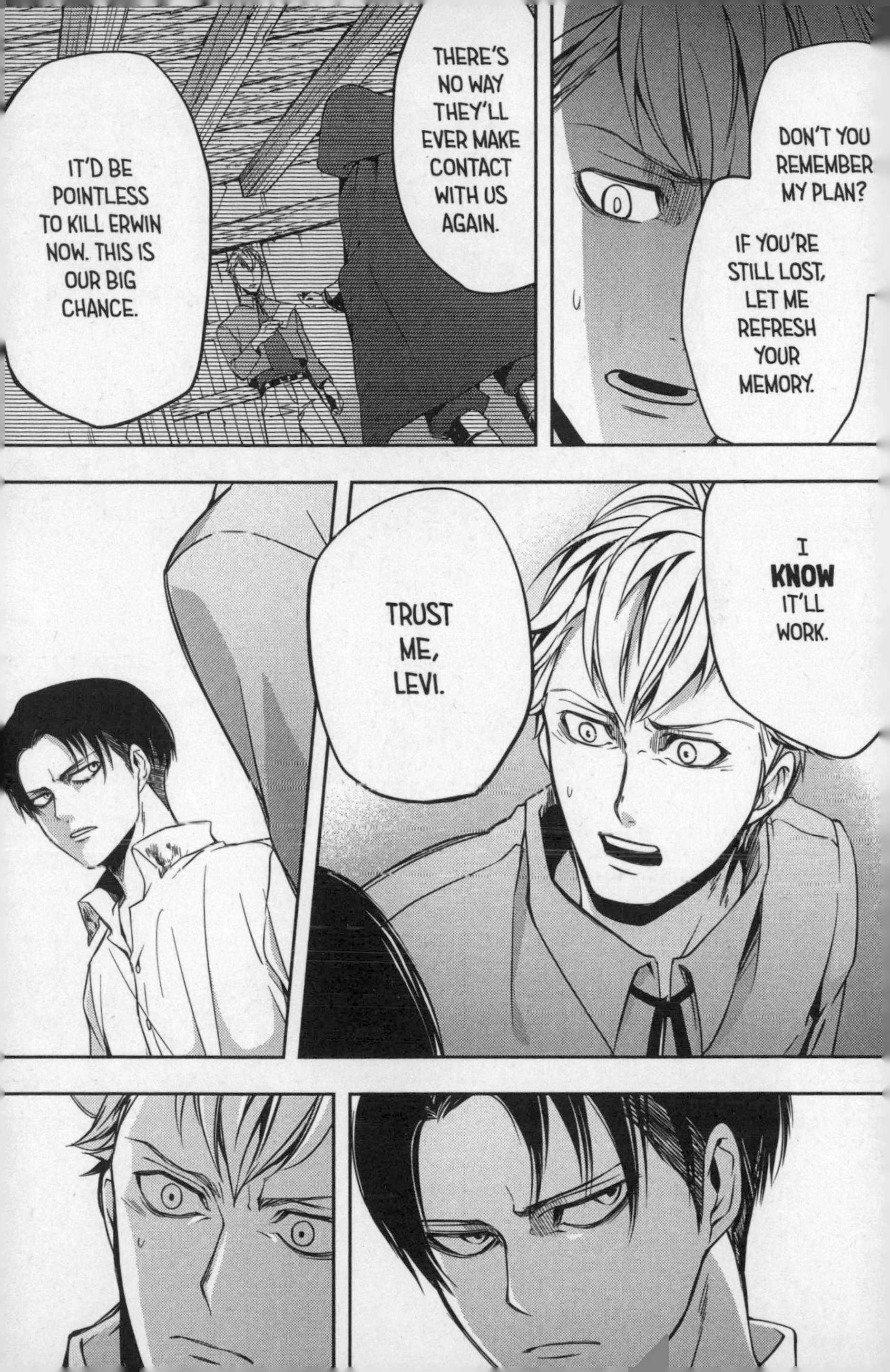
DON'T YOU REMEMBER MY PLAN?
IF YOU'RE STILL LOST, LET ME REFRESH YOUR MEMORY.
THERE'S NO WAY THEY'LL EVER MAKE CONTACT WITH US AGAIN.
IT'D BE POINTLESS TO KILL ERWIN NOW. THIS IS OUR BIG CHANCE.
I **KNOW** IT'LL WORK.
TRUST ME, LEVI.

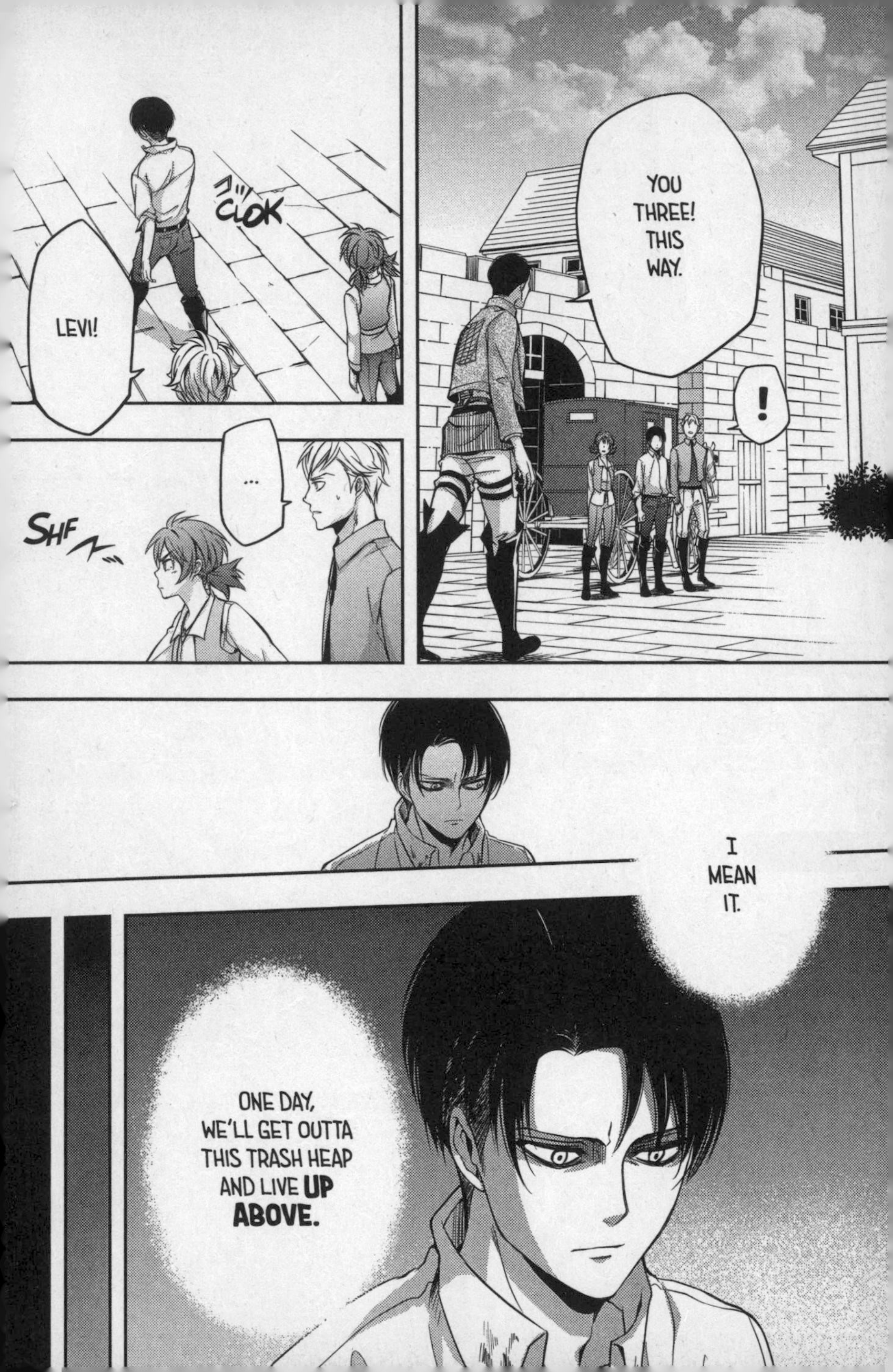
YOU THREE! THIS WAY.
!
CLOK
LEVI!
...
SHF
I MEAN IT.
ONE DAY, WE'LL GET OUTTA THIS TRASH HEAP AND LIVE **UP ABOVE.**

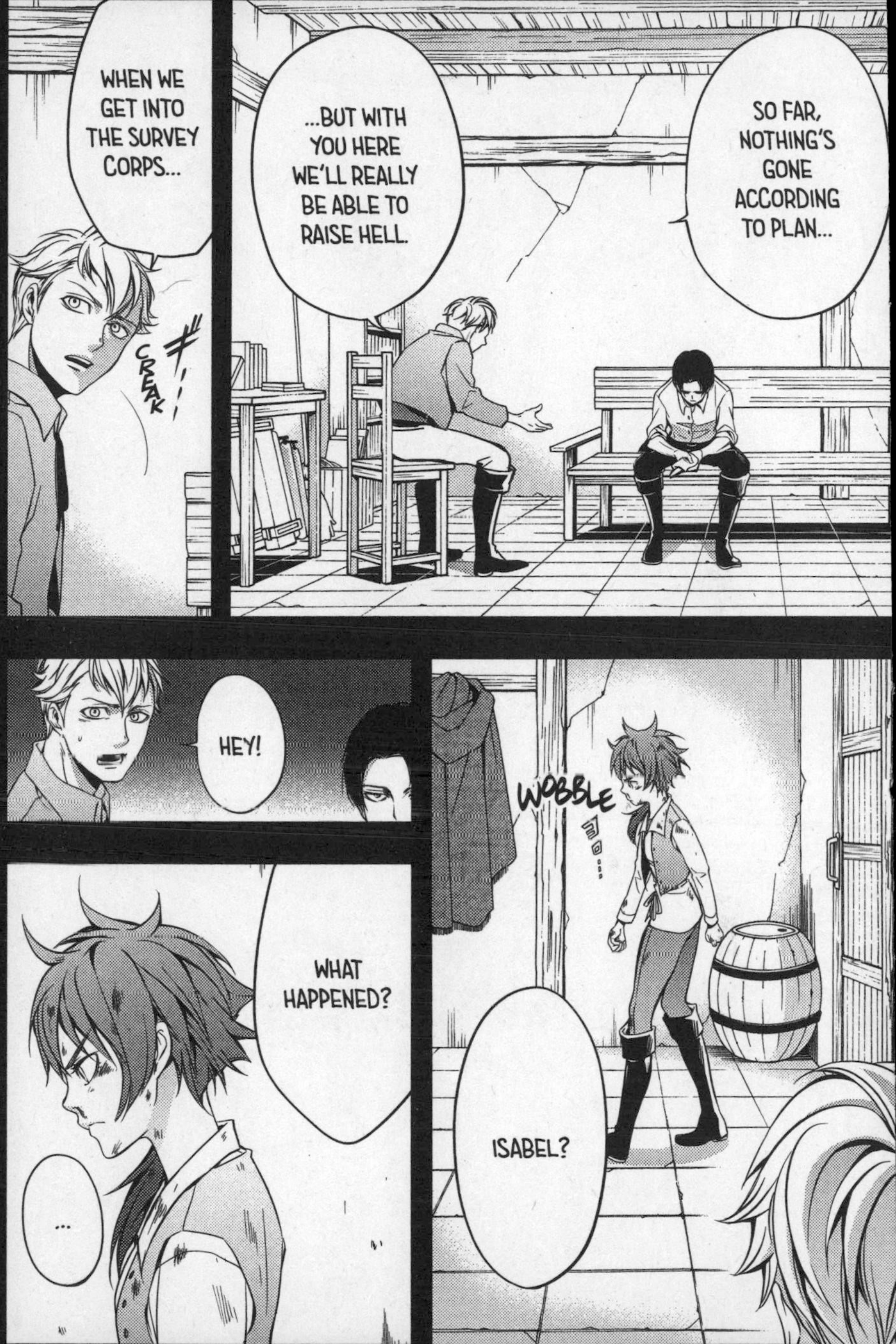
SO FAR, NOTHING'S GONE ACCORDING TO PLAN...
...BUT WITH YOU HERE WE'LL REALLY BE ABLE TO RAISE HELL.
WHEN WE GET INTO THE SURVEY CORPS...
CREAK
WOBBLE
ISABEL?
HEY!
WHAT HAPPENED?
...

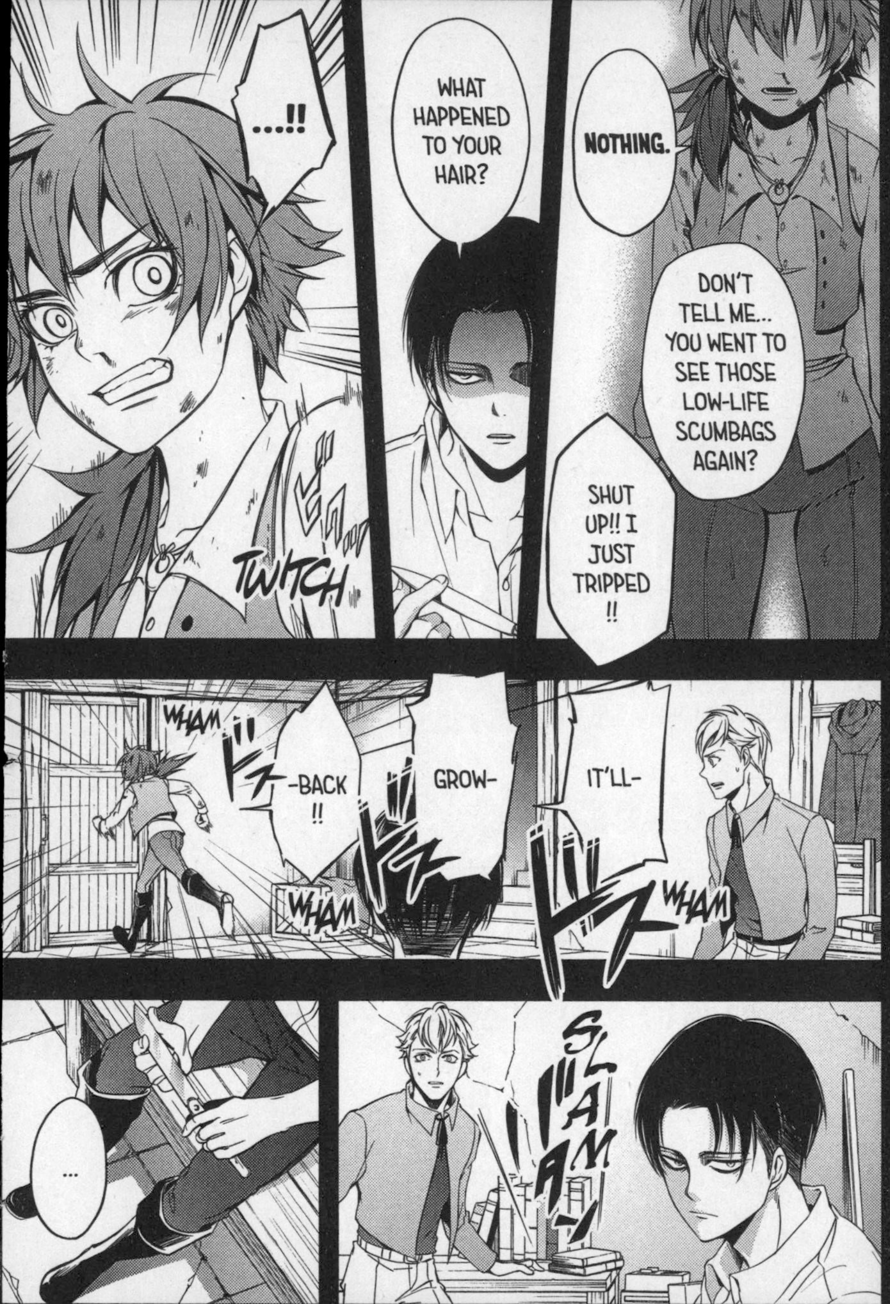
NOTHING.
DON'T TELL ME... YOU WENT TO SEE THOSE LOW-LIFE SCUMBAGS AGAIN?
SHUT UP!! I JUST TRIPPED !!
WHAT HAPPENED TO YOUR HAIR?
...!!
TWITCH
IT'LL-
WHAM
GROW-
WHAM
-BACK !!
WHAM
SLAM
...

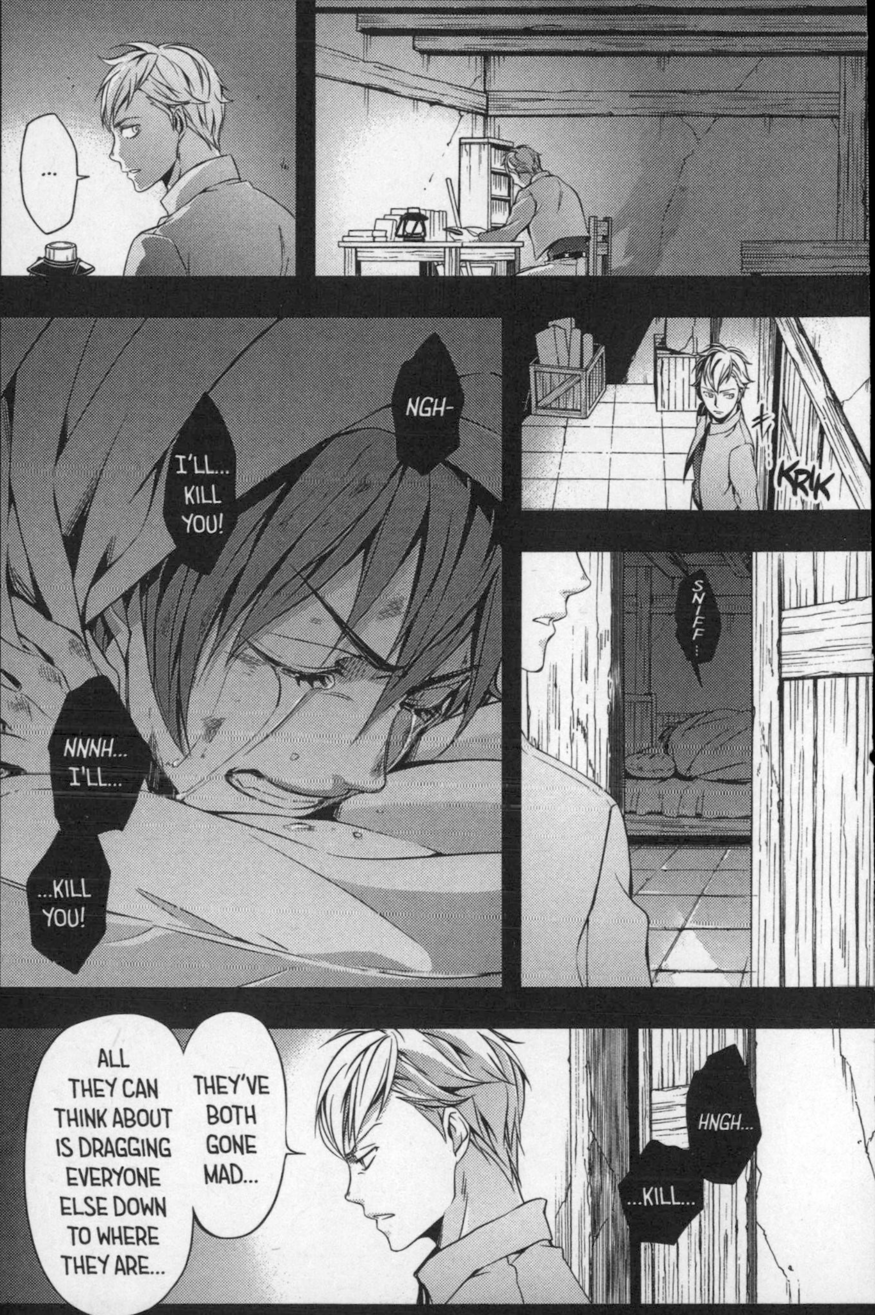
...
KRIK
SNIFF...
NGH-
I'LL... KILL YOU!
NNNH... I'LL...
...KILL YOU!
HNGH...
...KILL...
THEY'VE BOTH GONE MAD...
ALL THEY CAN THINK ABOUT IS DRAGGING EVERYONE ELSE DOWN TO WHERE THEY ARE...

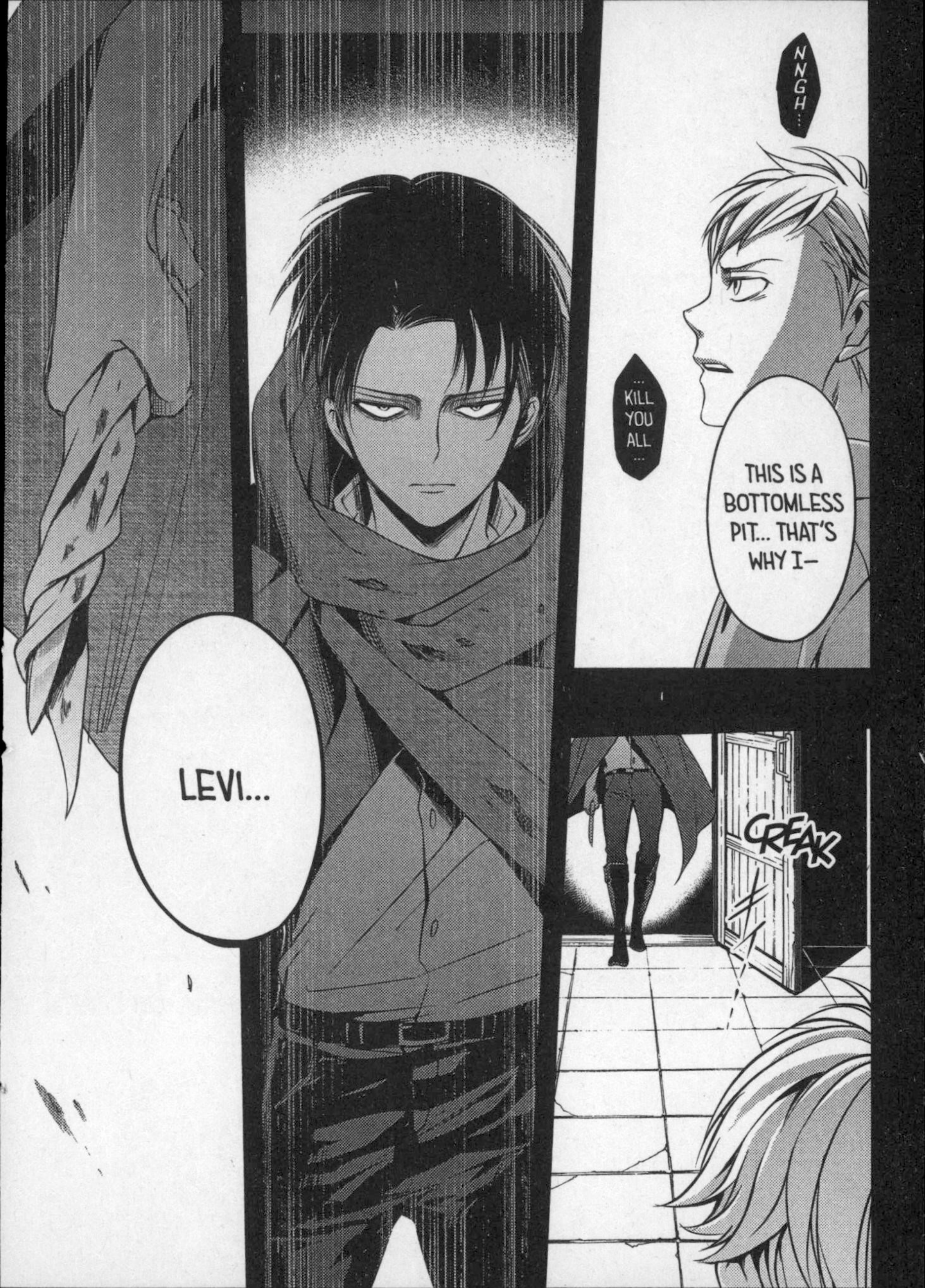
NNGH…
…KILL YOU ALL…
THIS IS A BOTTOMLESS PIT… THAT'S WHY I—
CREAK
LEVI…

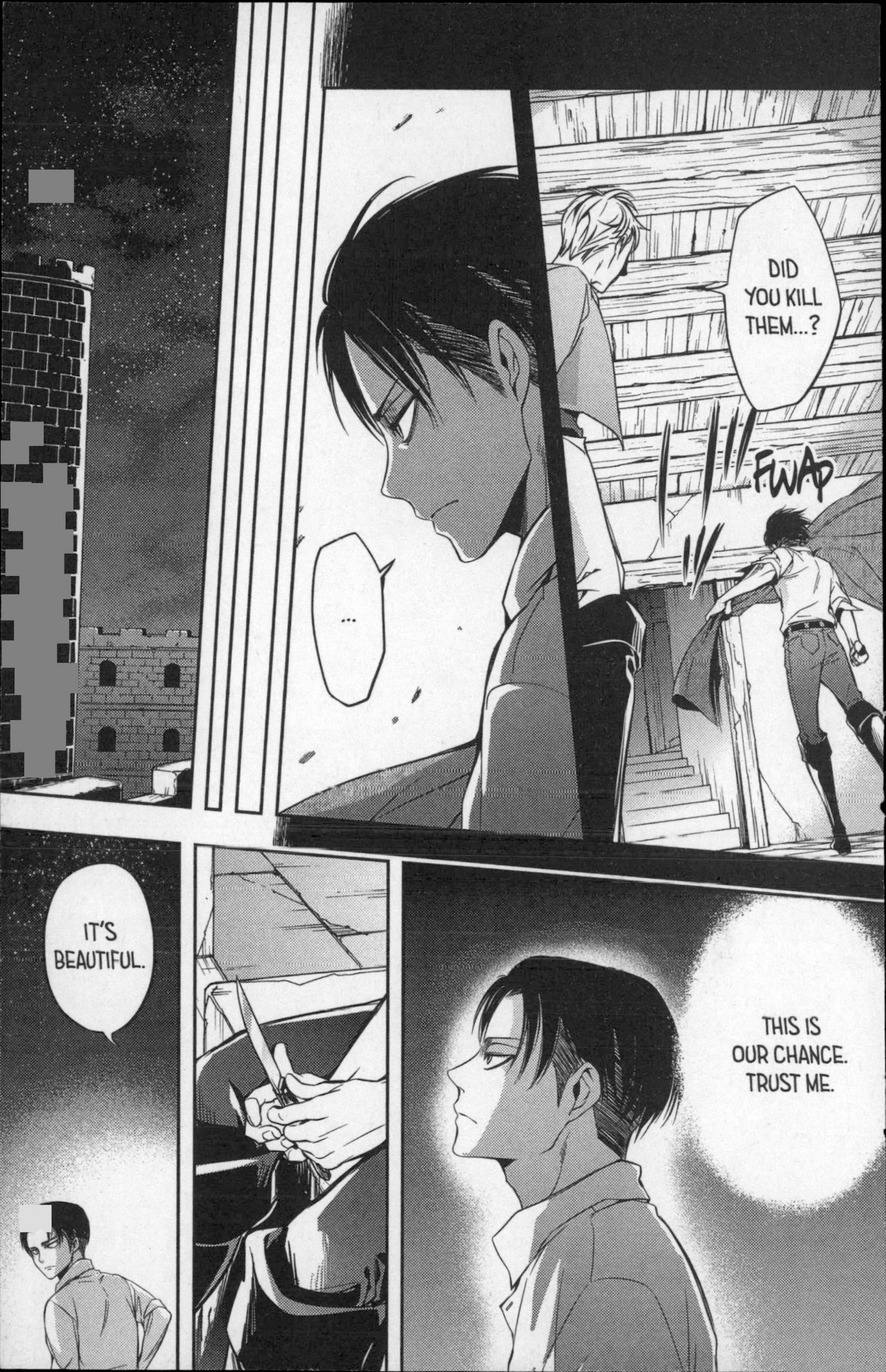
DID YOU KILL THEM...?
FWAP
...
THIS IS OUR CHANCE. TRUST ME.
IT'S BEAUTIFUL.

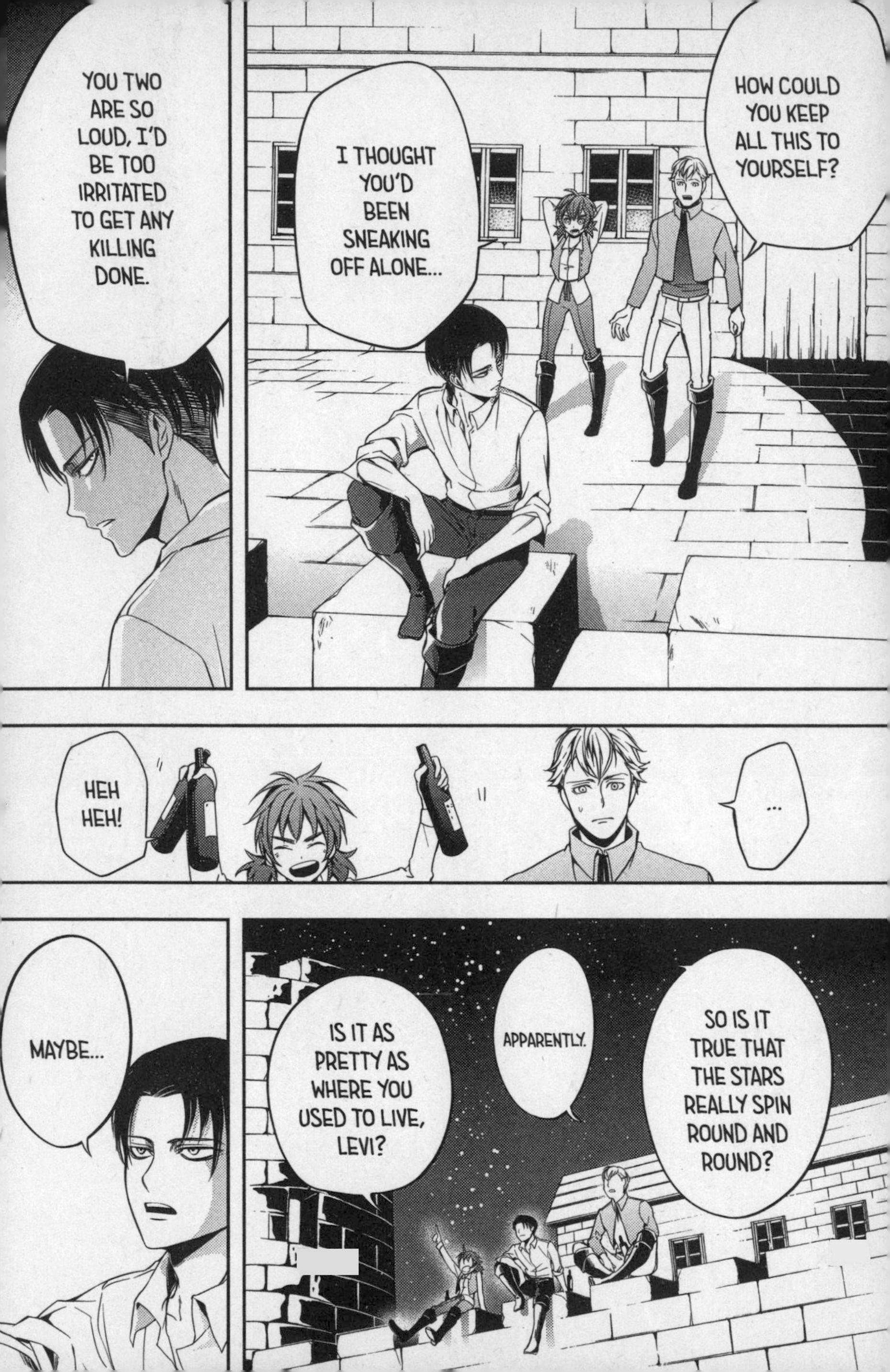
HOW COULD YOU KEEP ALL THIS TO YOURSELF?
I THOUGHT YOU'D BEEN SNEAKING OFF ALONE...
YOU TWO ARE SO LOUD, I'D BE TOO IRRITATED TO GET ANY KILLING DONE.
...
HEH HEH!
SO IS IT TRUE THAT THE STARS REALLY SPIN ROUND AND ROUND?
APPARENTLY.
IS IT AS PRETTY AS WHERE YOU USED TO LIVE, LEVI?
MAYBE...

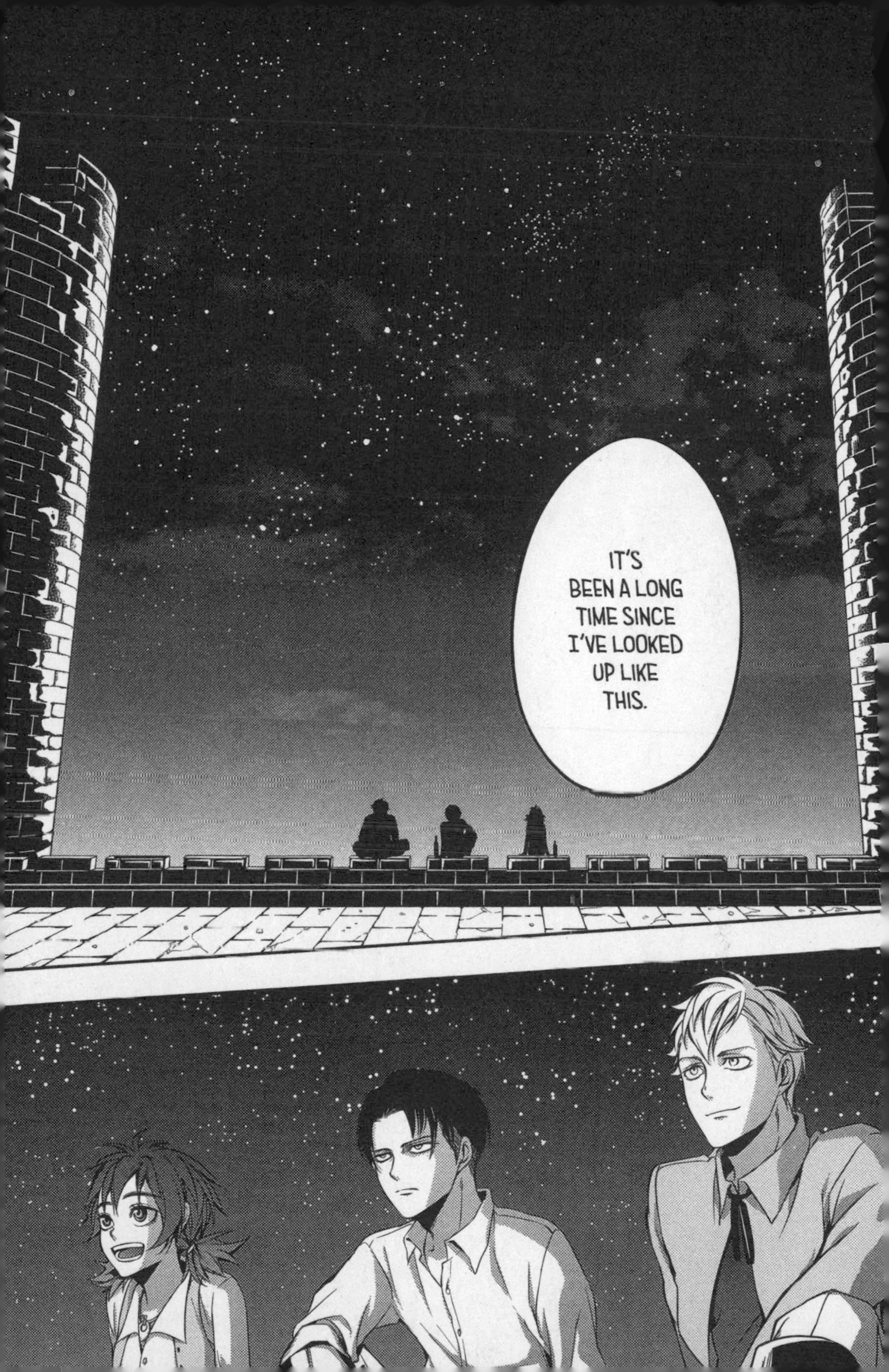
IT'S BEEN A LONG TIME SINCE I'VE LOOKED UP LIKE THIS.

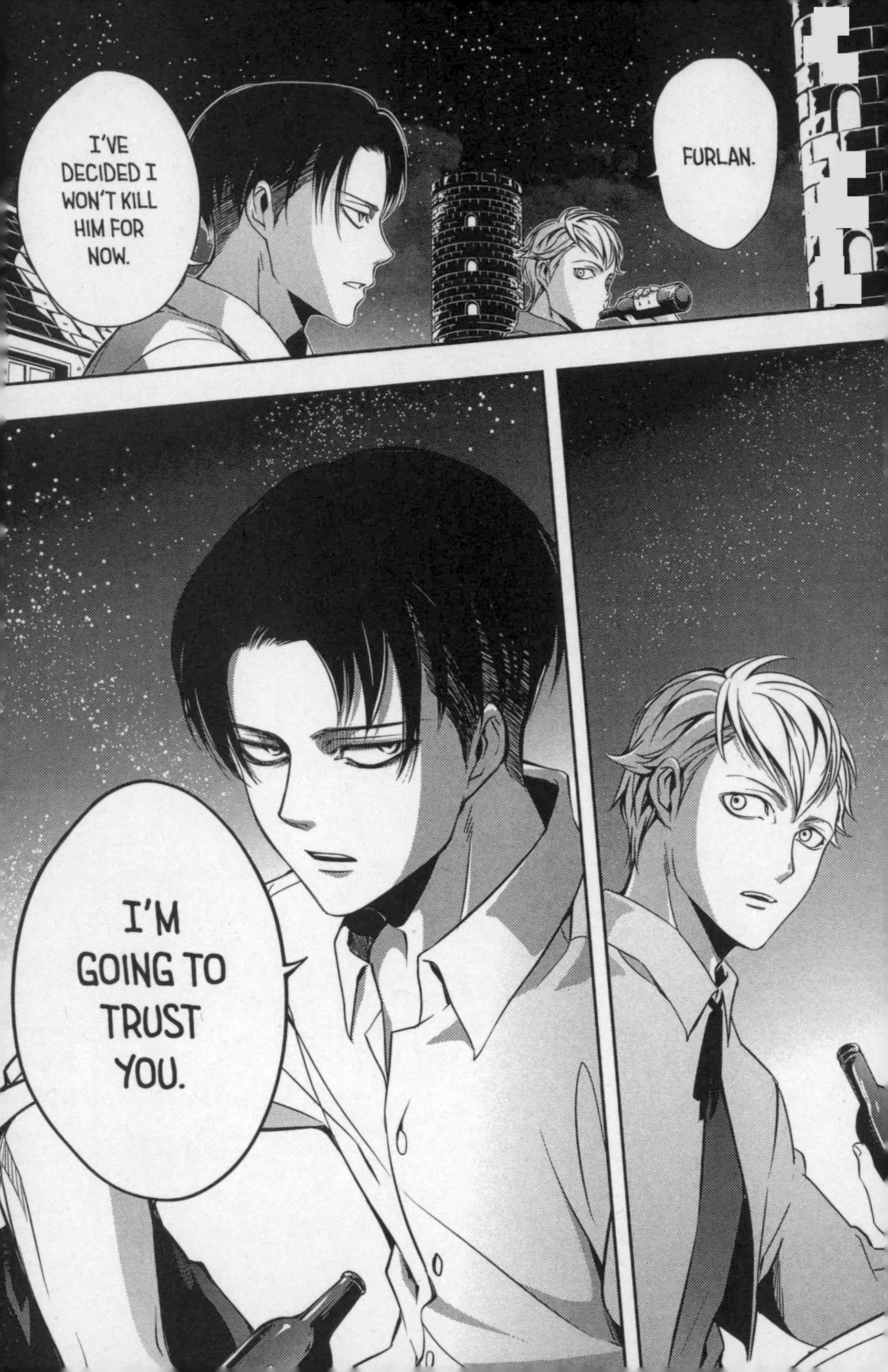
FURLAN.
I'VE DECIDED I WON'T KILL HIM FOR NOW.
I'M GOING TO TRUST YOU.

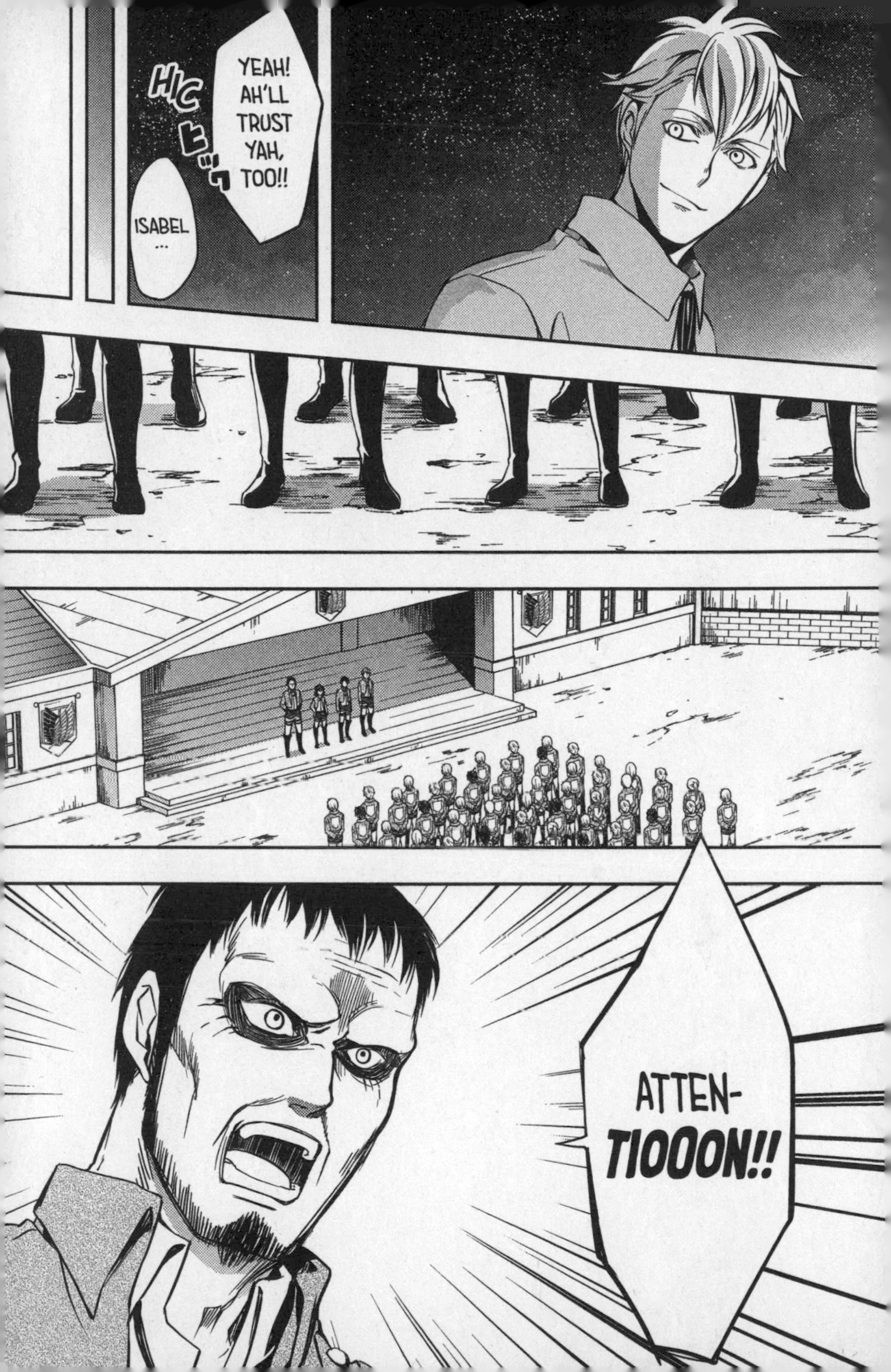
YEAH! AH'LL TRUST YAH, TOO!!
HIC
ヒッ
ISABEL ...
ATTEN-TIOOON!!

ATTACK on TITAN
NO REGRETS

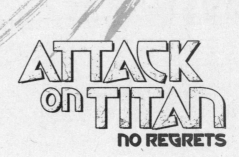

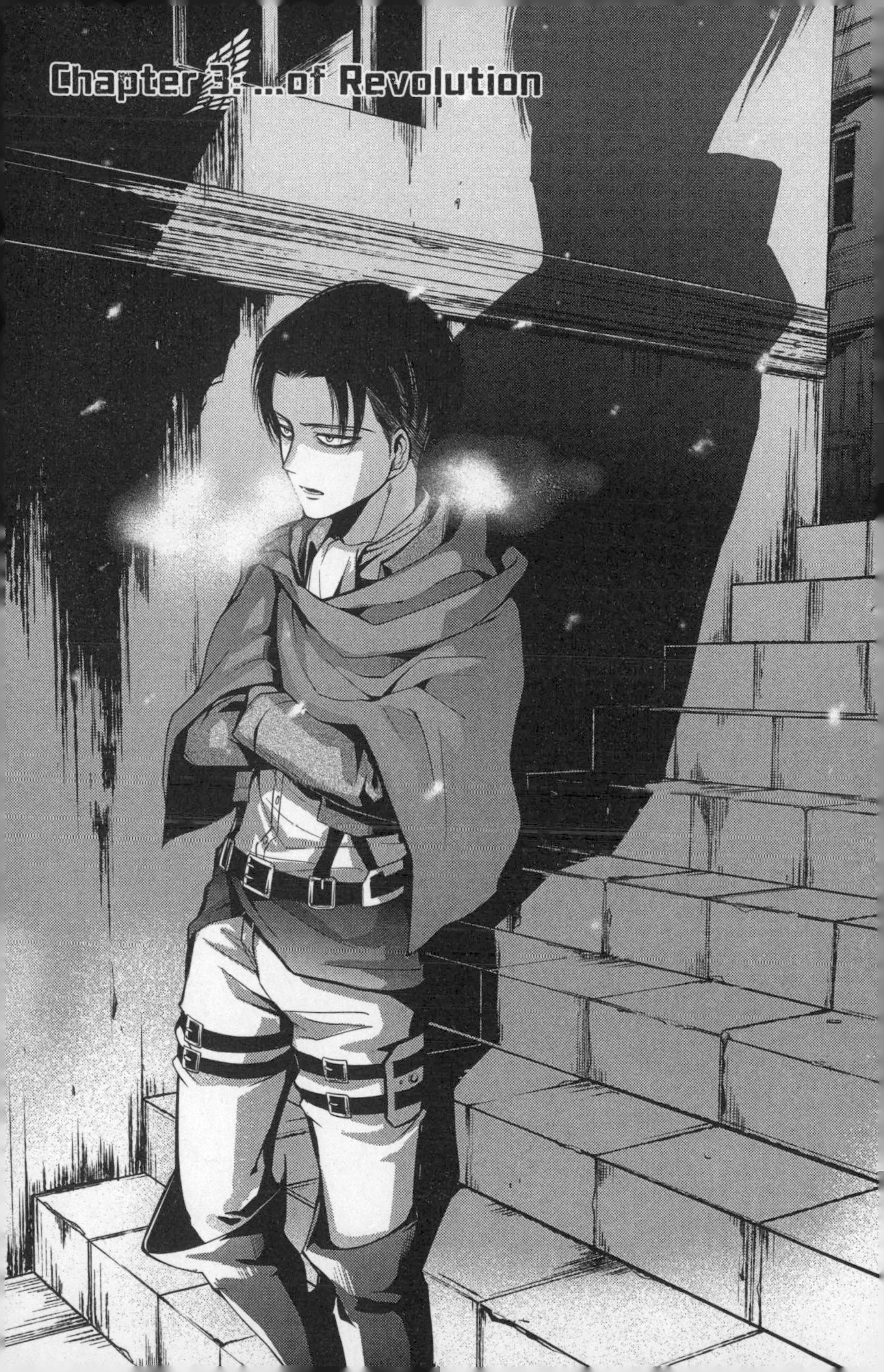
Chapter 3: ...of Revolution

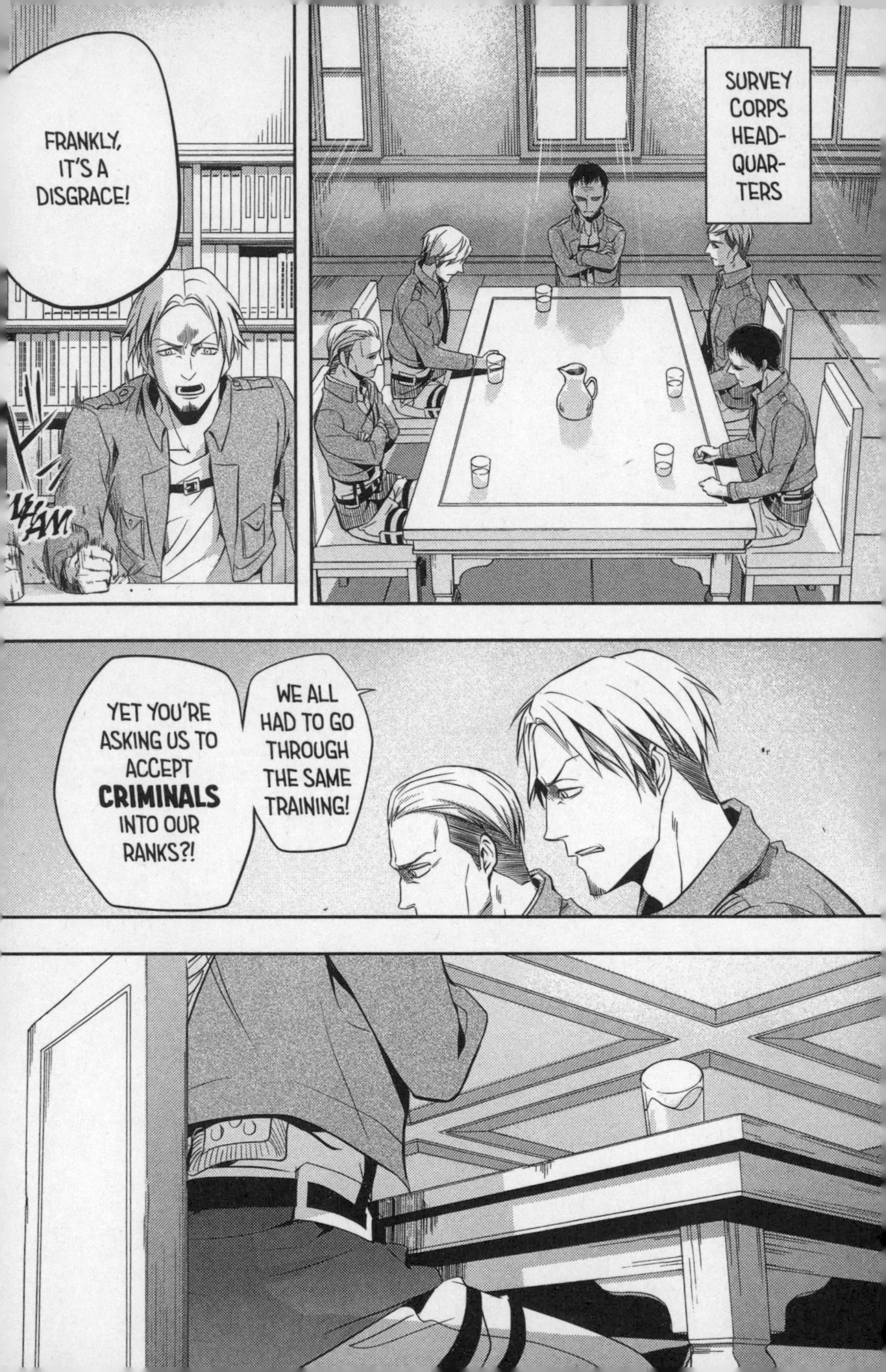
SURVEY CORPS HEAD-QUARTERS
FRANKLY, IT'S A DISGRACE!
WHAM!
WE ALL HAD TO GO THROUGH THE SAME TRAINING!
YET YOU'RE ASKING US TO ACCEPT **CRIMINALS** INTO OUR RANKS?!

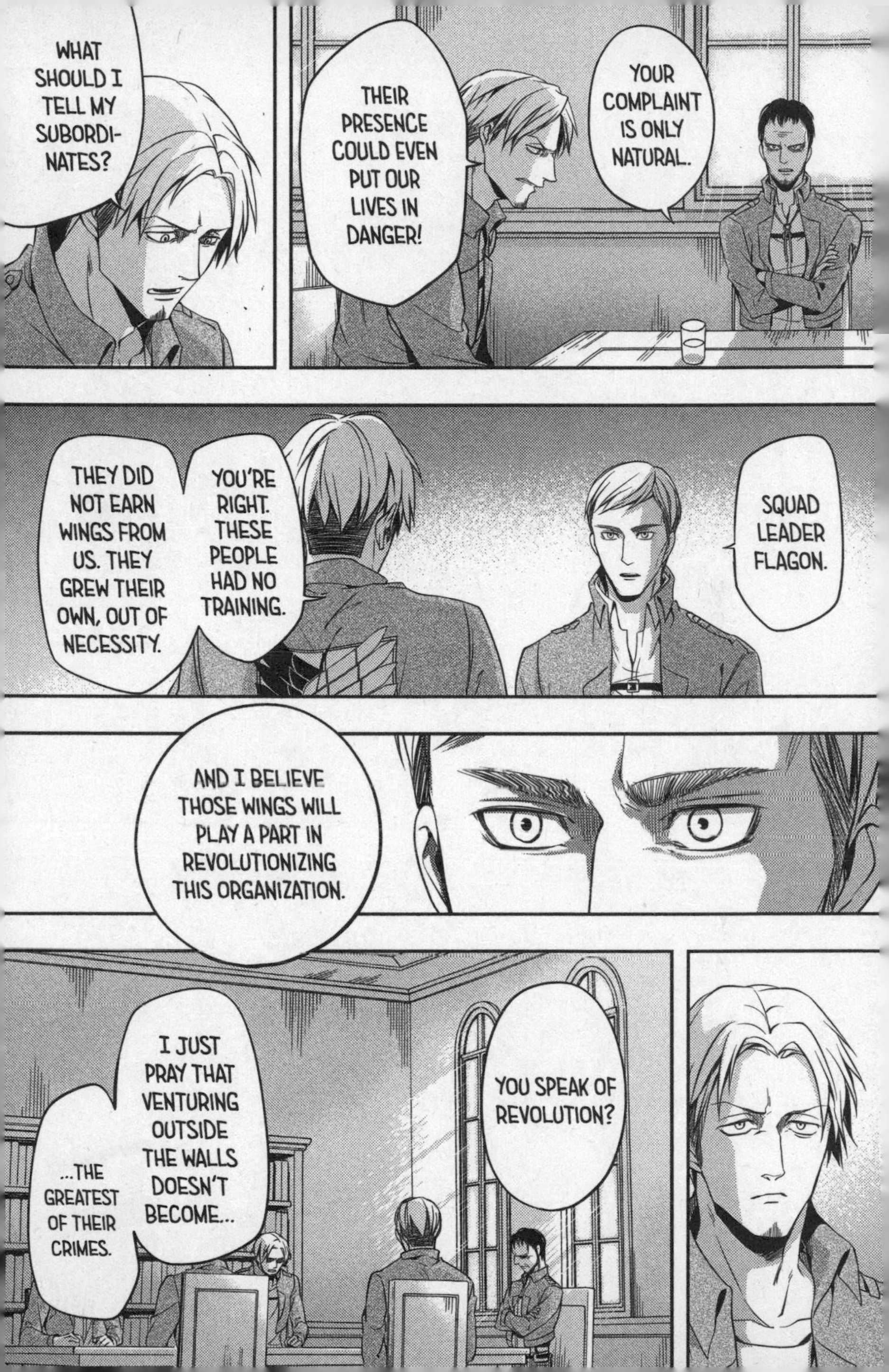
YOUR COMPLAINT IS ONLY NATURAL.
THEIR PRESENCE COULD EVEN PUT OUR LIVES IN DANGER!
WHAT SHOULD I TELL MY SUBORDI-NATES?
SQUAD LEADER FLAGON.
YOU'RE RIGHT. THESE PEOPLE HAD NO TRAINING.
THEY DID NOT EARN WINGS FROM US. THEY GREW THEIR OWN, OUT OF NECESSITY.
AND I BELIEVE THOSE WINGS WILL PLAY A PART IN REVOLUTIONIZING THIS ORGANIZATION.
YOU SPEAK OF REVOLUTION?
I JUST PRAY THAT VENTURING OUTSIDE THE WALLS DOESN'T BECOME...
...THE GREATEST OF THEIR CRIMES.

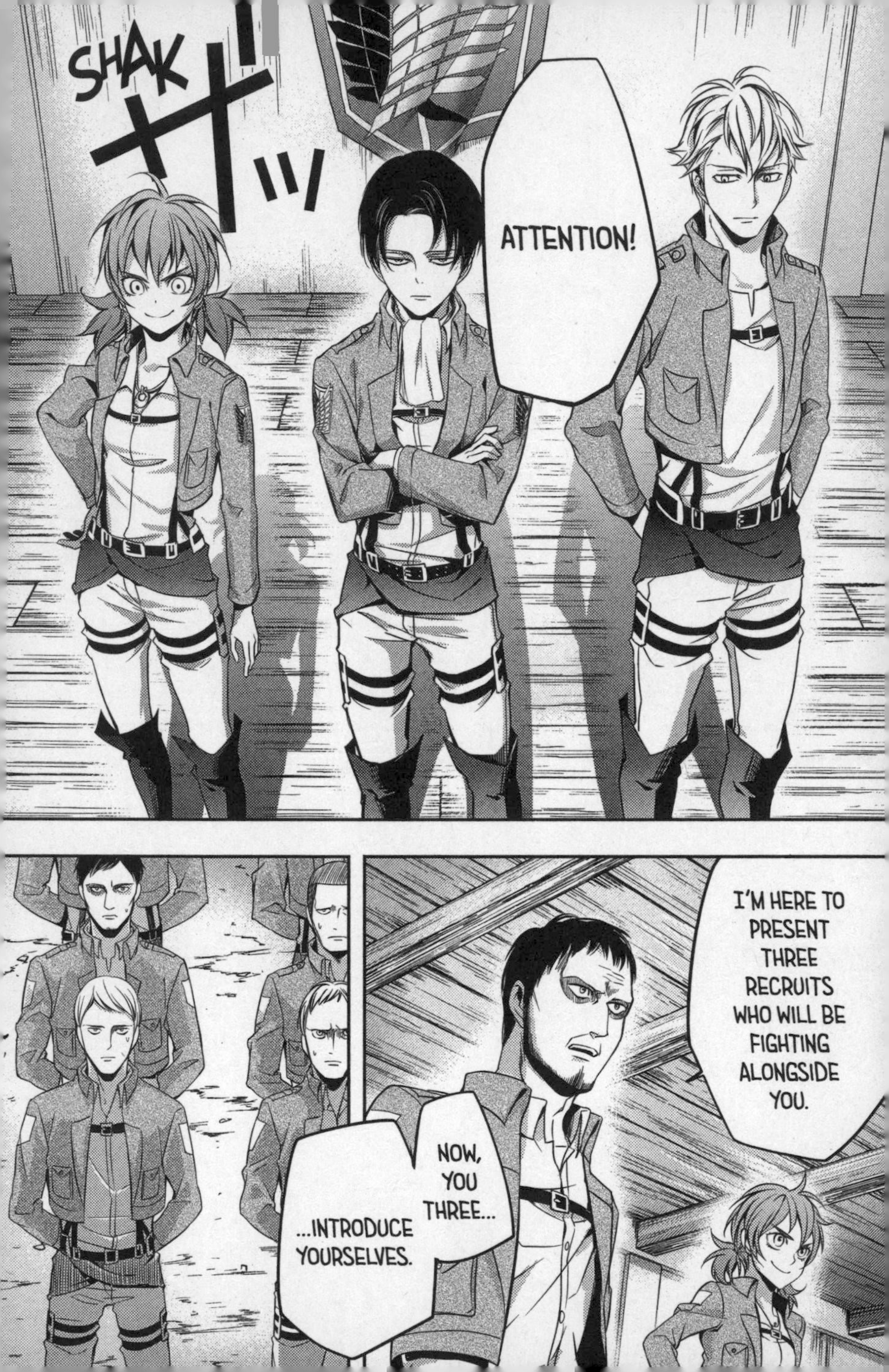
SHAK
ATTENTION!
I'M HERE TO PRESENT THREE RECRUITS WHO WILL BE FIGHTING ALONGSIDE YOU.
NOW, YOU THREE...
...INTRODUCE YOURSELVES.

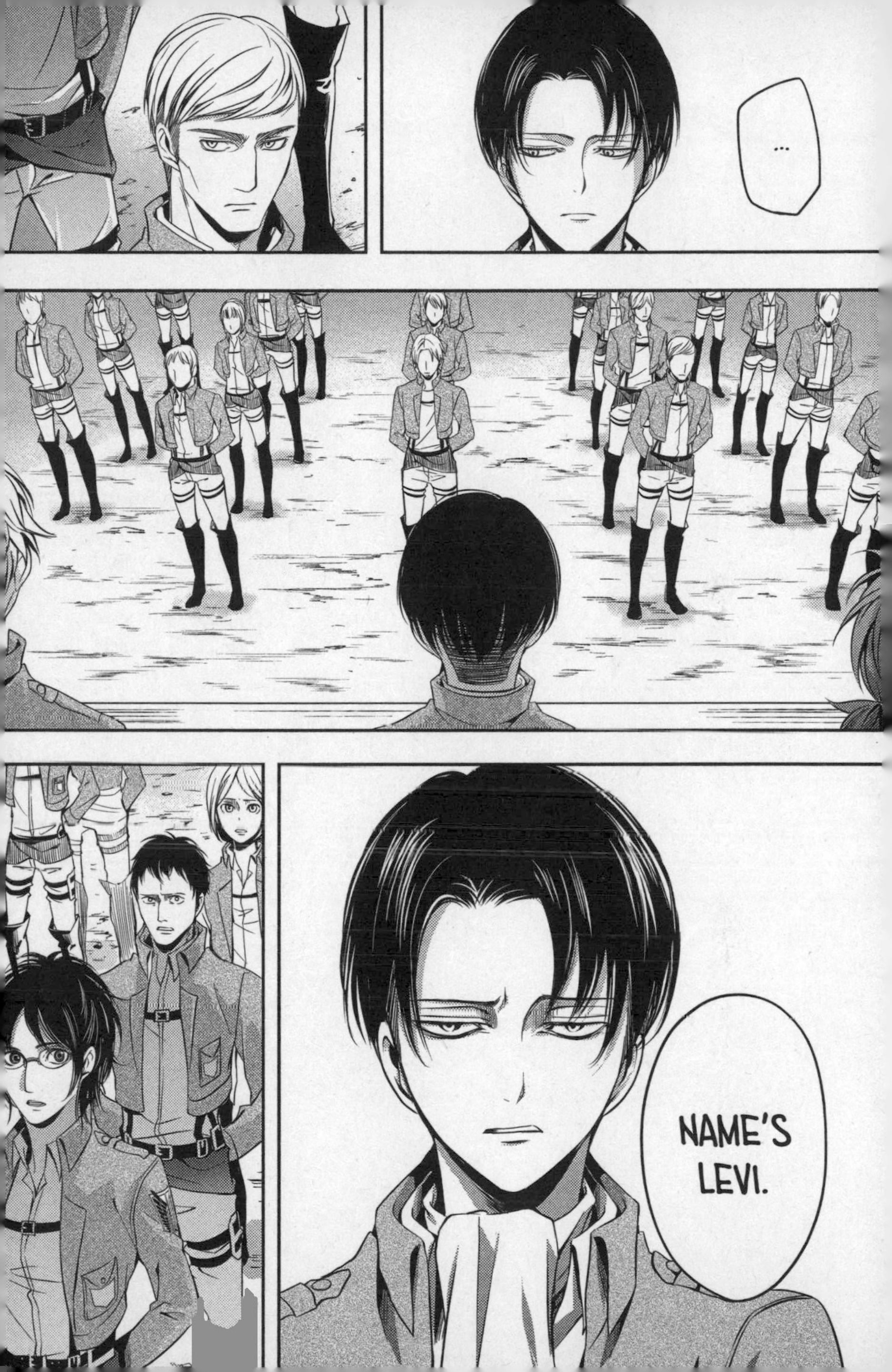
...
NAME'S LEVI.

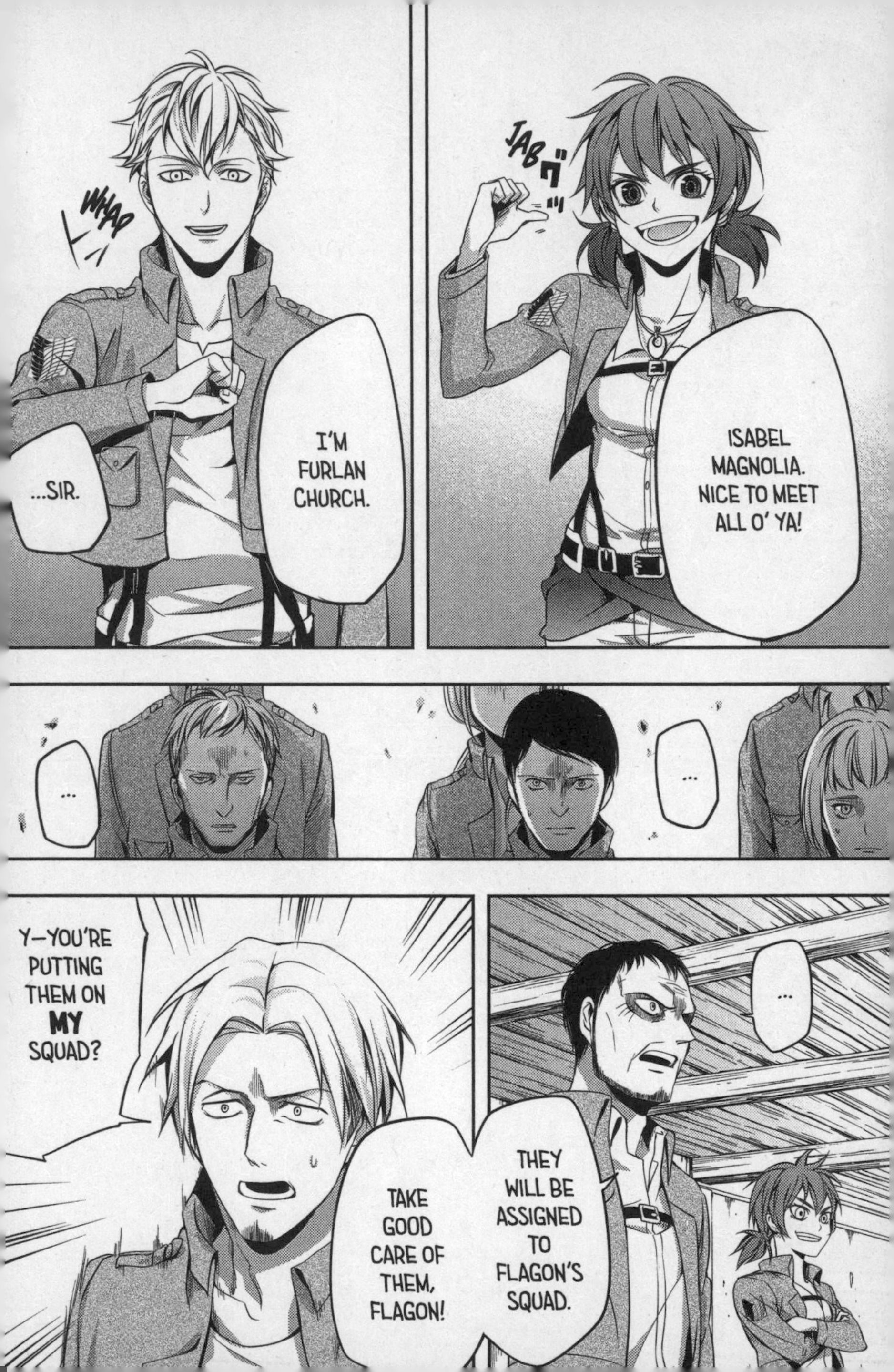
JAB
ISABEL MAGNOLIA. NICE TO MEET ALL O' YA!
WHAP
I'M FURLAN CHURCH.
...SIR.
...
...
...
THEY WILL BE ASSIGNED TO FLAGON'S SQUAD.
TAKE GOOD CARE OF THEM, FLAGON!
Y—YOU'RE PUTTING THEM ON **MY** SQUAD?

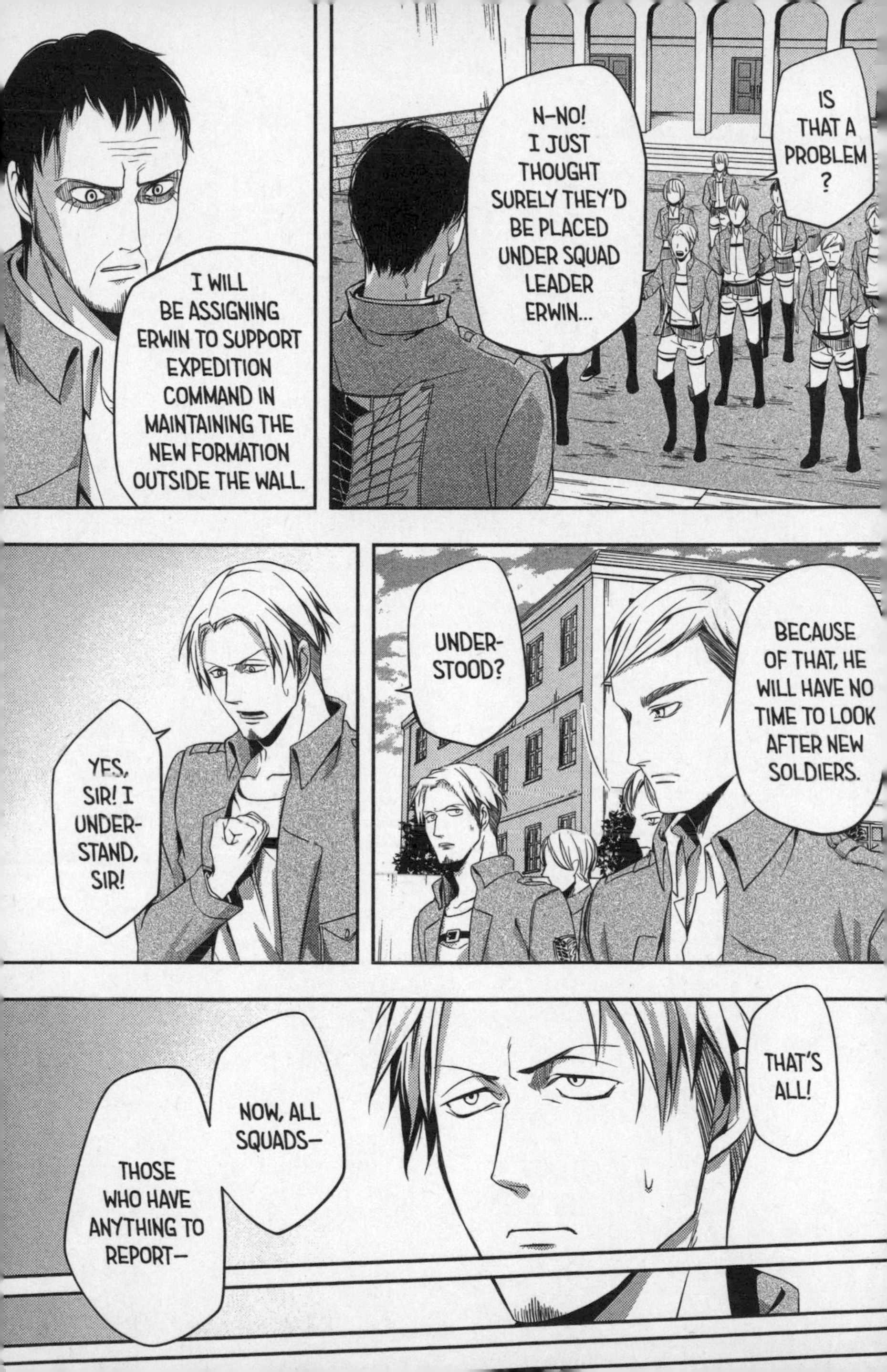
IS THAT A PROBLEM ?
N-NO! I JUST THOUGHT SURELY THEY'D BE PLACED UNDER SQUAD LEADER ERWIN...
I WILL BE ASSIGNING ERWIN TO SUPPORT EXPEDITION COMMAND IN MAINTAINING THE NEW FORMATION OUTSIDE THE WALL.
BECAUSE OF THAT, HE WILL HAVE NO TIME TO LOOK AFTER NEW SOLDIERS.
UNDER-STOOD?
YES, SIR! I UNDER-STAND, SIR!
THAT'S ALL!
NOW, ALL SQUADS—
THOSE WHO HAVE ANYTHING TO REPORT—

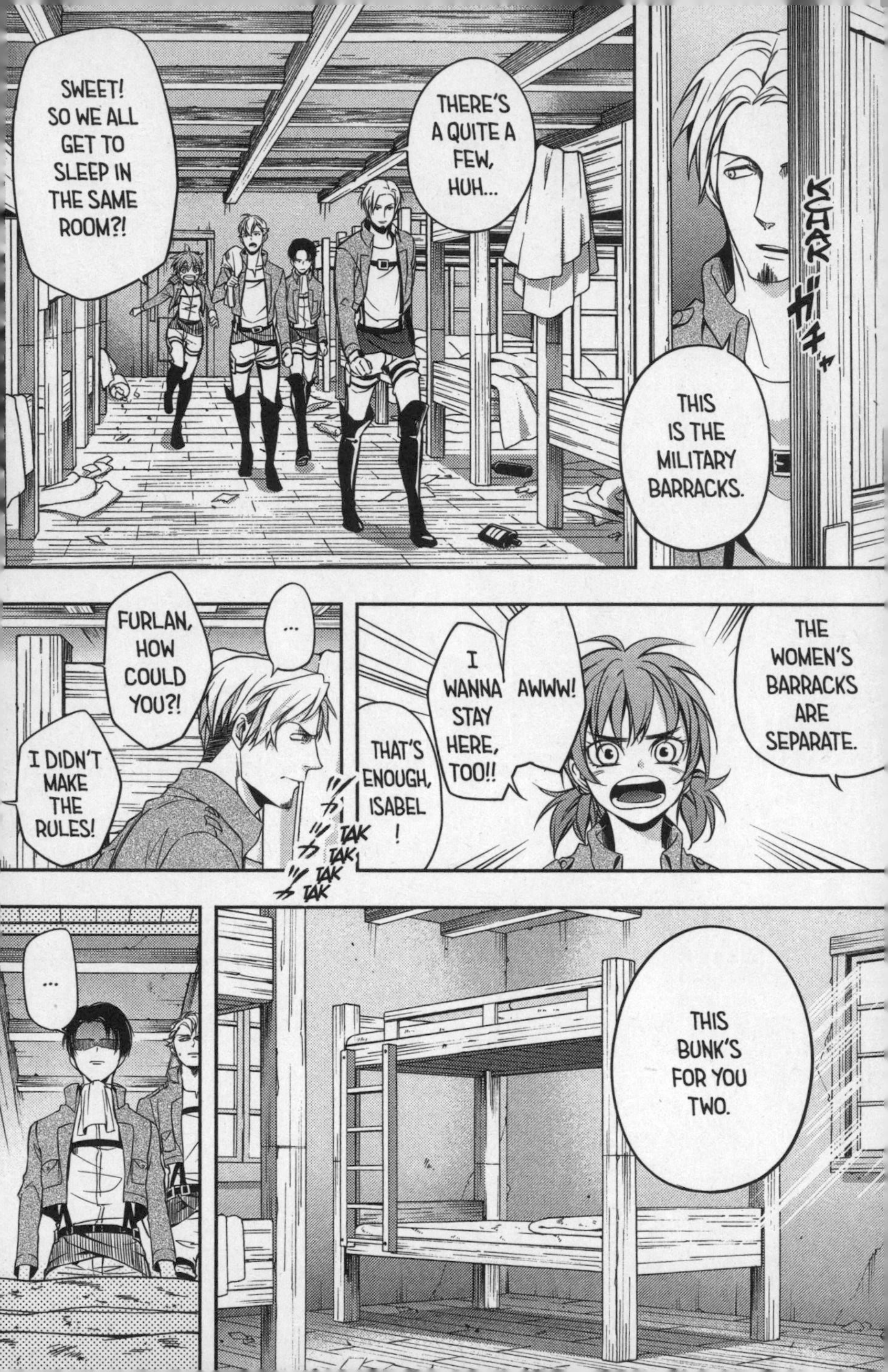
KCHAK
ガチャ
THIS IS THE MILITARY BARRACKS.
THERE'S A QUITE A FEW, HUH...
SWEET! SO WE ALL GET TO SLEEP IN THE SAME ROOM?!
THE WOMEN'S BARRACKS ARE SEPARATE.
AWWW!
I WANNA STAY HERE, TOO!!
THAT'S ENOUGH, ISABEL!
...
FURLAN, HOW COULD YOU?!
I DIDN'T MAKE THE RULES!
TAK TAK TAK TAK
THIS BUNK'S FOR YOU TWO.
...

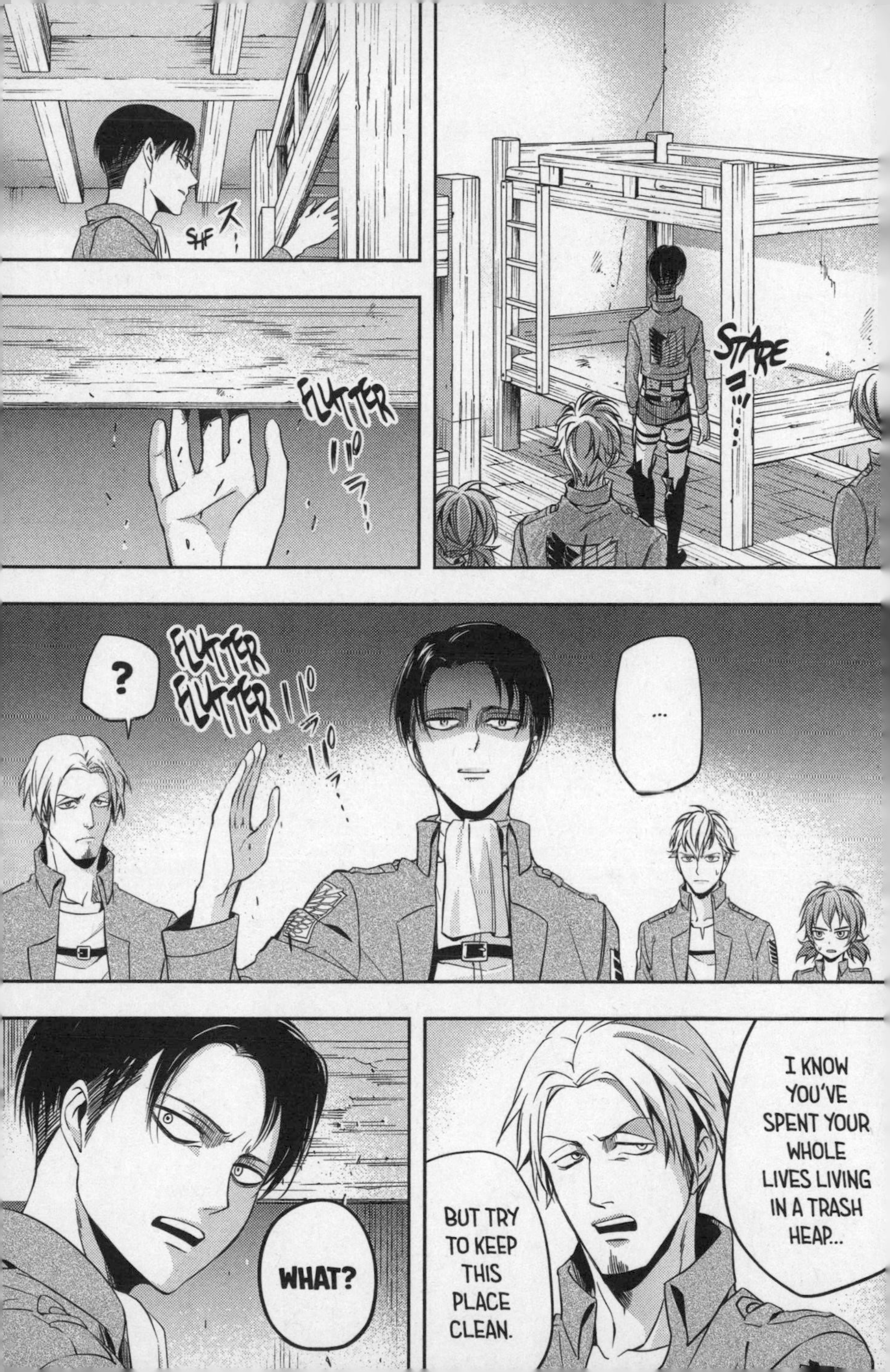
STARE
SHF
FLUTTER
...
FLUTTER FLUTTER
?
I KNOW YOU'VE SPENT YOUR WHOLE LIVES LIVING IN A TRASH HEAP...
BUT TRY TO KEEP THIS PLACE CLEAN.
WHAT?

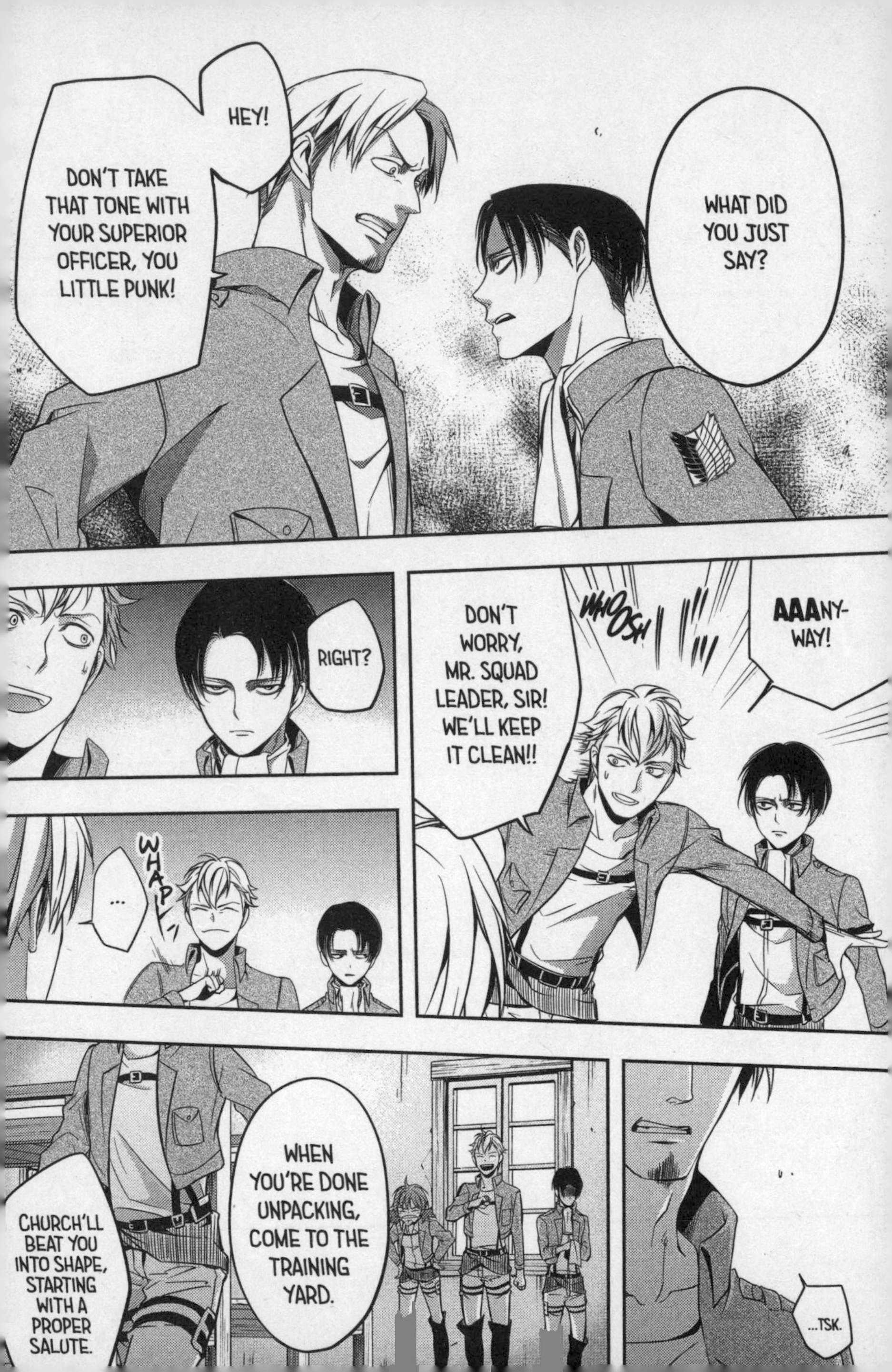
WHAT DID YOU JUST SAY?
HEY!
DON'T TAKE THAT TONE WITH YOUR SUPERIOR OFFICER, YOU LITTLE PUNK!
AAANY-WAY!
WHOOSH
DON'T WORRY, MR. SQUAD LEADER, SIR! WE'LL KEEP IT CLEAN!!
RIGHT?
WHAP
...
...TSK.
WHEN YOU'RE DONE UNPACKING, COME TO THE TRAINING YARD.
CHURCH'LL BEAT YOU INTO SHAPE, STARTING WITH A PROPER SALUTE.

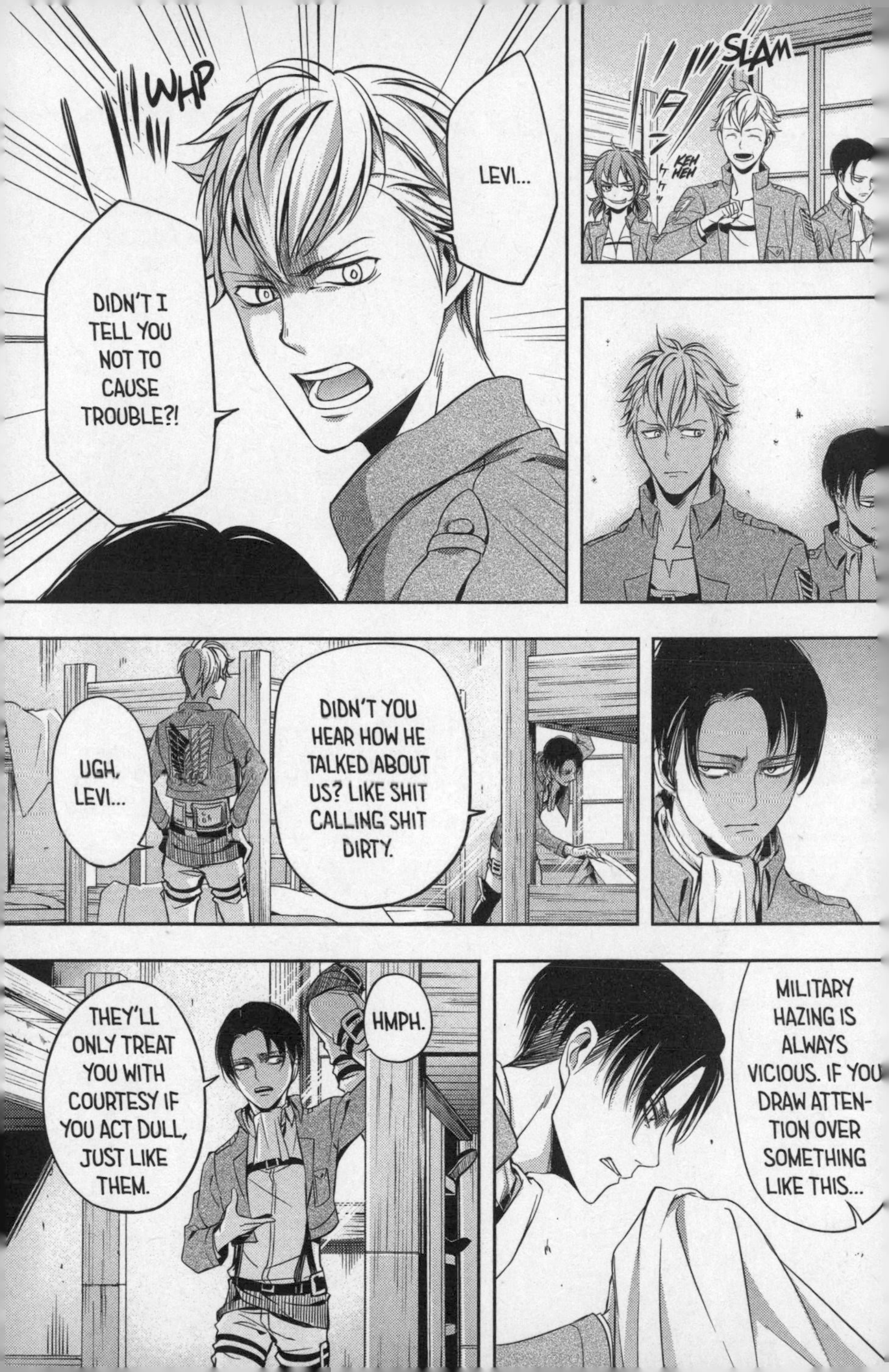
SLAM
KEH HEH
LEVI...
WHP
DIDN'T I TELL YOU NOT TO CAUSE TROUBLE?!
DIDN'T YOU HEAR HOW HE TALKED ABOUT US? LIKE SHIT CALLING SHIT DIRTY.
UGH, LEVI...
MILITARY HAZING IS ALWAYS VICIOUS. IF YOU DRAW ATTEN-TION OVER SOMETHING LIKE THIS...
HMPH.
THEY'LL ONLY TREAT YOU WITH COURTESY IF YOU ACT DULL, JUST LIKE THEM.

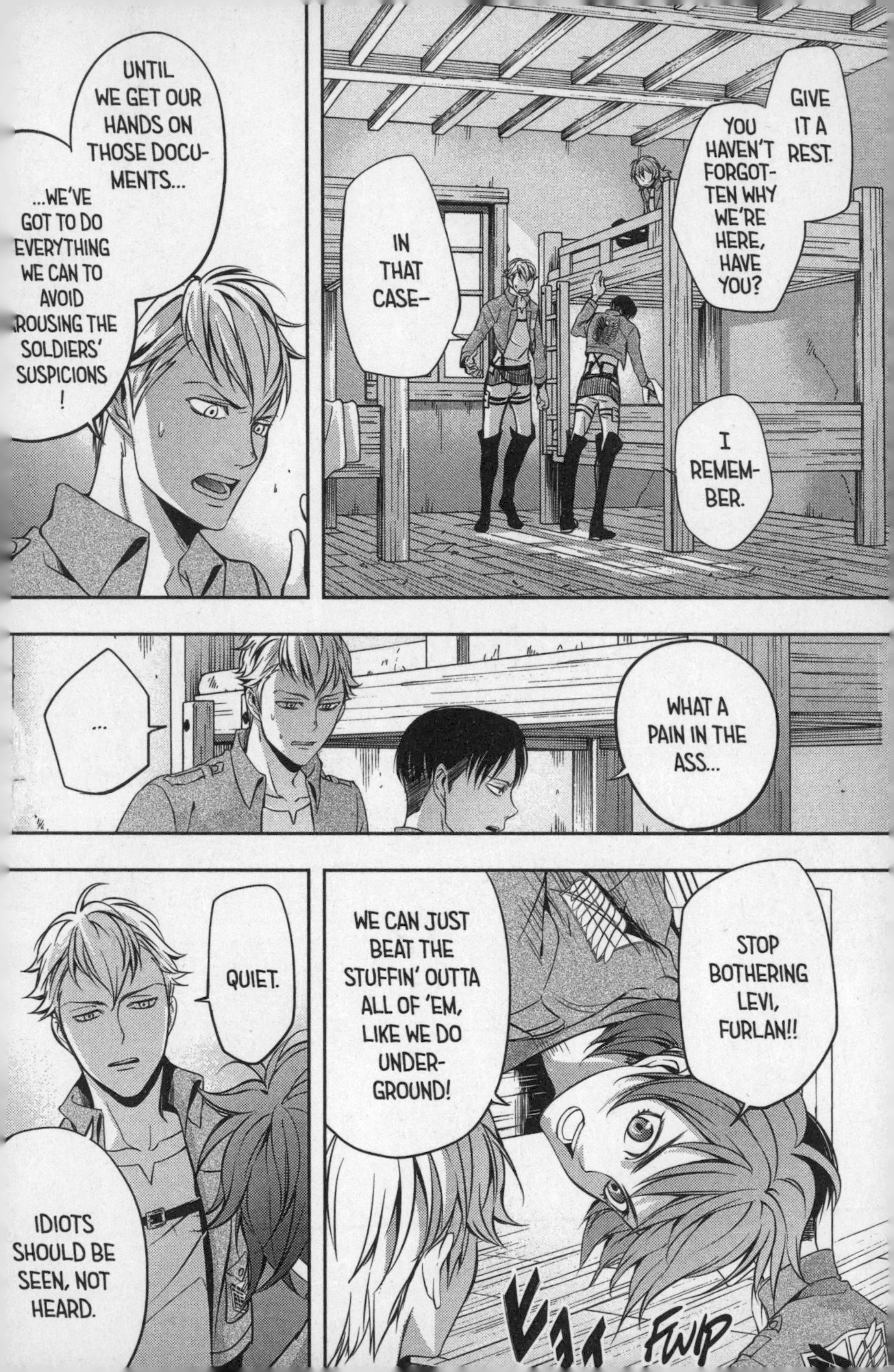
GIVE IT A REST.
YOU HAVEN'T FORGOTTEN WHY WE'RE HERE, HAVE YOU?
I REMEMBER.
IN THAT CASE-
UNTIL WE GET OUR HANDS ON THOSE DOCUMENTS...
...WE'VE GOT TO DO EVERYTHING WE CAN TO AVOID AROUSING THE SOLDIERS' SUSPICIONS!
WHAT A PAIN IN THE ASS...
...
STOP BOTHERING LEVI, FURLAN!!
WE CAN JUST BEAT THE STUFFIN' OUTTA ALL OF 'EM, LIKE WE DO UNDERGROUND!
FWIP
QUIET.
IDIOTS SHOULD BE SEEN, NOT HEARD.

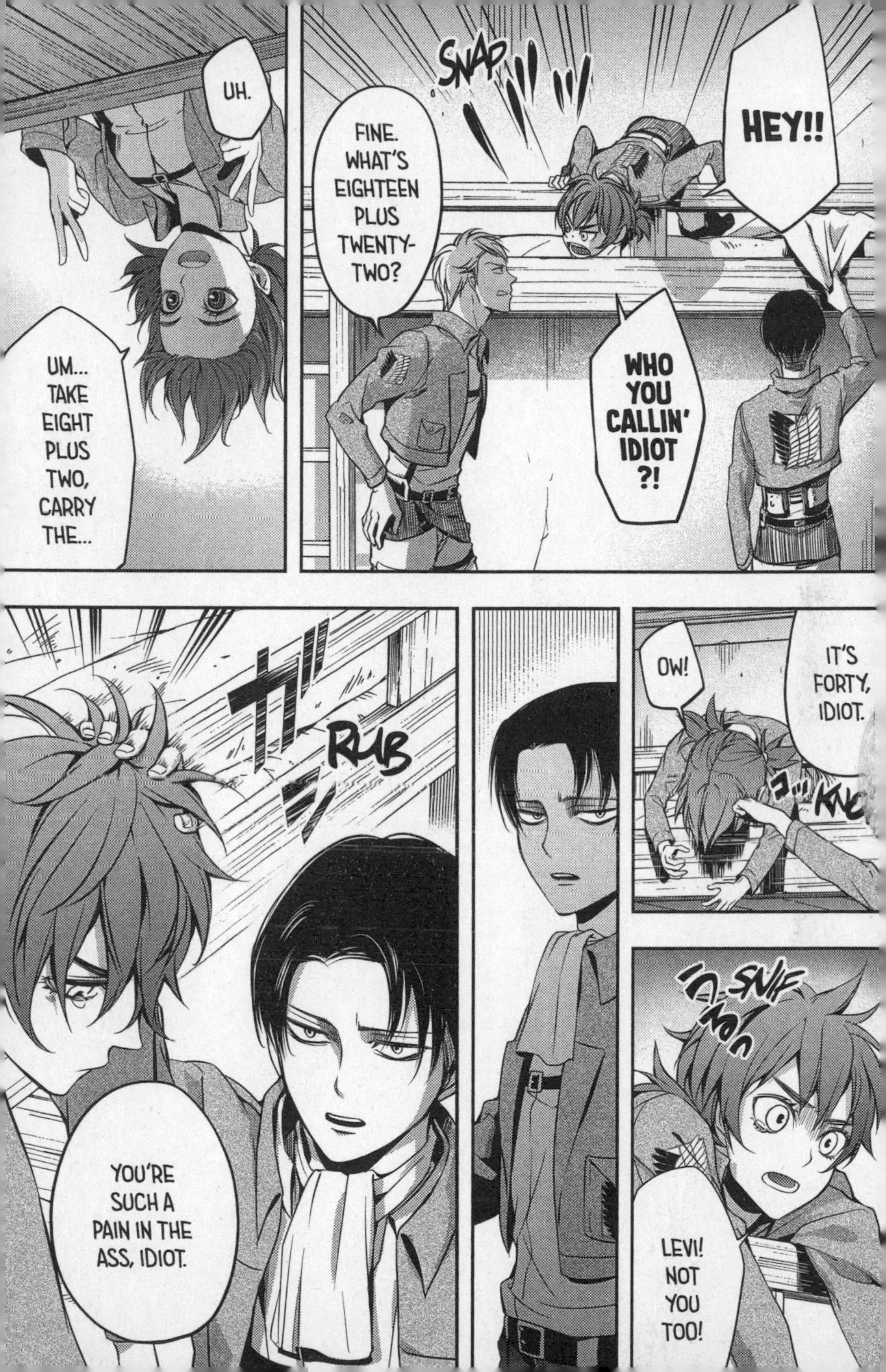
HEY!!
SNAP
FINE. WHAT'S EIGHTEEN PLUS TWENTY-TWO?
WHO YOU CALLIN' IDIOT ?!
UH.
UM... TAKE EIGHT PLUS TWO, CARRY THE...
IT'S FORTY, IDIOT.
OW!
SNIF
LEVI! NOT YOU TOO!
RUB
YOU'RE SUCH A PAIN IN THE ASS, IDIOT.

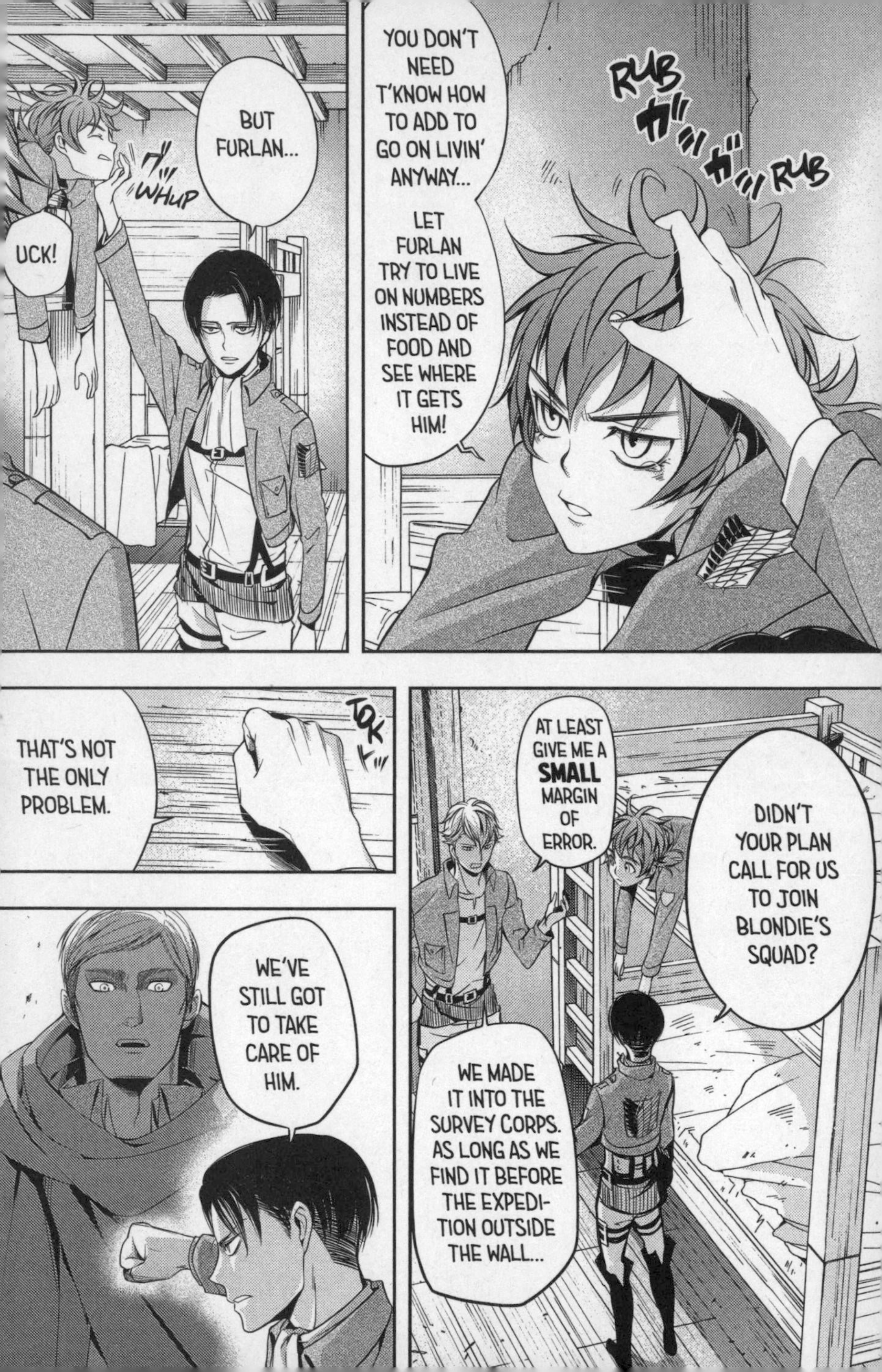
RUB
ガ
ガ
RUB
YOU DON'T NEED T'KNOW HOW TO ADD TO GO ON LIVIN' ANYWAY...
LET FURLAN TRY TO LIVE ON NUMBERS INSTEAD OF FOOD AND SEE WHERE IT GETS HIM!
BUT FURLAN...
WHUP
UCK!
DIDN'T YOUR PLAN CALL FOR US TO JOIN BLONDIE'S SQUAD?
AT LEAST GIVE ME A **SMALL** MARGIN OF ERROR.
WE MADE IT INTO THE SURVEY CORPS. AS LONG AS WE FIND IT BEFORE THE EXPEDITION OUTSIDE THE WALL...
TOK
THAT'S NOT THE ONLY PROBLEM.
WE'VE STILL GOT TO TAKE CARE OF HIM.

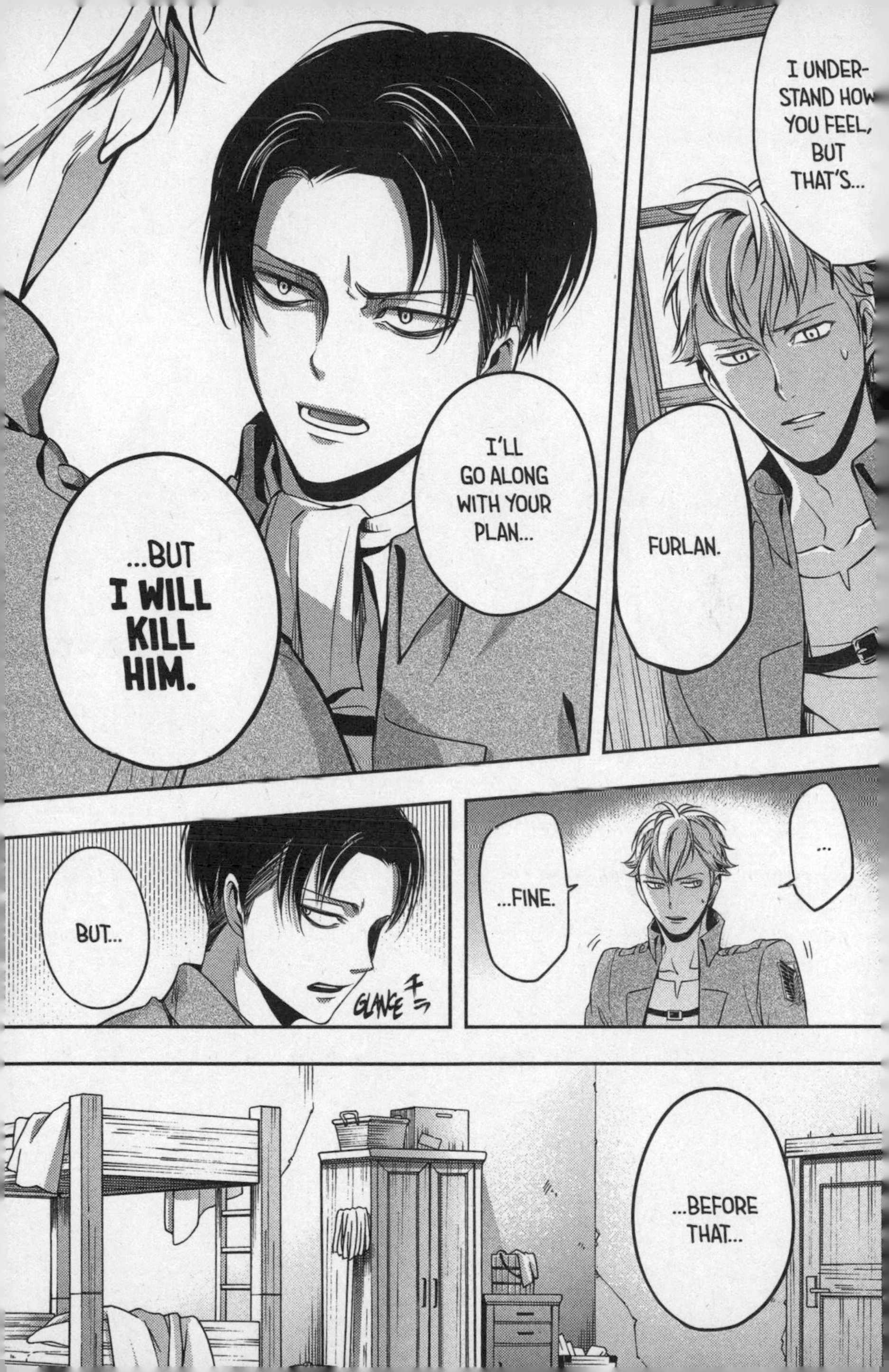
I UNDER-STAND HOW YOU FEEL, BUT THAT'S...
FURLAN.
I'LL GO ALONG WITH YOUR PLAN...
...BUT I WILL KILL HIM.
...
...FINE.
BUT...
GLANCE
...BEFORE THAT...

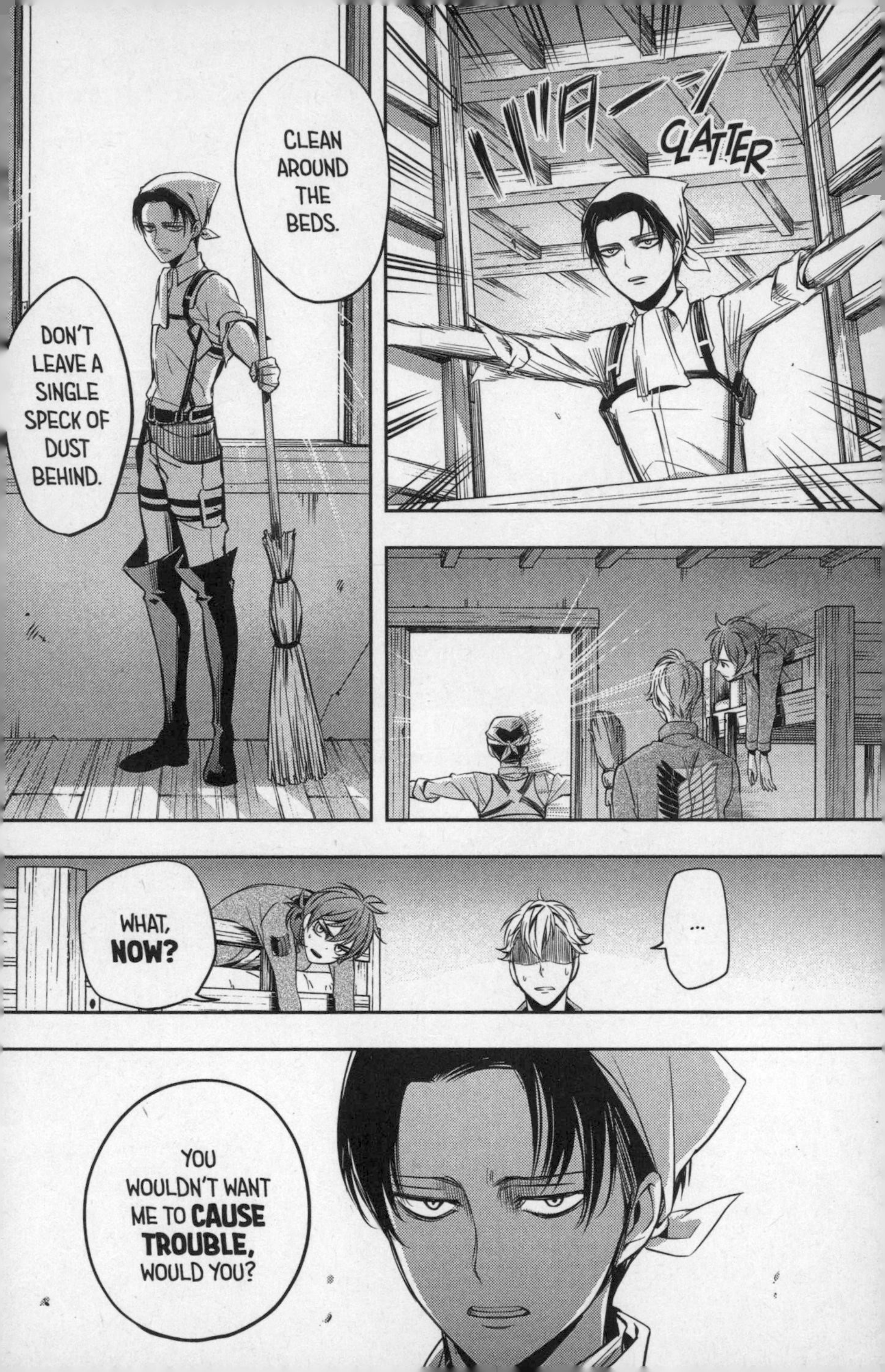
CLATTER
CLEAN AROUND THE BEDS.
DON'T LEAVE A SINGLE SPECK OF DUST BEHIND.
...
WHAT, **NOW?**
YOU WOULDN'T WANT ME TO **CAUSE TROUBLE,** WOULD YOU?

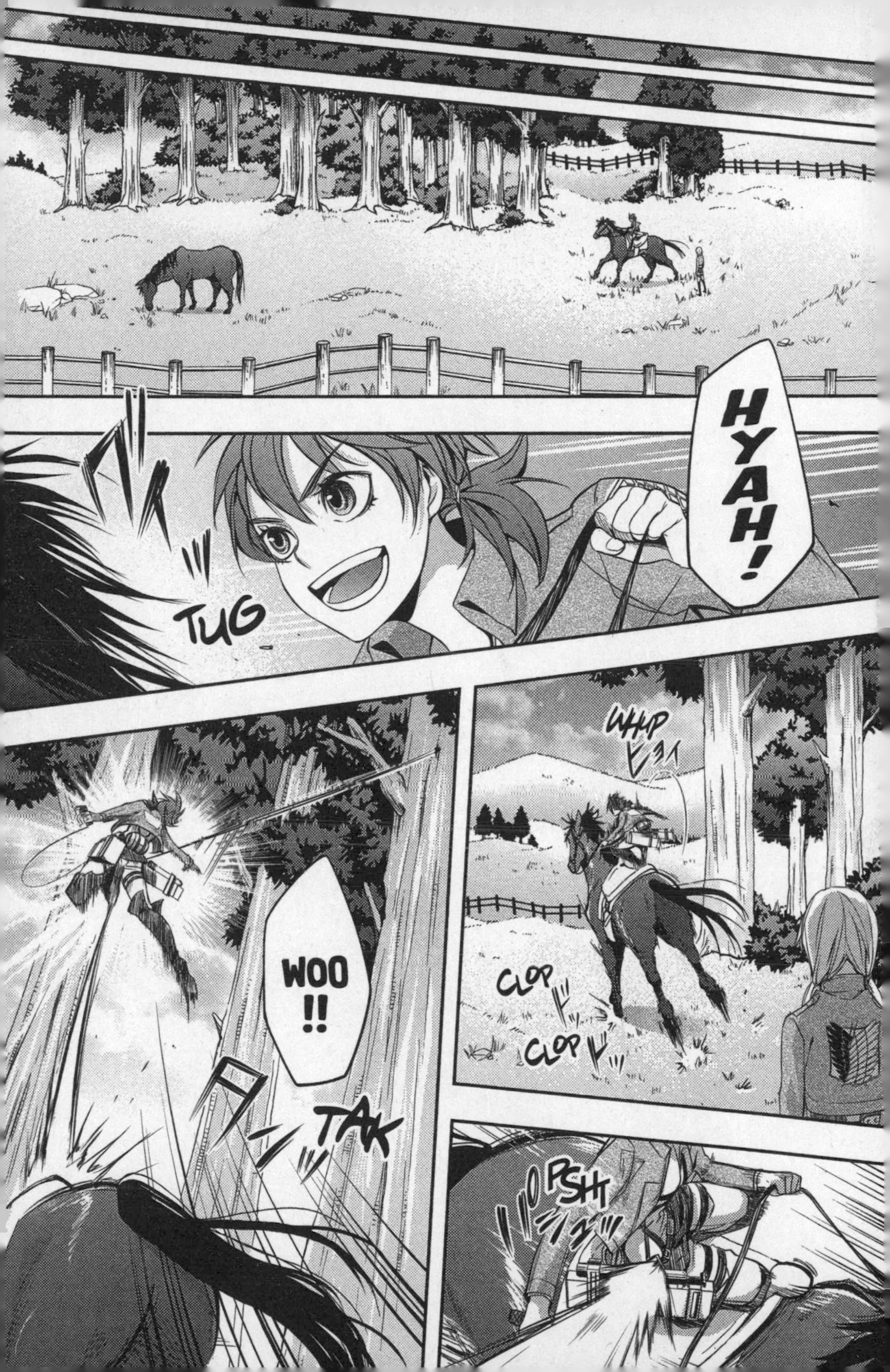
HYAH!
TUG
WHIP
CLOP
CLOP
PSHT
WOO!!
TAK

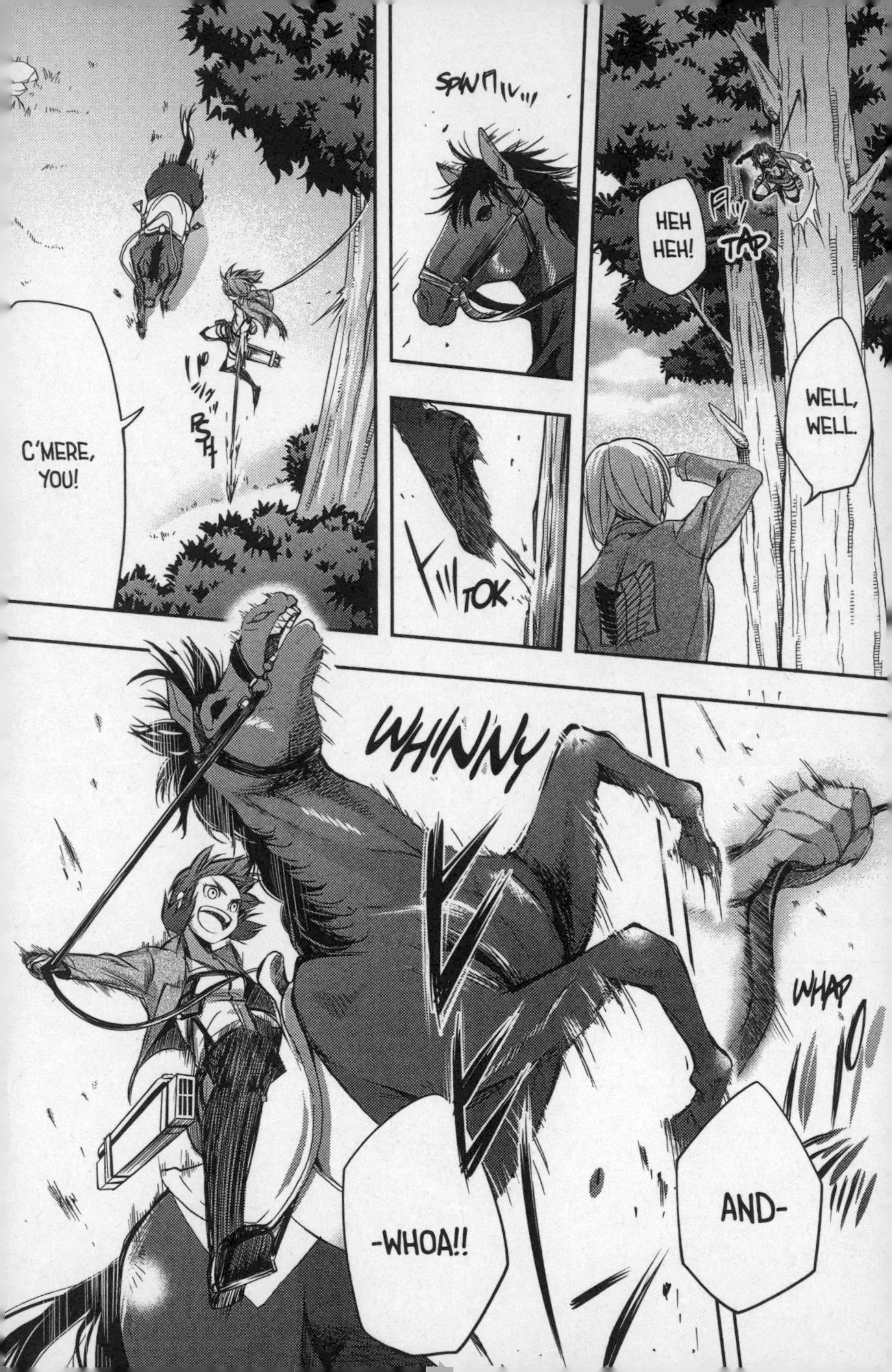
HEH HEH!
TAP
WELL, WELL.
SPIN
TOK
C'MERE, YOU!
AND-
WHAP
WHINNY
-WHOA!!

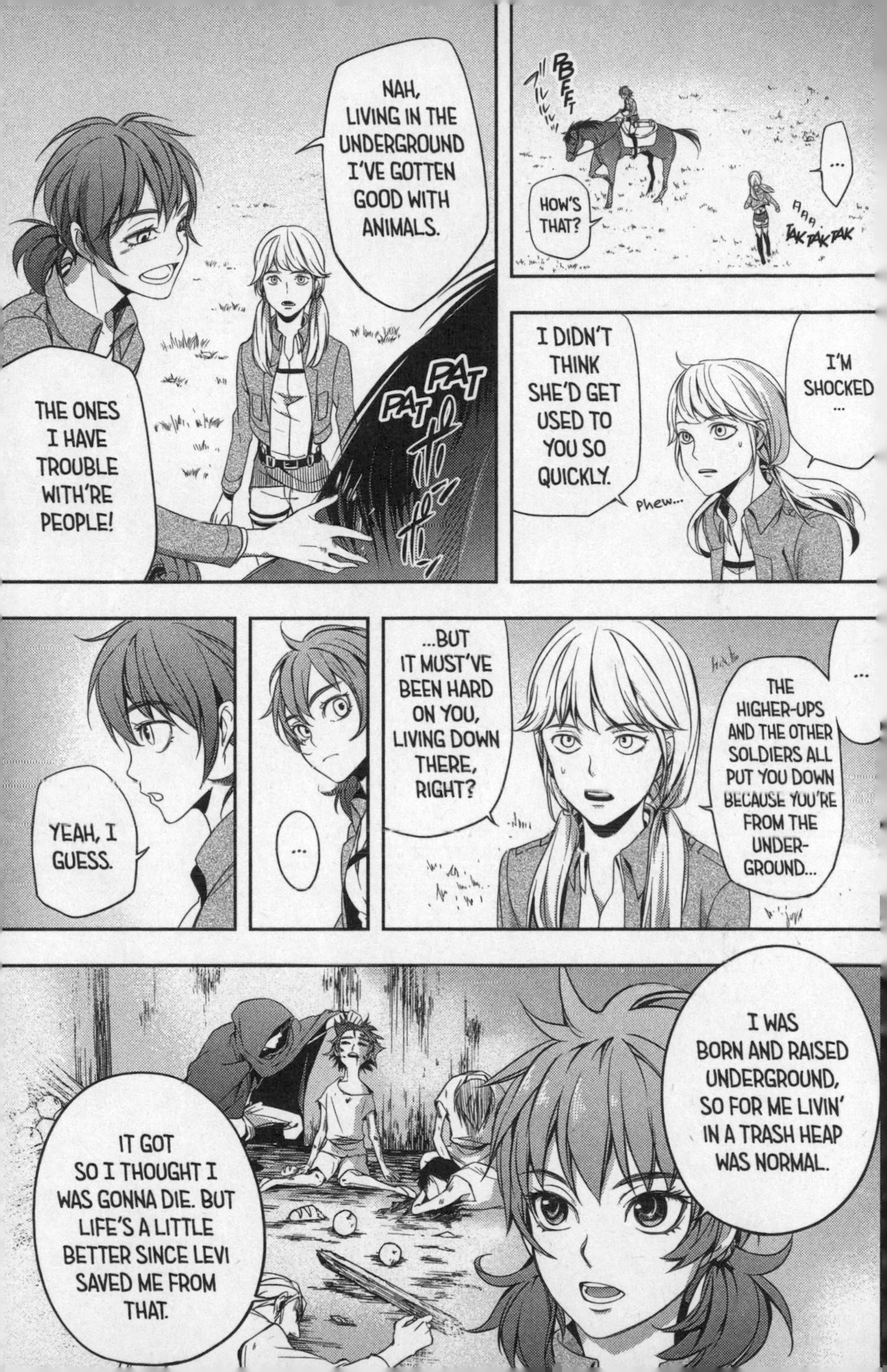
PBBFFT
...
HOW'S THAT?
TAKTAKTAK
I'M SHOCKED ...
I DIDN'T THINK SHE'D GET USED TO YOU SO QUICKLY.
Phew...
NAH, LIVING IN THE UNDERGROUND I'VE GOTTEN GOOD WITH ANIMALS.
PAT PAT
THE ONES I HAVE TROUBLE WITH'RE PEOPLE!
...
THE HIGHER-UPS AND THE OTHER SOLDIERS ALL PUT YOU DOWN BECAUSE YOU'RE FROM THE UNDER-GROUND...
...BUT IT MUST'VE BEEN HARD ON YOU, LIVING DOWN THERE, RIGHT?
...
YEAH, I GUESS.
I WAS BORN AND RAISED UNDERGROUND, SO FOR ME LIVIN' IN A TRASH HEAP WAS NORMAL.
IT GOT SO I THOUGHT I WAS GONNA DIE. BUT LIFE'S A LITTLE BETTER SINCE LEVI SAVED ME FROM THAT.

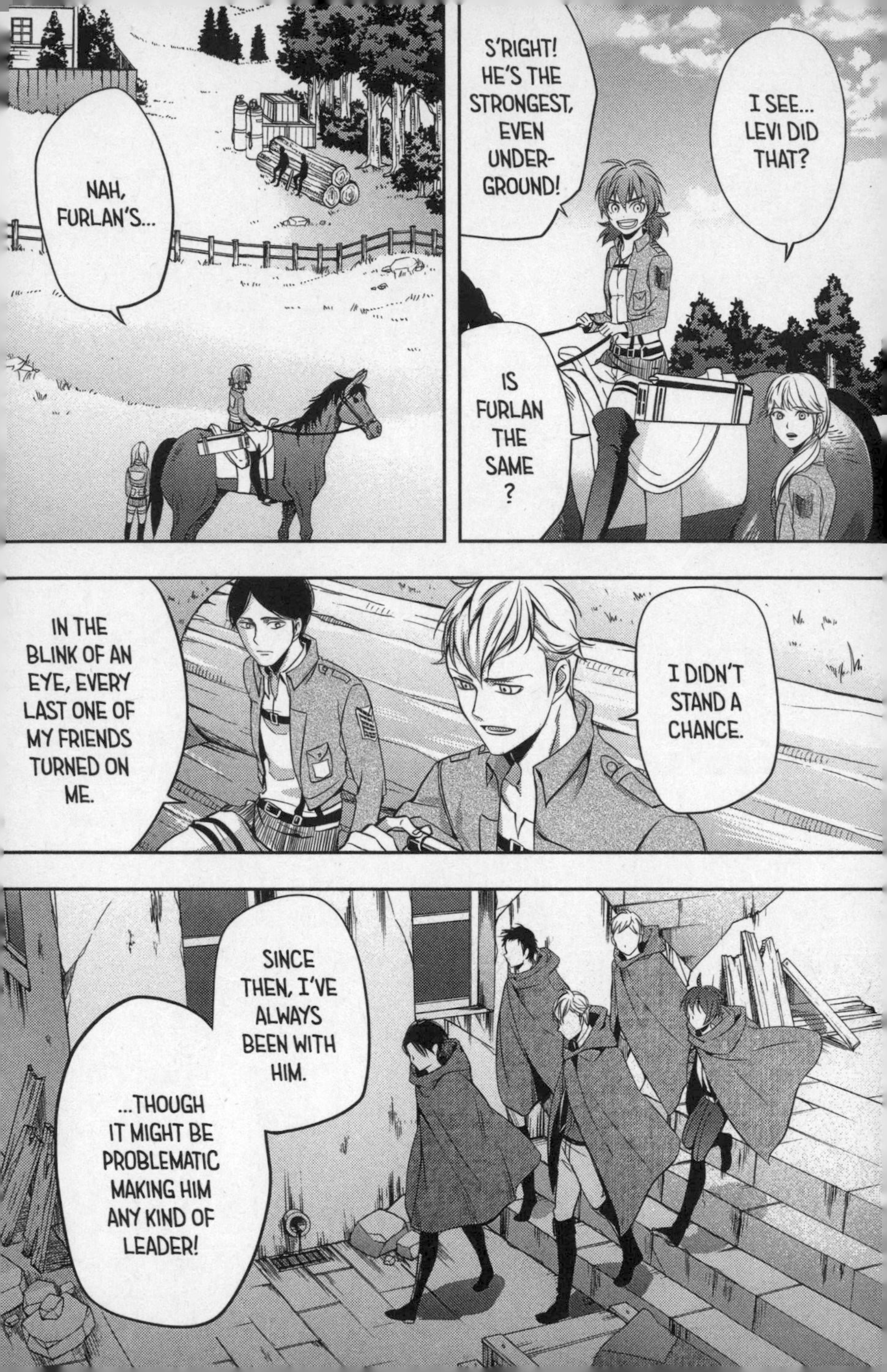
I SEE... LEVI DID THAT?
S'RIGHT! HE'S THE STRONGEST, EVEN UNDER-GROUND!
IS FURLAN THE SAME?
NAH, FURLAN'S...
I DIDN'T STAND A CHANCE.
IN THE BLINK OF AN EYE, EVERY LAST ONE OF MY FRIENDS TURNED ON ME.
SINCE THEN, I'VE ALWAYS BEEN WITH HIM.
...THOUGH IT MIGHT BE PROBLEMATIC MAKING HIM ANY KIND OF LEADER!

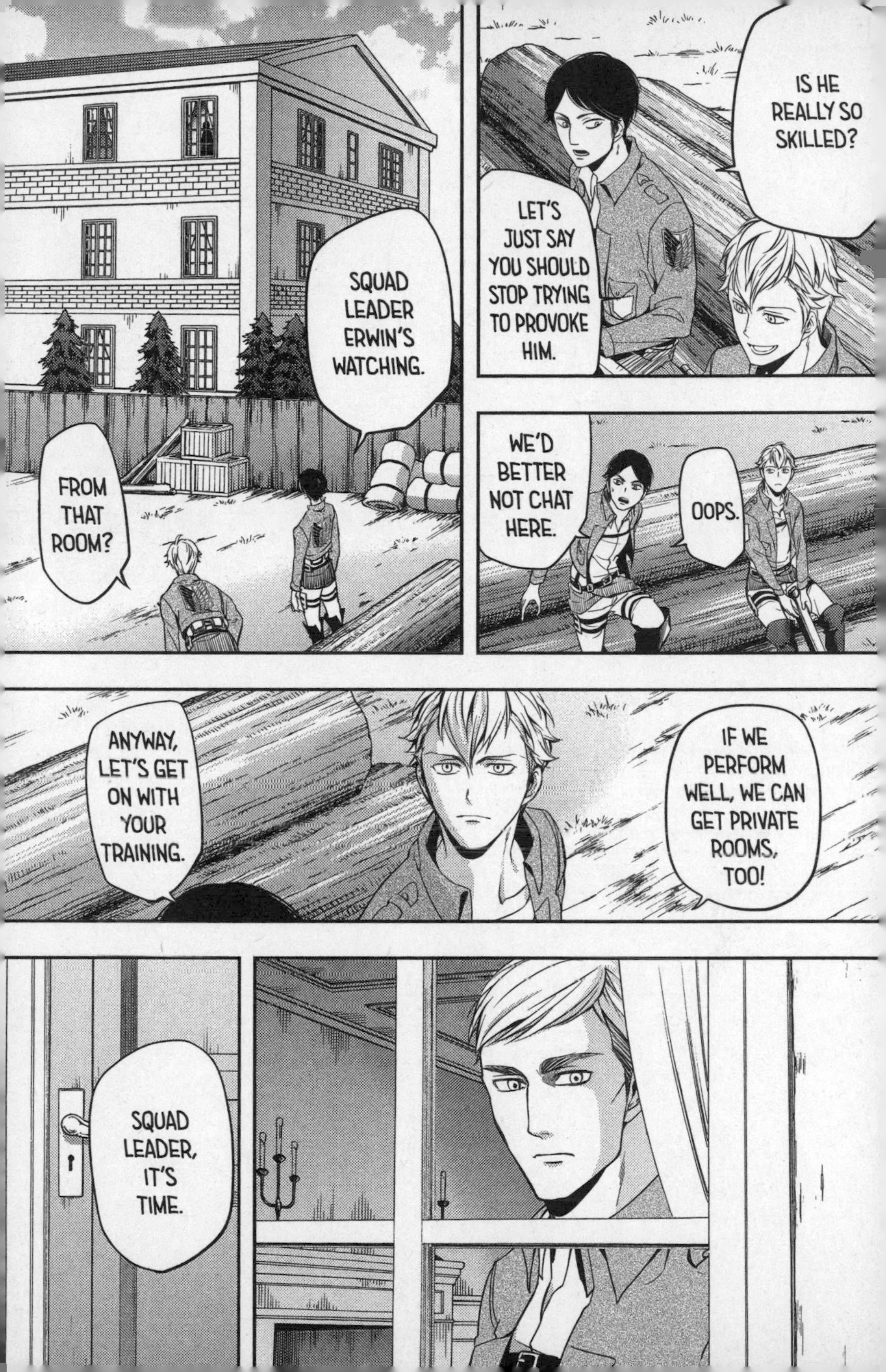
IS HE REALLY SO SKILLED?
LET'S JUST SAY YOU SHOULD STOP TRYING TO PROVOKE HIM.
WE'D BETTER NOT CHAT HERE.
OOPS.
SQUAD LEADER ERWIN'S WATCHING.
FROM THAT ROOM?
IF WE PERFORM WELL, WE CAN GET PRIVATE ROOMS, TOO!
ANYWAY, LET'S GET ON WITH YOUR TRAINING.
SQUAD LEADER, IT'S TIME.

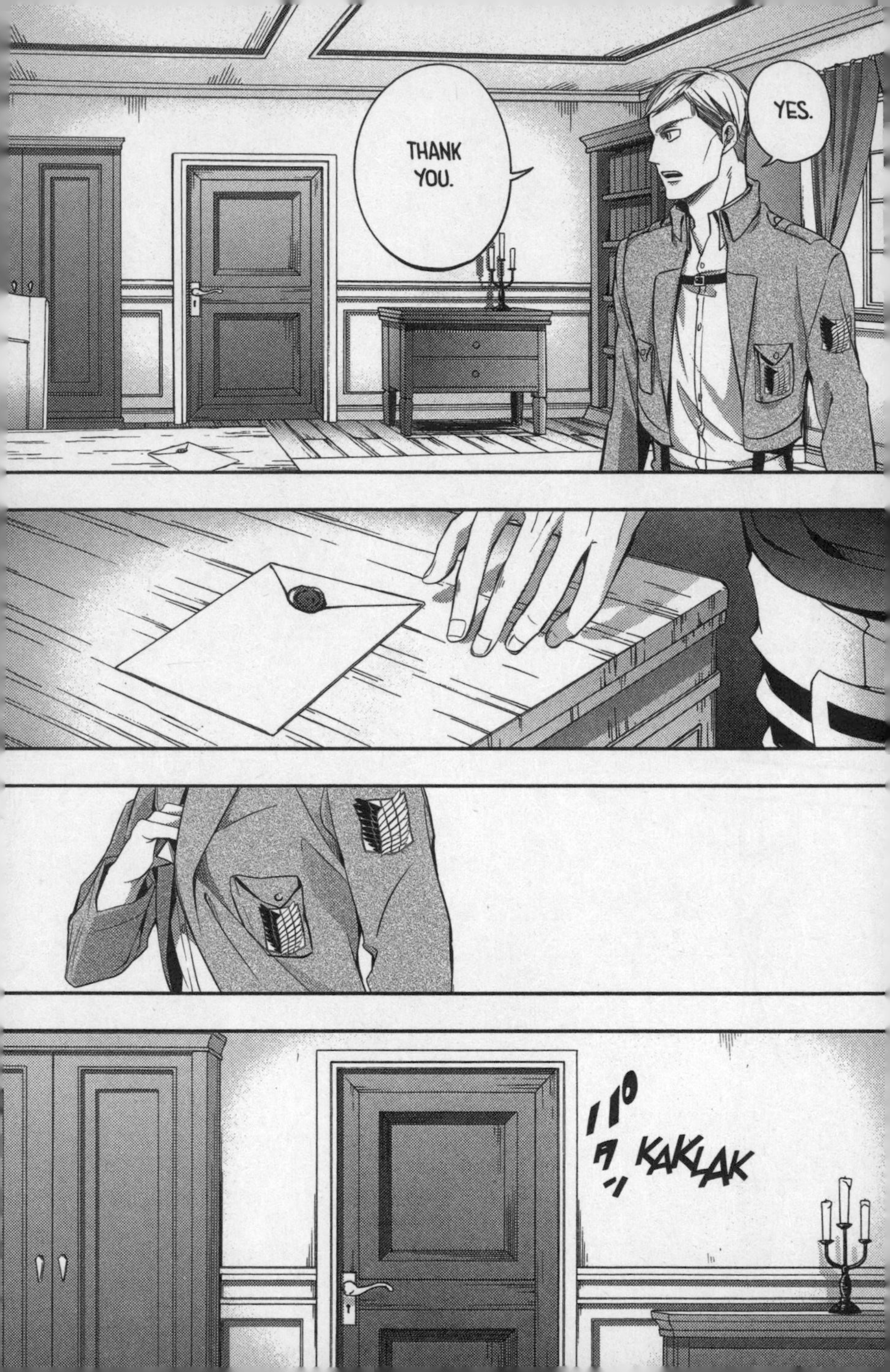
YES.
THANK YOU.
KAKLAK

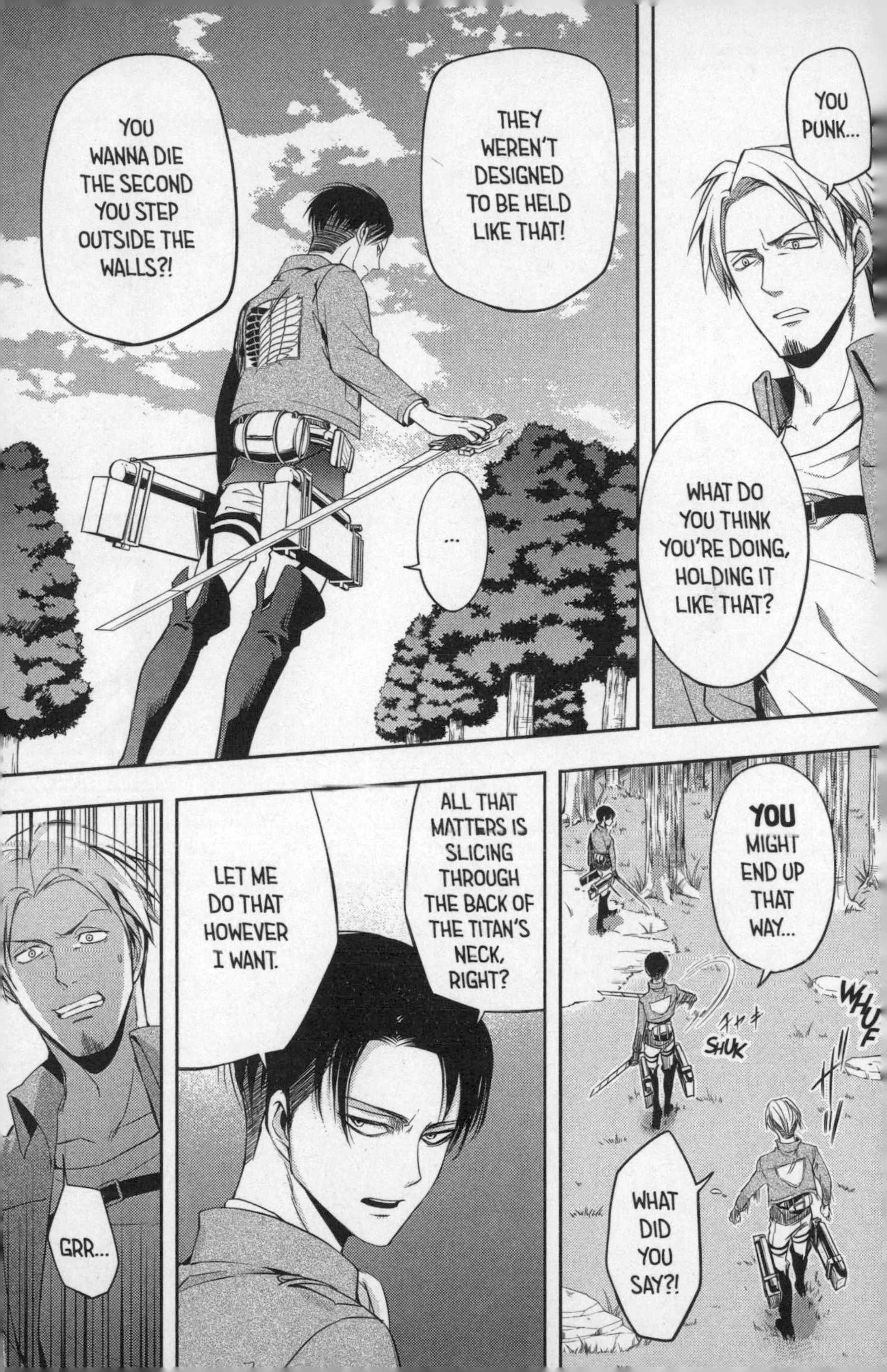
YOU PUNK...
WHAT DO YOU THINK YOU'RE DOING, HOLDING IT LIKE THAT?
THEY WEREN'T DESIGNED TO BE HELD LIKE THAT!
YOU WANNA DIE THE SECOND YOU STEP OUTSIDE THE WALLS?!
...
YOU MIGHT END UP THAT WAY...
WHUF
SHUK
WHAT DID YOU SAY?!
ALL THAT MATTERS IS SLICING THROUGH THE BACK OF THE TITAN'S NECK, RIGHT?
LET ME DO THAT HOWEVER I WANT.
GRR...

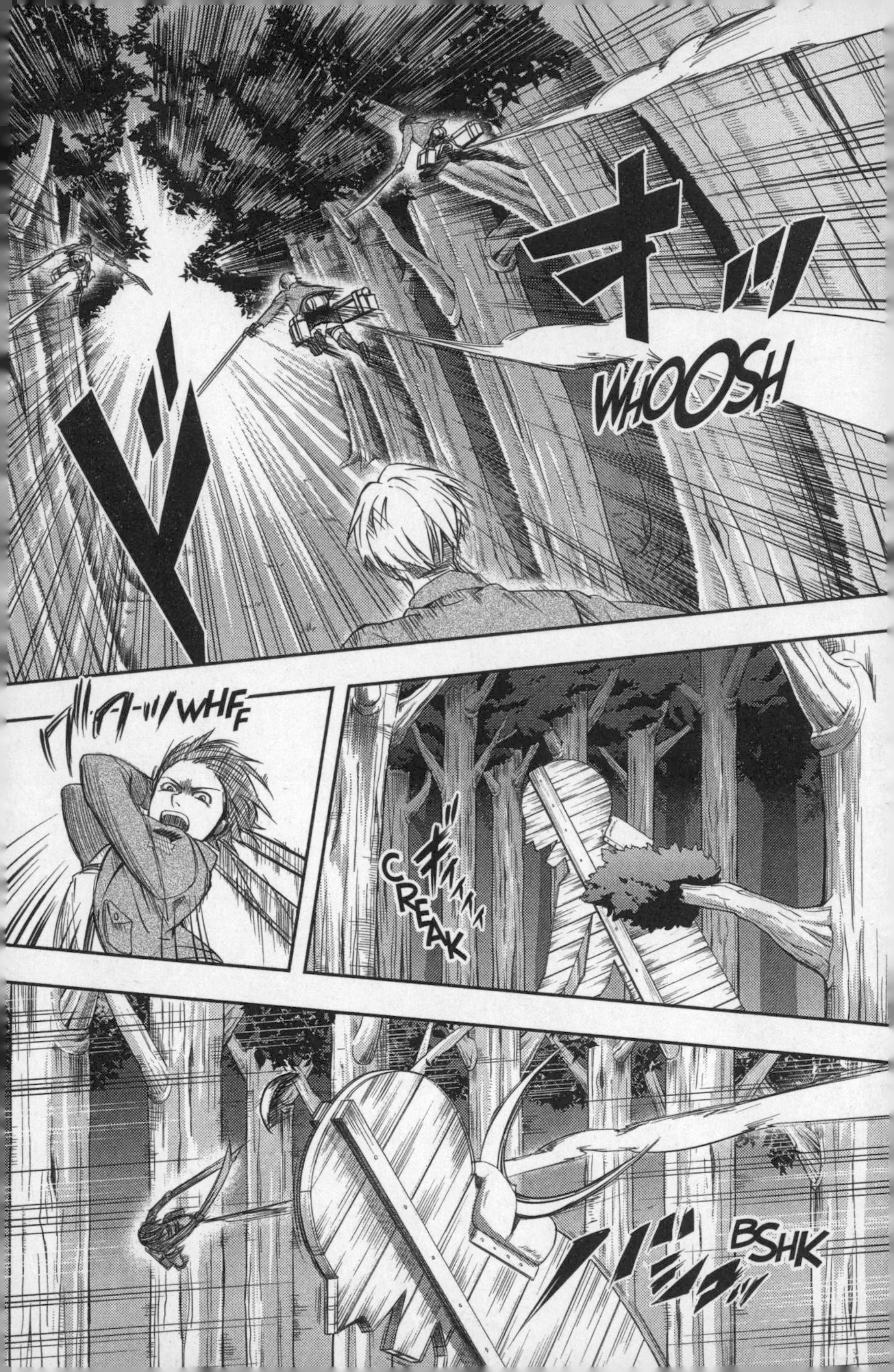
WHOOSH
CREAK
WHFF
BSHK

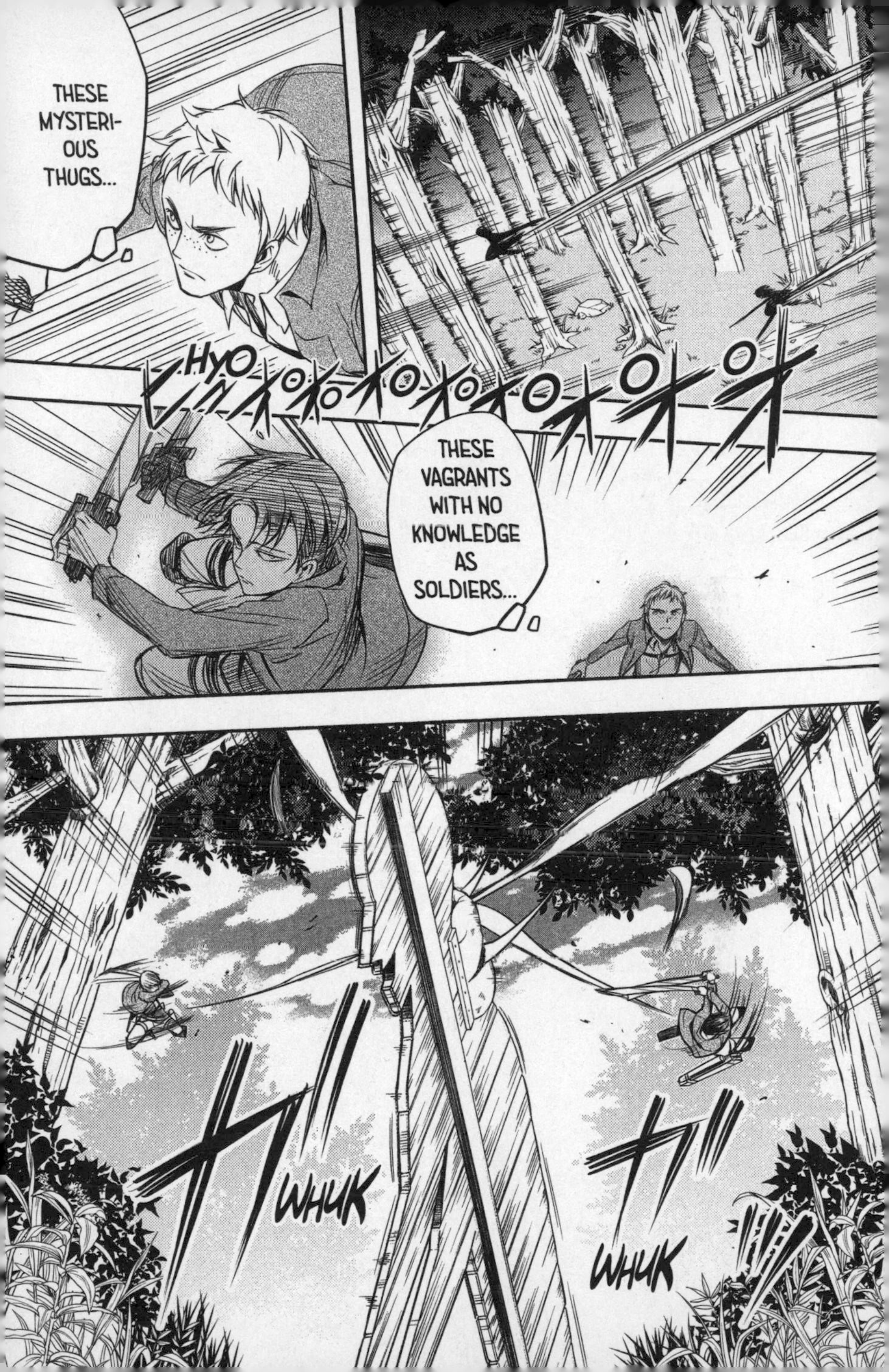
THESE MYSTERIOUS THUGS...
HYO
THESE VAGRANTS WITH NO KNOWLEDGE AS SOLDIERS...
WHUK
WHUK

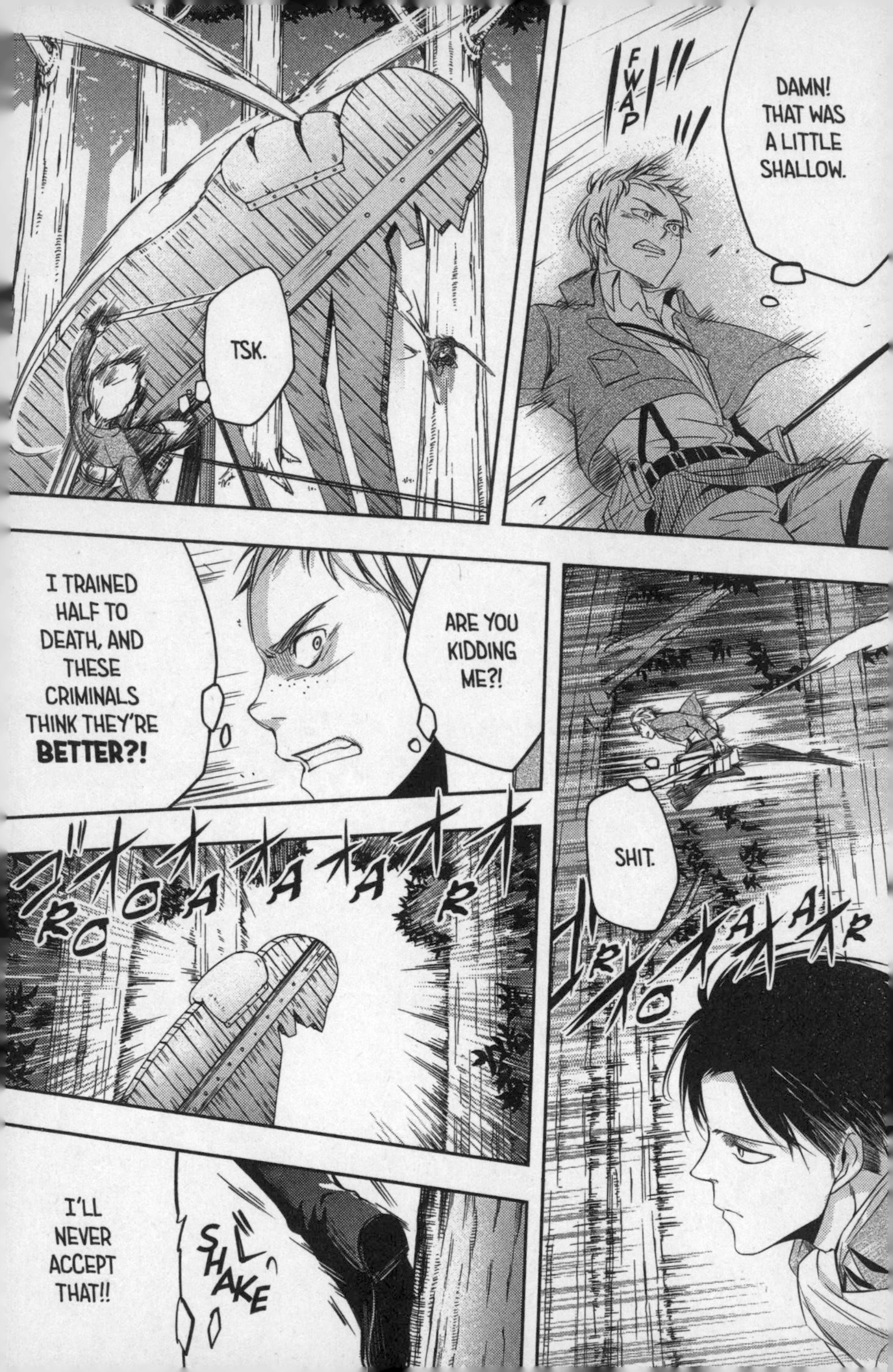
FWAP
DAMN! THAT WAS A LITTLE SHALLOW.
TSK.
SHIT.
ROAAR
ARE YOU KIDDING ME?!
I TRAINED HALF TO DEATH, AND THESE CRIMINALS THINK THEY'RE **BETTER?!**
ROOAAAR
SHAKE
I'LL NEVER ACCEPT THAT!!

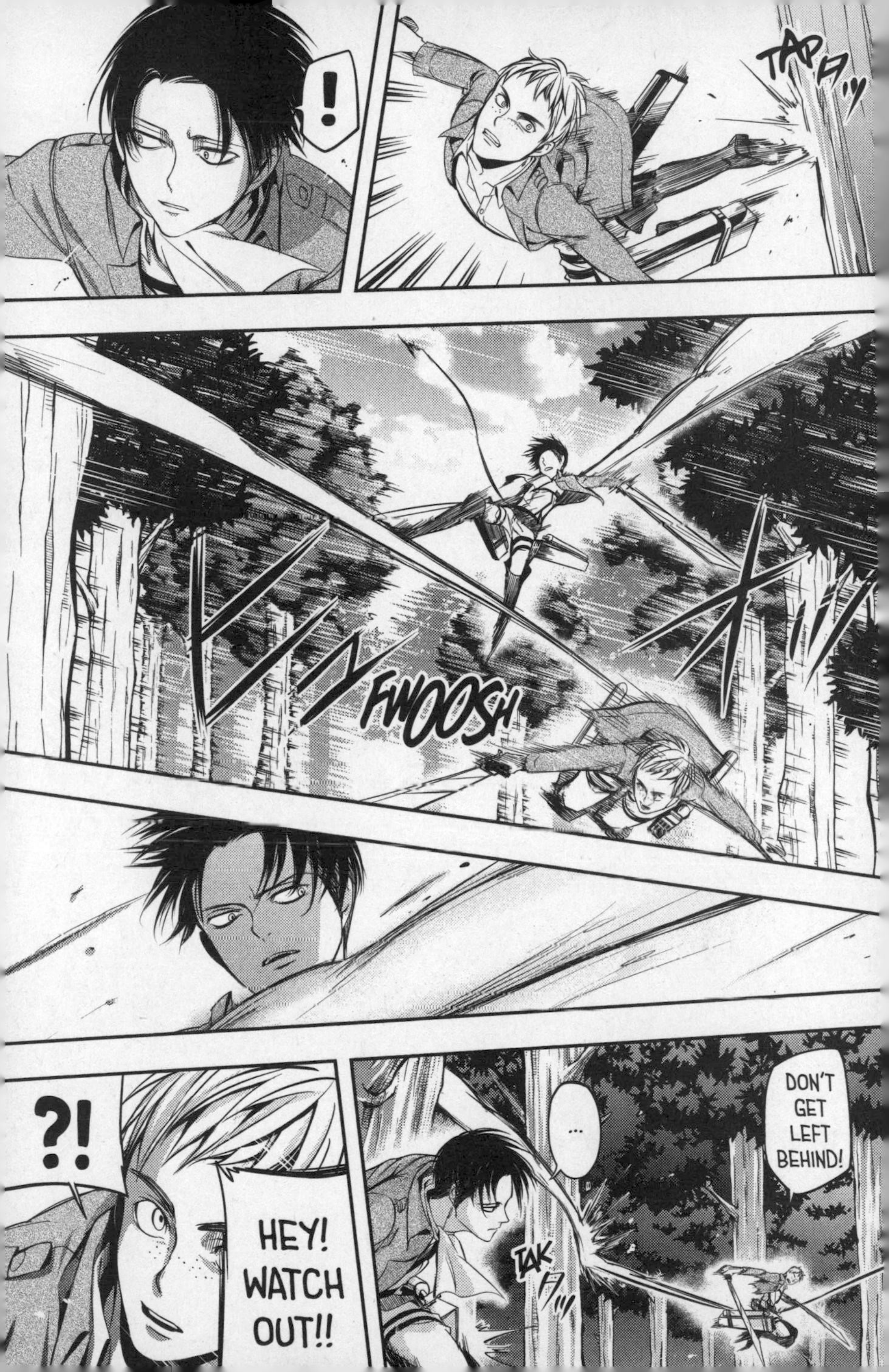
TAP
!
FWOOSH
DON'T GET LEFT BEHIND!
...
TAK
?!
HEY! WATCH OUT!!

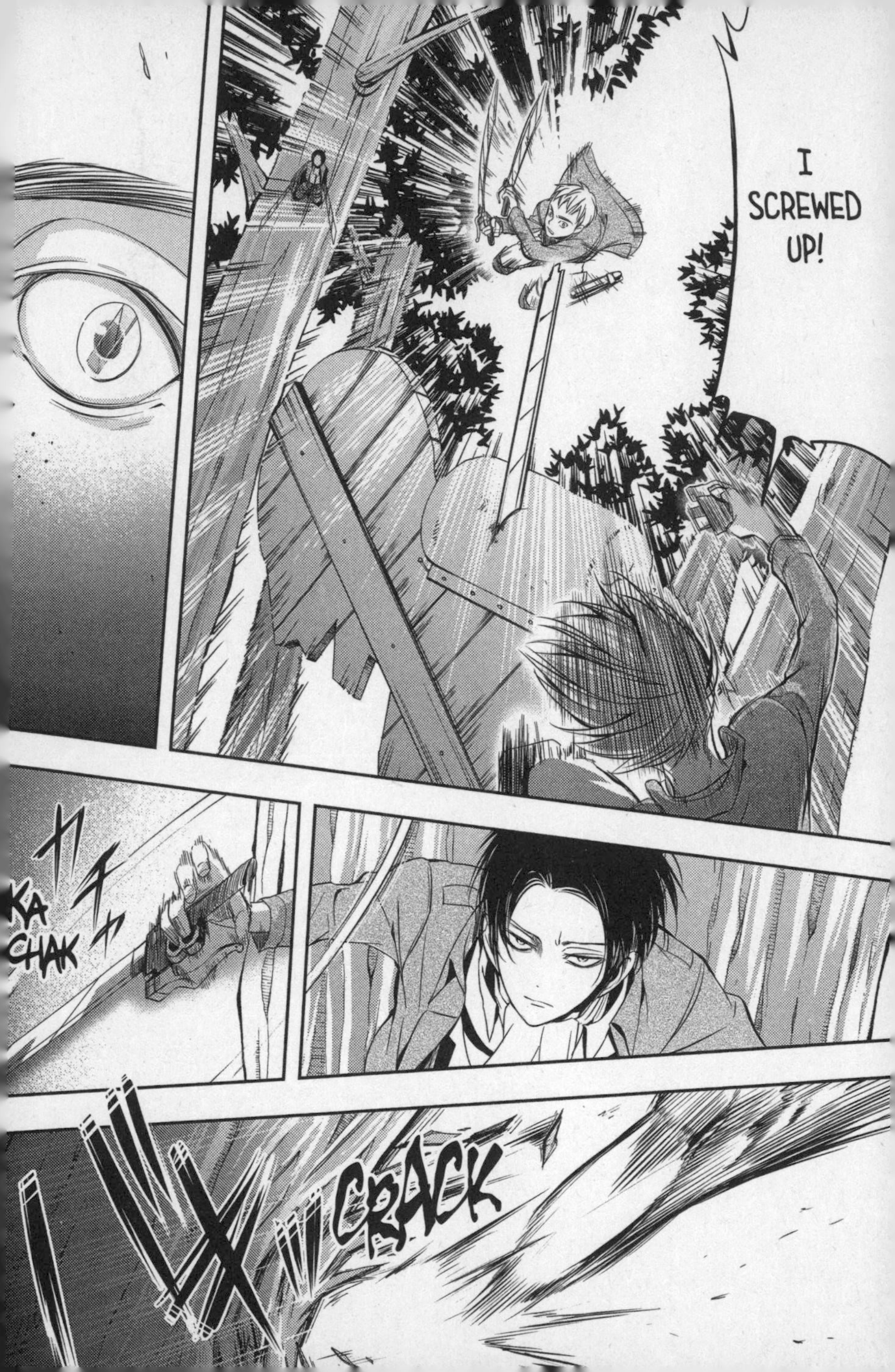
I SCREWED UP!
KA CHAK
CRACK

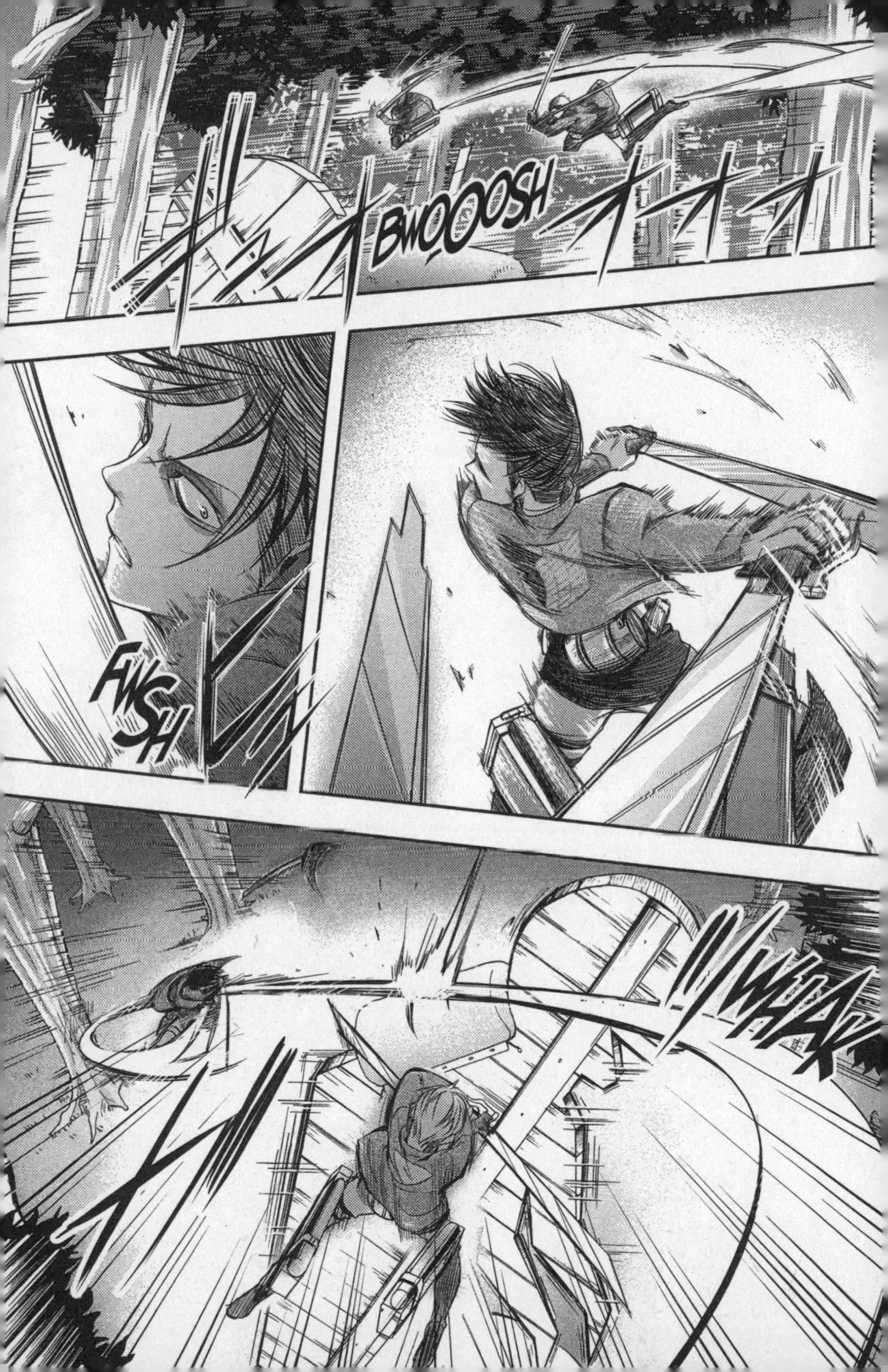
BWOOOSH
FWSH
WHAK

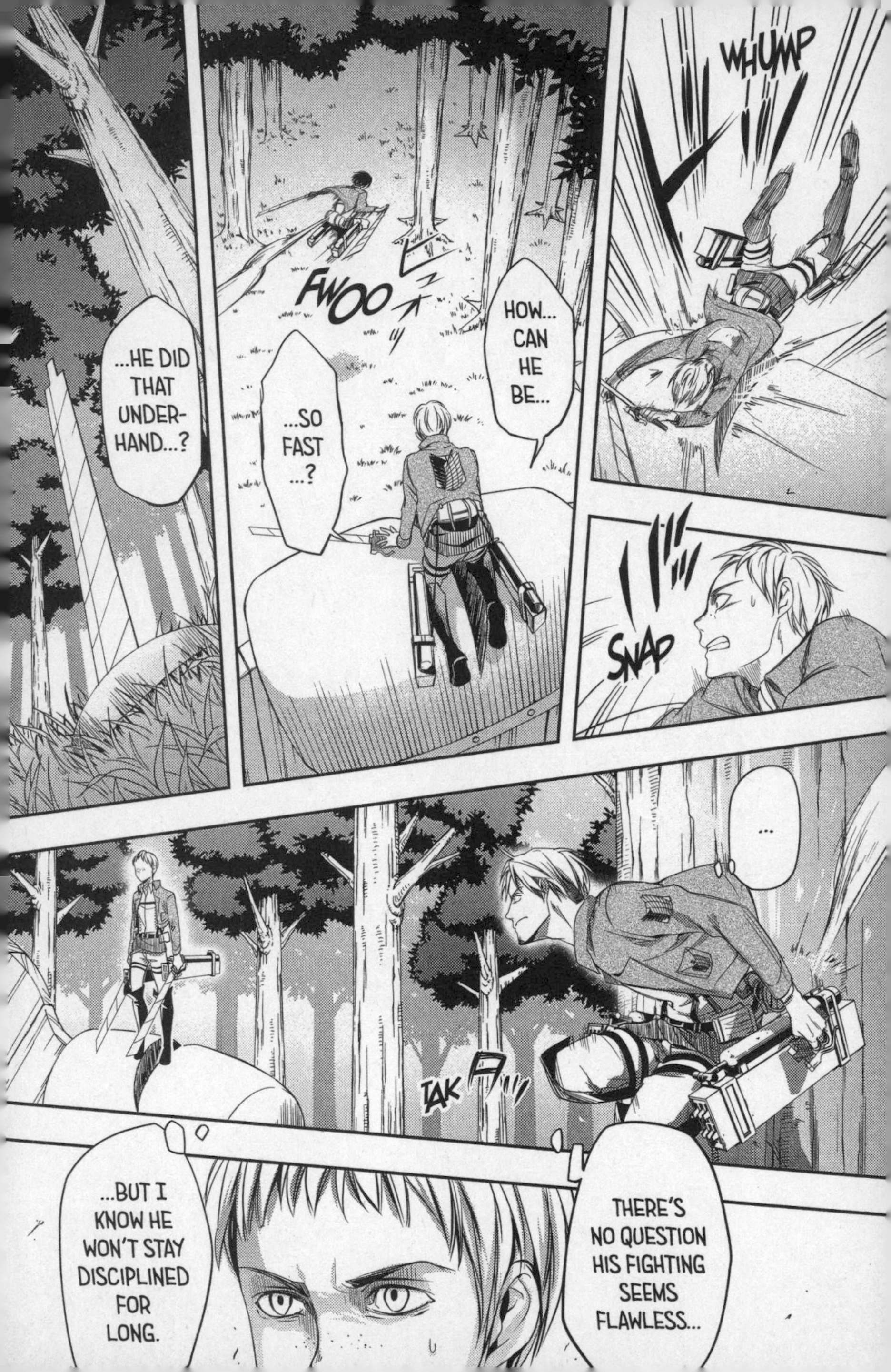
WHUMP
SNAP
HOW... CAN HE BE...
FWOO
...SO FAST...?
...HE DID THAT UNDER-HAND...?
...
TAK
THERE'S NO QUESTION HIS FIGHTING SEEMS FLAWLESS...
...BUT I KNOW HE WON'T STAY DISCIPLINED FOR LONG.

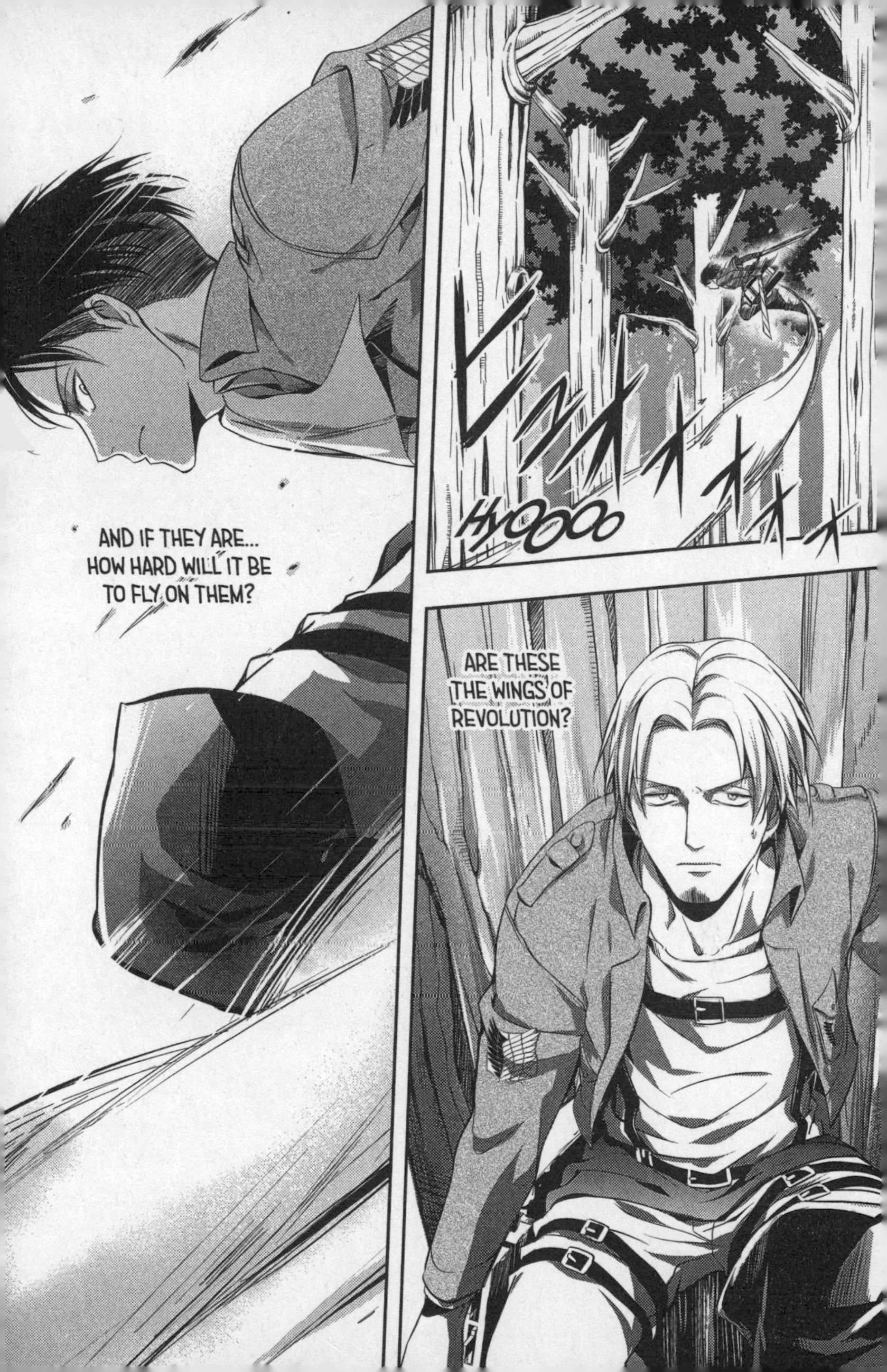
KYOOOO
ARE THESE THE WINGS OF REVOLUTION?
AND IF THEY ARE... HOW HARD WILL IT BE TO FLY ON THEM?

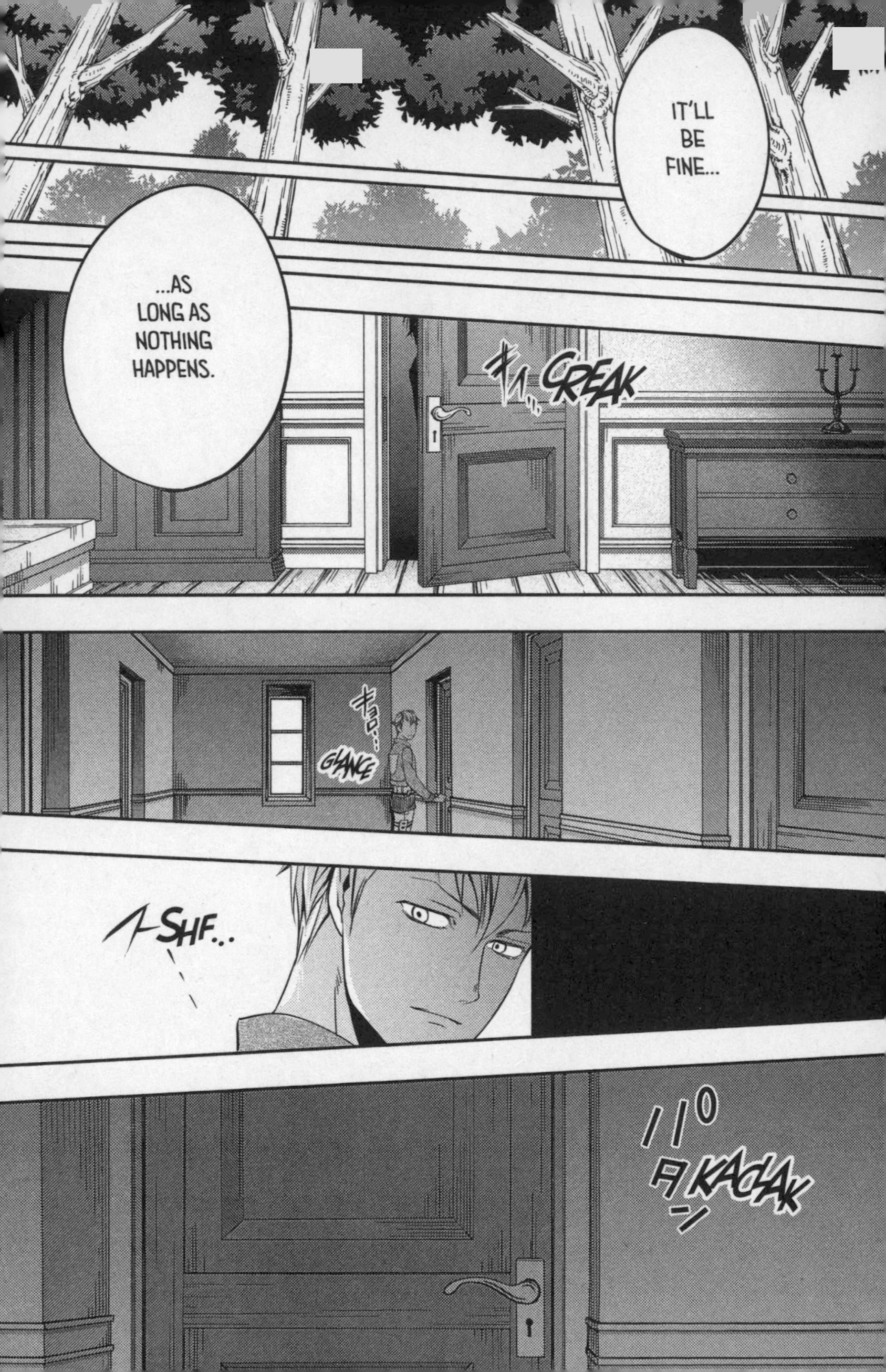
IT'LL BE FINE...
...AS LONG AS NOTHING HAPPENS.
CREAK
GLANCE
SHF...
KACLAK

ATTACK on TITAN

NO REGRETS

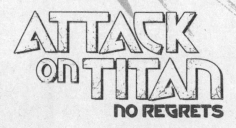

ATTACK on TITAN

NO REGRETS

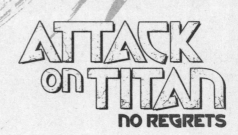

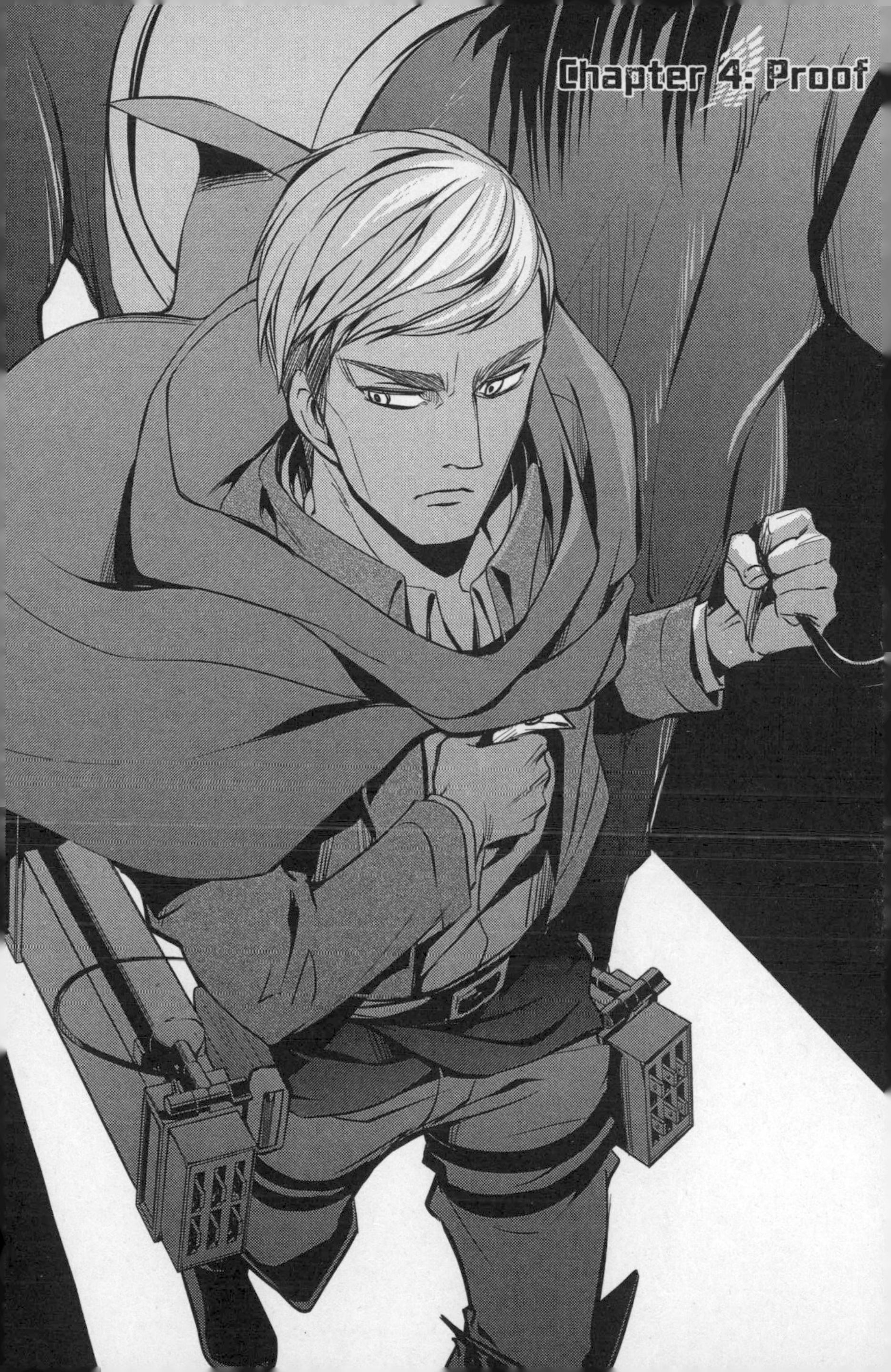
Chapter 4: Proof

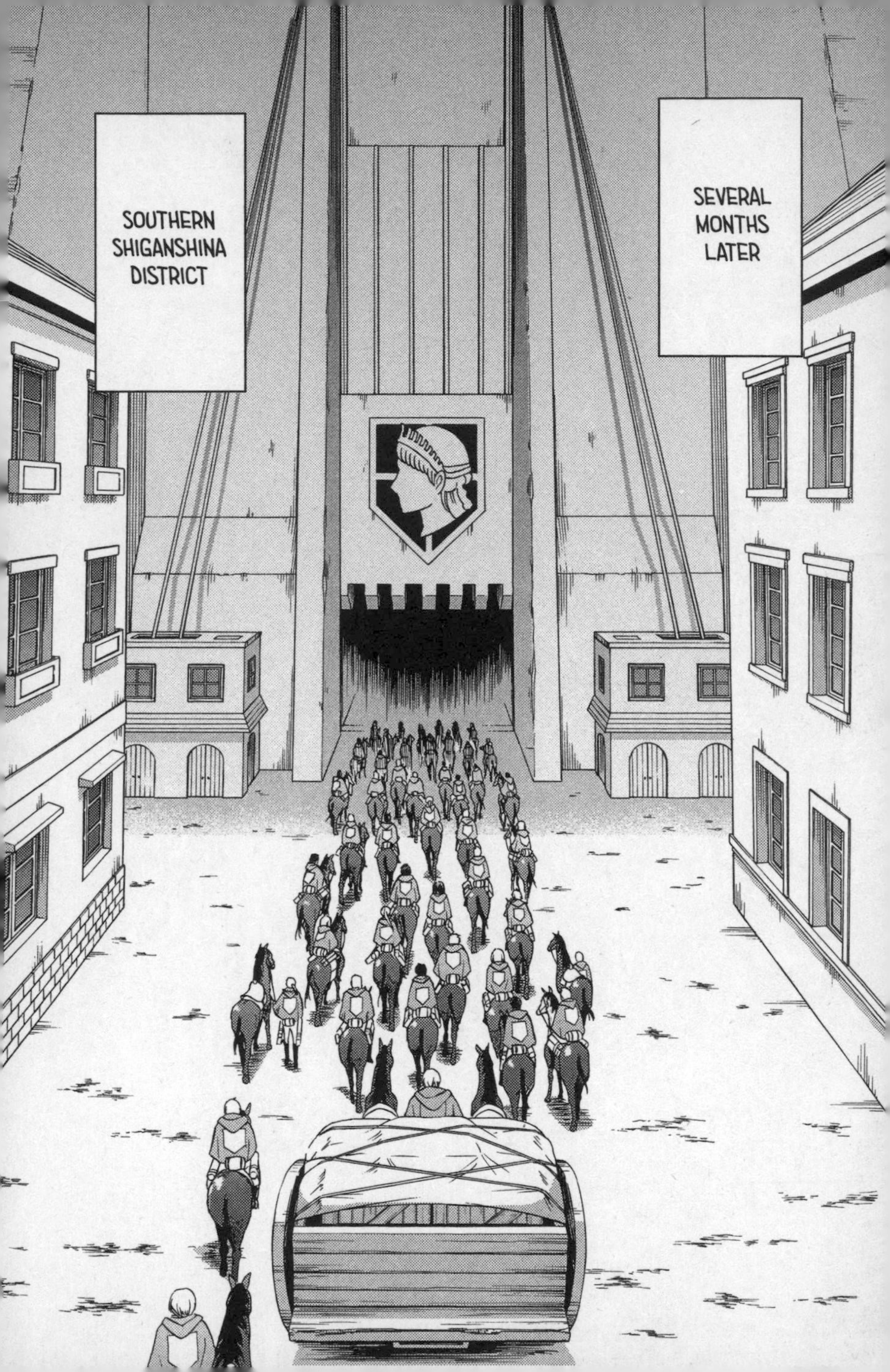
SEVERAL MONTHS LATER
SOUTHERN SHIGANSHINA DISTRICT

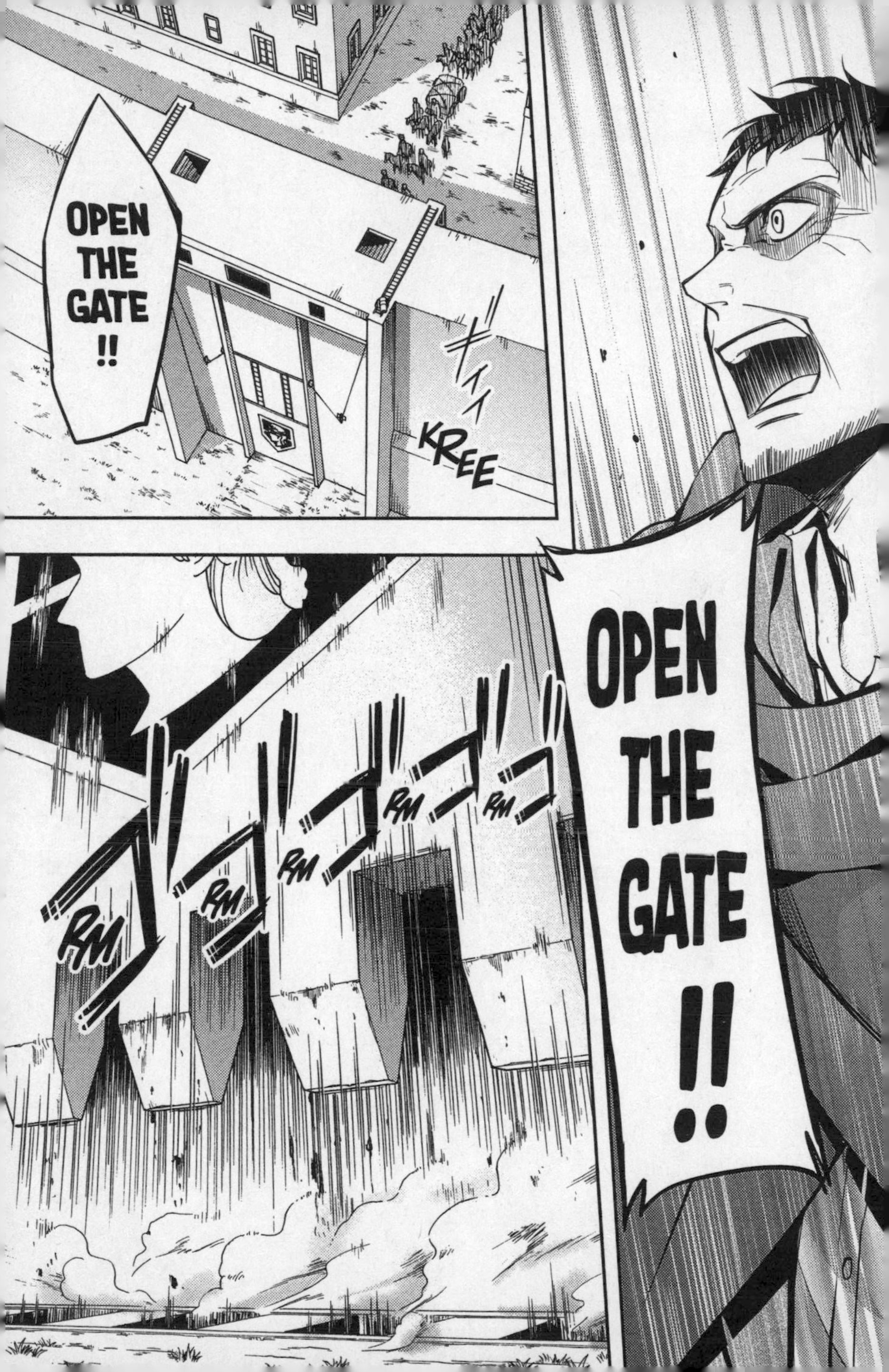

OPEN THE GATE!!
OPEN THE GATE!!
KREE
RM RM RM RM RM

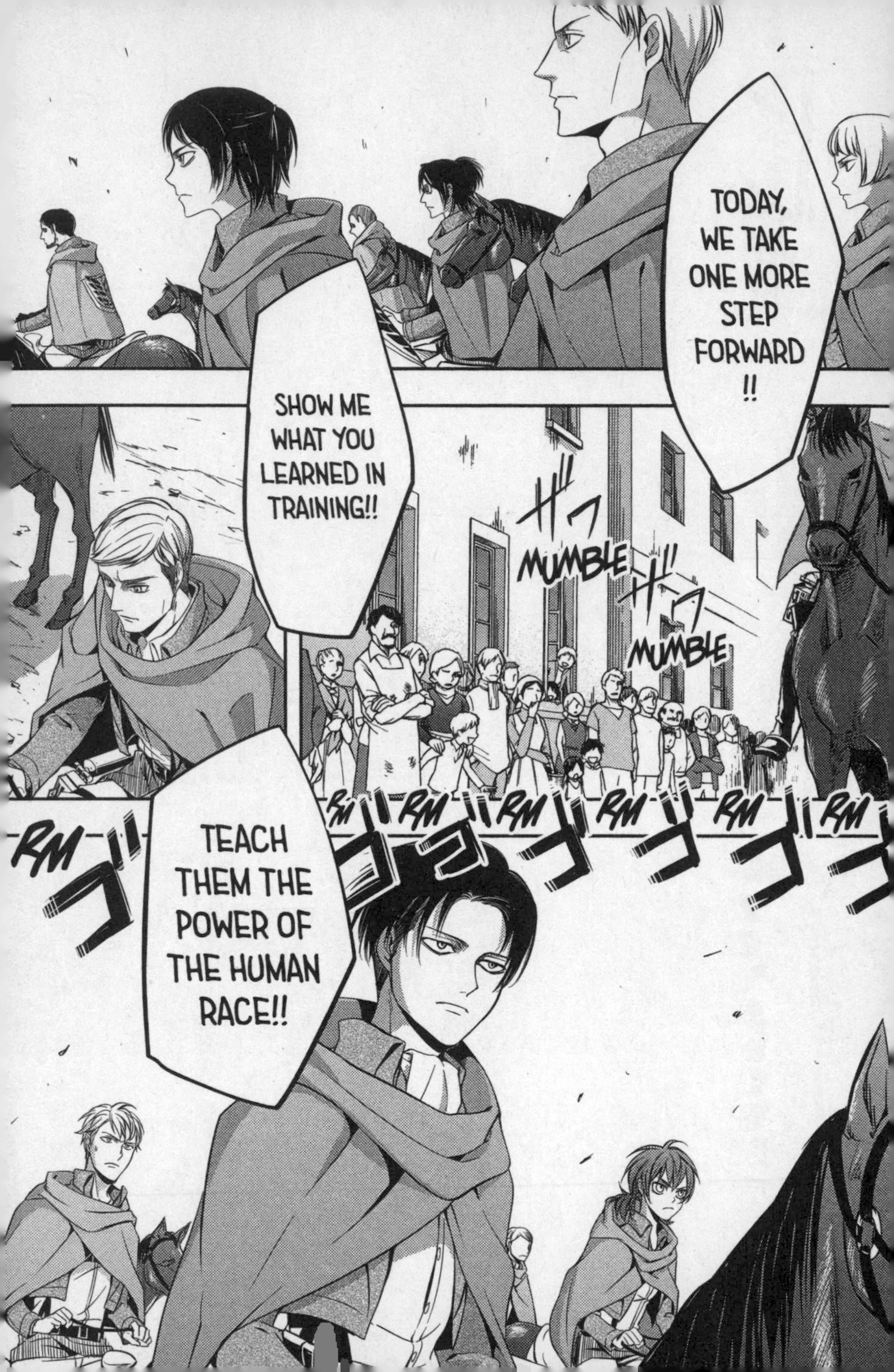
TODAY, WE TAKE ONE MORE STEP FORWARD!!
SHOW ME WHAT YOU LEARNED IN TRAINING!!
MUMBLE
MUMBLE
RM
RM
RM
RM
RM
RM
RM
TEACH THEM THE POWER OF THE HUMAN RACE!!

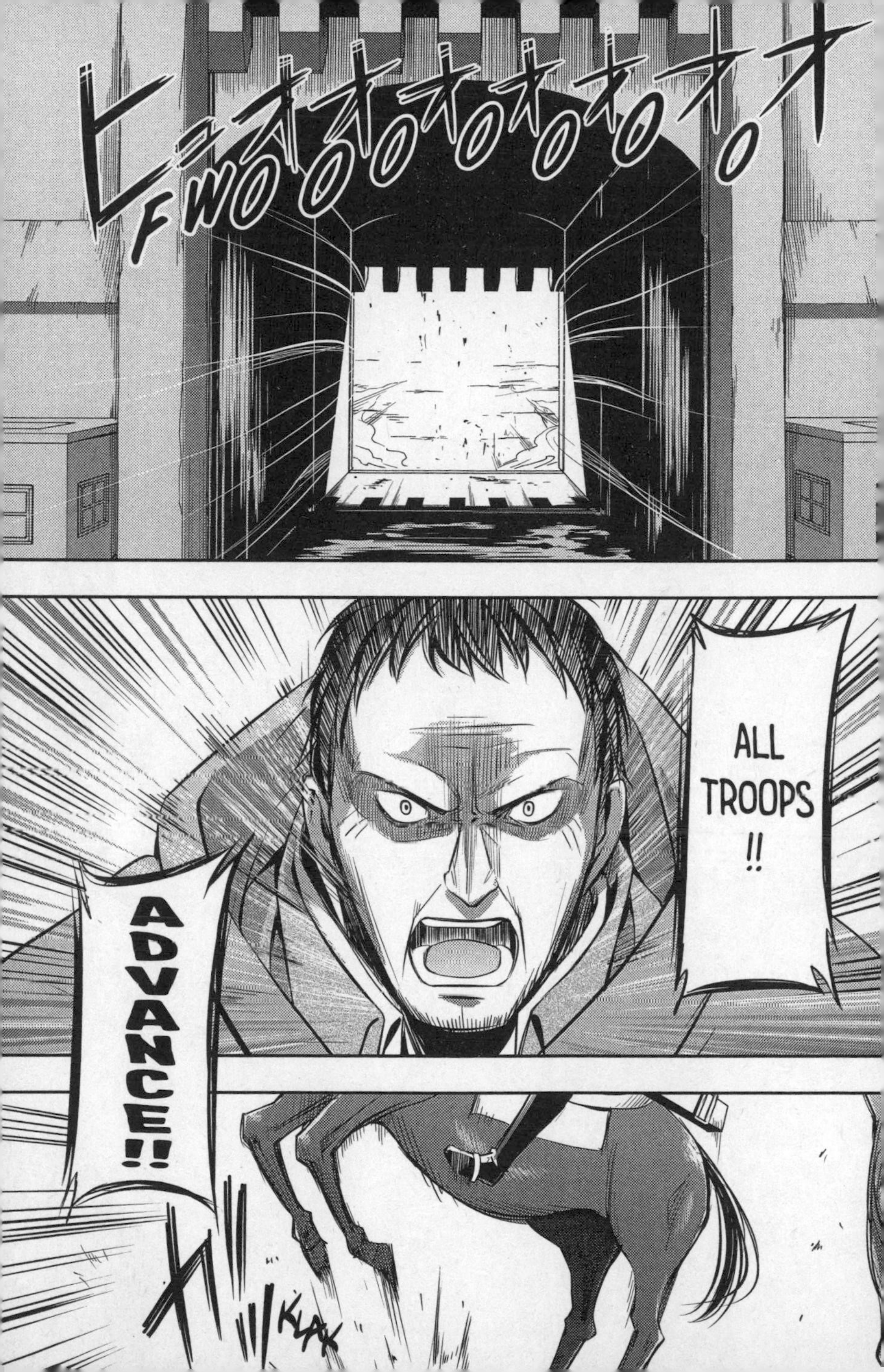
FWOOOOOOO
ALL TROOPS !!
ADVANCE!!
KLAK

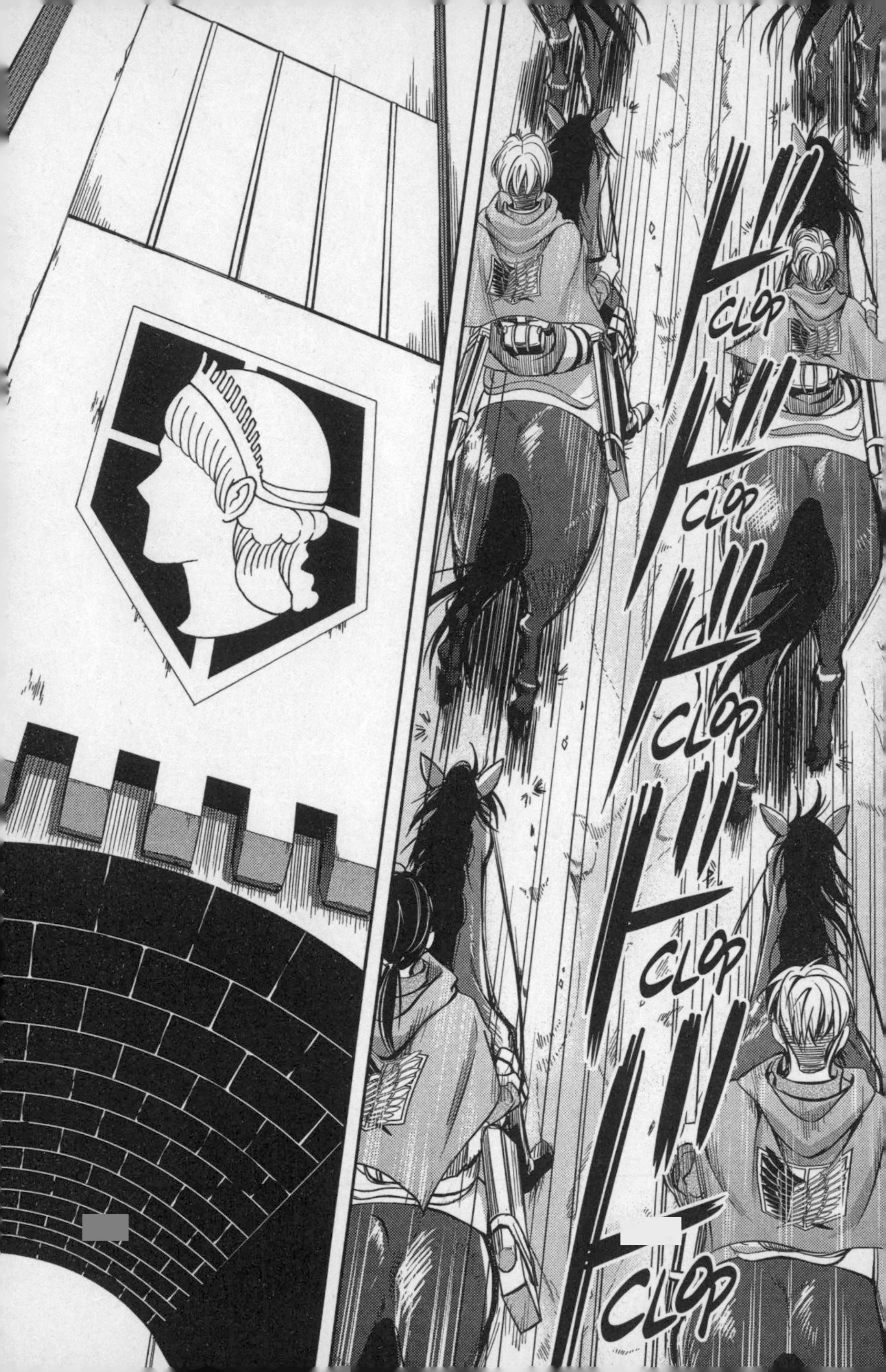
CLOP
CLOP
CLOP
CLOP
CLOP

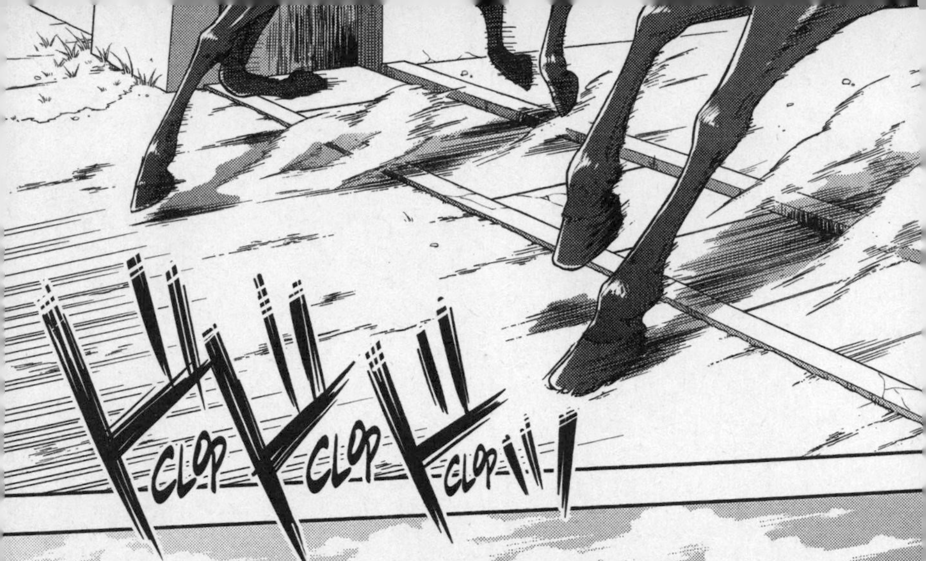
CLOP CLOP CLOP
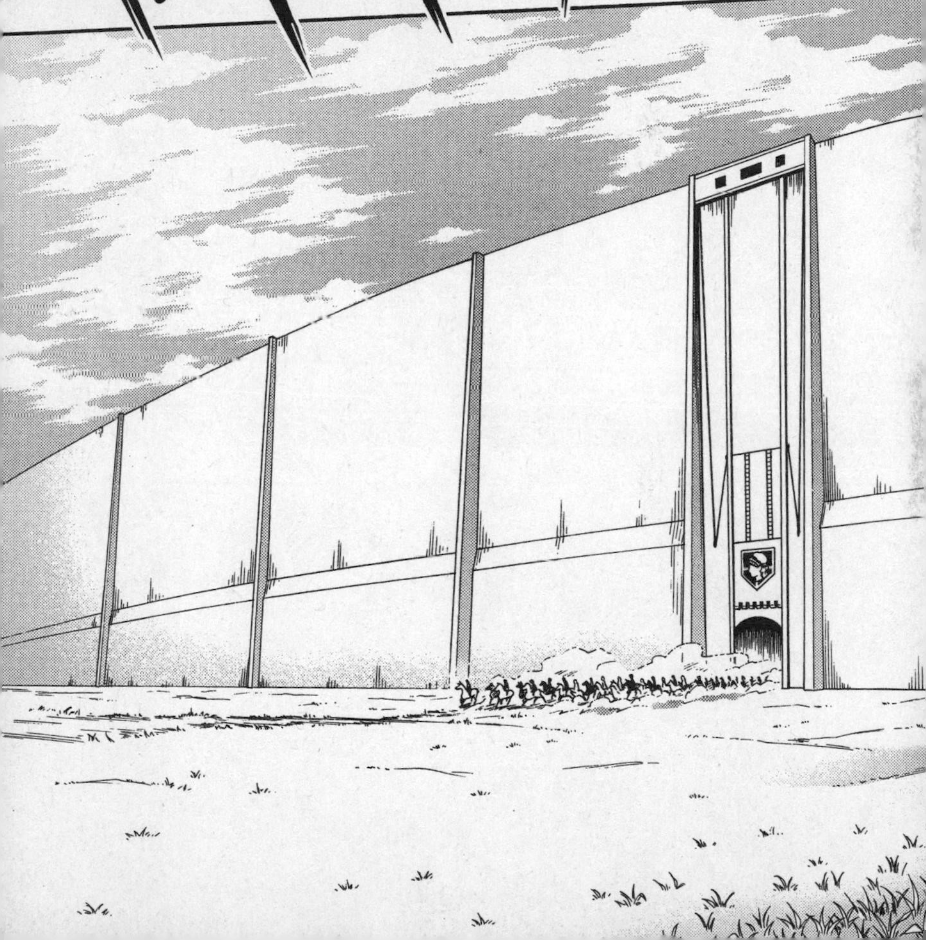

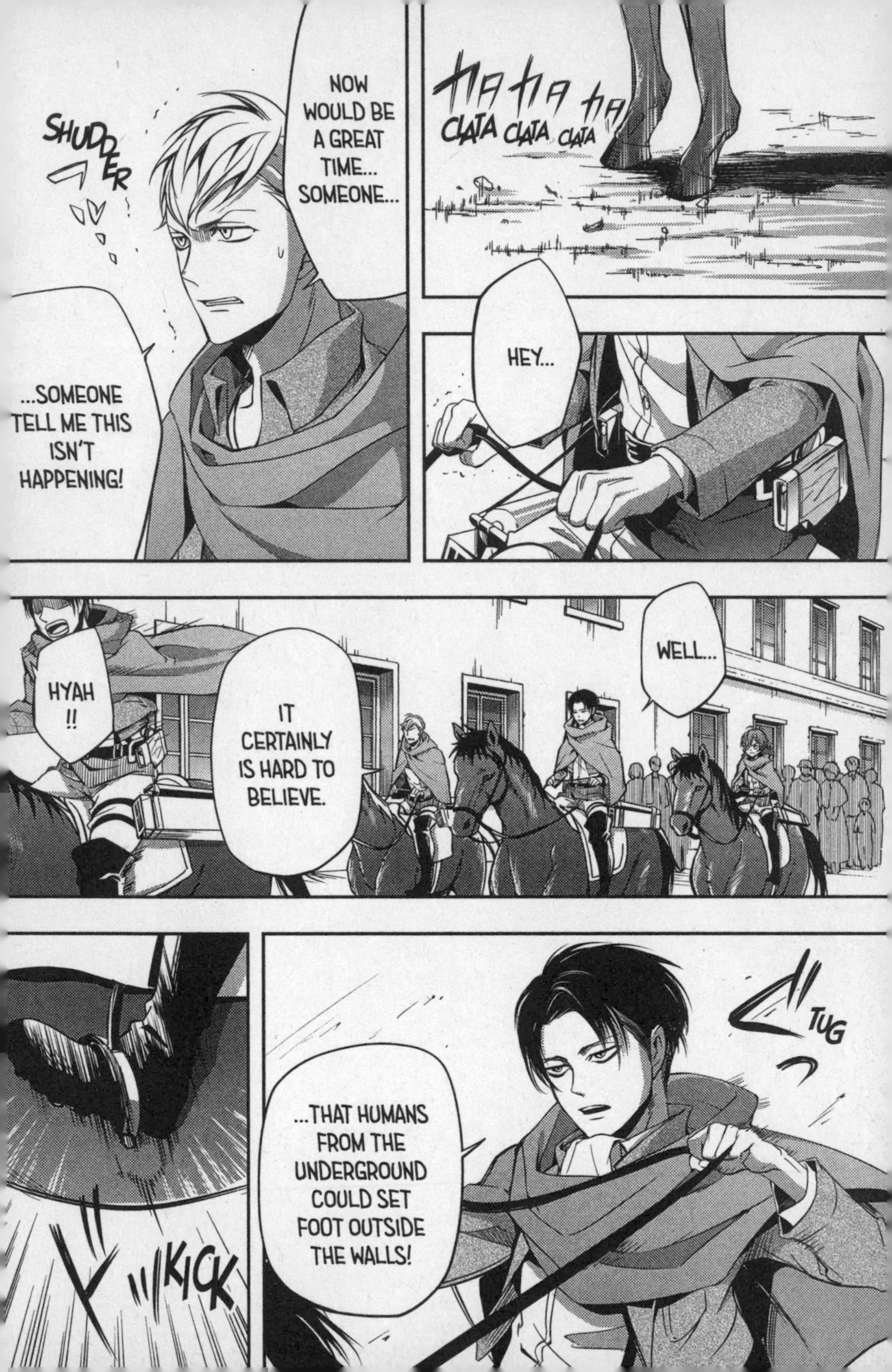
CLATA CLATA CLATA
HEY...
NOW WOULD BE A GREAT TIME... SOMEONE...
SHUDDER
...SOMEONE TELL ME THIS ISN'T HAPPENING!
WELL...
IT CERTAINLY IS HARD TO BELIEVE.
HYAH!!
TUG
...THAT HUMANS FROM THE UNDERGROUND COULD SET FOOT OUTSIDE THE WALLS!
KICK

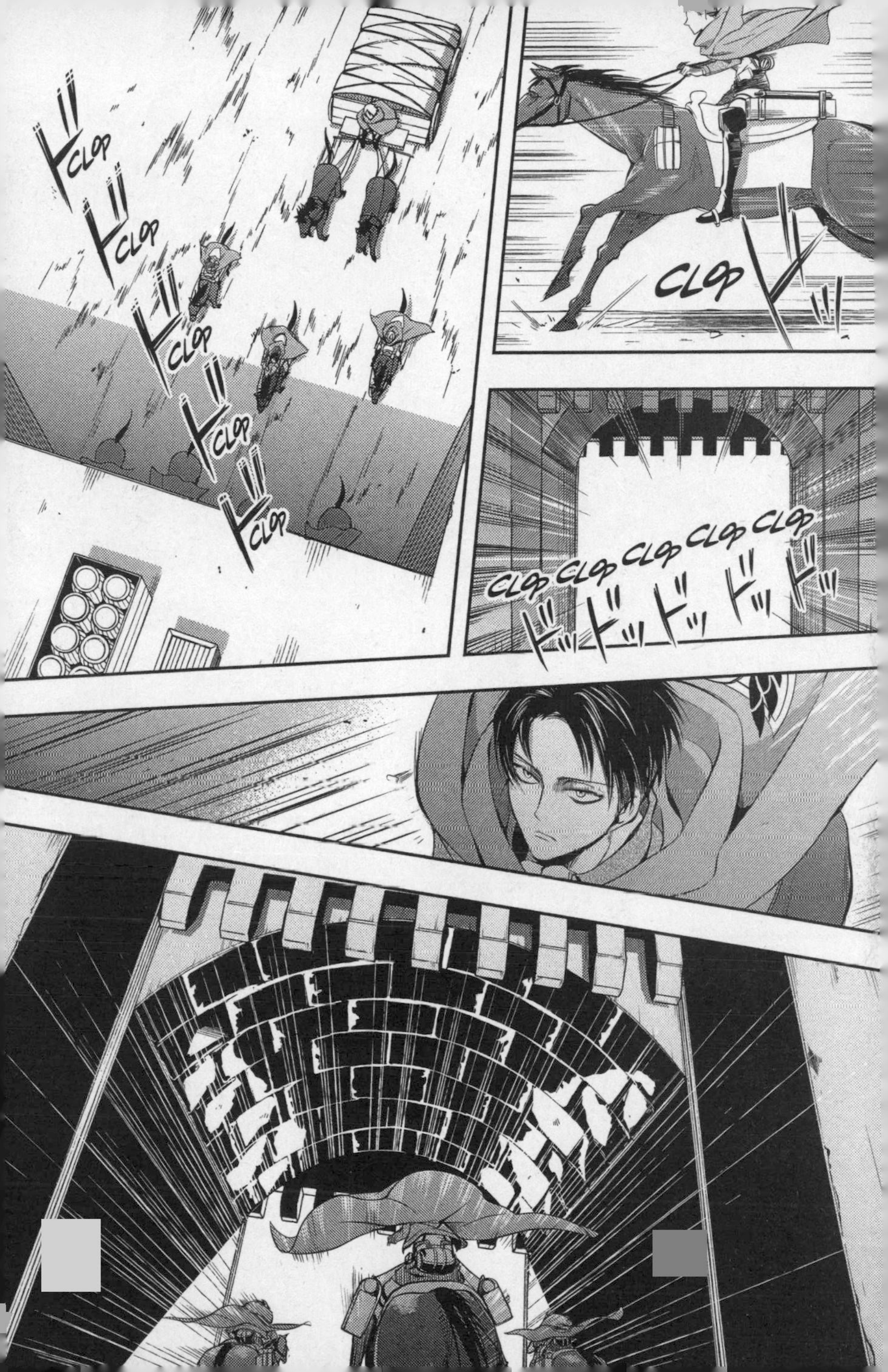
ドッ
CLOP
CLOP CLOP CLOP CLOP CLOP
ドッドッドッドッドッ
ドッ CLOP
ドッ CLOP
ドッ CLOP
ドッ CLOP
ドッ CLOP

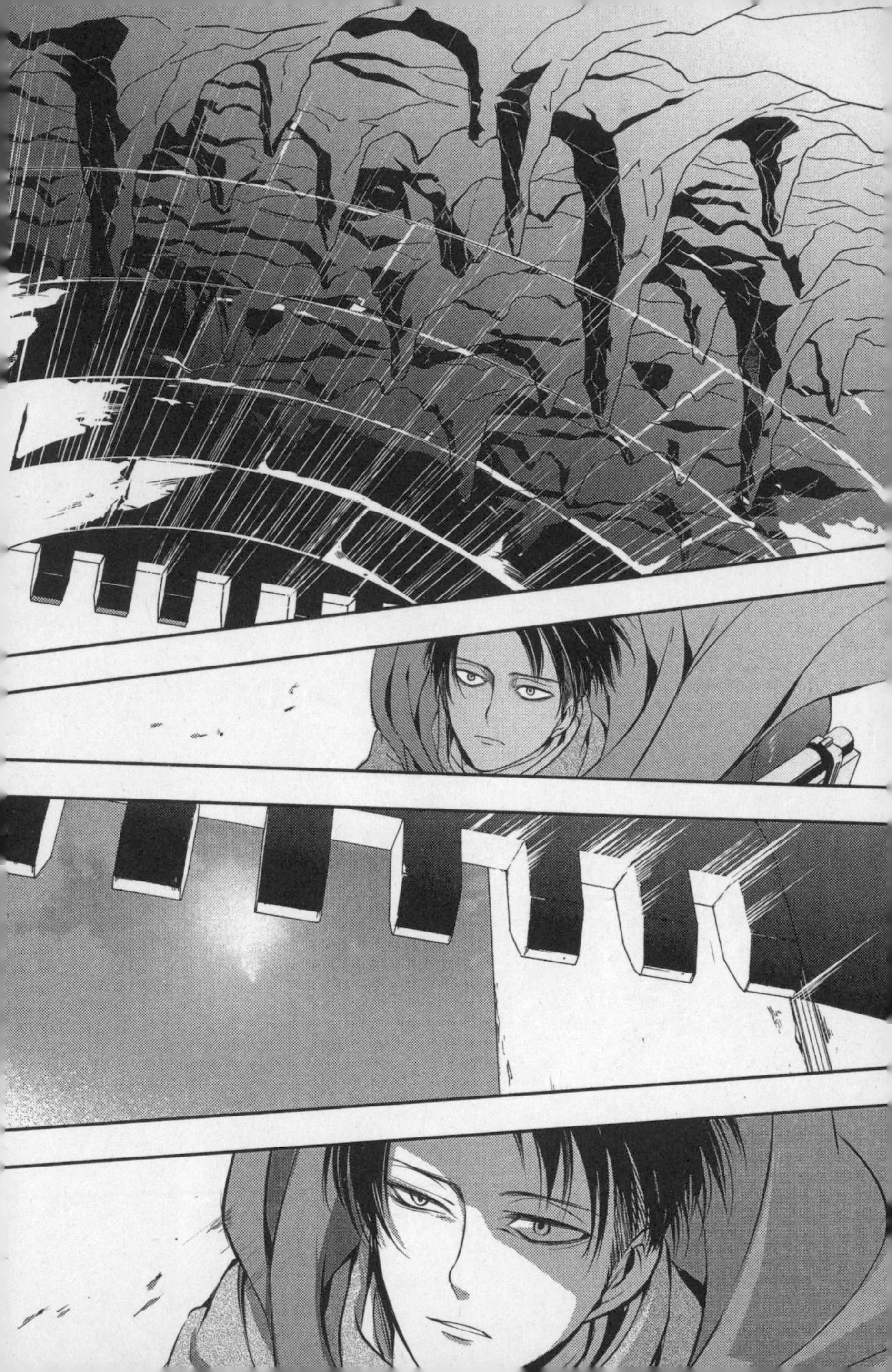

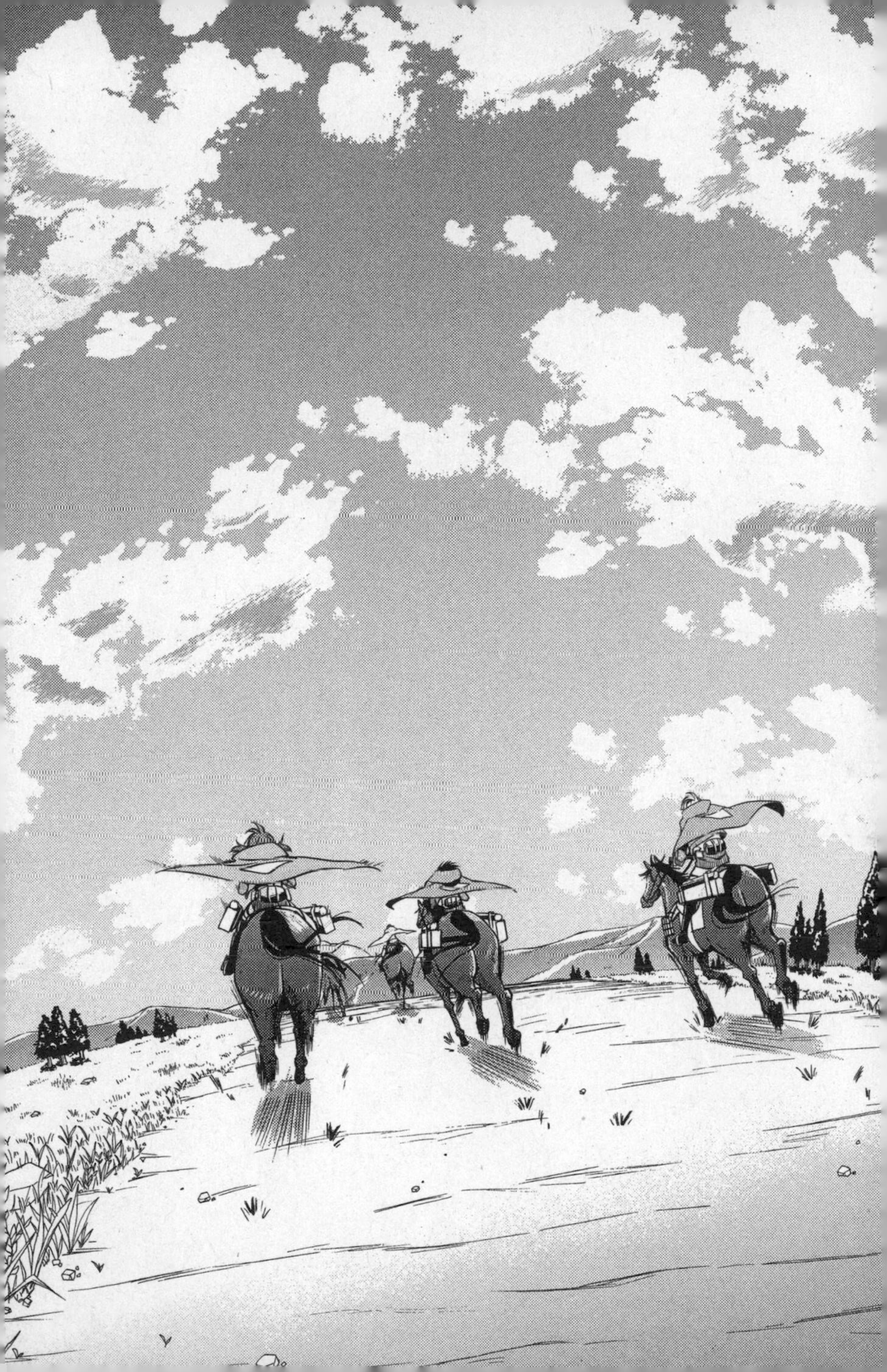

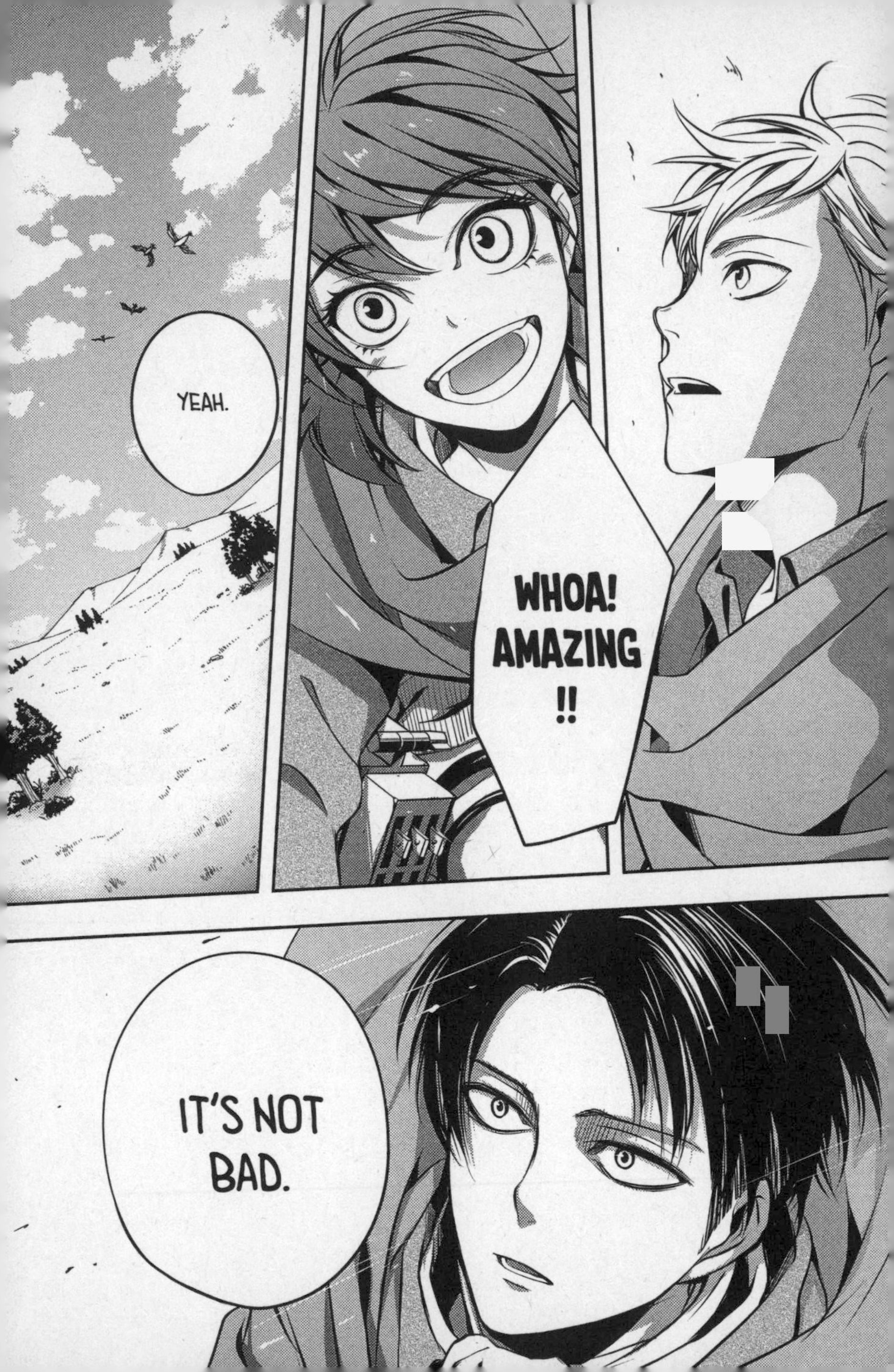
WHOA! AMAZING !!
YEAH.
IT'S NOT BAD.

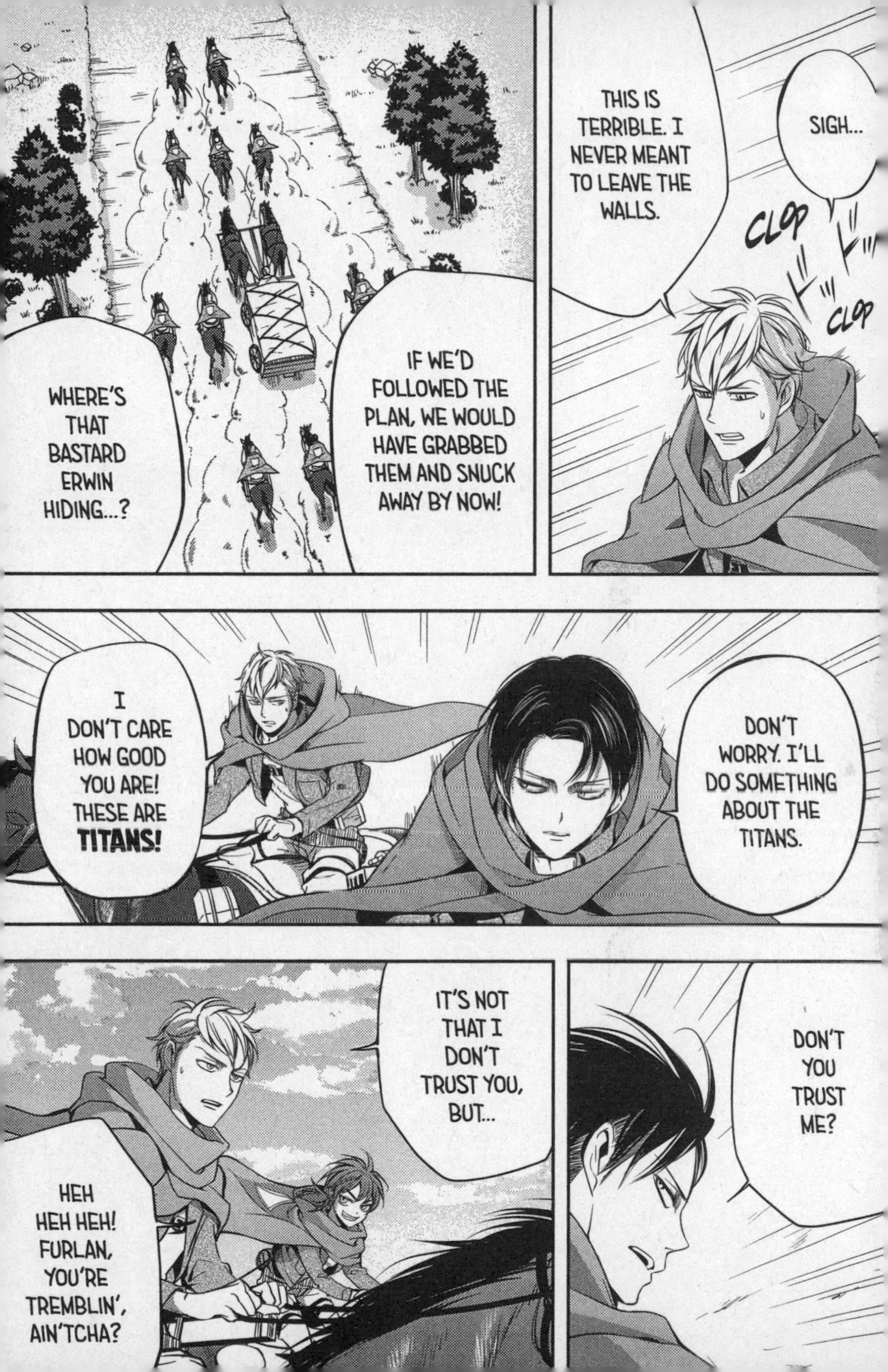
SIGH...
CLOP
CLOP
THIS IS TERRIBLE. I NEVER MEANT TO LEAVE THE WALLS.
IF WE'D FOLLOWED THE PLAN, WE WOULD HAVE GRABBED THEM AND SNUCK AWAY BY NOW!
WHERE'S THAT BASTARD ERWIN HIDING...?
DON'T WORRY. I'LL DO SOMETHING ABOUT THE TITANS.
I DON'T CARE HOW GOOD YOU ARE! THESE ARE **TITANS!**
DON'T YOU TRUST ME?
IT'S NOT THAT I DON'T TRUST YOU, BUT...
HEH HEH HEH! FURLAN, YOU'RE TREMBLIN', AIN'TCHA?

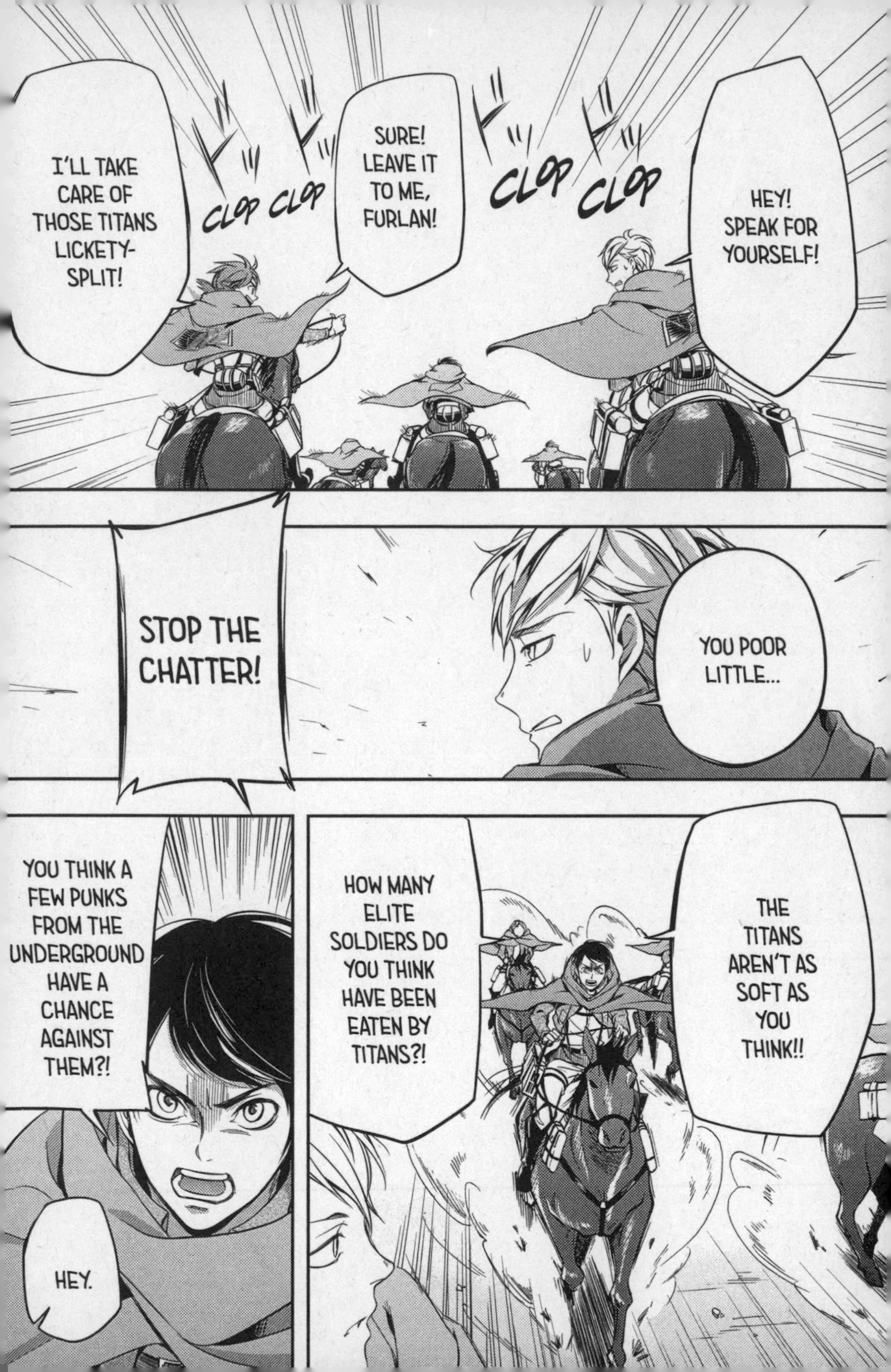
HEY! SPEAK FOR YOURSELF!
CLOP CLOP
SURE! LEAVE IT TO ME, FURLAN!
CLOP CLOP
I'LL TAKE CARE OF THOSE TITANS LICKETY-SPLIT!
YOU POOR LITTLE...
STOP THE CHATTER!
THE TITANS AREN'T AS SOFT AS YOU THINK!!
HOW MANY ELITE SOLDIERS DO YOU THINK HAVE BEEN EATEN BY TITANS?!
YOU THINK A FEW PUNKS FROM THE UNDERGROUND HAVE A CHANCE AGAINST THEM?!
HEY.

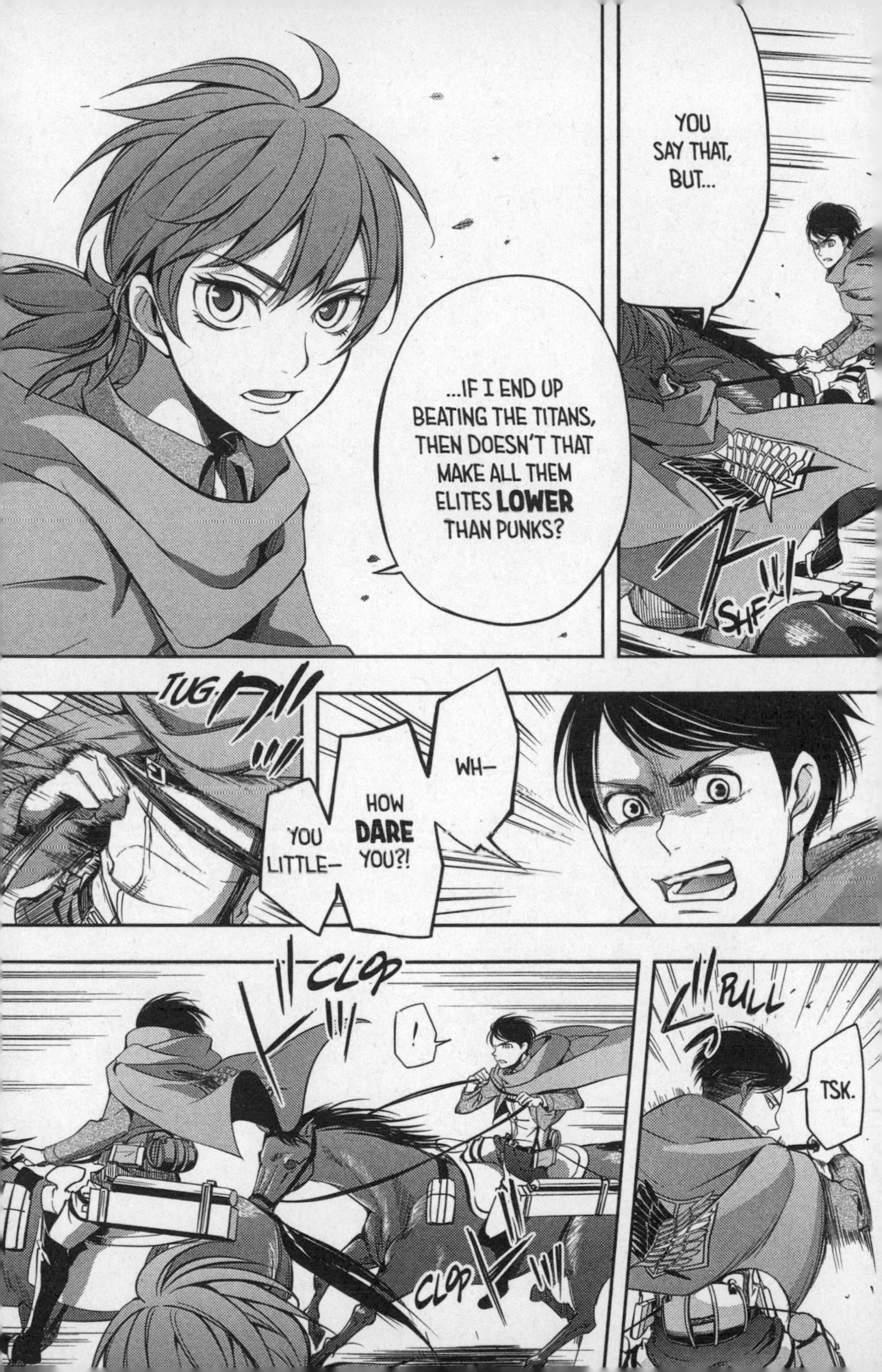
YOU SAY THAT, BUT...
SHF
...IF I END UP BEATING THE TITANS, THEN DOESN'T THAT MAKE ALL THEM ELITES **LOWER** THAN PUNKS?
TUG
WH-
HOW **DARE** YOU?!
YOU LITTLE-
PULL
TSK.
CLOP
!
CLOP

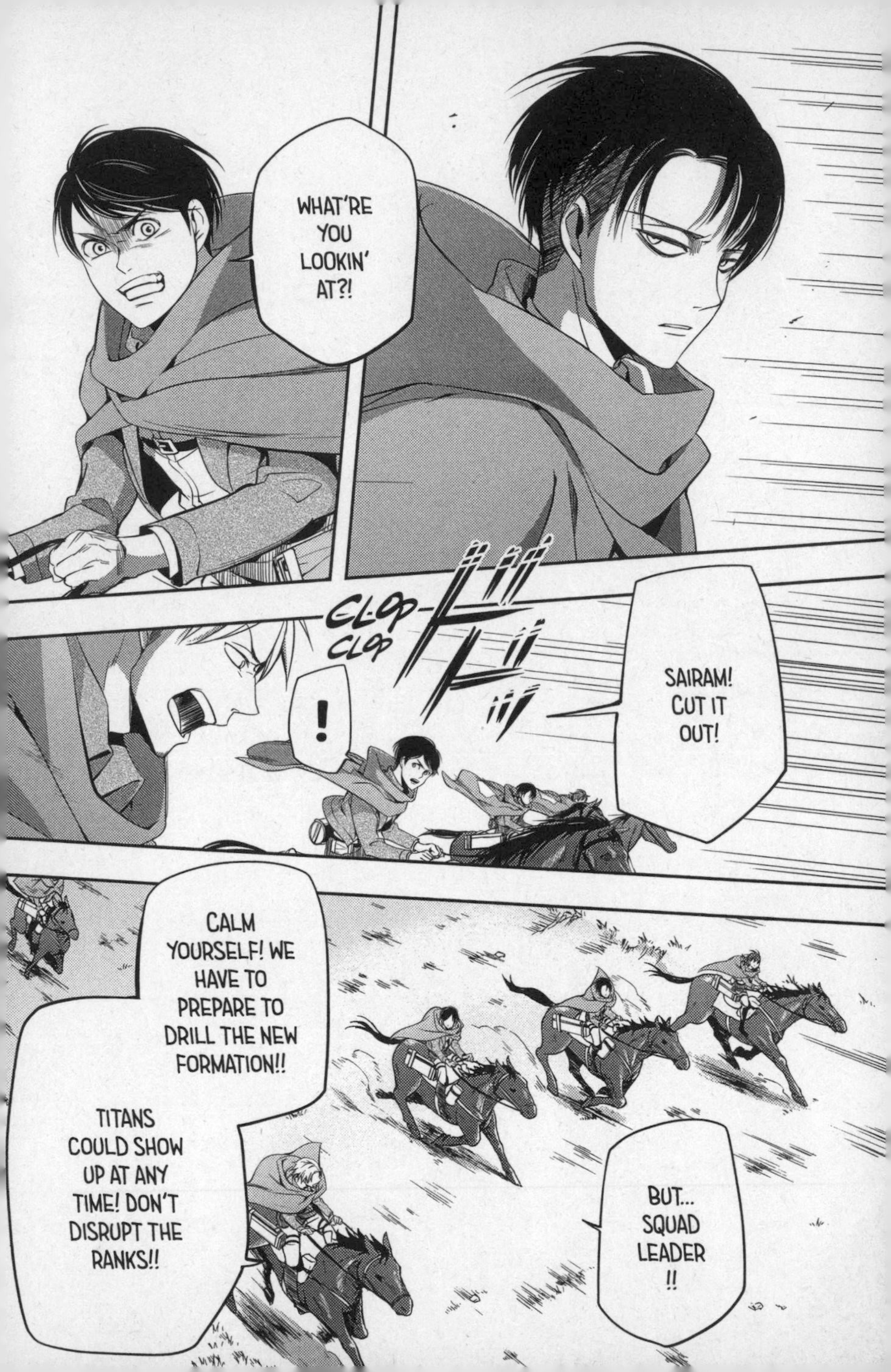
WHAT'RE YOU LOOKIN' AT?!
SAIRAM! CUT IT OUT!
CLOP CLOP
!
BUT... SQUAD LEADER!!
CALM YOURSELF! WE HAVE TO PREPARE TO DRILL THE NEW FORMATION!!
TITANS COULD SHOW UP AT ANY TIME! DON'T DISRUPT THE RANKS!!

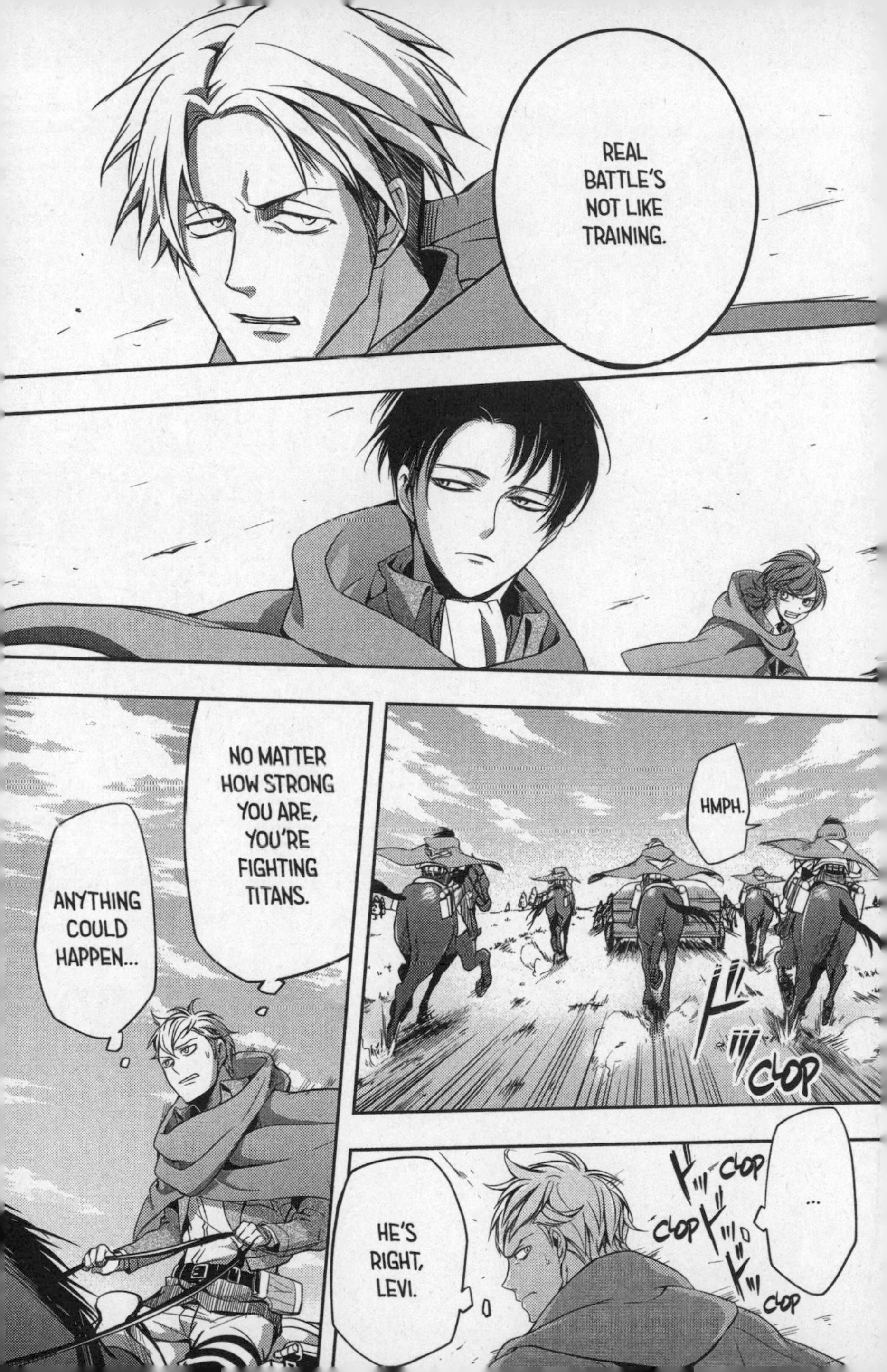
REAL BATTLE'S NOT LIKE TRAINING.
HMPH.
CLOP
...
CLOP
CLOP
CLOP
HE'S RIGHT, LEVI.
NO MATTER HOW STRONG YOU ARE, YOU'RE FIGHTING TITANS.
ANYTHING COULD HAPPEN...

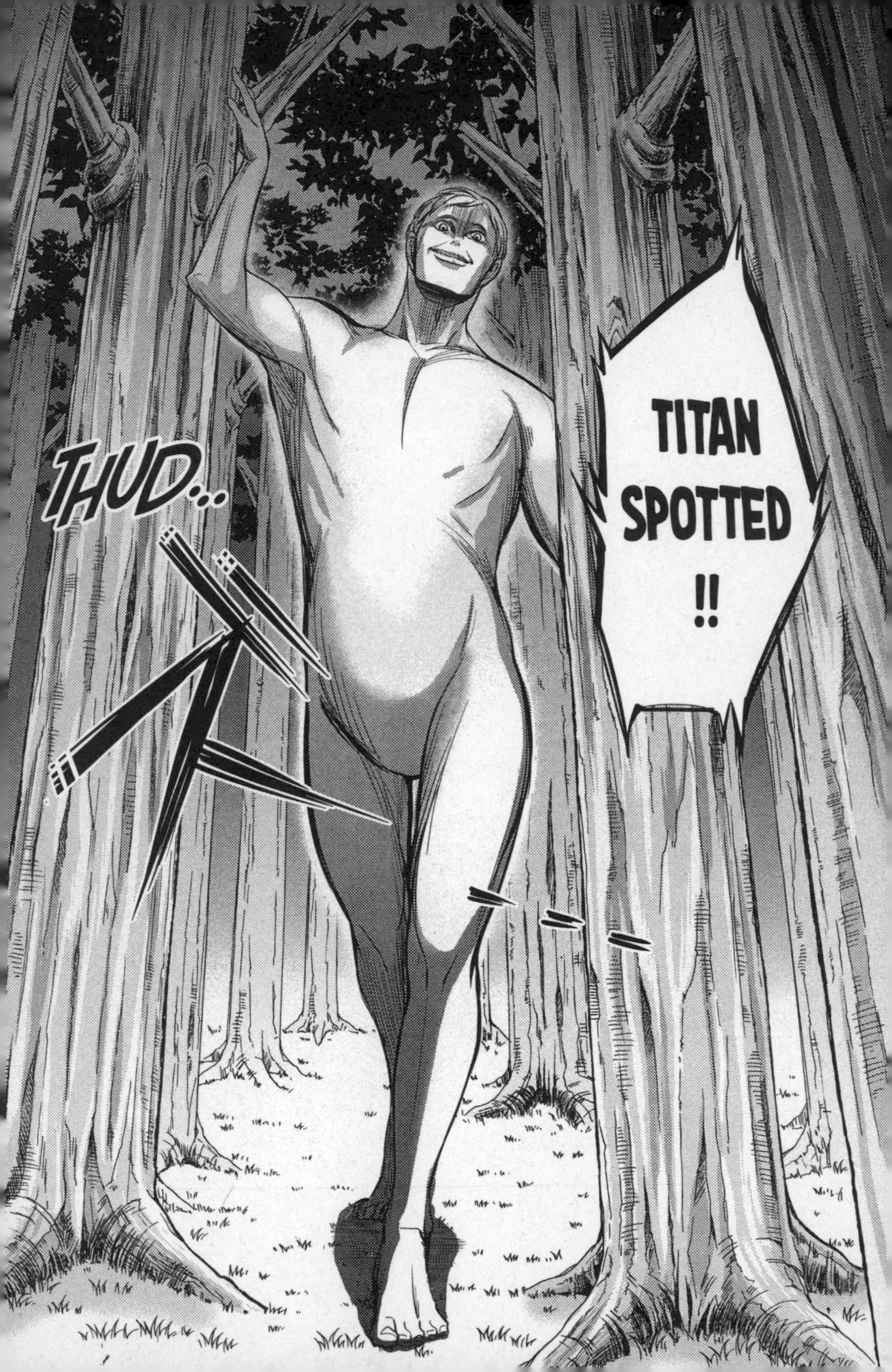
TITAN SPOTTED !!
THUD...

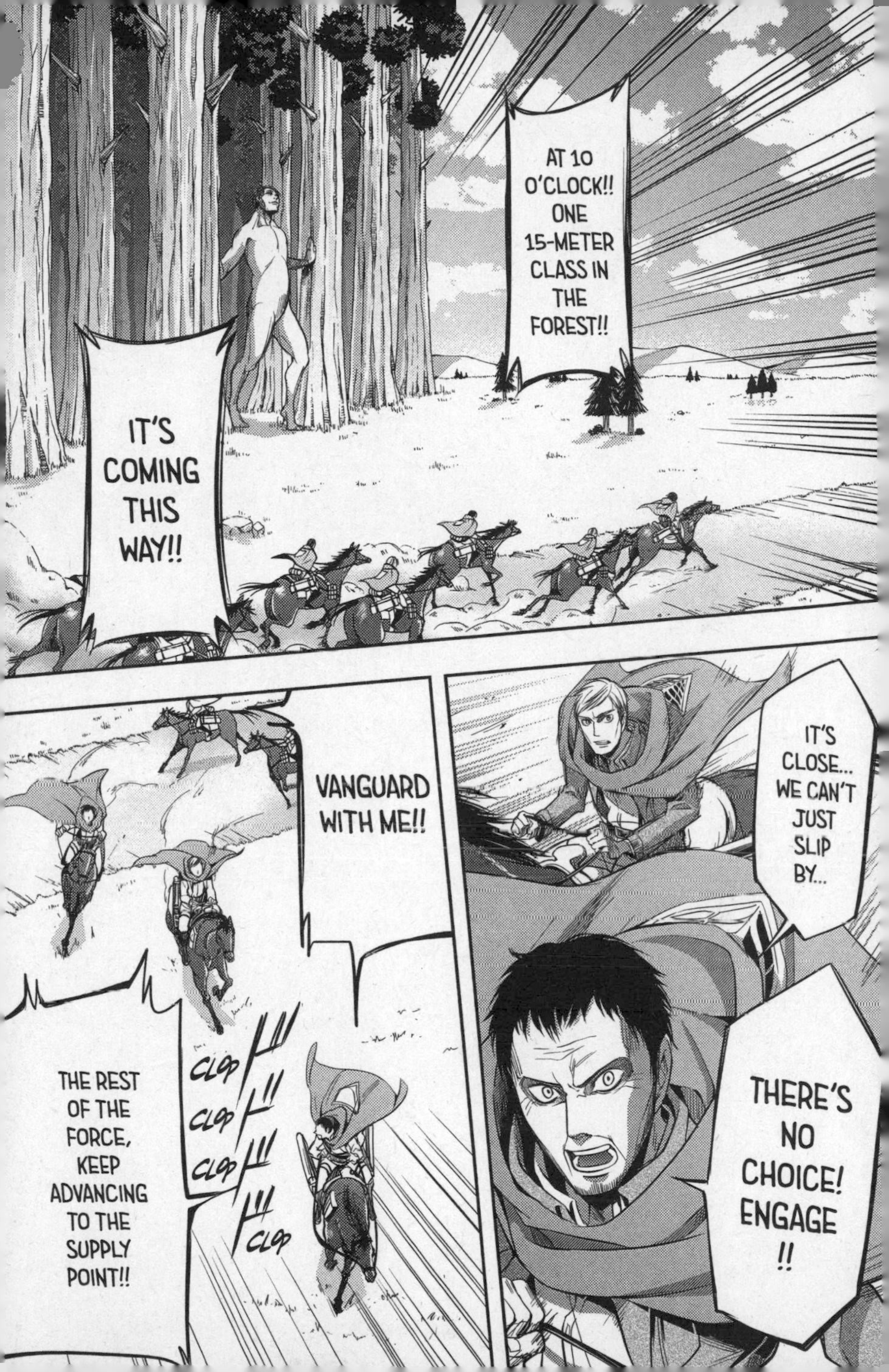
AT 10 O'CLOCK!! ONE 15-METER CLASS IN THE FOREST!!
IT'S COMING THIS WAY!!
IT'S CLOSE... WE CAN'T JUST SLIP BY...
THERE'S NO CHOICE! ENGAGE!!
VANGUARD WITH ME!!
THE REST OF THE FORCE, KEEP ADVANCING TO THE SUPPLY POINT!!
CLOP
CLOP
CLOP
CLOP

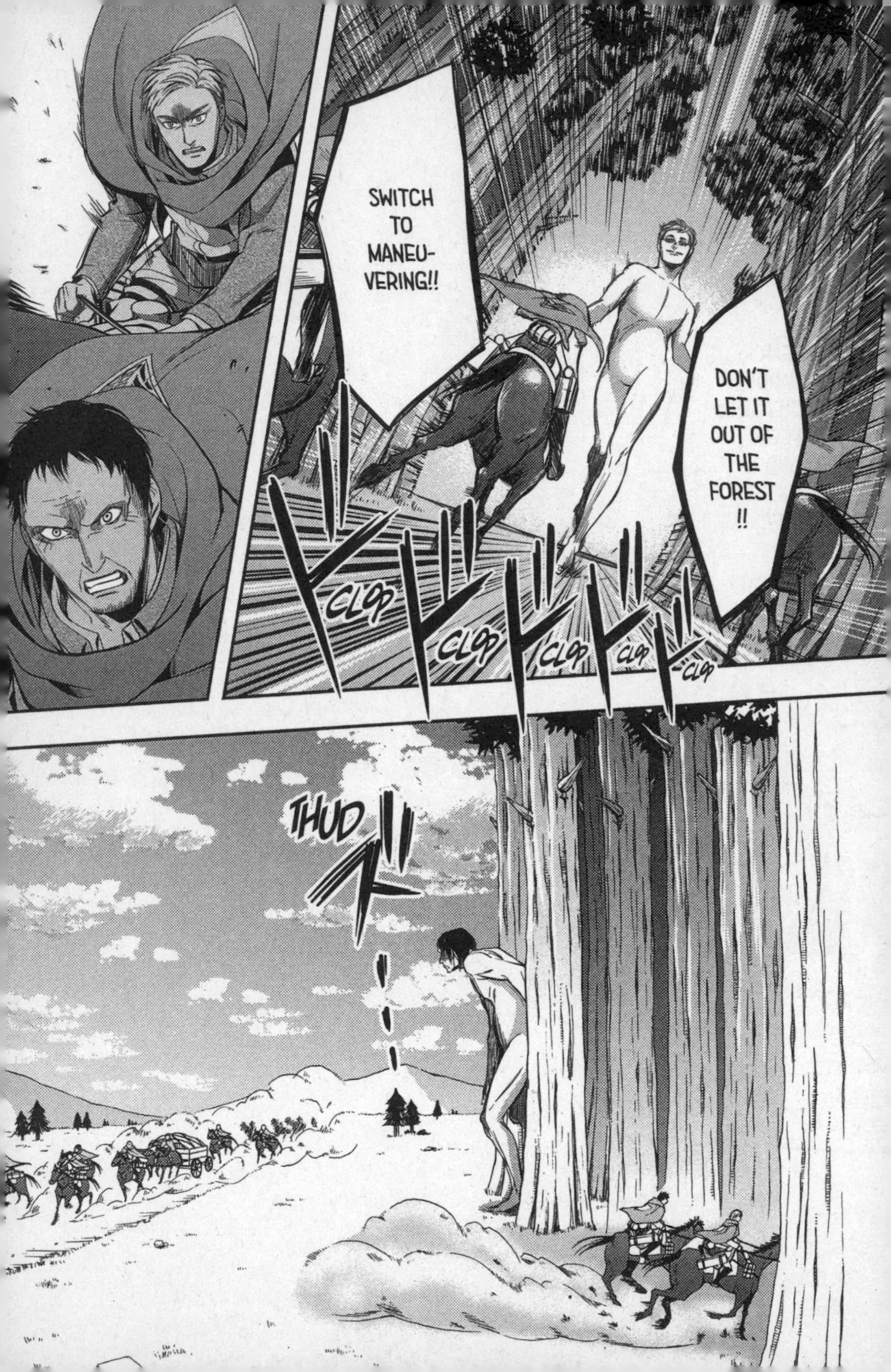
SWITCH TO MANEU-VERING!!
DON'T LET IT OUT OF THE FOREST !!
CLOP
CLOP
CLOP
CLOP
CLOP
THUD

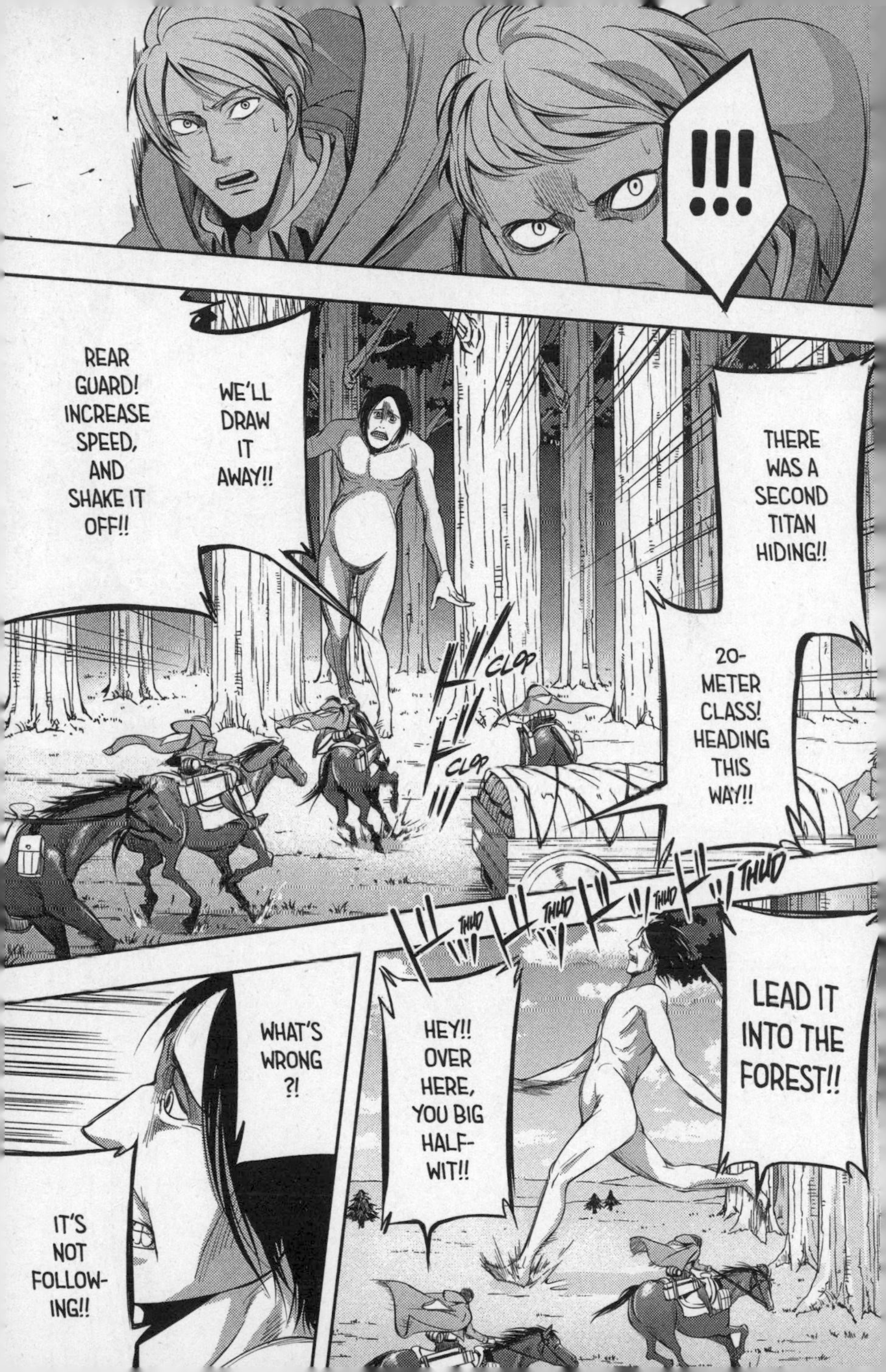
!!!
THERE WAS A SECOND TITAN HIDING!!
20-METER CLASS! HEADING THIS WAY!!
WE'LL DRAW IT AWAY!!
REAR GUARD! INCREASE SPEED, AND SHAKE IT OFF!!
CLOP
CLOP
THUD
THUD
THUD
THUD
LEAD IT INTO THE FOREST!!
HEY!! OVER HERE, YOU BIG HALF-WIT!!
WHAT'S WRONG?!
IT'S NOT FOLLOWING!!

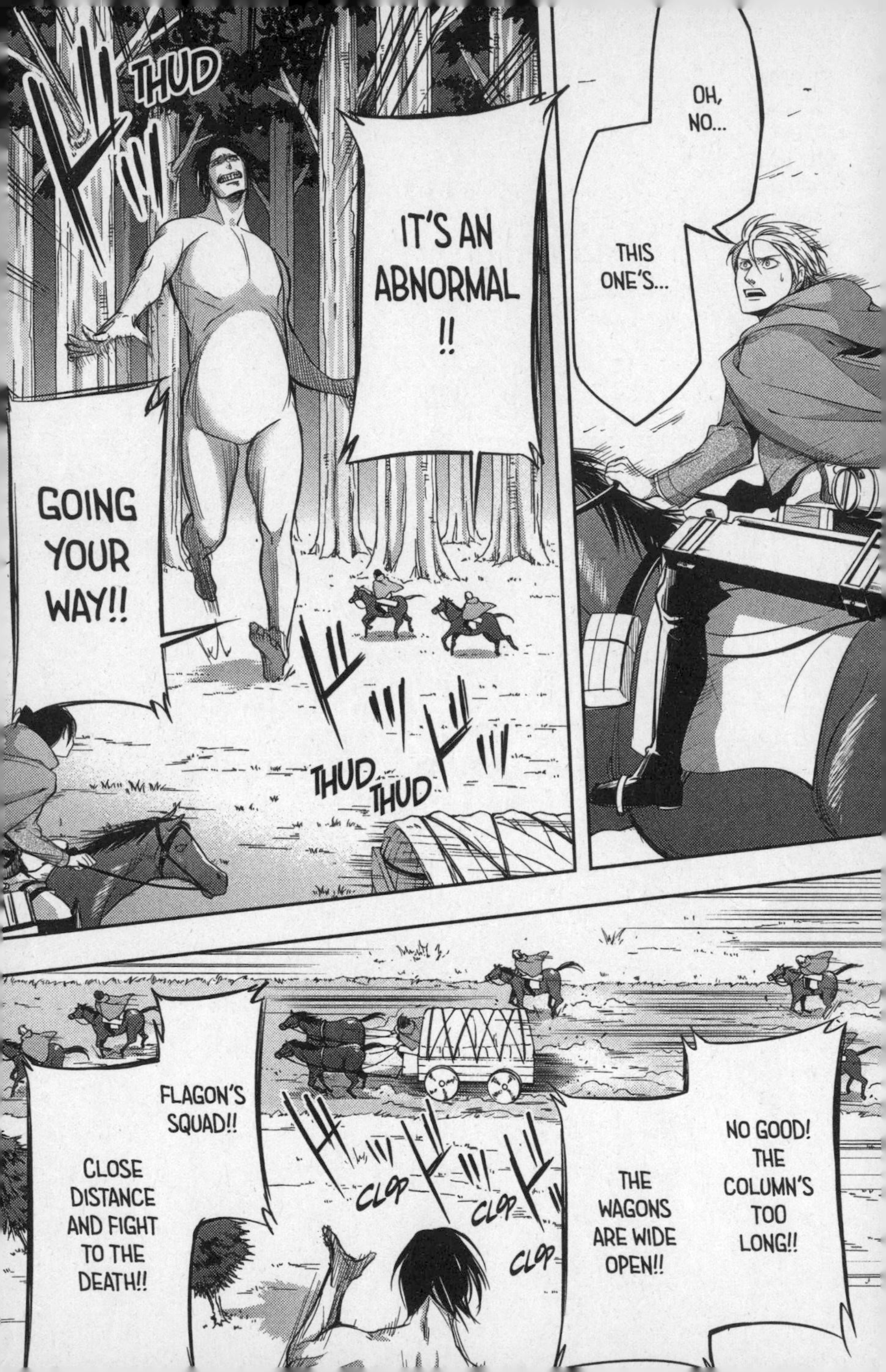
OH, NO...
THIS ONE'S...
THUD
IT'S AN ABNORMAL!!
GOING YOUR WAY!!
THUD THUD
NO GOOD! THE COLUMN'S TOO LONG!!
THE WAGONS ARE WIDE OPEN!!
CLOP CLOP CLOP
FLAGON'S SQUAD!!
CLOSE DISTANCE AND FIGHT TO THE DEATH!!

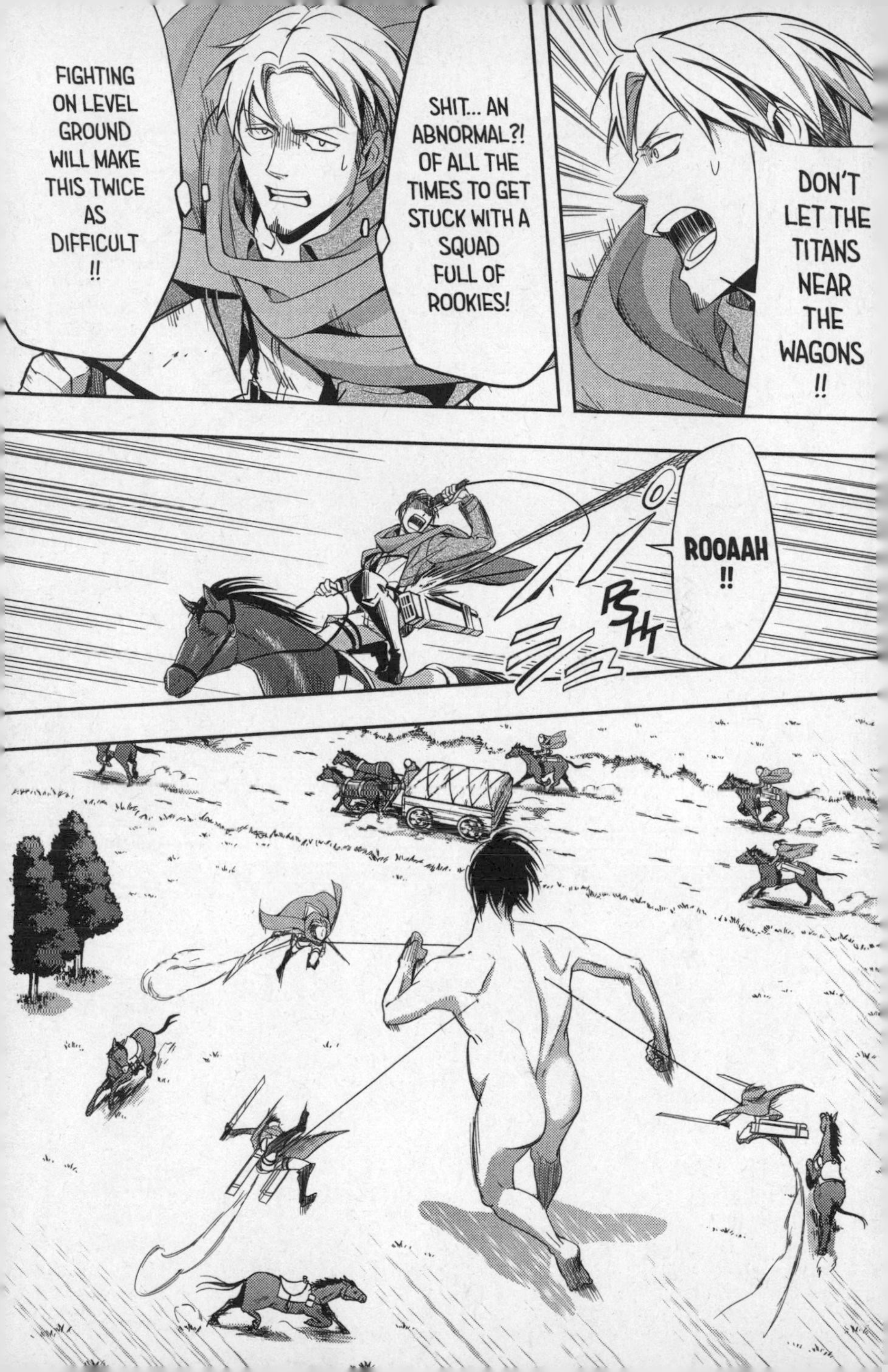
DON'T LET THE TITANS NEAR THE WAGONS!!
SHIT... AN ABNORMAL?! OF ALL THE TIMES TO GET STUCK WITH A SQUAD FULL OF ROOKIES!
FIGHTING ON LEVEL GROUND WILL MAKE THIS TWICE AS DIFFICULT!!
ROOAAH!!
PSHK

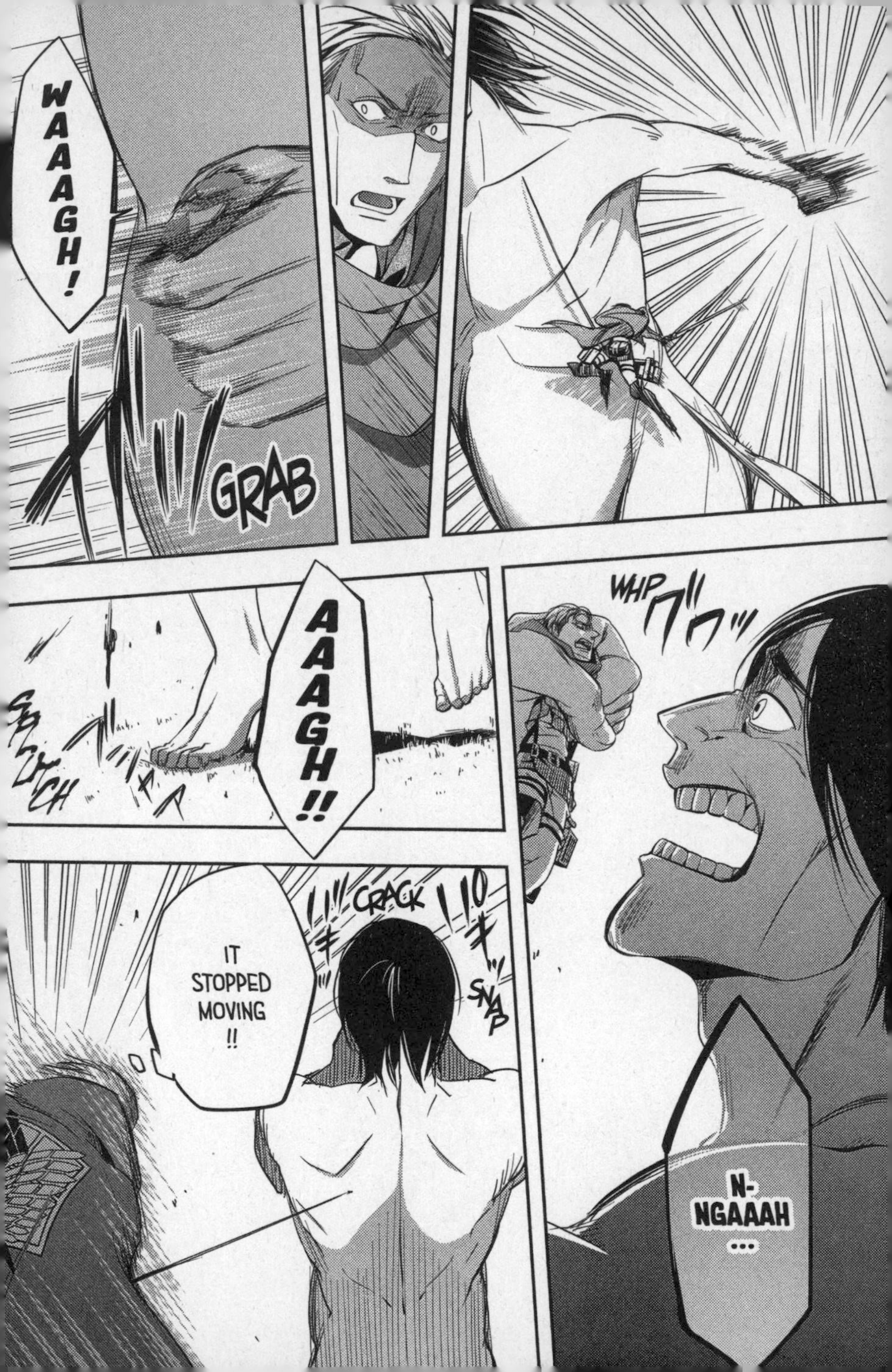

WAAAAGH!
GRAB
WHP
N-NGAAAH ...
AAAAGH!!
CRACK
SNAP
IT STOPPED MOVING !!

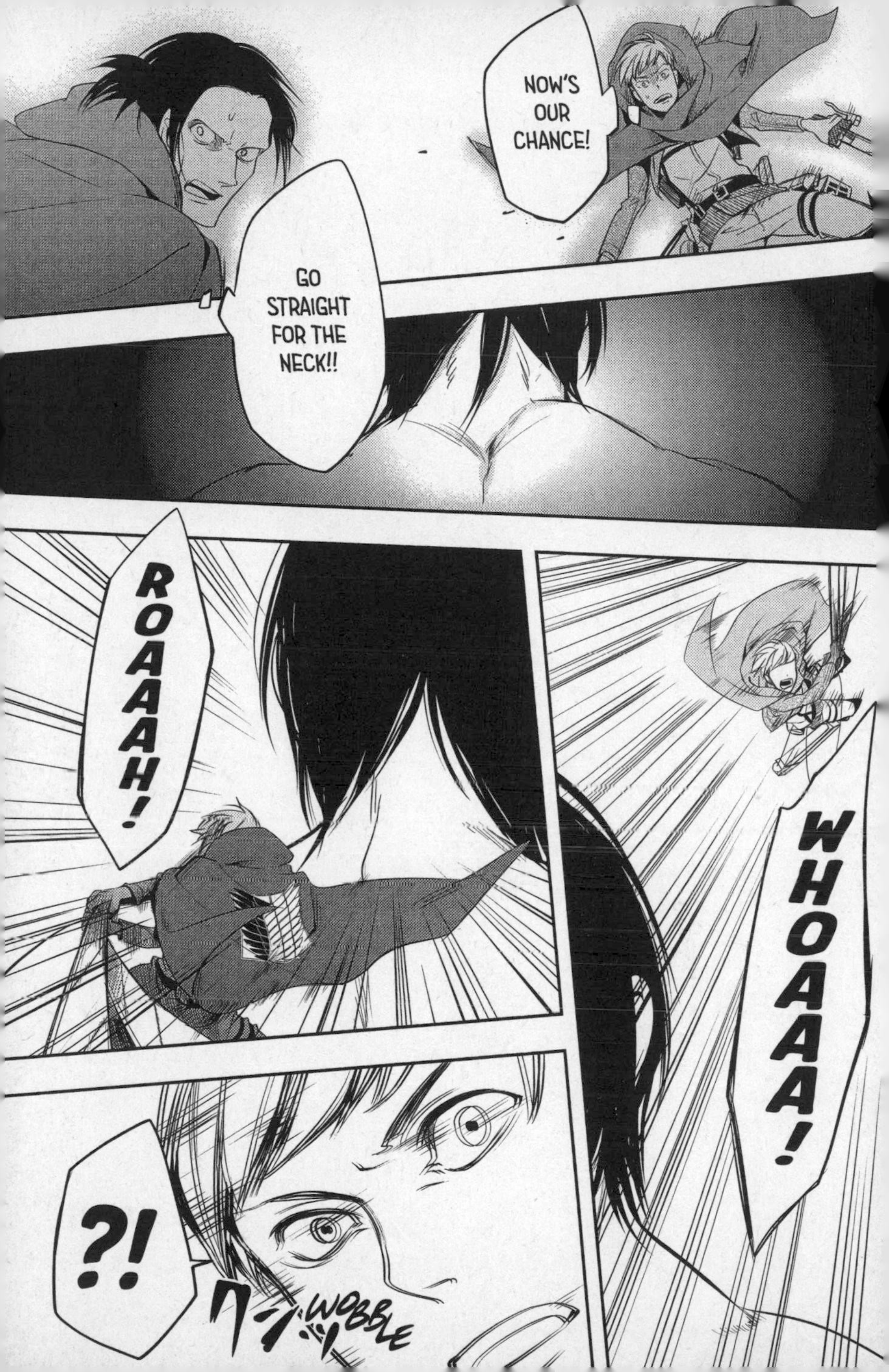
NOW'S OUR CHANCE!
GO STRAIGHT FOR THE NECK!!
WHOAAA!
ROAAAH!
?!
WOBBLE

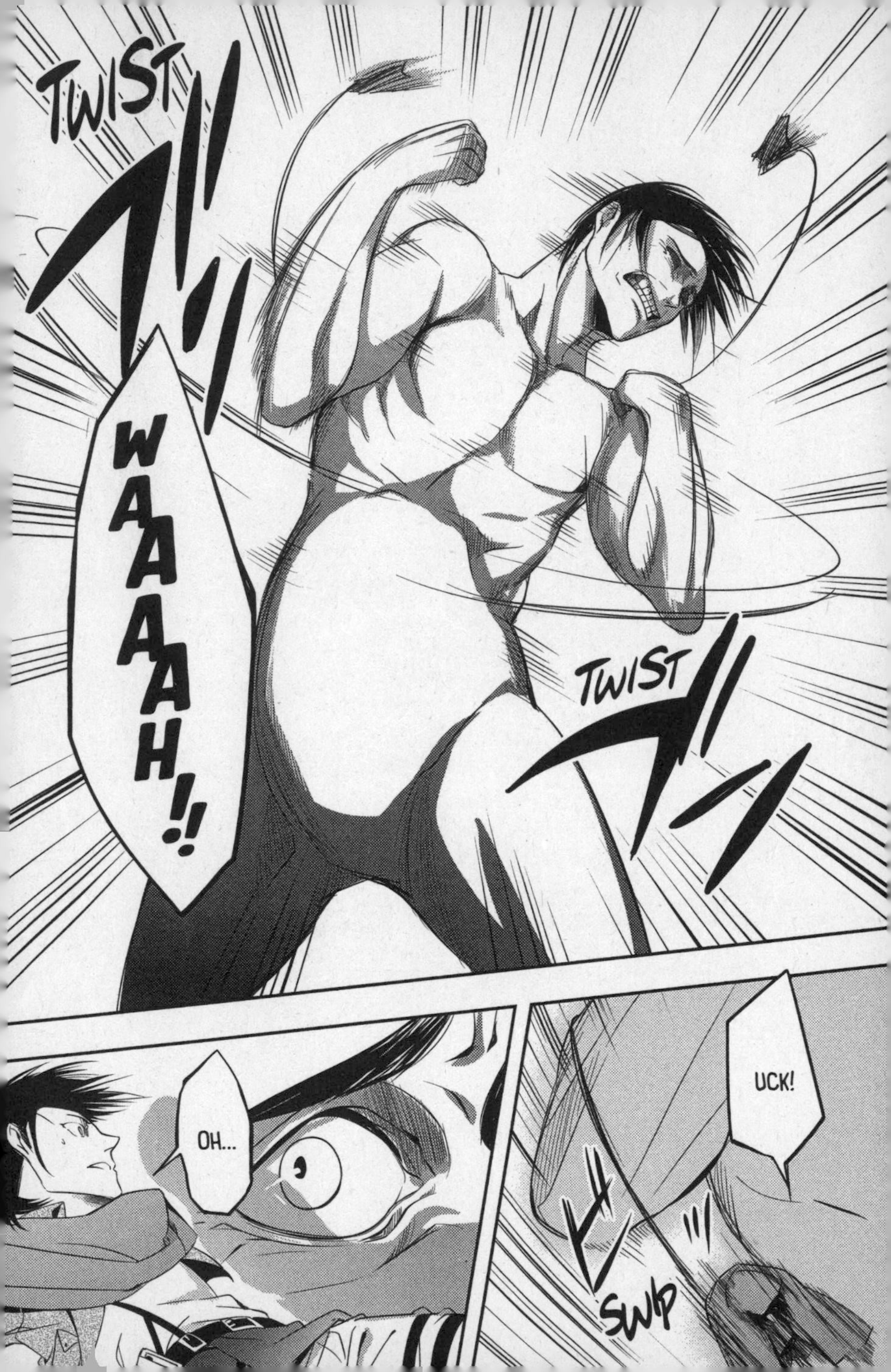
TWIST
WAAAAH!!
TWIST
UCK!
SWIP
OH...

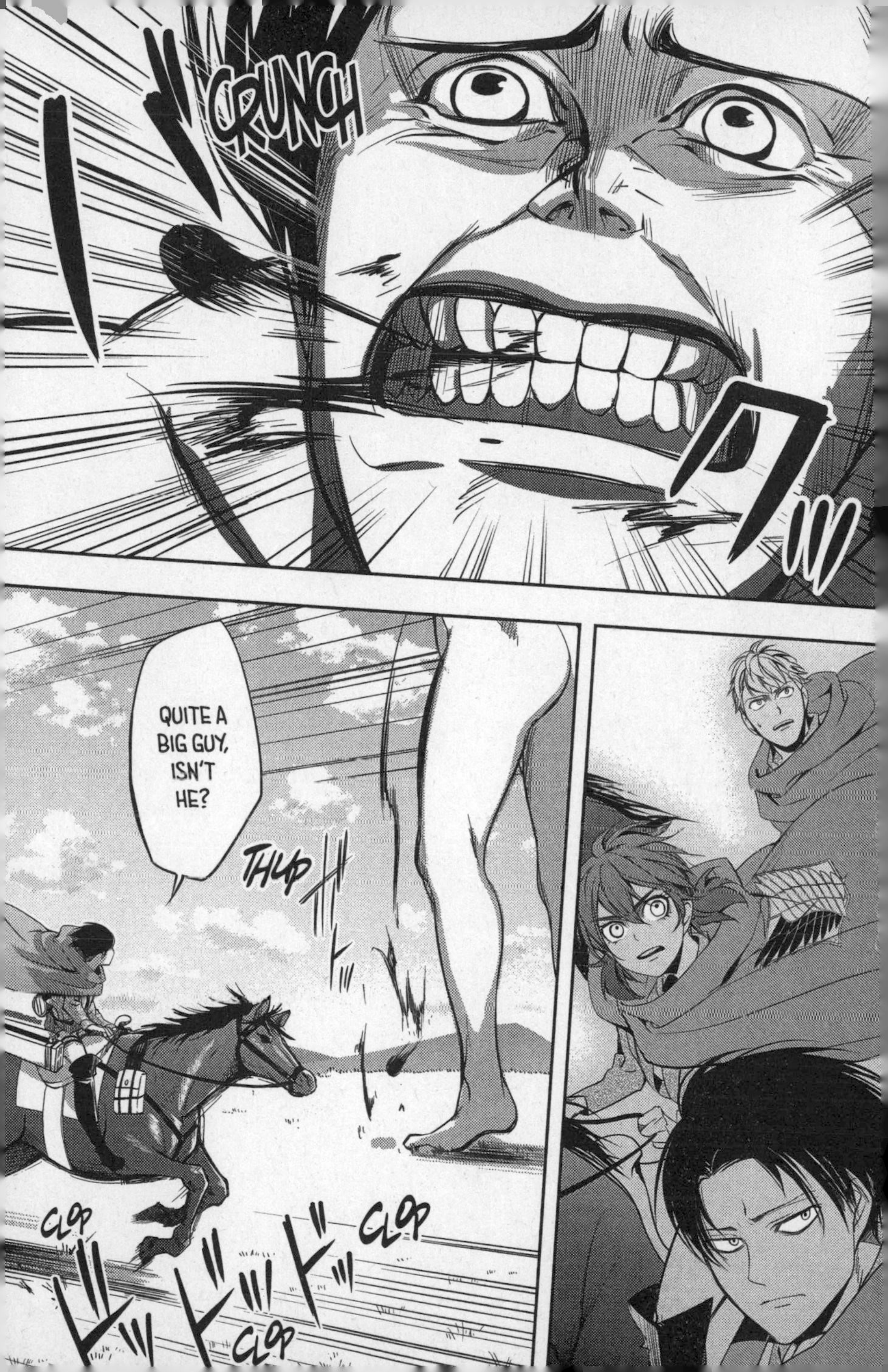
CRUNCH
QUITE A BIG GUY, ISN'T HE?
THUD
CLOP
CLOP
CLOP

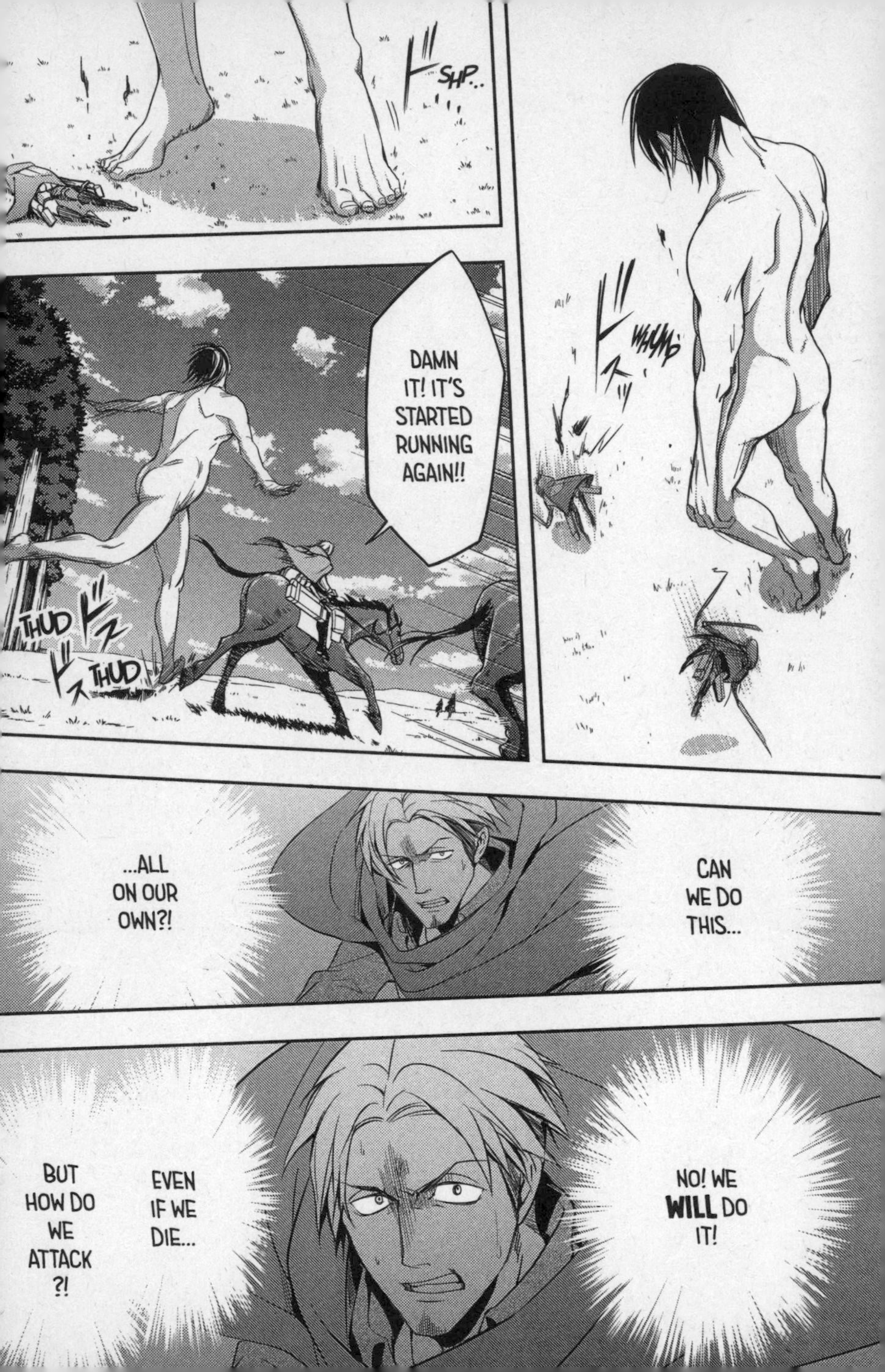
WHUMP
SHP...
DAMN IT! IT'S STARTED RUNNING AGAIN!!
THUD
THUD
CAN WE DO THIS...
...ALL ON OUR OWN?!
NO! WE **WILL** DO IT!
EVEN IF WE DIE...
BUT HOW DO WE ATTACK?!

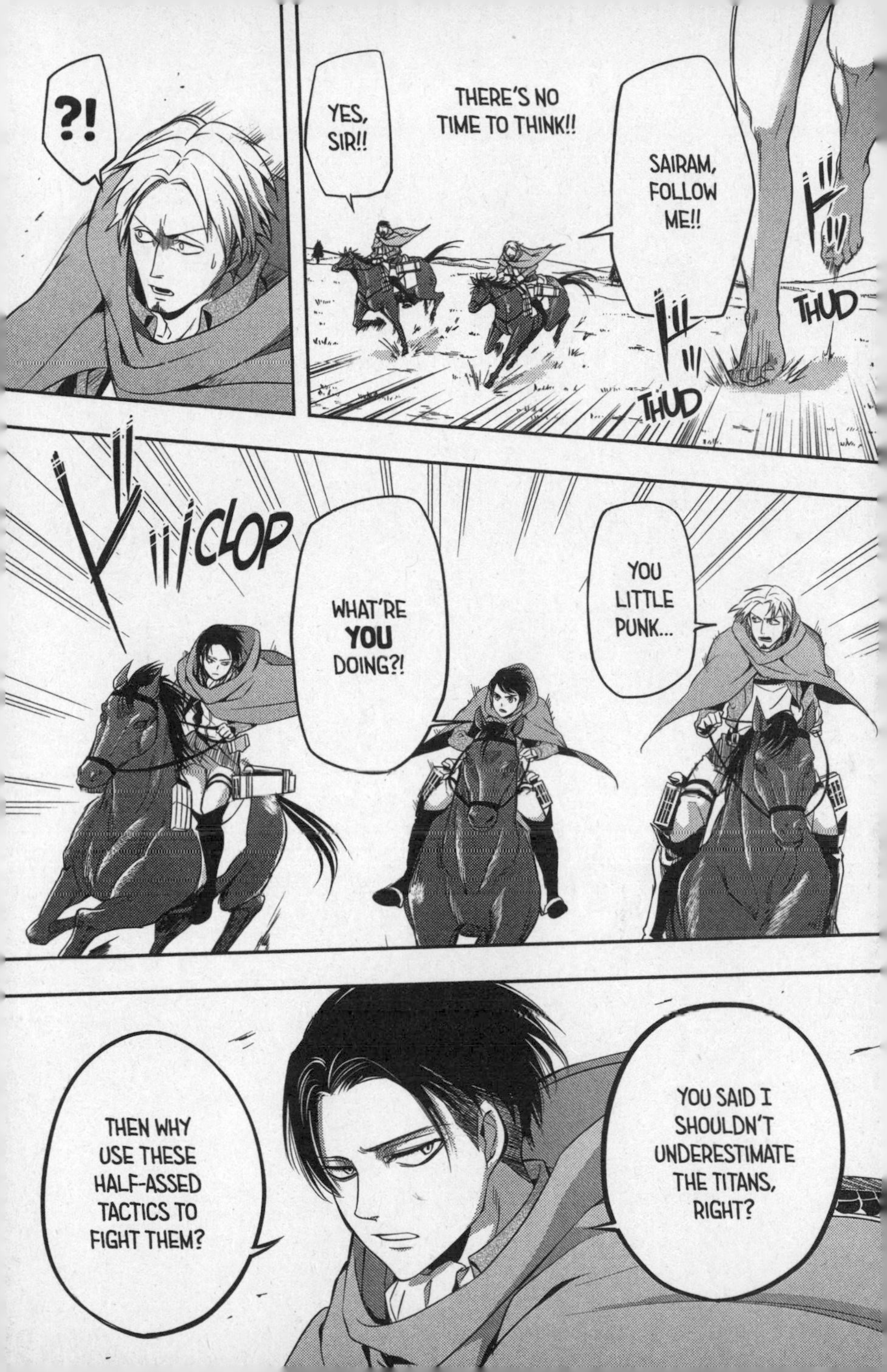
SAIRAM, FOLLOW ME!!
THUD
THUD
THERE'S NO TIME TO THINK!!
YES, SIR!!
?!
YOU LITTLE PUNK...
WHAT'RE **YOU** DOING?!
CLOP
YOU SAID I SHOULDN'T UNDERESTIMATE THE TITANS, RIGHT?
THEN WHY USE THESE HALF-ASSED TACTICS TO FIGHT THEM?

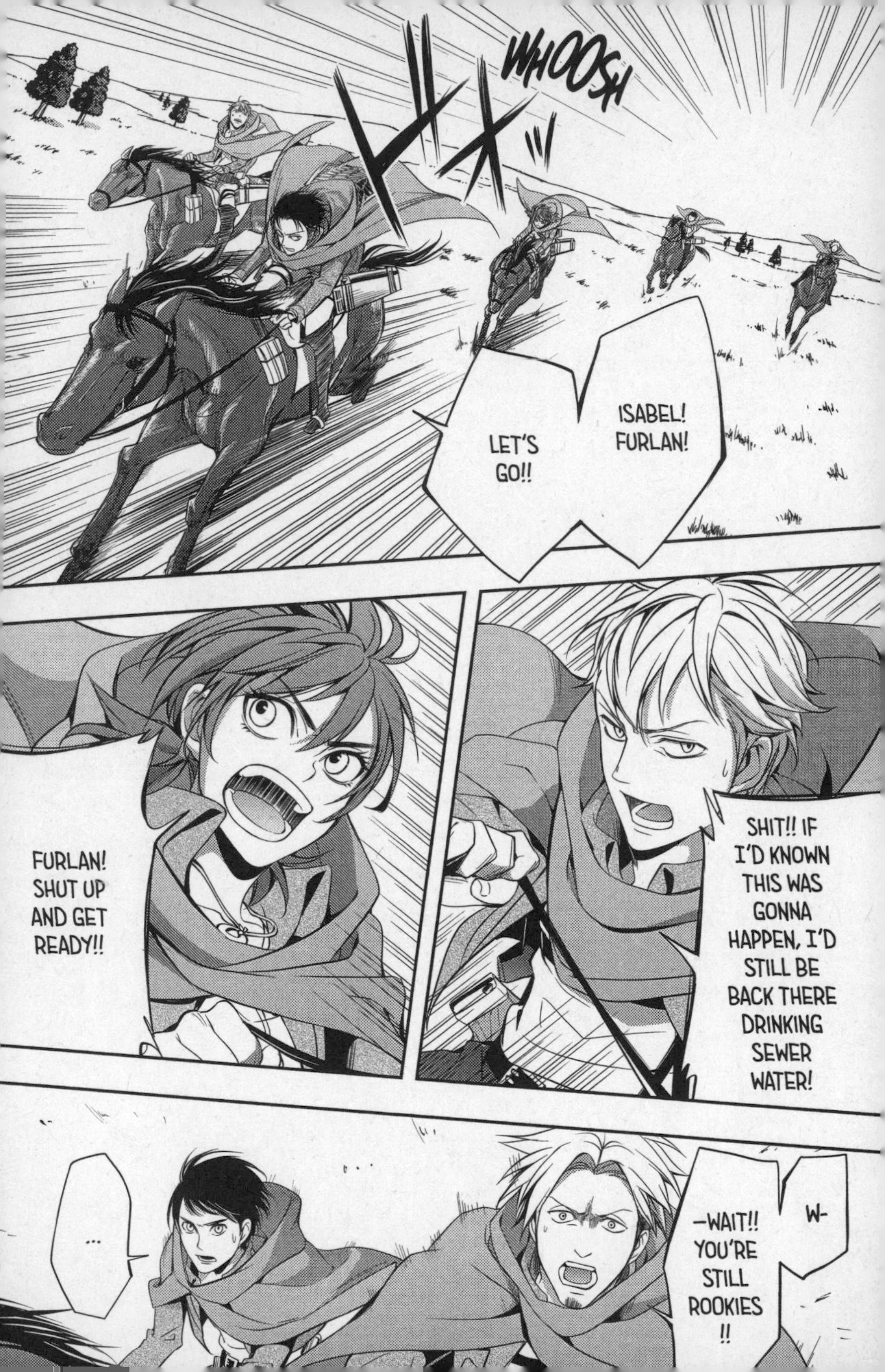
WHOOSH
ISABEL! FURLAN! LET'S GO!!
SHIT!! IF I'D KNOWN THIS WAS GONNA HAPPEN, I'D STILL BE BACK THERE DRINKING SEWER WATER!
FURLAN! SHUT UP AND GET READY!!
W- —WAIT!! YOU'RE STILL ROOKIES!!
...

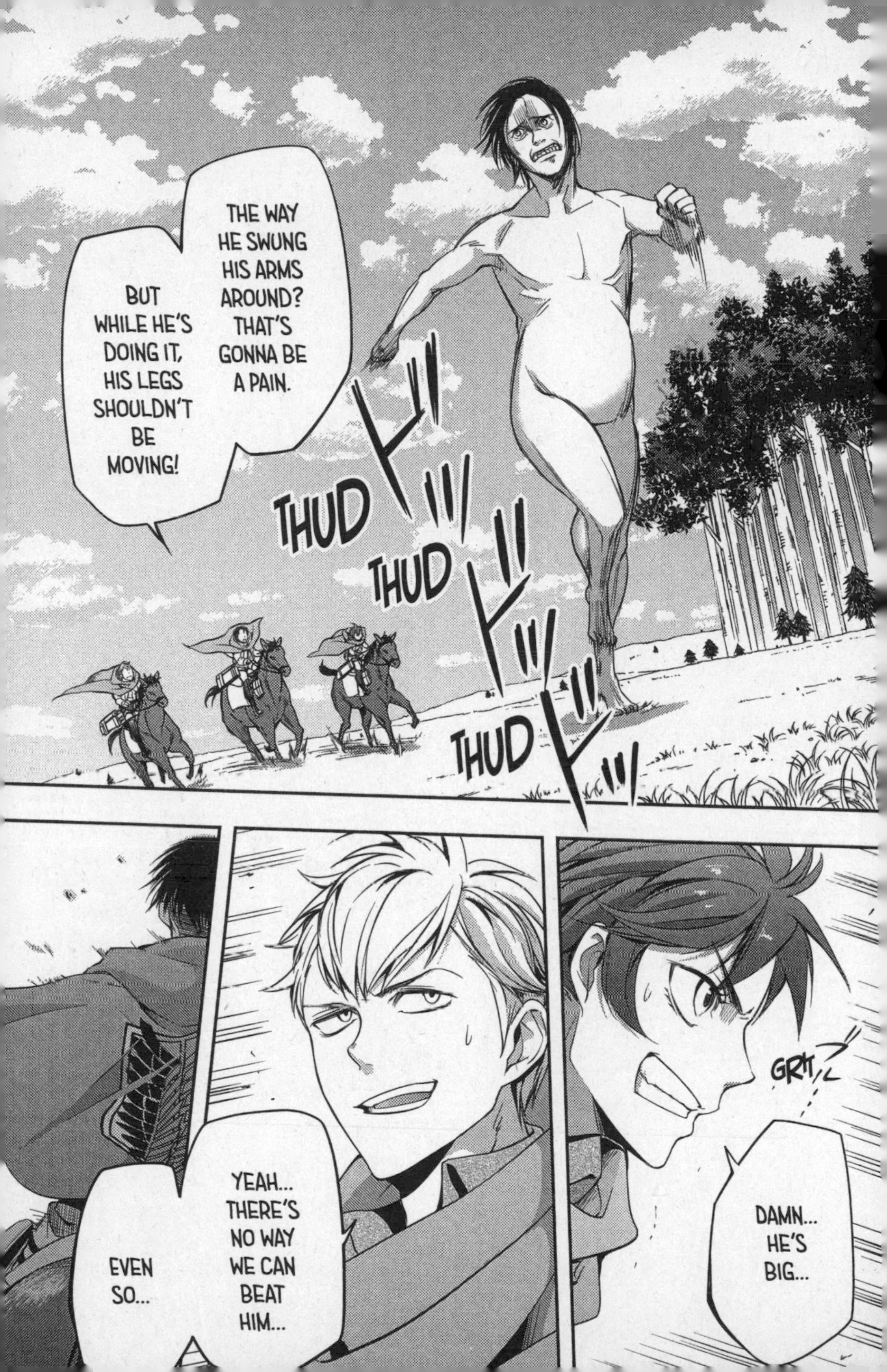
THE WAY HE SWUNG HIS ARMS AROUND? THAT'S GONNA BE A PAIN.
BUT WHILE HE'S DOING IT, HIS LEGS SHOULDN'T BE MOVING!
THUD
THUD
THUD
GRIT
DAMN... HE'S BIG...
YEAH... THERE'S NO WAY WE CAN BEAT HIM...
EVEN SO...

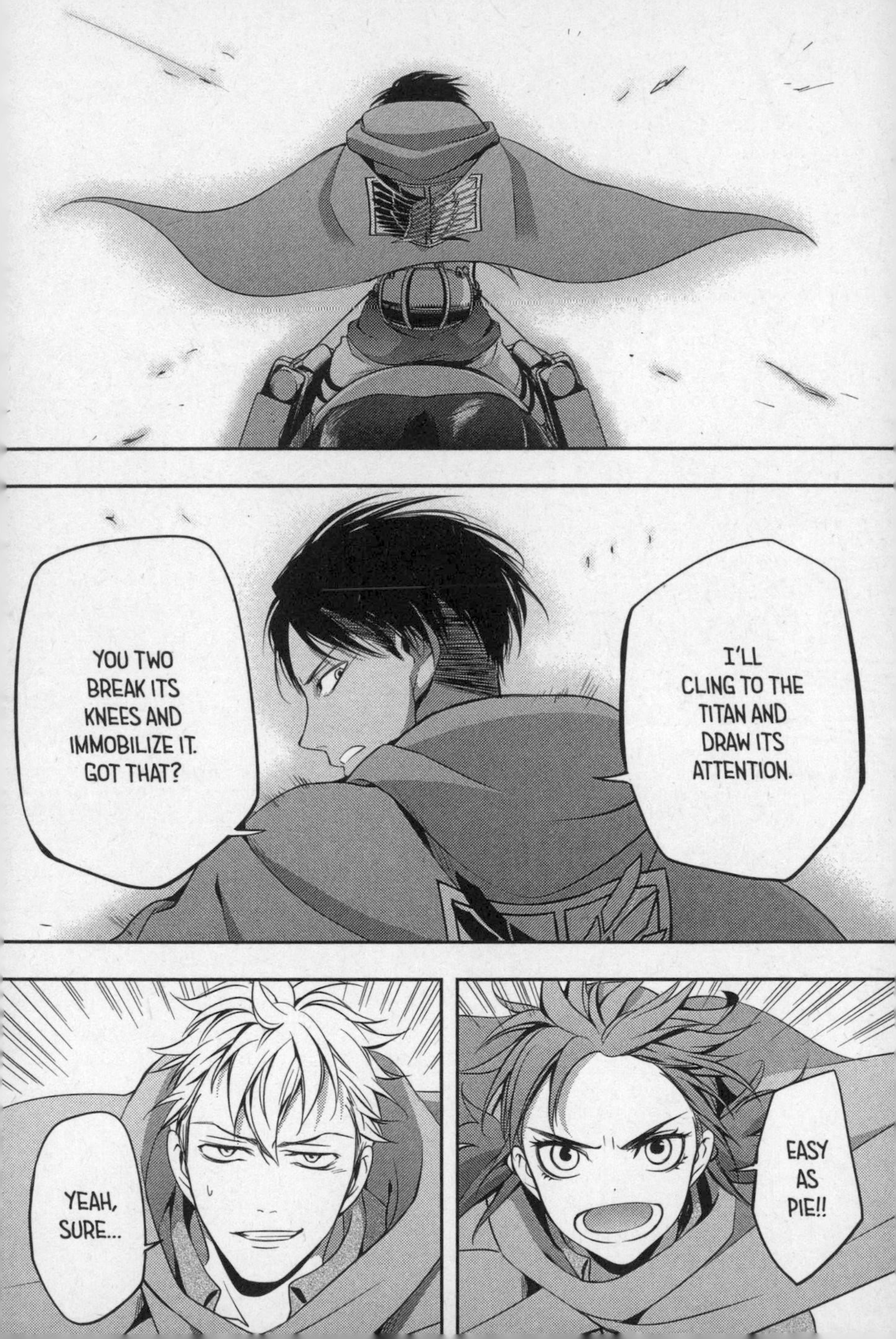
I'LL CLING TO THE TITAN AND DRAW ITS ATTENTION.
YOU TWO BREAK ITS KNEES AND IMMOBILIZE IT. GOT THAT?
EASY AS PIE!!
YEAH, SURE...

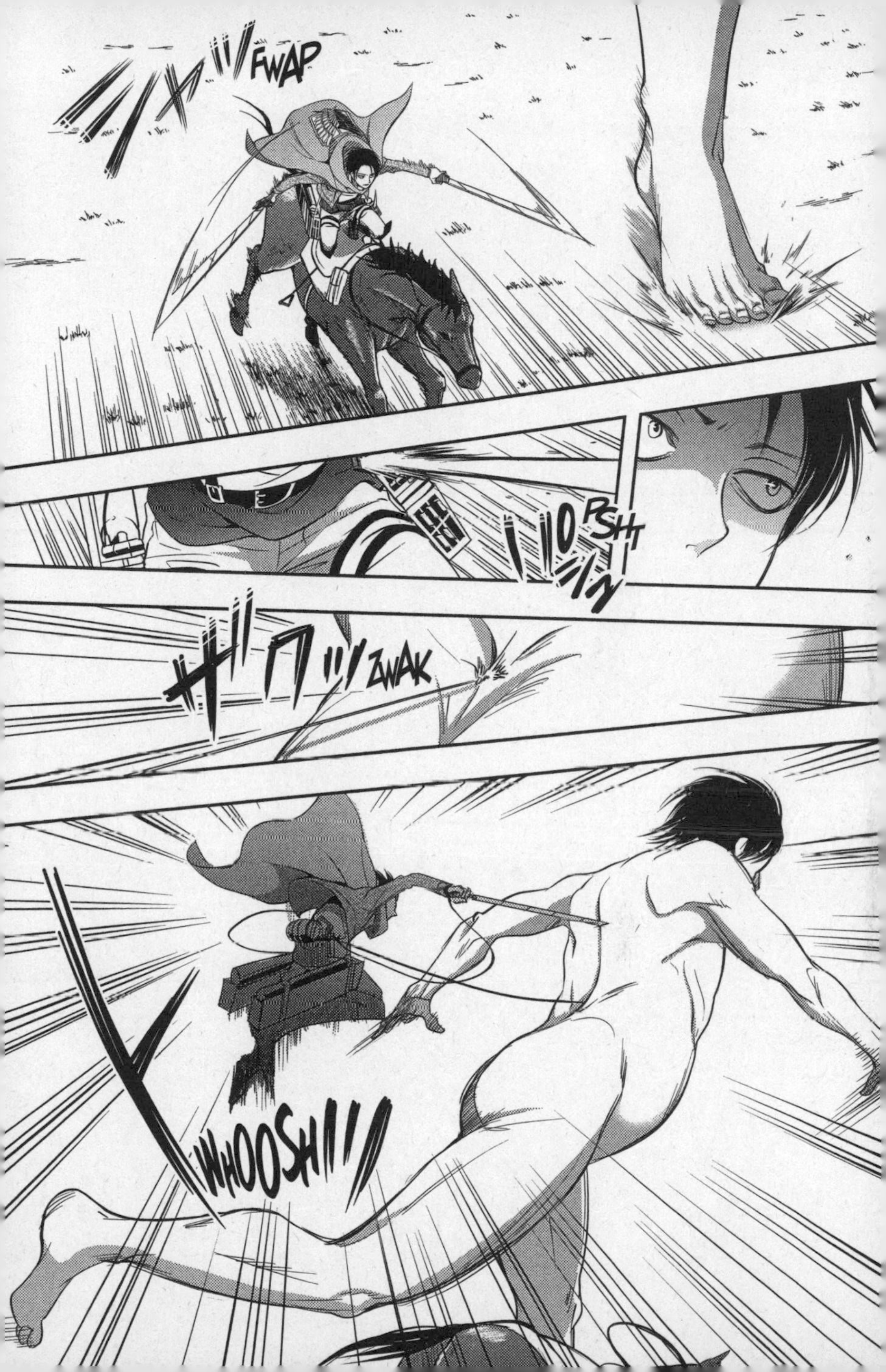
FWAP
PSHT
ZWAK
WHOOSH

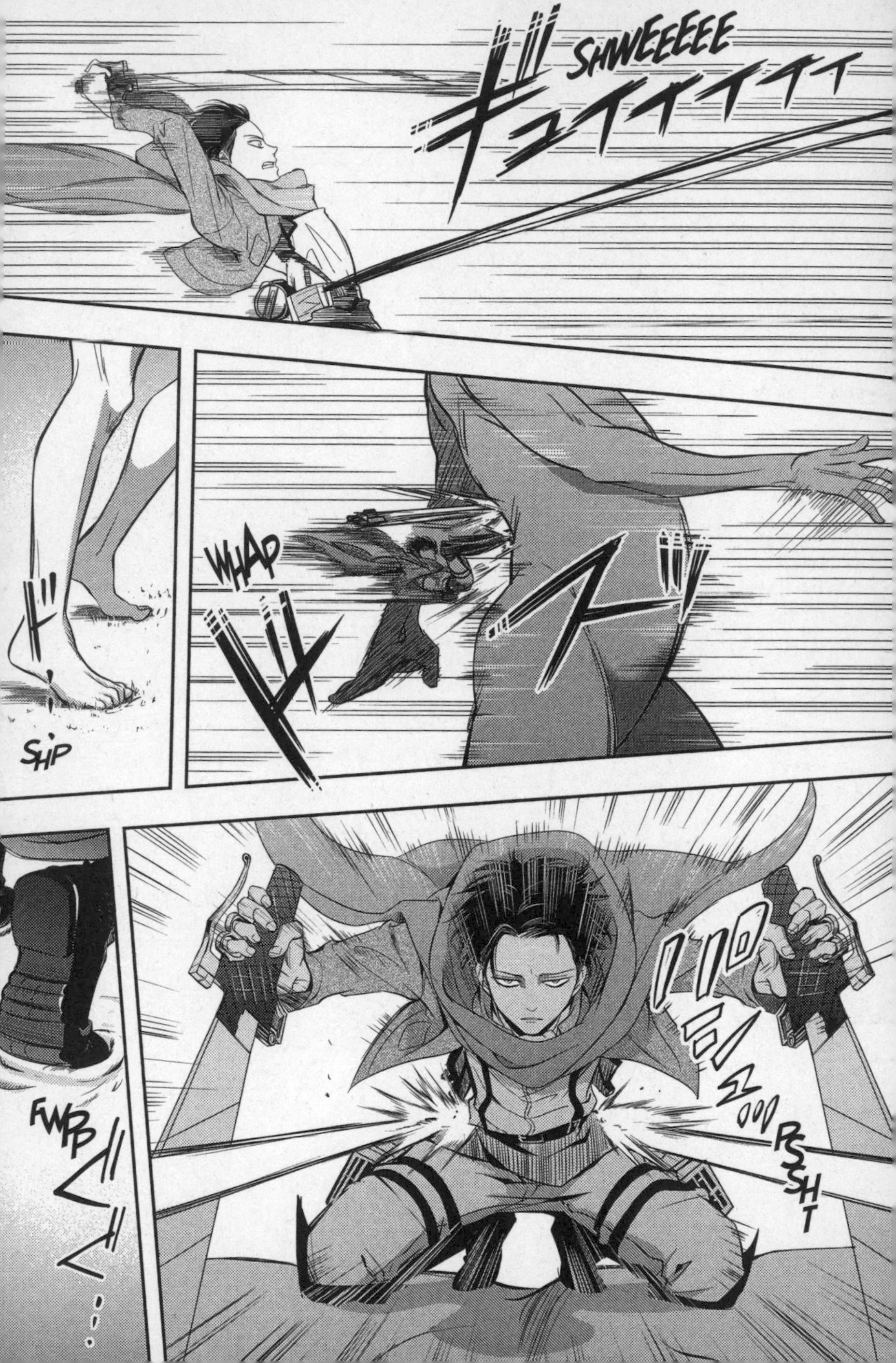
SHWEEEEE
ギュイイイイイ
WHAP
SHIP
PSSHT
FWPP

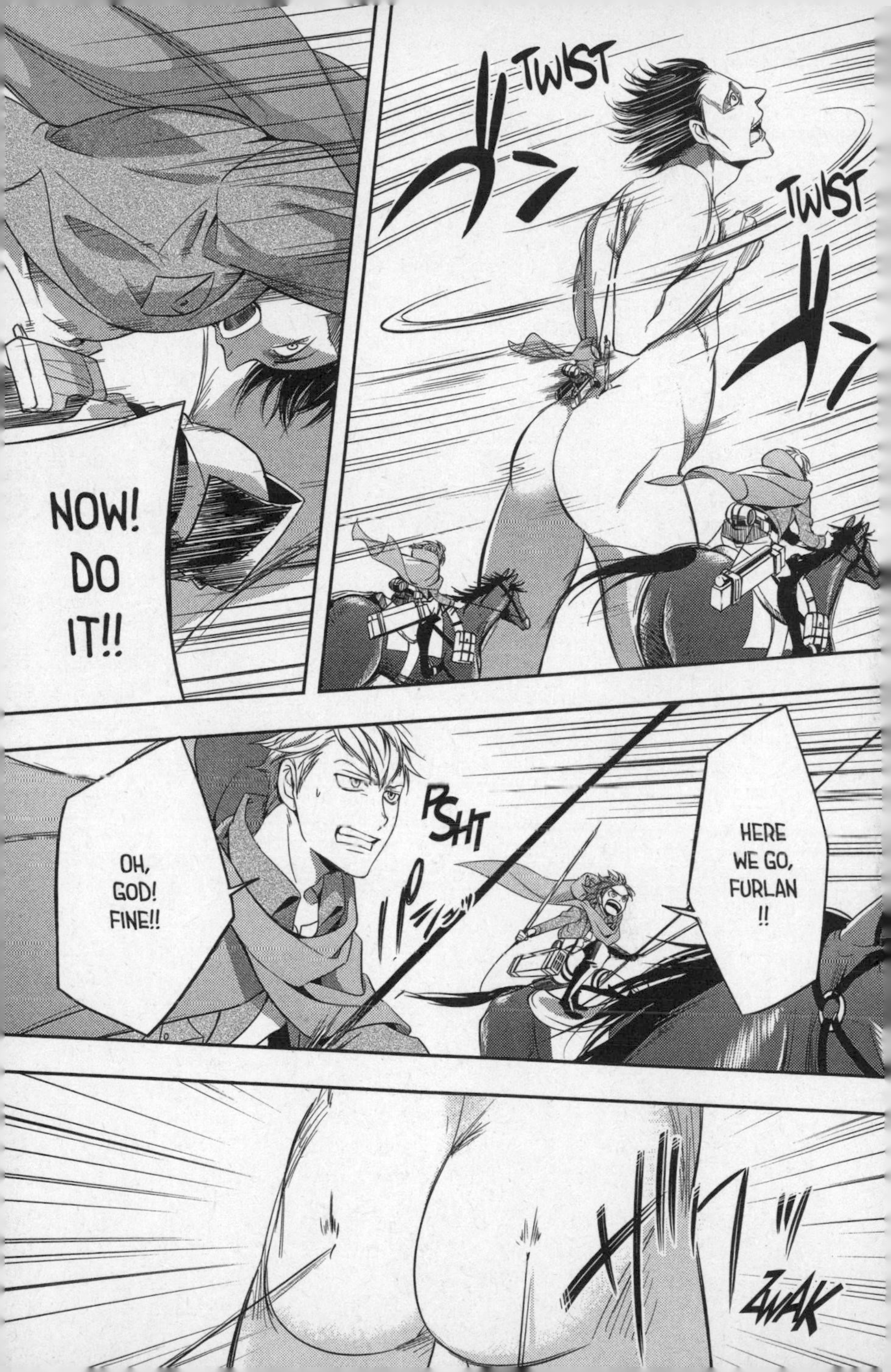
TWIST
TWIST
NOW! DO IT!!
HERE WE GO, FURLAN !!
PSHT
OH, GOD! FINE!!
ZWAK

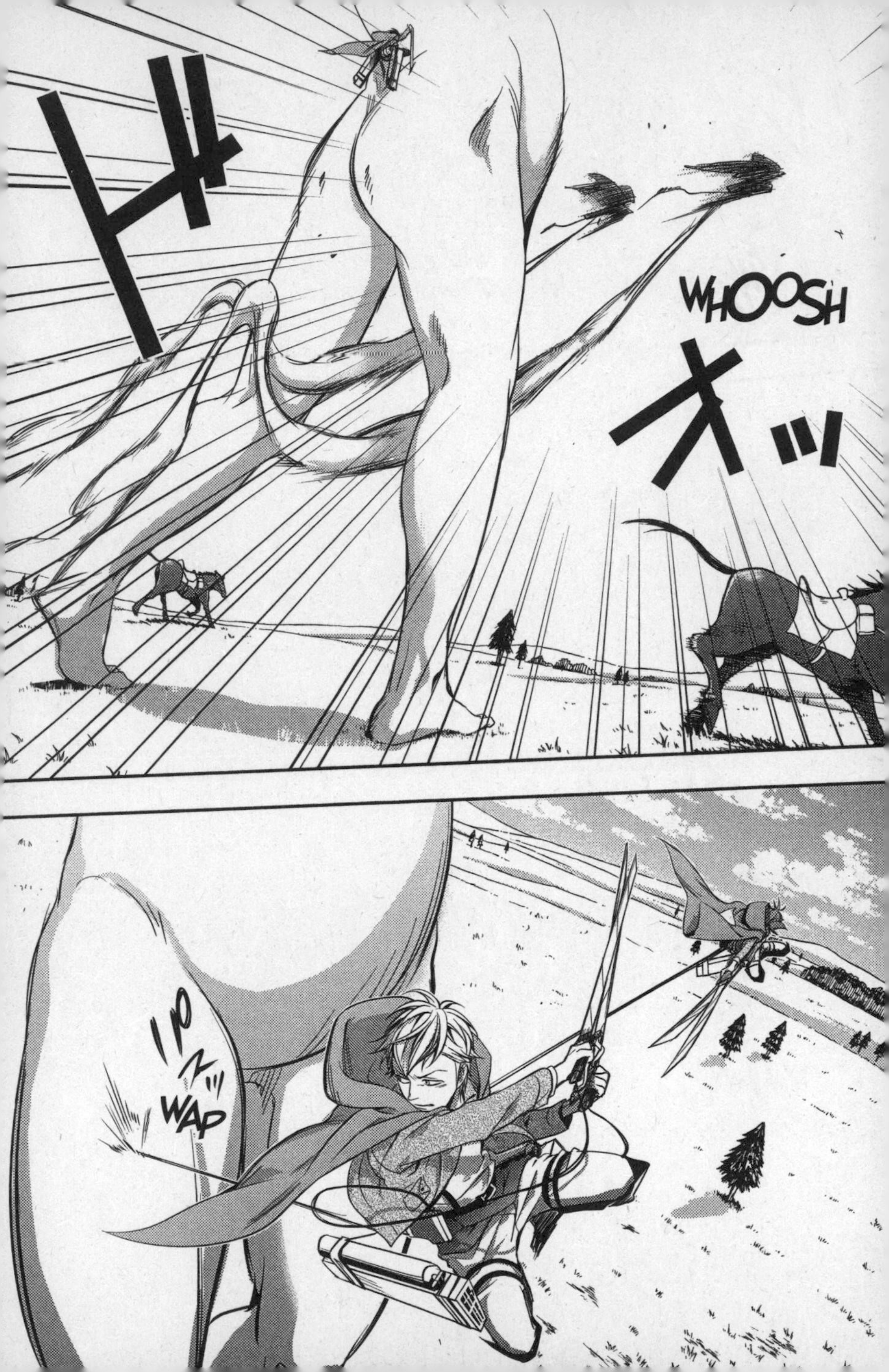
WHOOSH
WAP

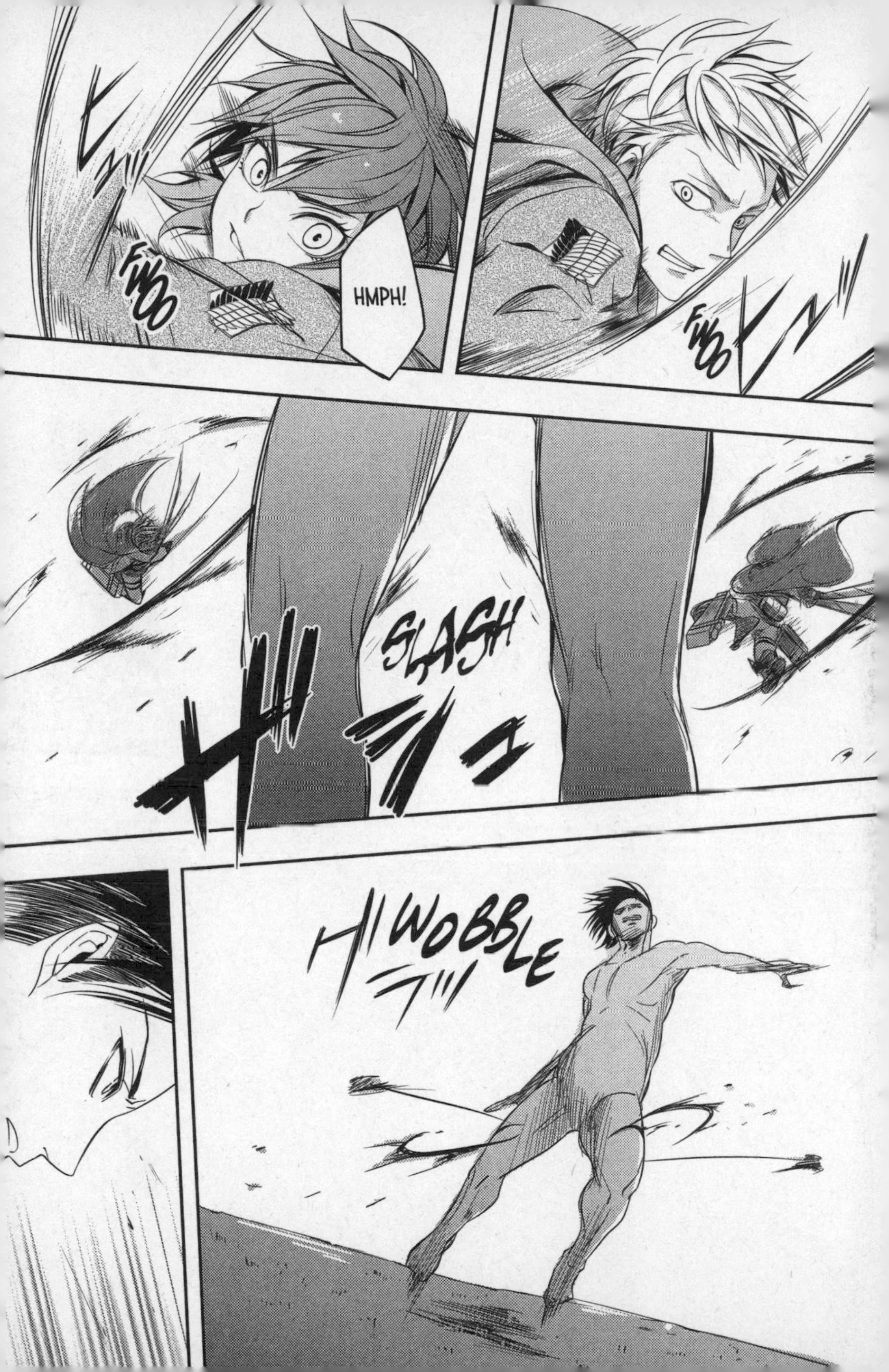
FWOO
FWOO
HMPH!
SLASH
WOBBLE

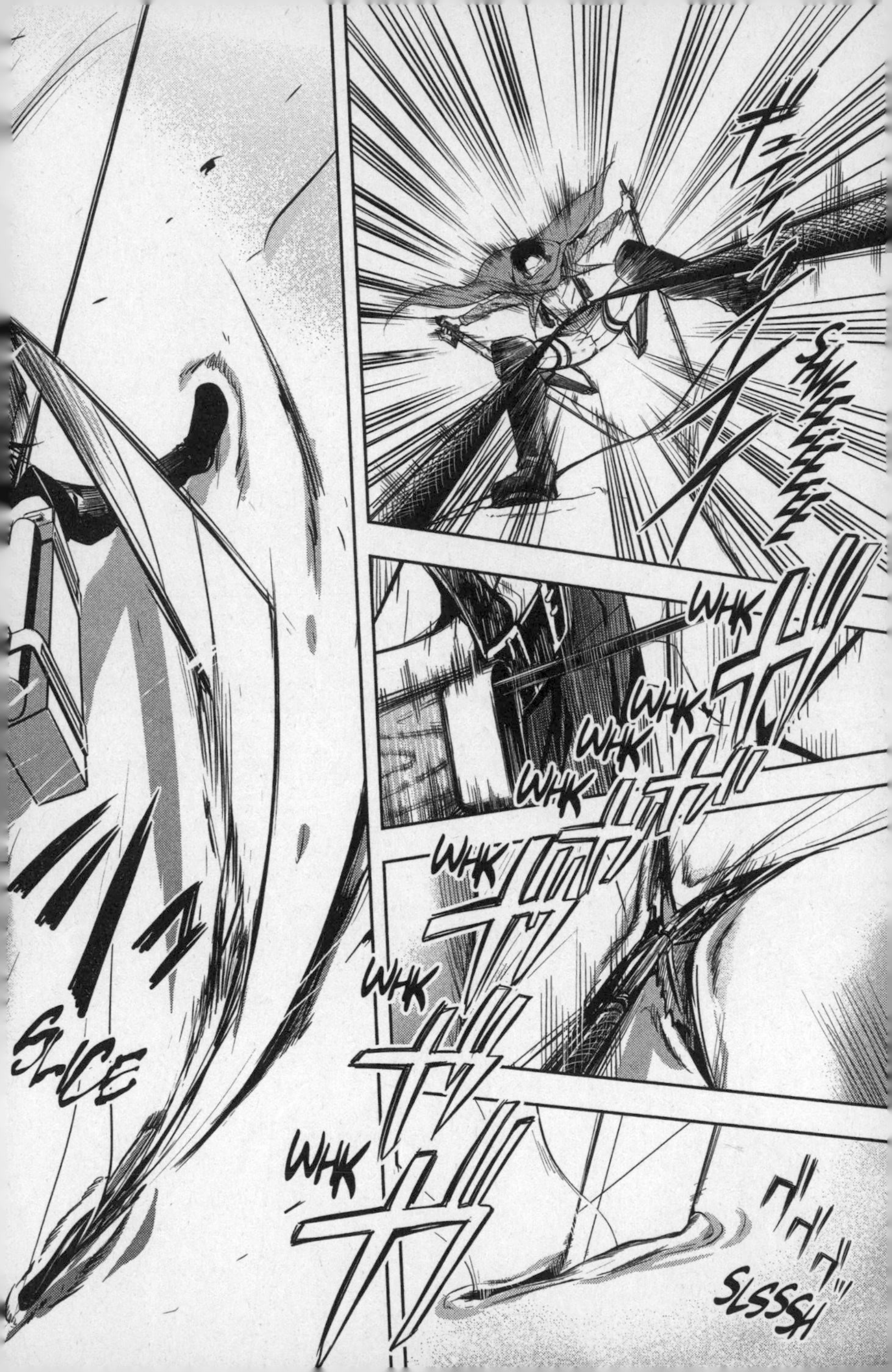
SHWEEEEEE
WHK
WHK
WHK
WHK
WHK
WHK
WHK
SLSSSH
SLICE

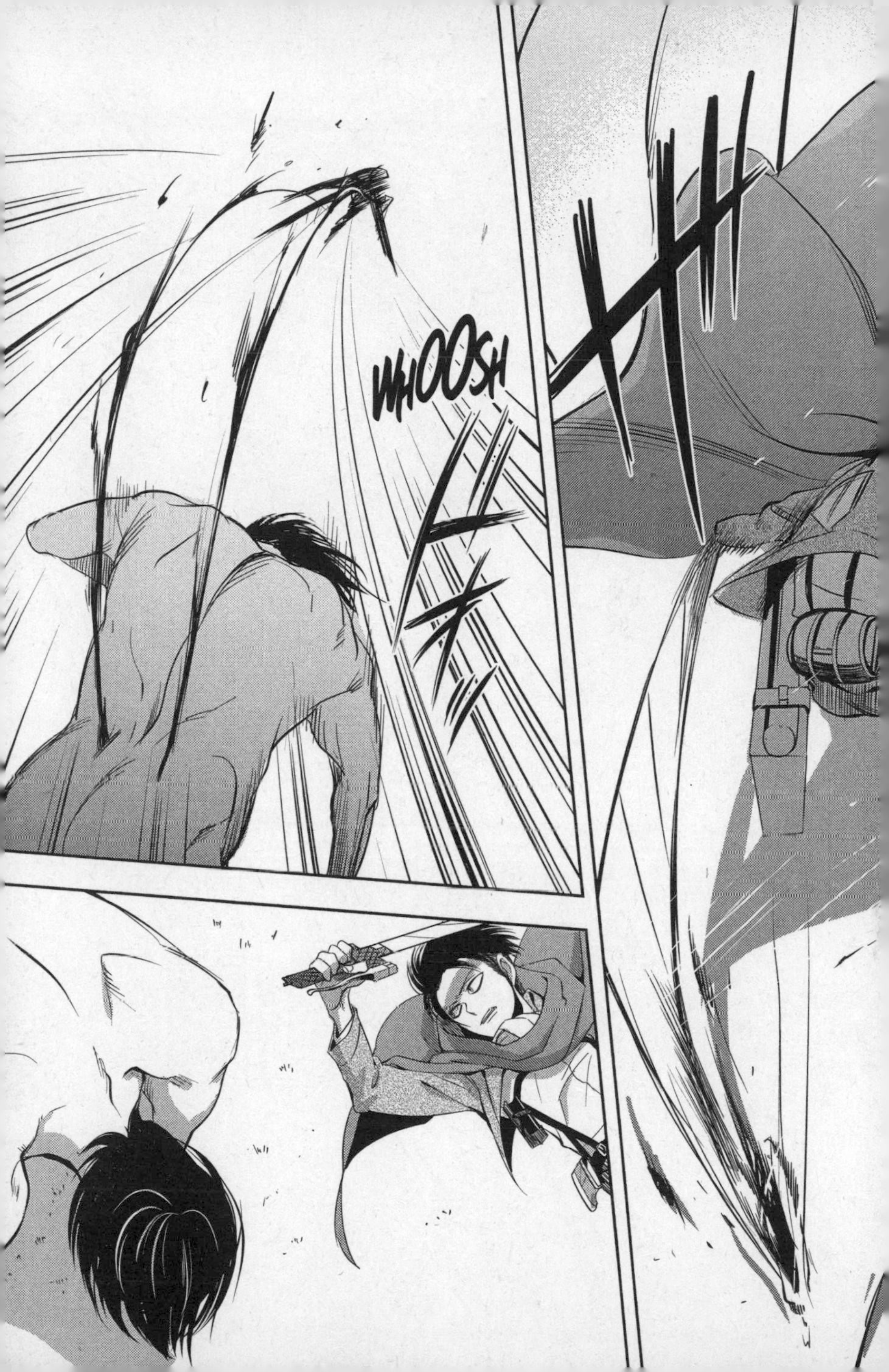
WHOOSH

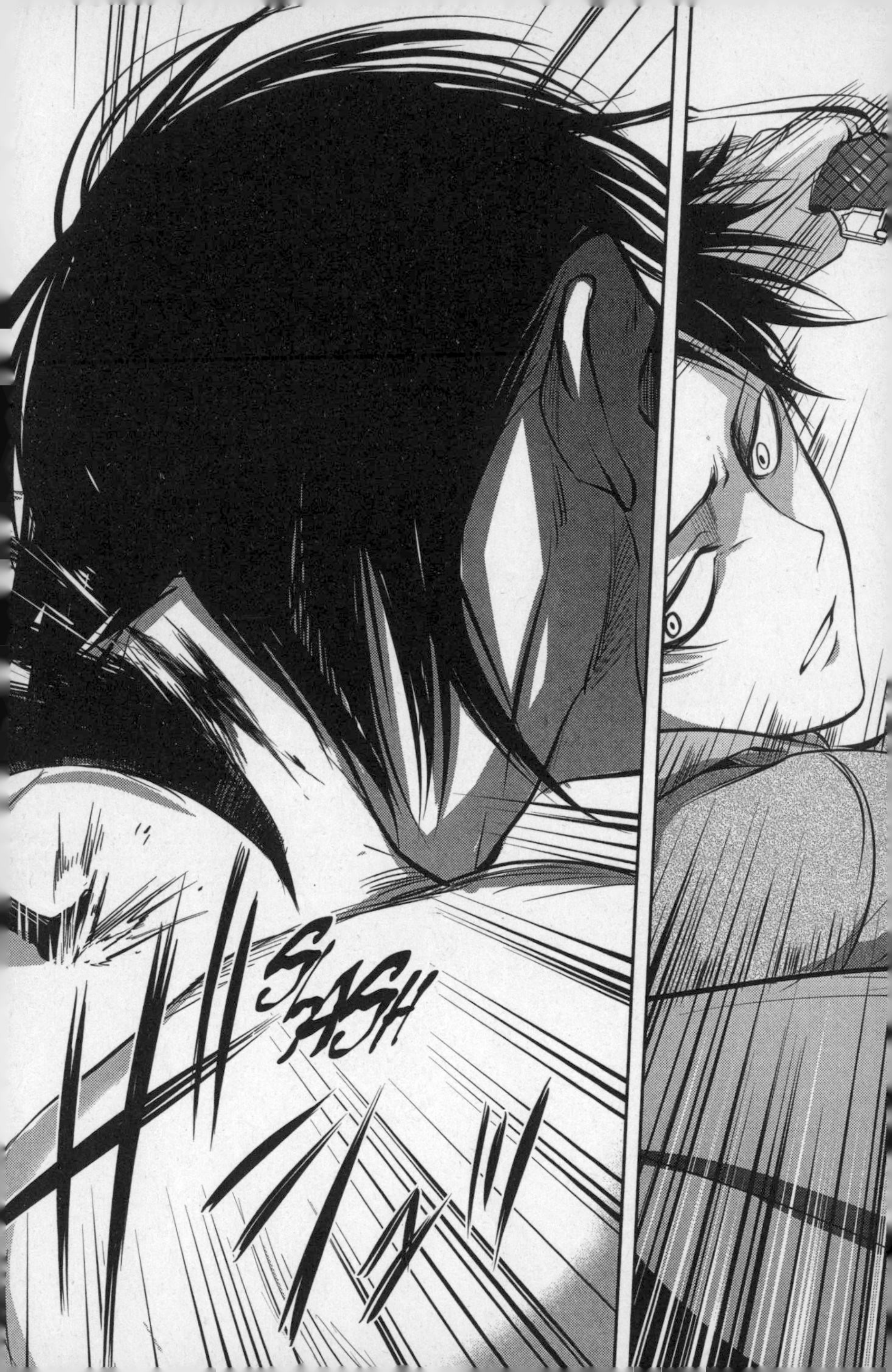
SLASH

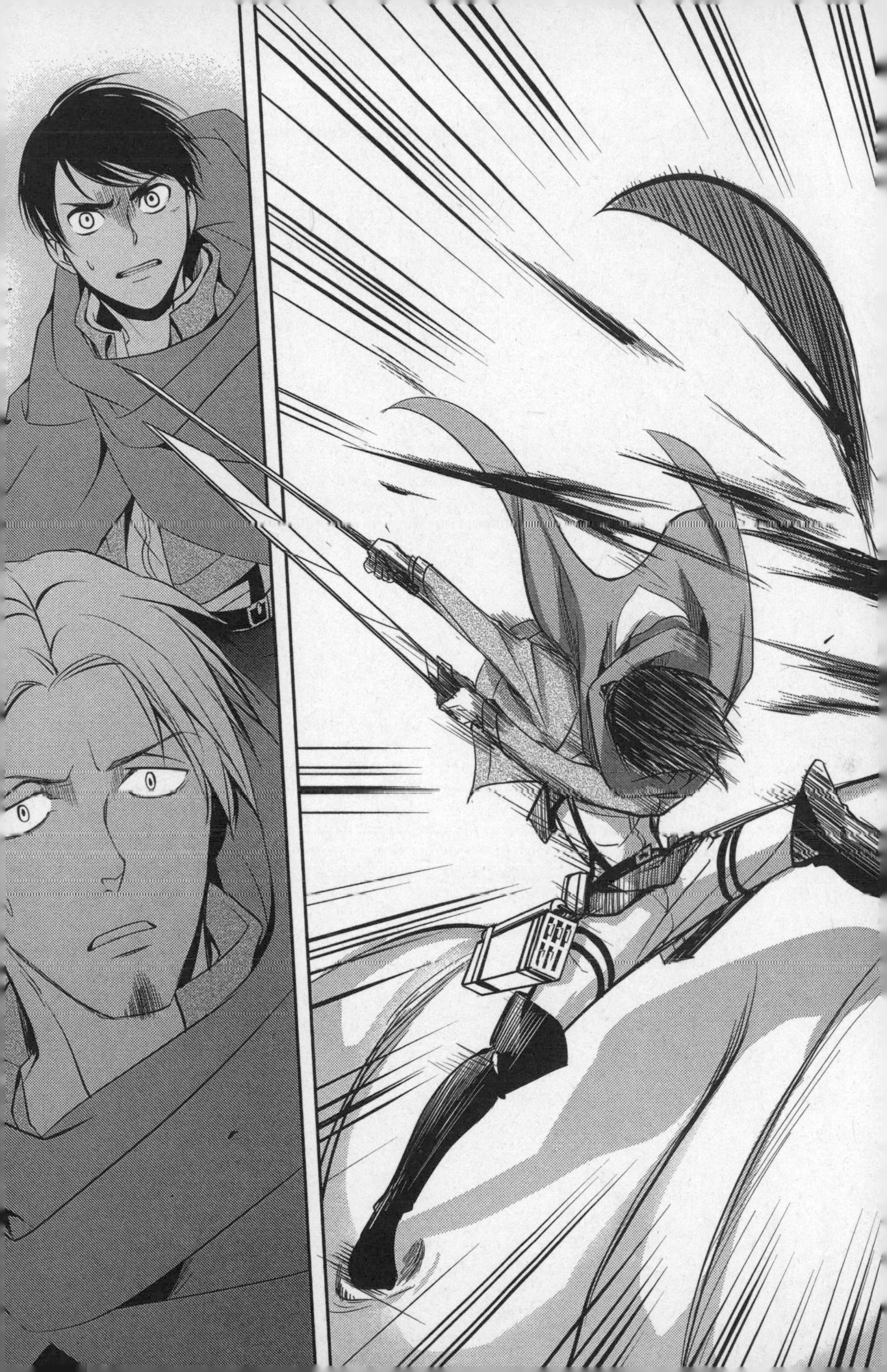

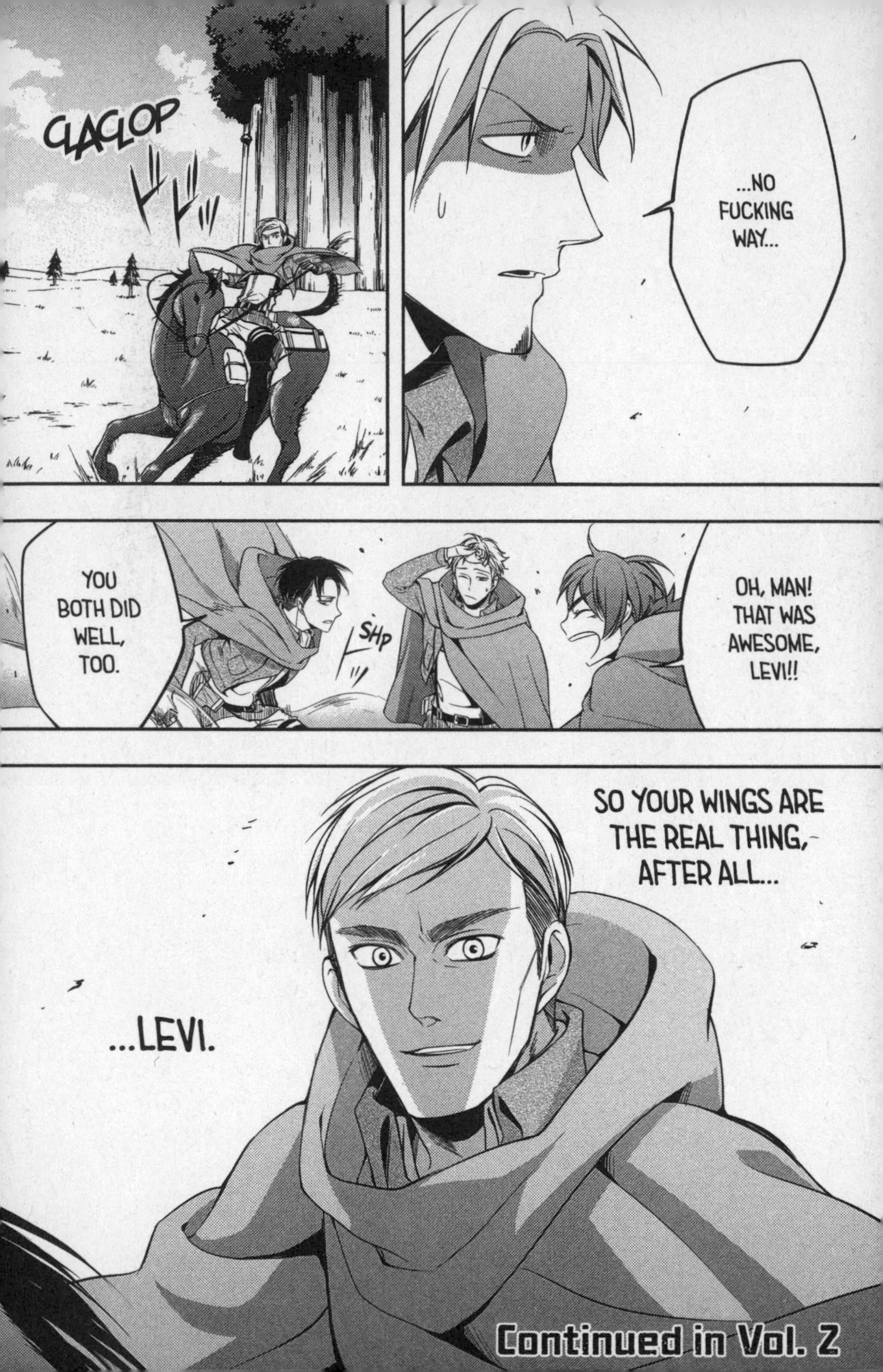
...NO FUCKING WAY...
CLACLOP
OH, MAN! THAT WAS AWESOME, LEVI!!
SHP
YOU BOTH DID WELL, TOO.
SO YOUR WINGS ARE THE REAL THING, AFTER ALL...
...LEVI.
Continued in Vol. 2

To be continued...

Hello there. My name is Hikaru Suruga.
Thank you so much for reading!

I love "Attack on Titan," and I am so happy to be
able to draw a Titan story. "No Regrets" was born
out of the additions Gun Snark of Nitroplus
made to Hajime Isayama's original world. I hope
they enjoy this manga version, which I drew
based on their work. I am grateful to everyone
who gave me this precious opportunity.

Before the manga began serialization, on the
advice of the editor-in-chief, I visited a place
called the Metropolitan Area Outer Underground
Discharge Channel for research, to fill out my
mental image of the Underground, where Levi and
his comrades live. It's a mysterious space, where a
lot of concrete pillars 18 meters (59 feet) high
stretch out toward the ceiling. While imagining
the atmosphere of the Underground, I grew
excited about the story of Levi and the others
that was about to begin.
The impact of actually experiencing that space
was totally different from that of seeing photos. I
was actually able to picture the massive size of an
18-meter class Titan.

The story's still going, so please look forward to
the rest. I'm going to keep working hard!

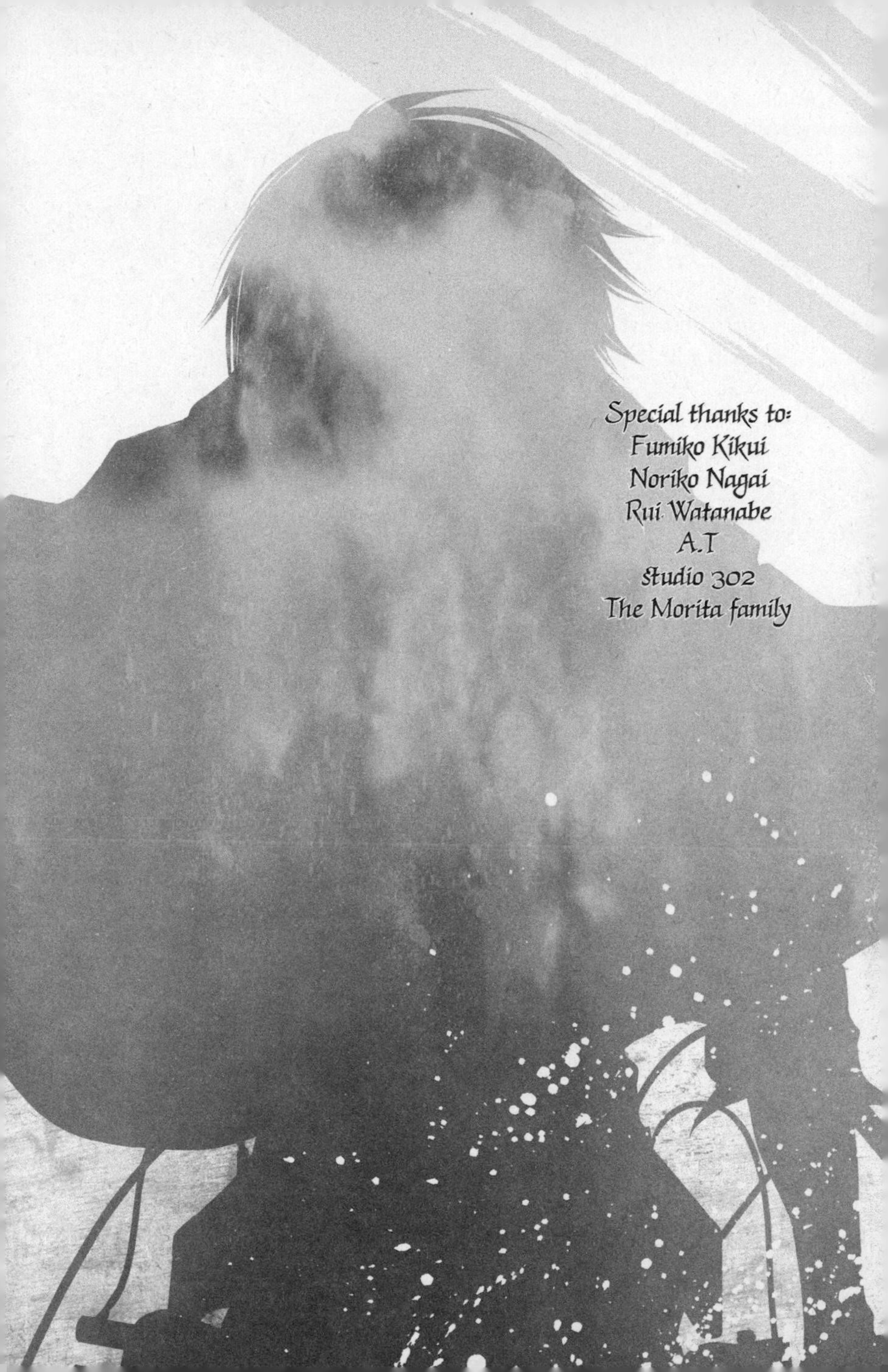

Special thanks to:
Fumiko Kikui
Noriko Nagai
Rui Watanabe
A.T
studio 302
The Morita family

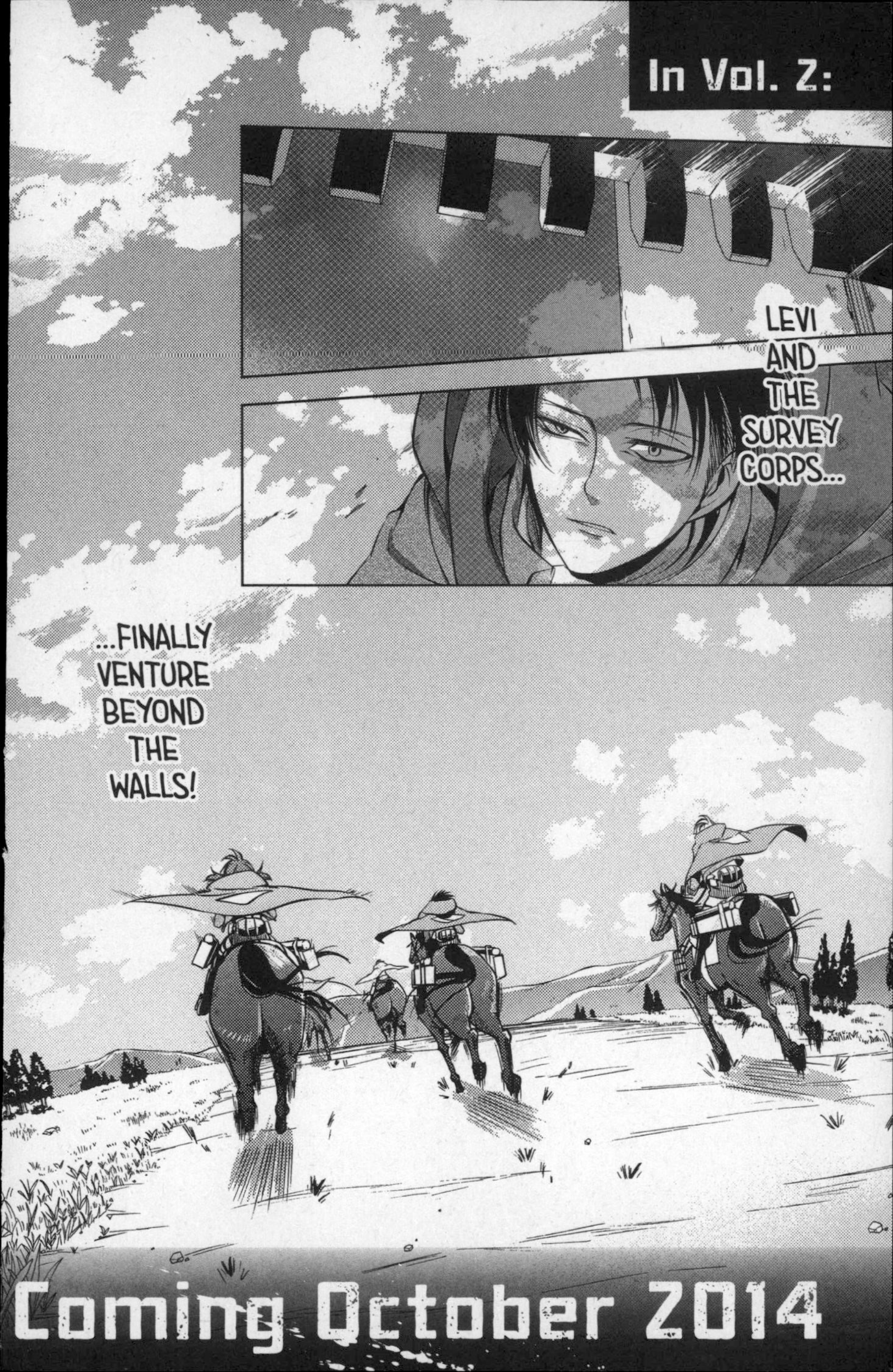
In Vol. 2:
LEVI AND THE SURVEY CORPS...
...FINALLY VENTURE BEYOND THE WALLS!
Coming October 2014

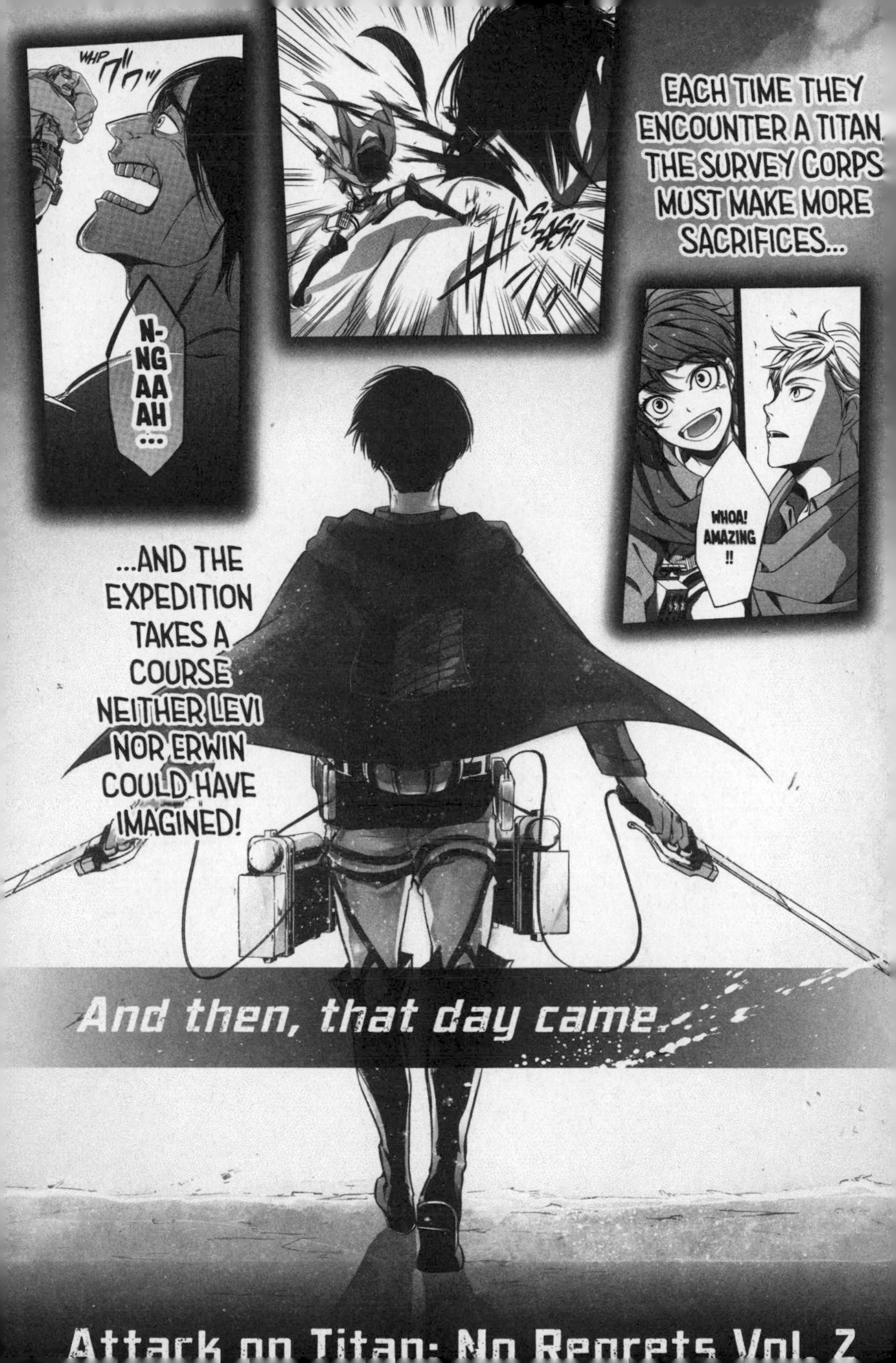

EACH TIME THEY ENCOUNTER A TITAN, THE SURVEY CORPS MUST MAKE MORE SACRIFICES...
SLASH
WHP
N-NGAAAH...
WHOA! AMAZING!!
...AND THE EXPEDITION TAKES A COURSE NEITHER LEVI NOR ERWIN COULD HAVE IMAGINED!
And then, that day came.
Attack on Titan: No Regrets Vol. 2

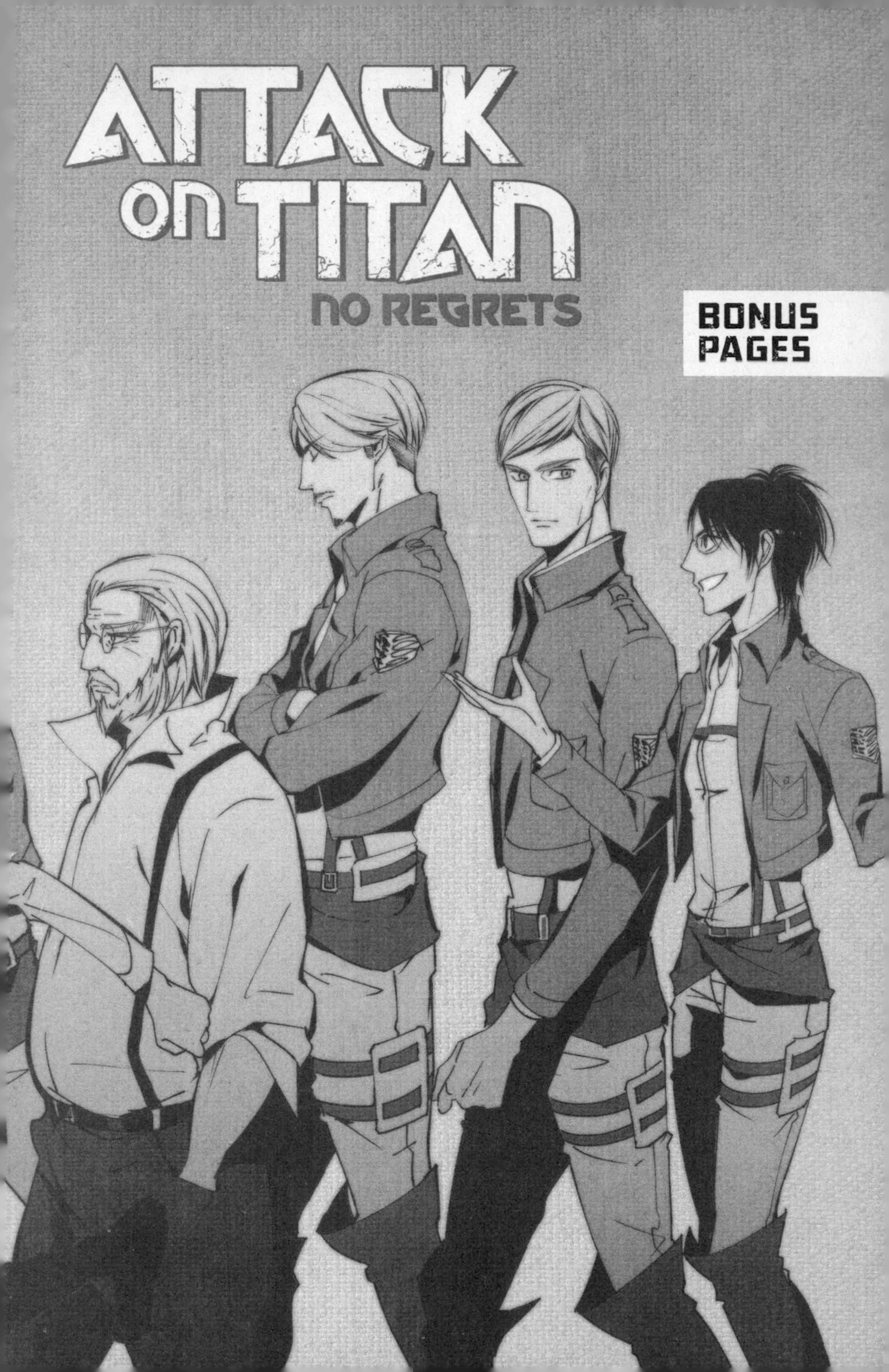
ATTACK on TITAN
NO REGRETS
BONUS PAGES

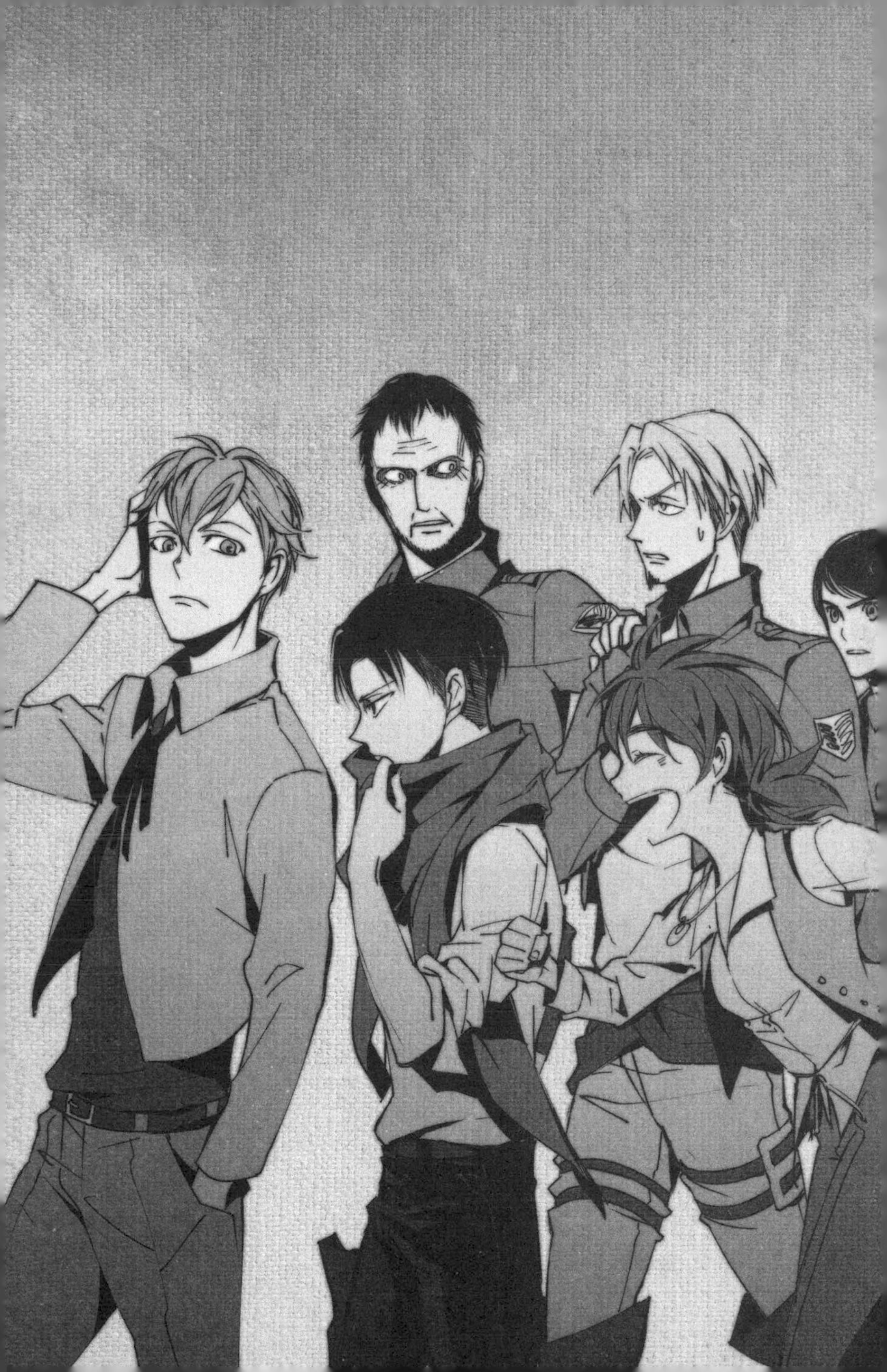

ATTACK on TITAN

NO REGRETS

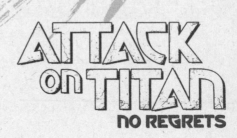

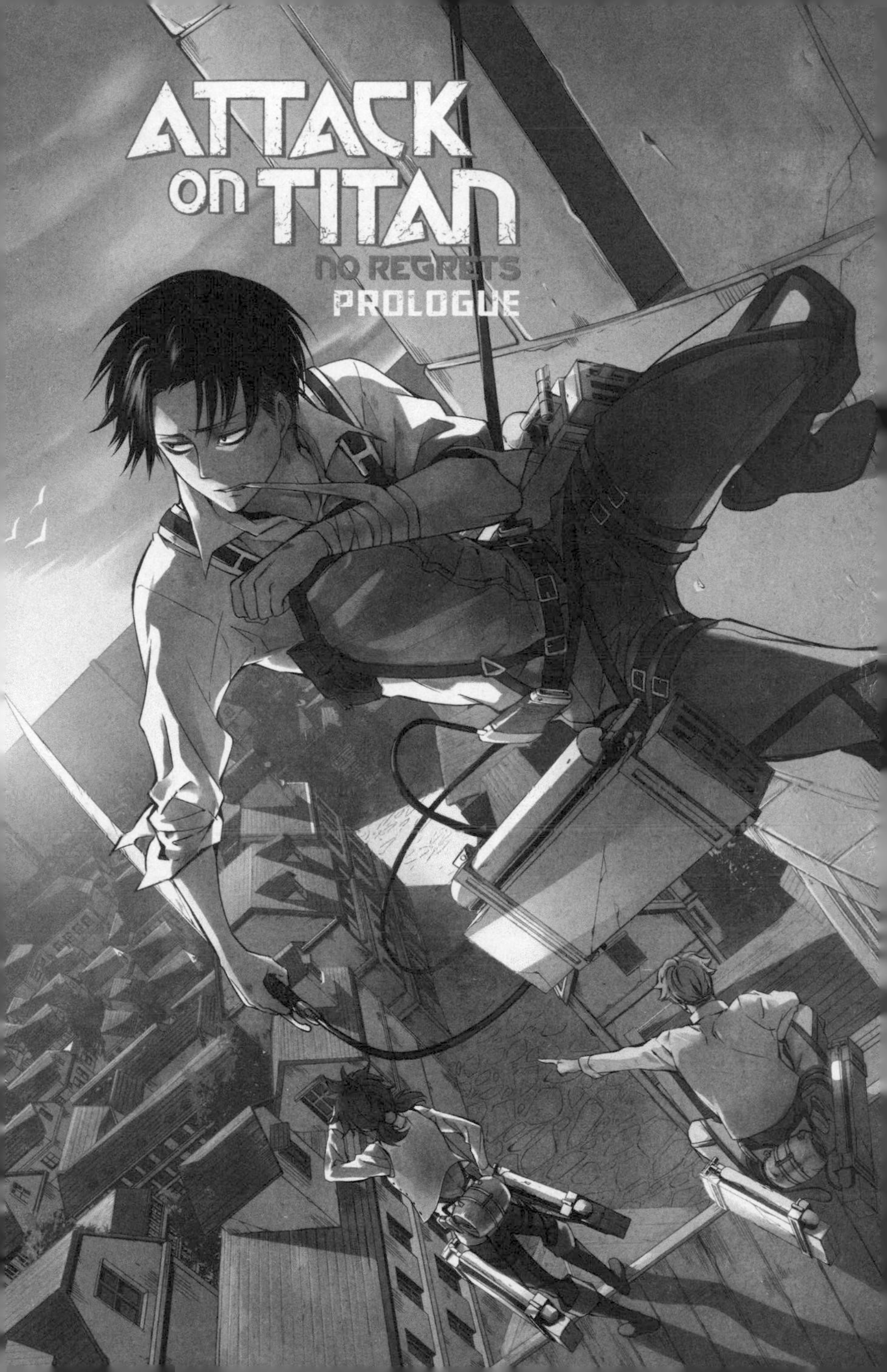
ATTACK on TITAN
NO REGRETS
PROLOGUE

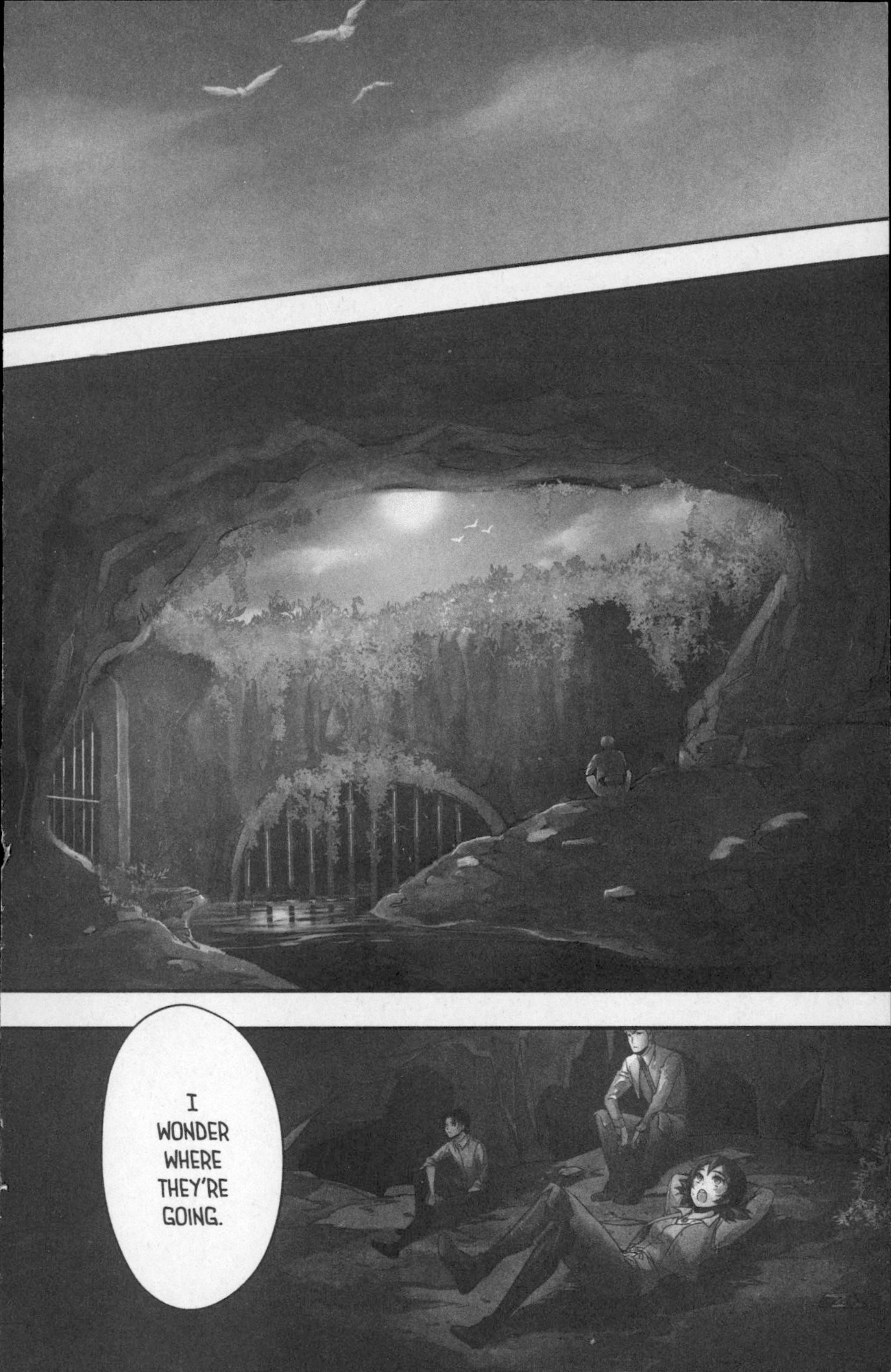
I WONDER WHERE THEY'RE GOING.

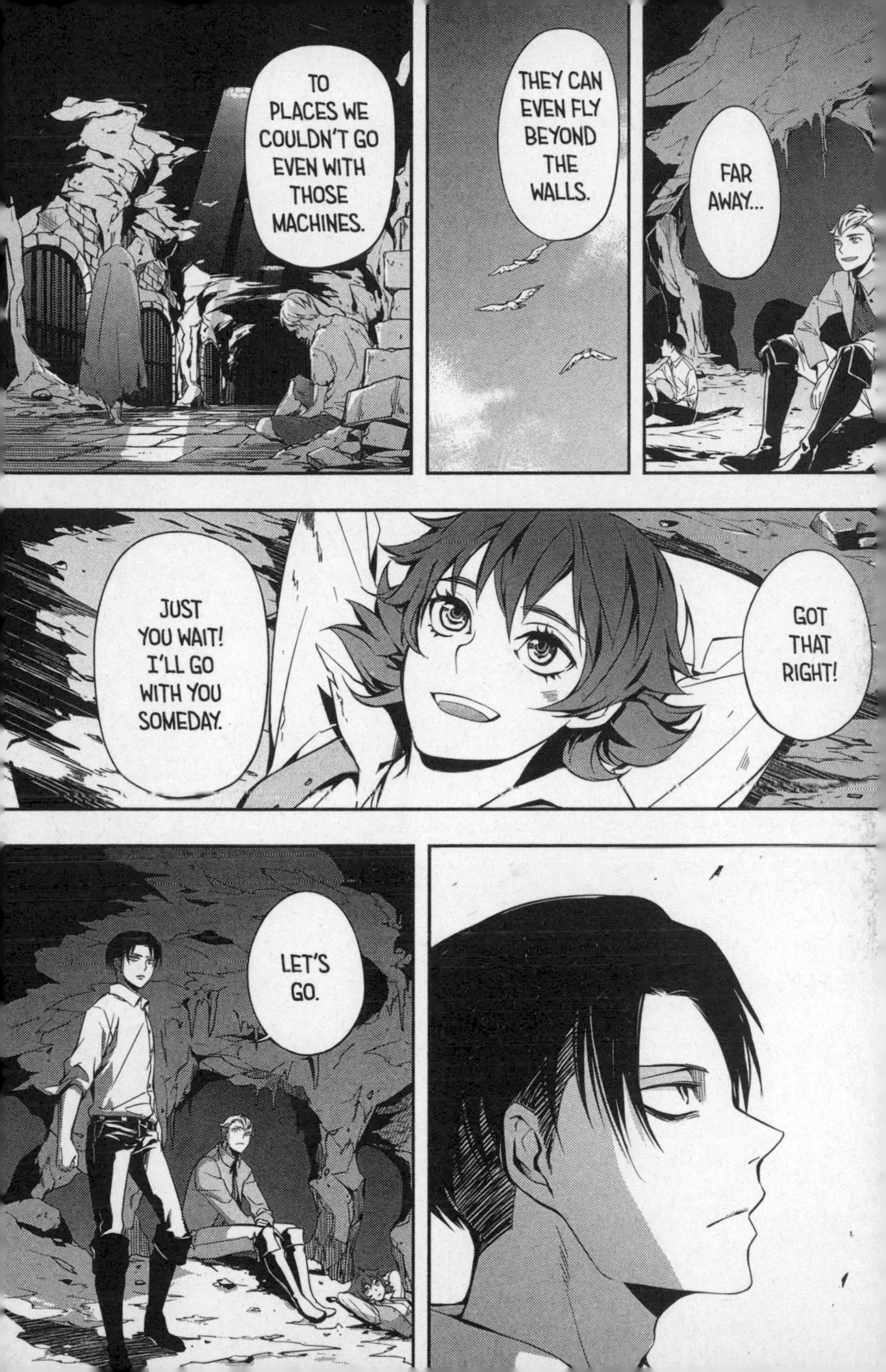
FAR AWAY...
THEY CAN EVEN FLY BEYOND THE WALLS.
TO PLACES WE COULDN'T GO EVEN WITH THOSE MACHINES.
GOT THAT RIGHT!
JUST YOU WAIT! I'LL GO WITH YOU SOMEDAY.
LET'S GO.

THE UNDER-
GROUND,
BENEATH
THE
ROYAL
CAPITAL

スッ SHF...

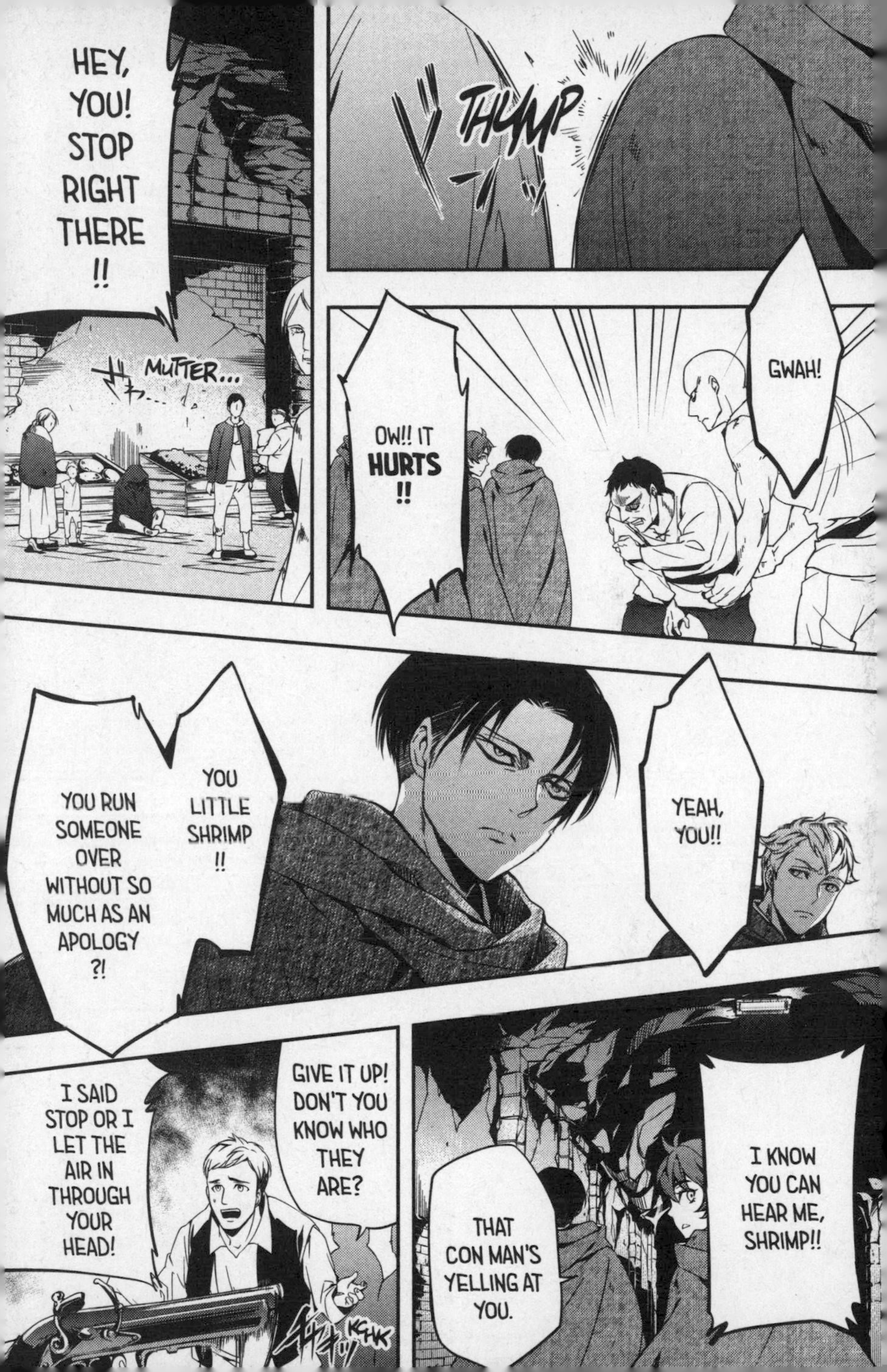
THUMP
GWAH!
OW!! IT HURTS!!
HEY, YOU! STOP RIGHT THERE!!
MUTTER...
YEAH, YOU!!
YOU LITTLE SHRIMP!!
YOU RUN SOMEONE OVER WITHOUT SO MUCH AS AN APOLOGY?!
I KNOW YOU CAN HEAR ME, SHRIMP!!
THAT CON MAN'S YELLING AT YOU.
GIVE IT UP! DON'T YOU KNOW WHO THEY ARE?
I SAID STOP OR I LET THE AIR IN THROUGH YOUR HEAD!
KCHK

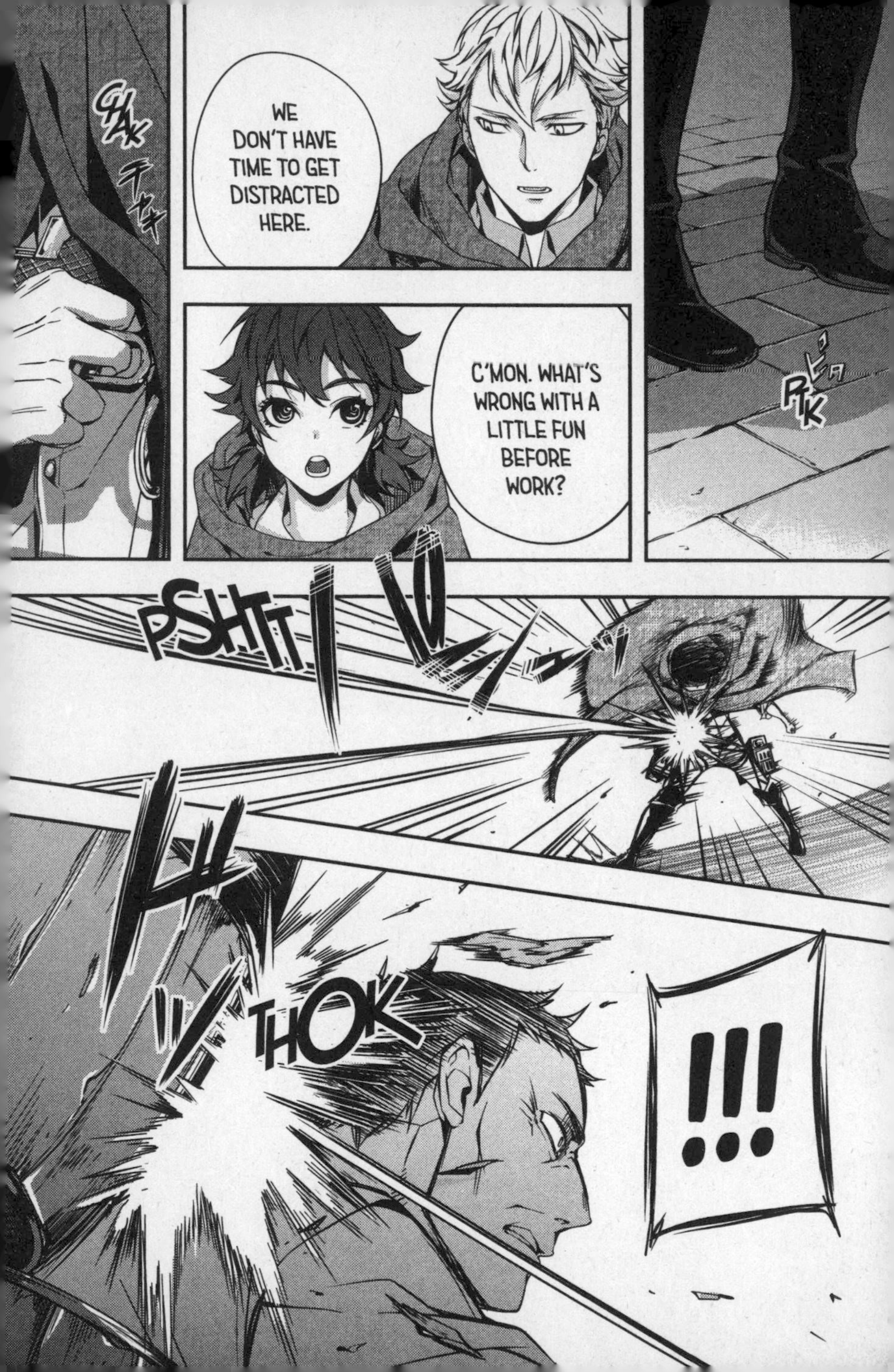
PIK
WE DON'T HAVE TIME TO GET DISTRACTED HERE.
C'MON. WHAT'S WRONG WITH A LITTLE FUN BEFORE WORK?
CHAK
PSHT
THOK
!!!

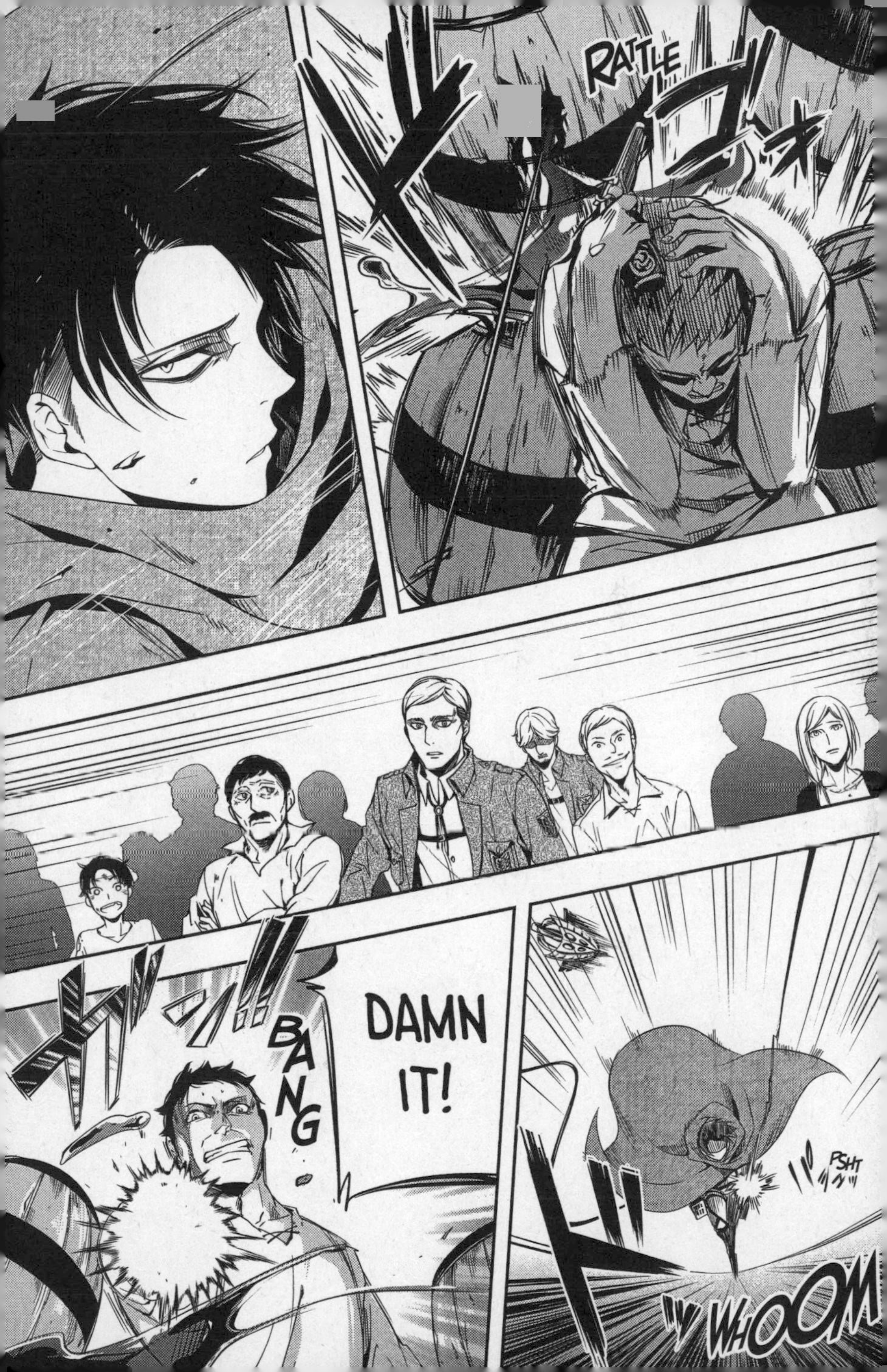
RATTLE
PSHT
WHOOM
BANG
DAMN IT!

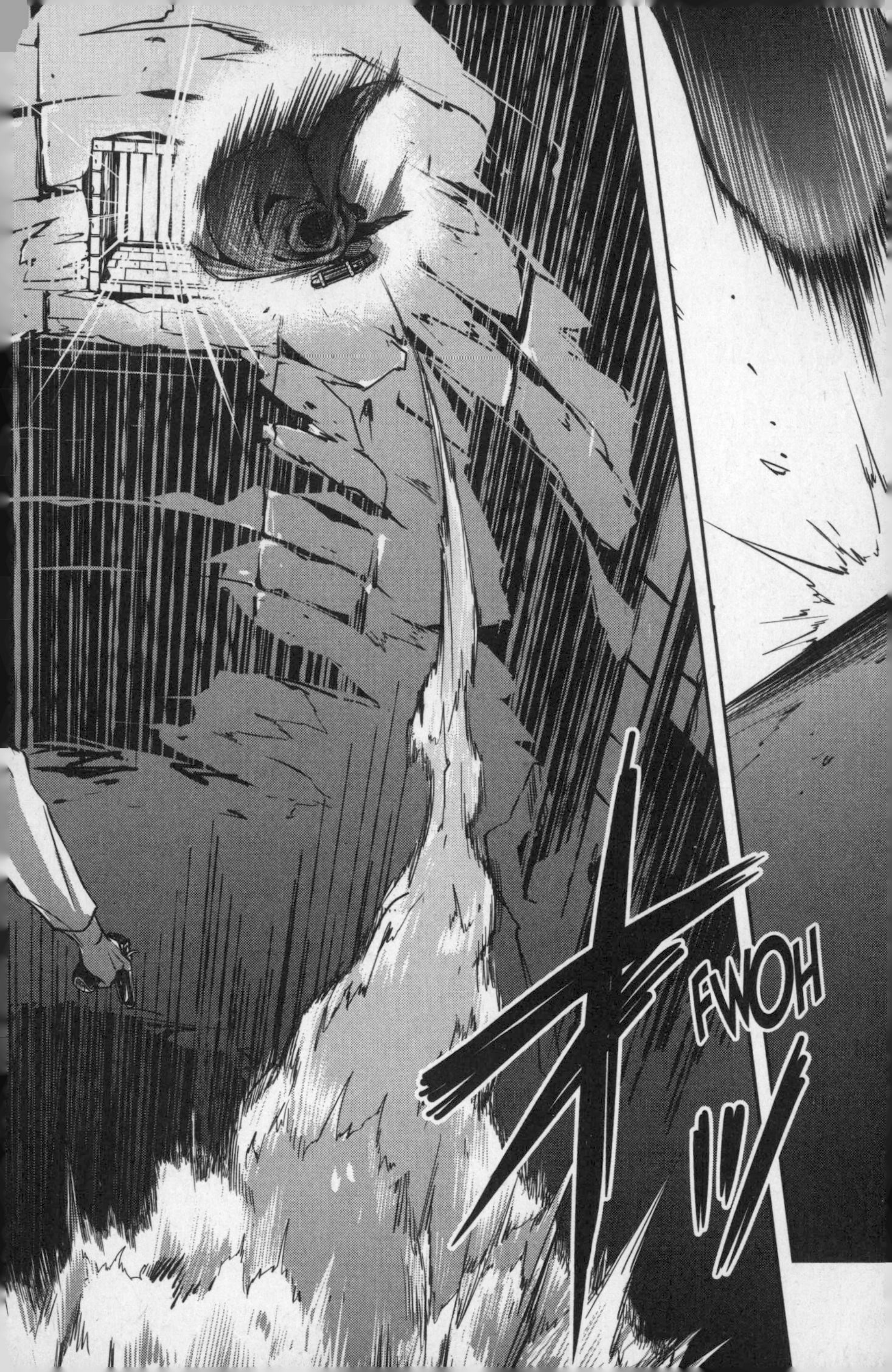
FWOH

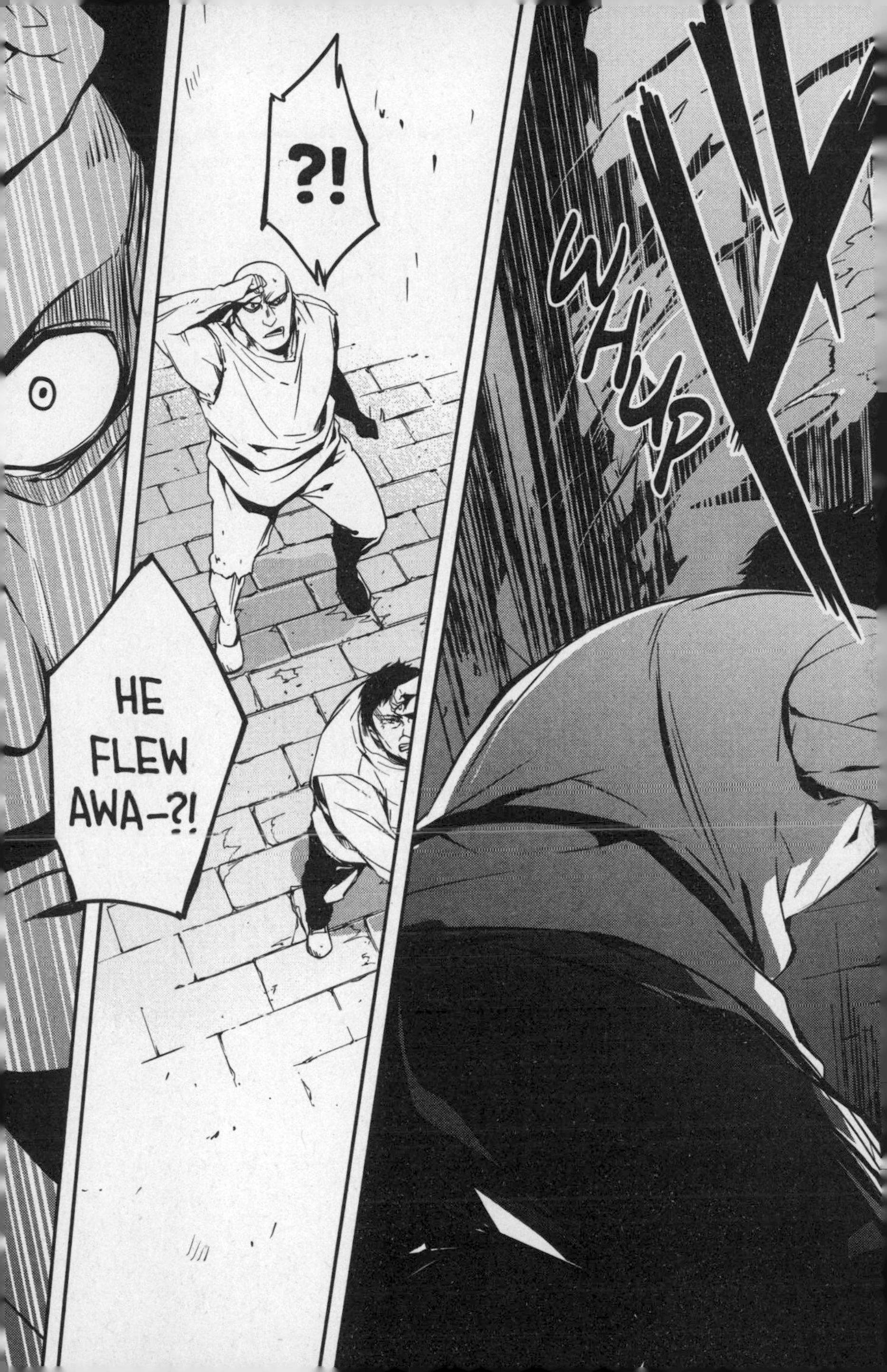
WHUP
?!
HE FLEW AWA-?!

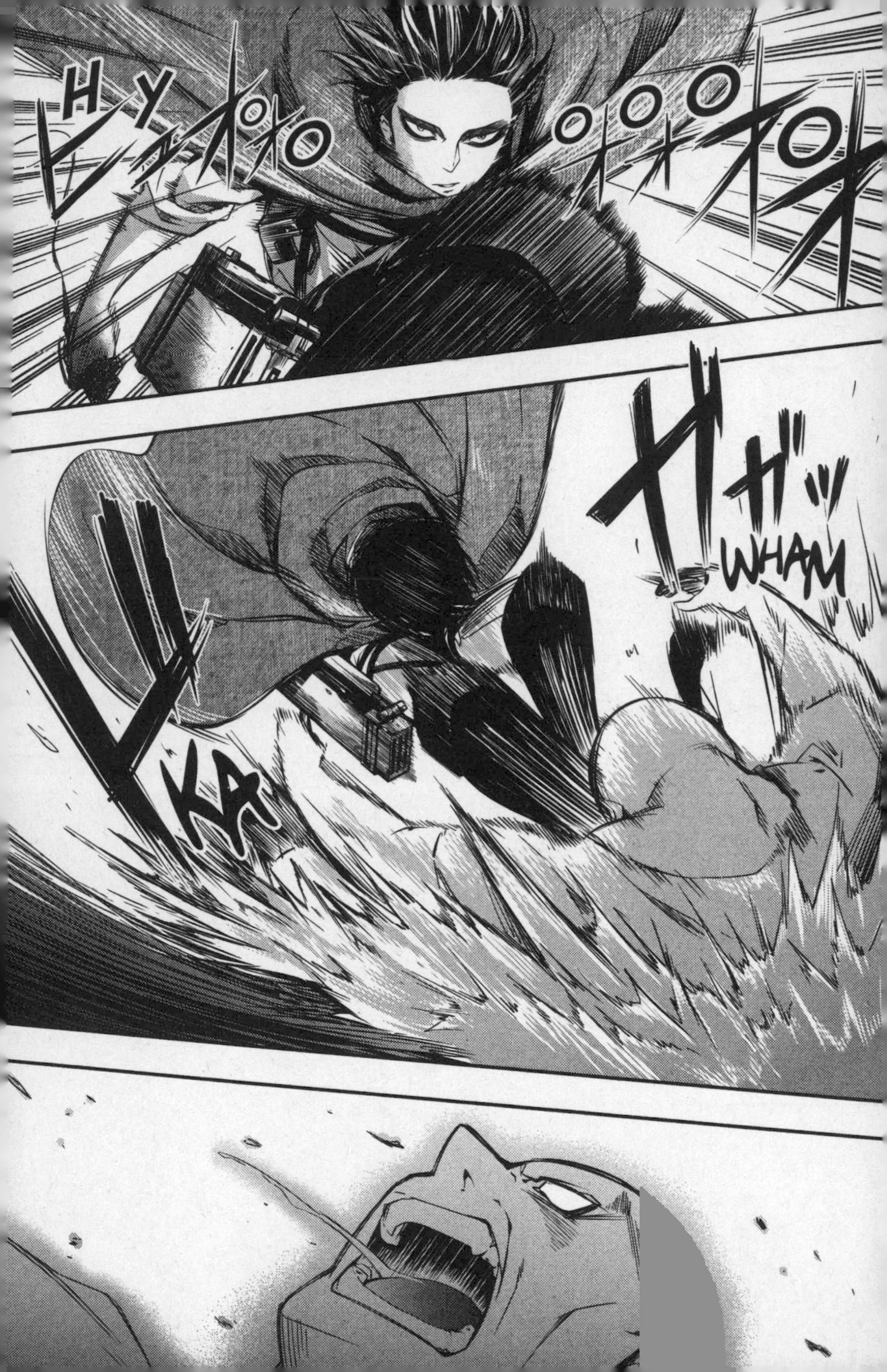
HYOOOOO
WHAM
KA

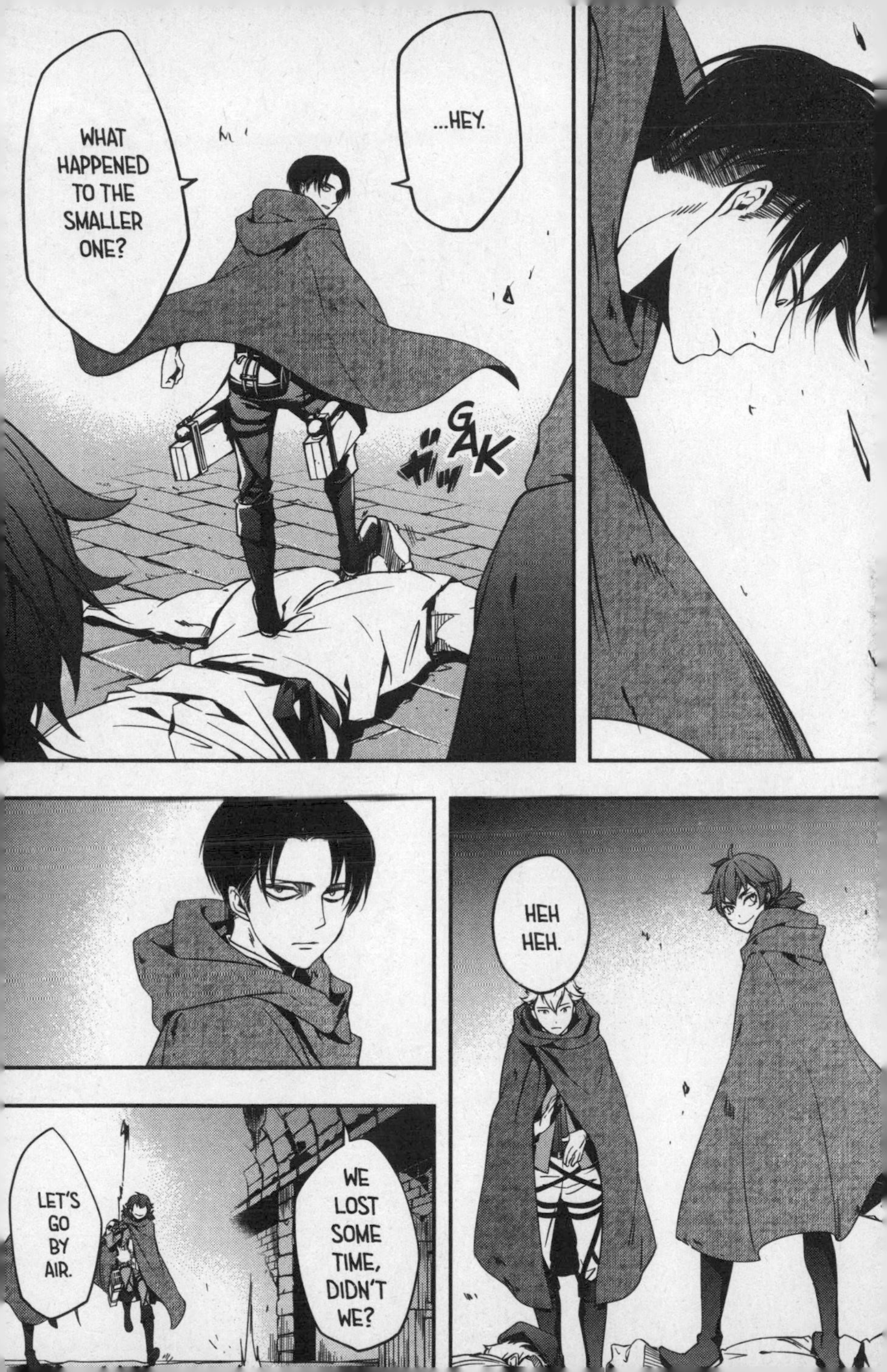
...HEY.
WHAT HAPPENED TO THE SMALLER ONE?
GAK
HEH HEH.
WE LOST SOME TIME, DIDN'T WE?
LET'S GO BY AIR.

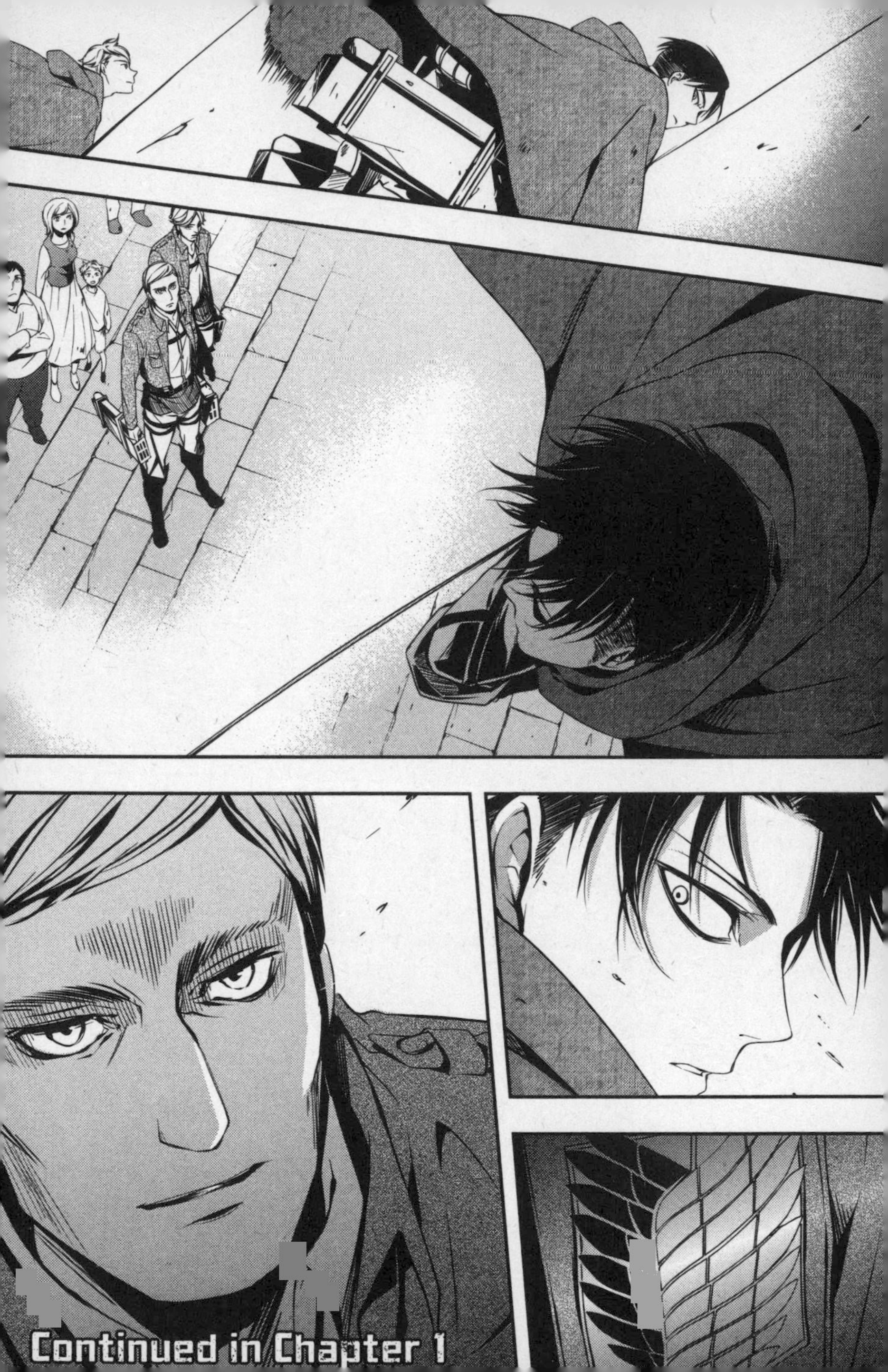
Continued in Chapter 1

CHARACTER SKETCHES

THREE MINOR CHARACTERS

THEY TOLD ME, "GIVE US THREE CHARACTER DESIGNS," MEANING LEVI'S GROUP, BUT I MISUNDERSTOOD, AND THIS WAS THE RESULT. -SURUGA

Levi

FOR LEVI, I WAS ALWAYS CAREFUL TO PRESERVE THE SPIRIT OF THE ORIGINAL. I AM STILL IN TRAINING. THE BESSATSU MAGAZINE EDITOR IN CHARGE OF "ATTACK ON TITAN," BACK, TOLD ME, "HE SHOULD BE SOMEWHAT YOUNGER THAN HE IS NOW, I THINK." SO I TRIED TO MAKE HIM LOOK YOUNGER. HE'S THE TYPE OF CHARACTER WHO DOESN'T SHOW A LOT OF EMOTION ON HIS FACE, SO I OFTEN WORRIED OVER WHAT EXPRESSION HE SHOULD BE WEARING AT DIFFERENT TIMES, BUT IN EVERY SCENE HE WAS FUN TO DRAW.

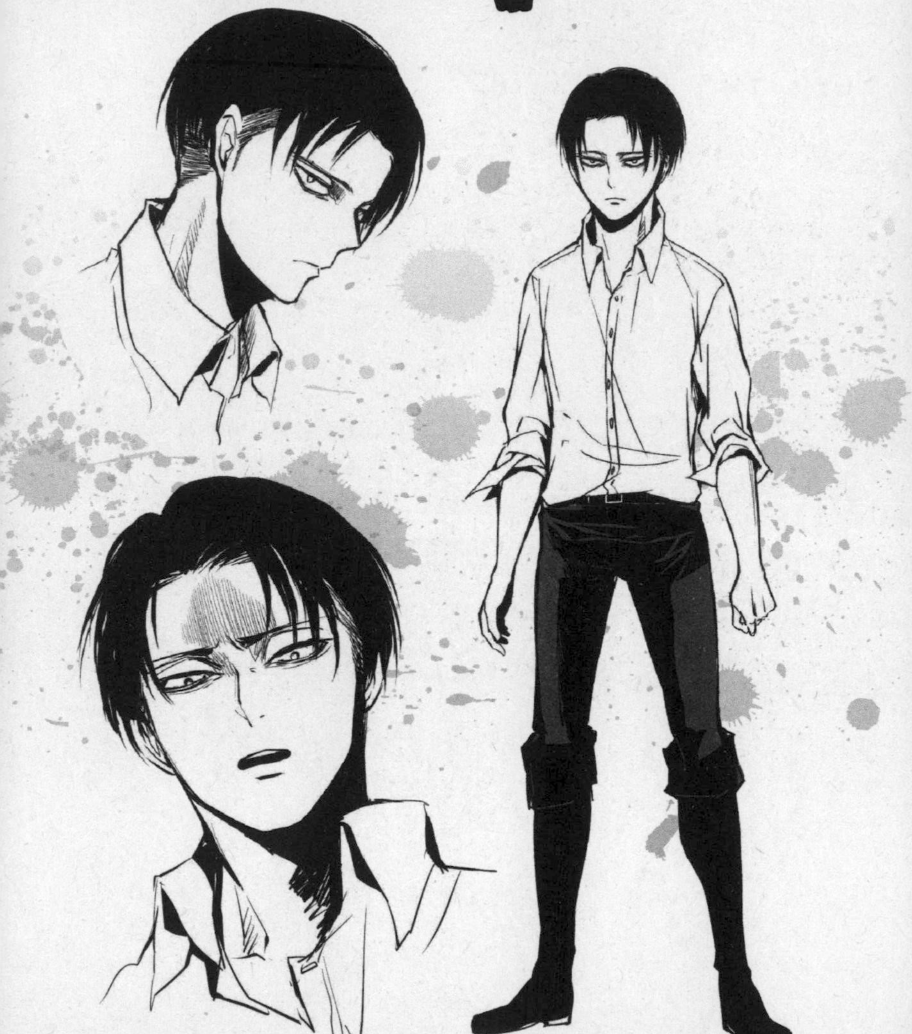

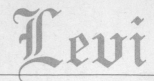

Isabel

THE CHARACTER DESIGN BY NAMANIKU ATK AT NITROPLUS WAS VERY CUTE, SO I AIMED FOR A LIVELY, ENERGETIC GIRL TO BRING THAT CUTENESS OUT. BUT I ALSO ALWAYS KEEP IN MIND THAT THIS IS AN EXPRESSIVE CHARACTER WHOSE STRENGTH EQUALS A MAN'S, AND WHO CAN STAND AGAINST THE TITANS JUST AS WELL.

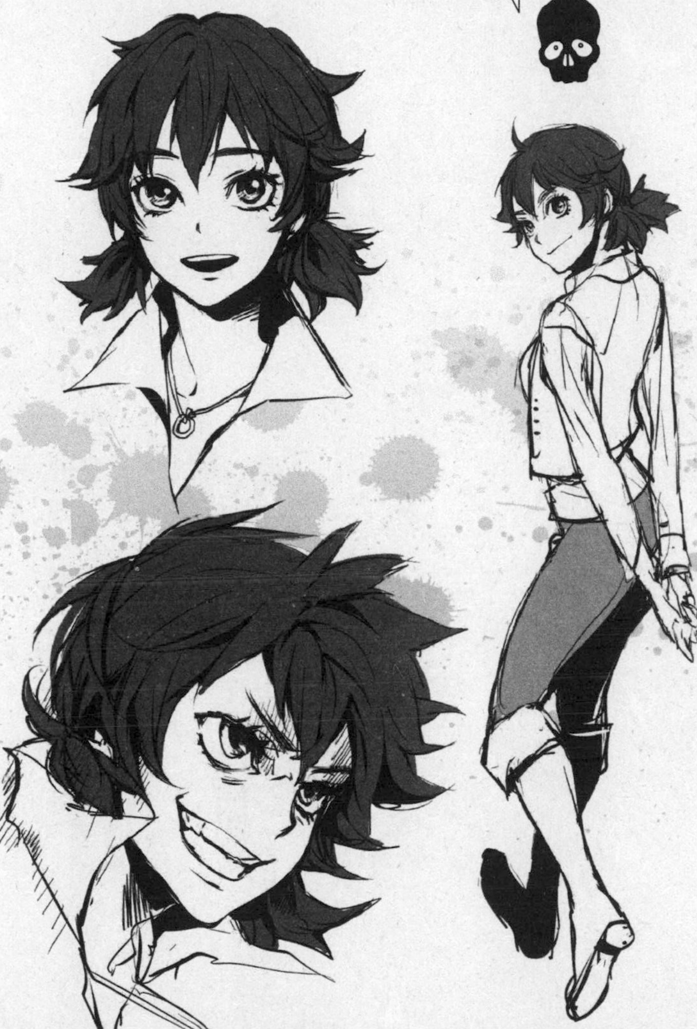

FURLAN WAS ALSO A CHARACTER DESIGNED BY NAMANIKU ATK FROM NITROPLUS. I WAS ABLE TO REPRODUCE HIS HAIRSTYLE UNEXPECTEDLY SMOOTHLY. HIS RECORD IS THAT OF A FORMER GANG LEADER, BUT I PICTURE HIM AS USING BRAINS BEFORE BRAWN. I FELT THAT I WANTED TO GIVE HIM FACIAL CHARACTERISTICS THAT WERE DIFFERENT FROM BOTH LEVI AND ISABEL, SO I WENT THROUGH A LOT OF TRIAL AND ERROR.

Furlan

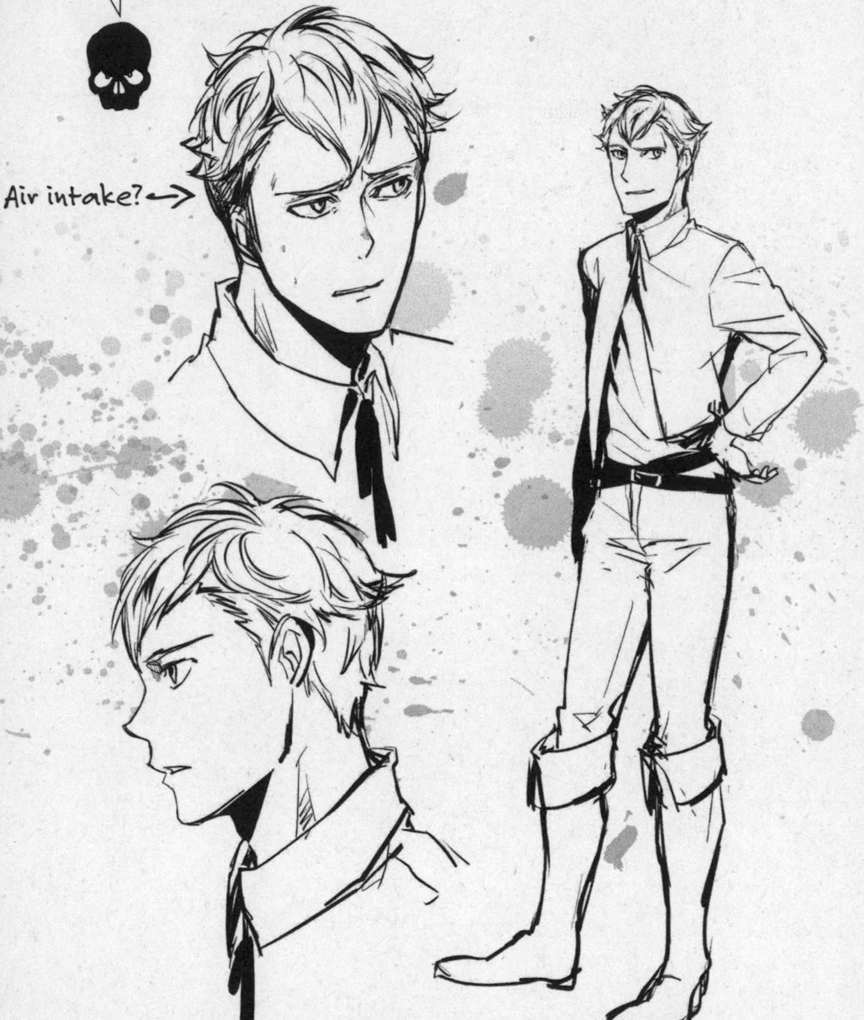
Air intake?

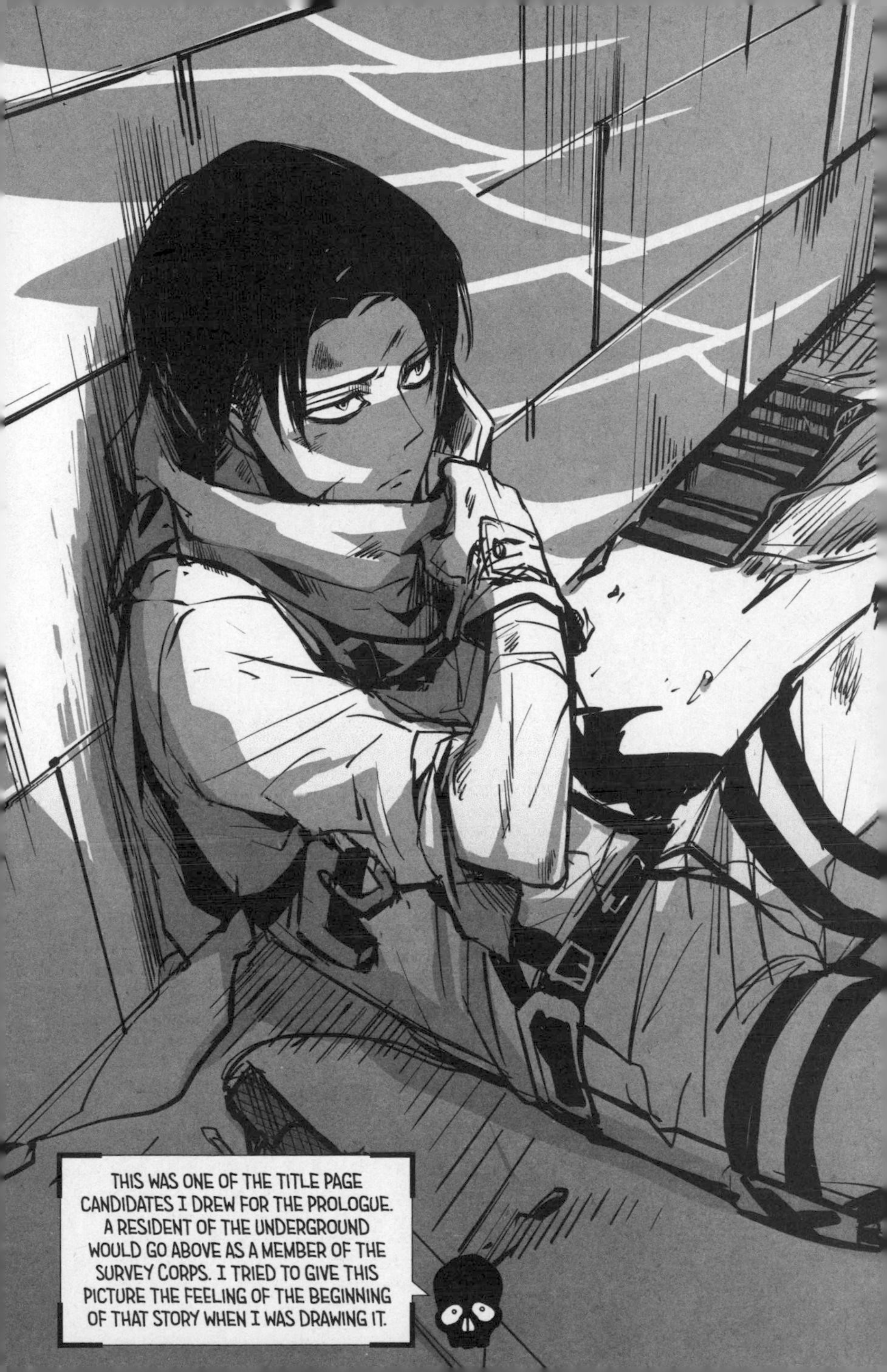
THIS WAS ONE OF THE TITLE PAGE CANDIDATES I DREW FOR THE PROLOGUE. A RESIDENT OF THE UNDERGROUND WOULD GO ABOVE AS A MEMBER OF THE SURVEY CORPS. I TRIED TO GIVE THIS PICTURE THE FEELING OF THE BEGINNING OF THAT STORY WHEN I WAS DRAWING IT.

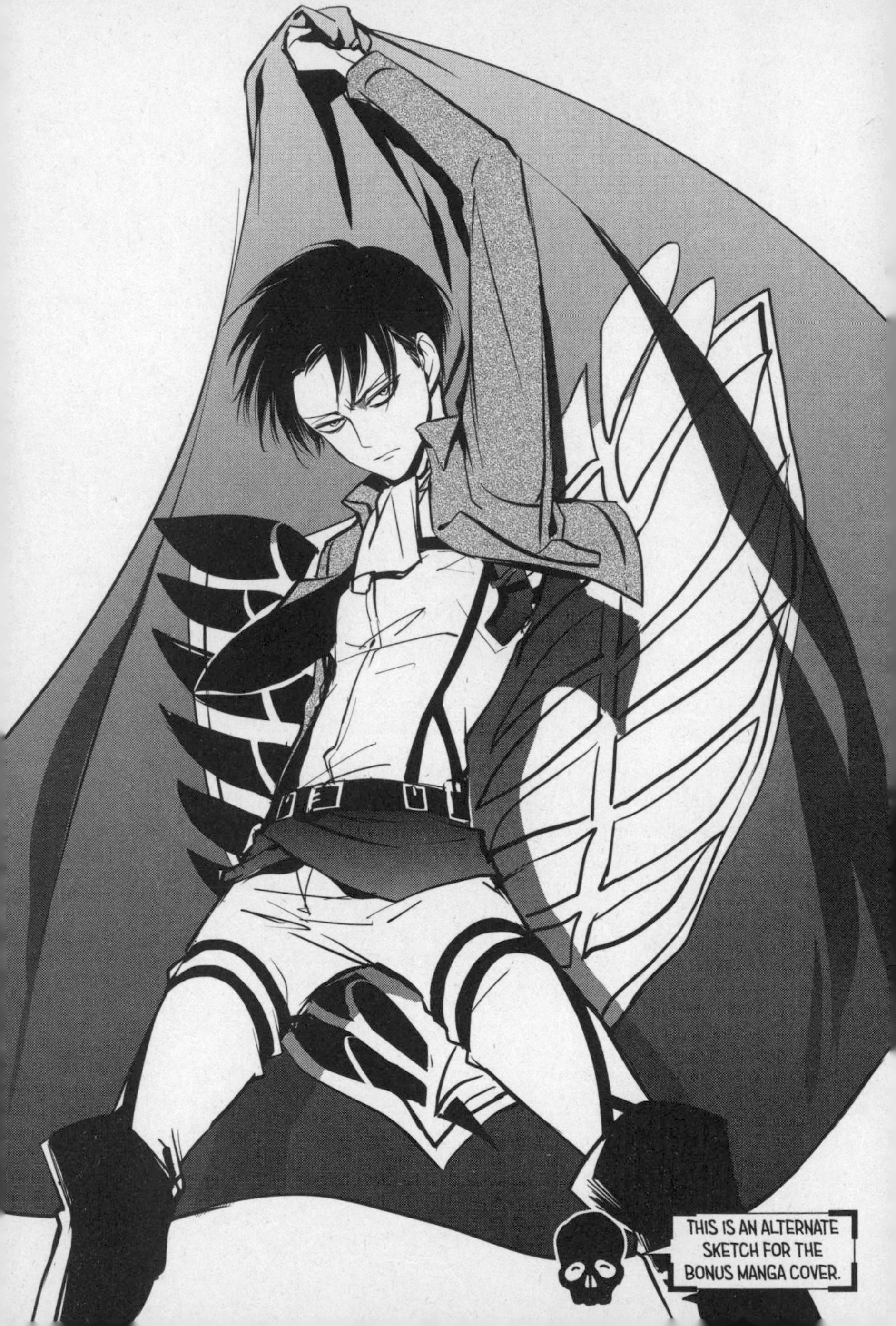
THIS IS AN ALTERNATE SKETCH FOR THE BONUS MANGA COVER.

ATTACK on TITAN
NO REGRETS

DON'T MISS THE MOST ACCLAIMED ACTION MANGA OF 2013!

"Gripping doesn't begin to describe Vinland Saga. 5 stars."
—ICv2

"Deeply engrossing... If you have any interest at all in Vikings, the Medieval period, or pirates, this is not a series you want to miss."
—Anime News Network

"The art is gorgeous, a combination of beautiful cartooning and realistic backgrounds. Yukimura is also a master of pacing, both in frenetic battle scenes and charged emotional moments."
—Faith Erin Hicks, *Friends With Boys*

"For those who love Berserk, you'll love this too... Worth the long wait."
—A Case Suitable for Treatment

"It will be impossible to stop watching this story unfold."
—Japan Media Arts Awards jury

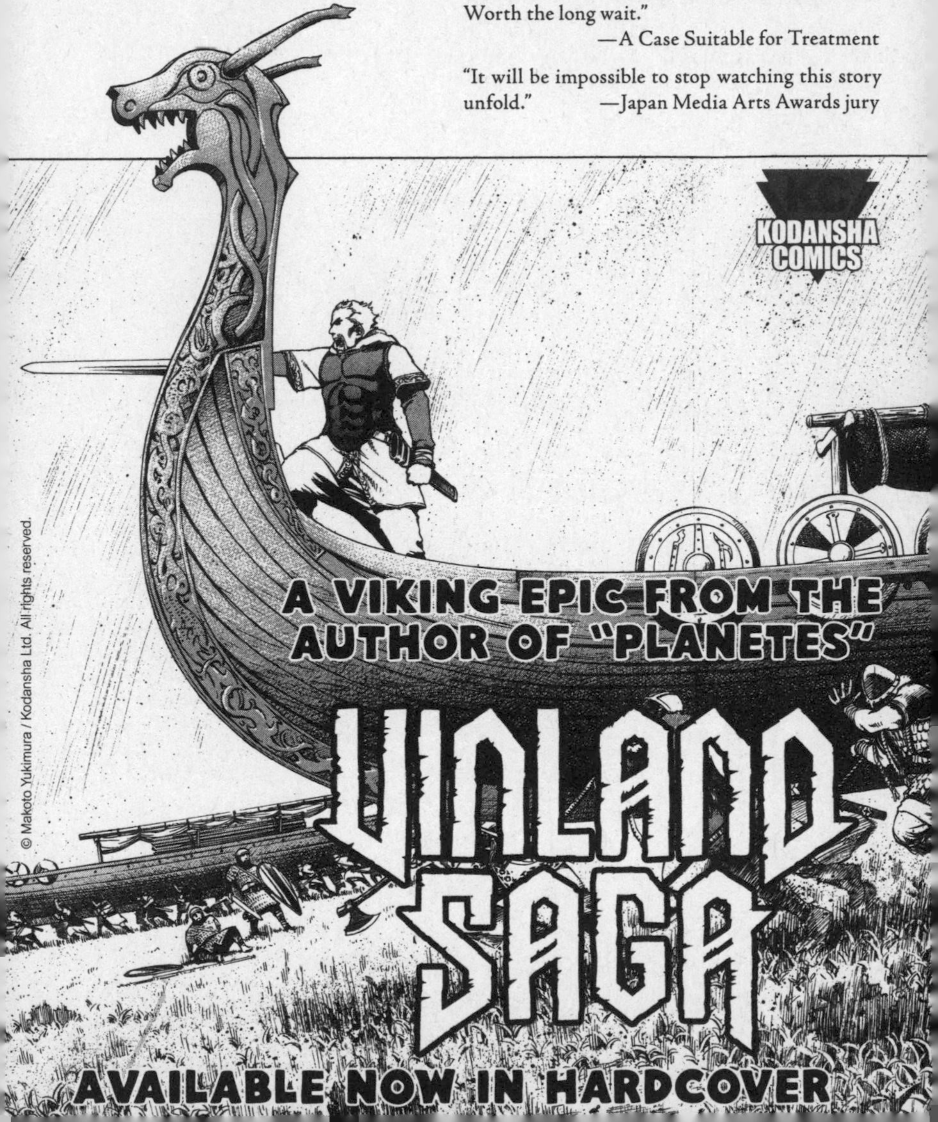

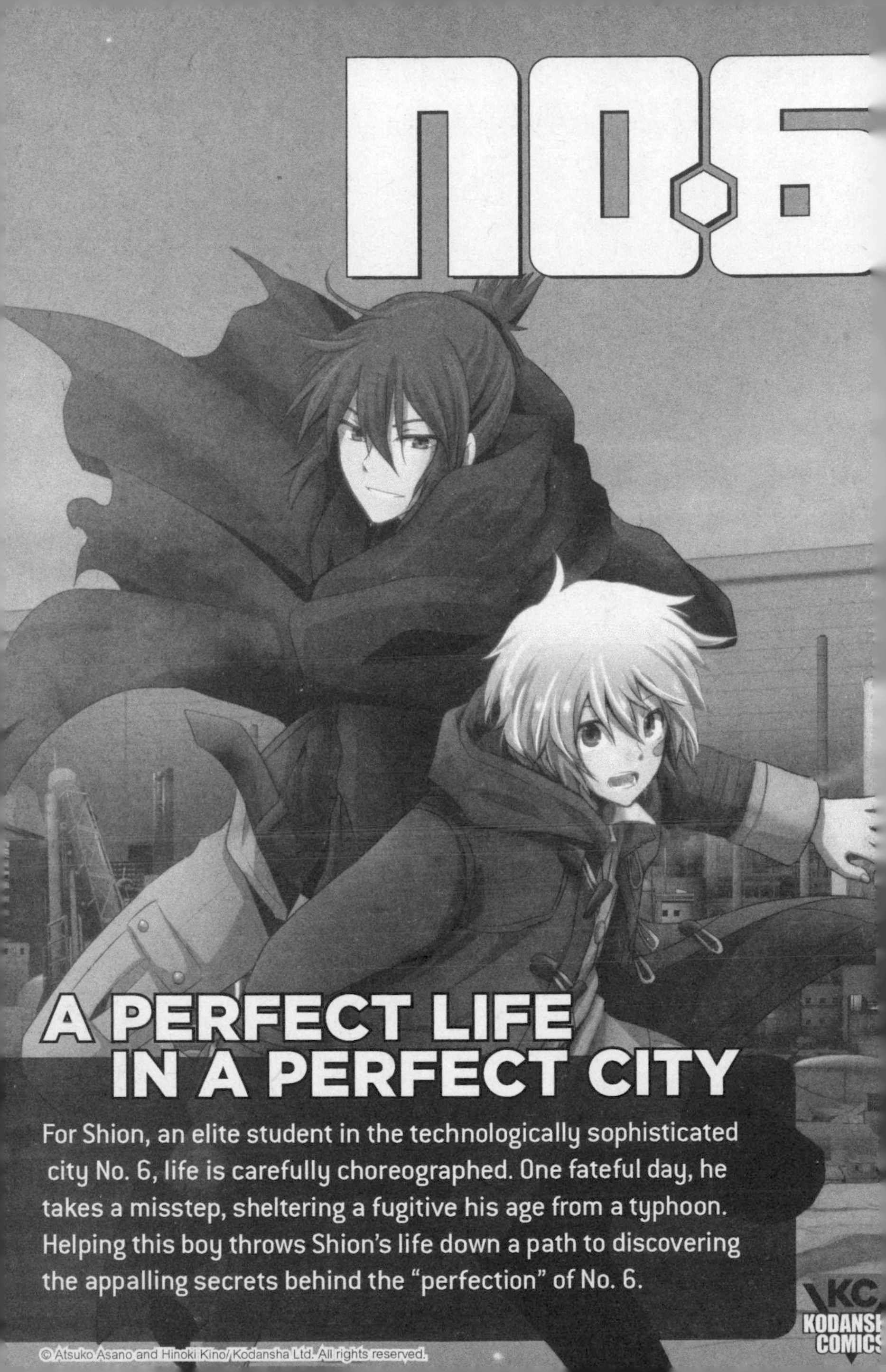
NO.6
A PERFECT LIFE
IN A PERFECT CITY
For Shion, an elite student in the technologically sophisticated city No. 6, life is carefully choreographed. One fateful day, he takes a misstep, sheltering a fugitive his age from a typhoon. Helping this boy throws Shion's life down a path to discovering the appalling secrets behind the "perfection" of No. 6.
KC
KODANSHA COMICS
© Atsuko Asano and Hinoki Kino/Kodansha Ltd. All rights reserved.

Mei Tachibana has no friends — and says she doesn't need them!

But everything changes when she accidentally roundhouse kicks the most popular boy in school! However, Yamato Kurosawa isn't angry in the slightest— in fact, he thinks his ordinary life could use an unusual girl like Mei. But winning Mei's trust will be a tough task. How long will she refuse to say, "I love you"?

A Kodansha Comics Trade Paperback Original
Attack on Titan: No Regrets volume 1 copyright © 2014 Hajime Isayama/
Hikaru Suruga/Kodansha, Ltd./"ATTACK ON TITAN" Production Committee
English translation copyright © 2014 Hajime Isayama/Hikaru Suruga/Kodansha, Ltd./
"ATTACK ON TITAN" Production Committee

Published in the United States by Kodansha Comics, an imprint of
Kodansha USA Publishing, LLC, New York.

Publication rights for this English edition arranged through
Kodansha Ltd, Tokyo.

First published in Japan in 2014 by Kodansha Ltd., Tokyo
as *Shingeki no kyojin kuinaki sentaku*, volume 1.

ISBN 978-1-61262-941-4

Story by Gun Snark (Nitroplus)
Original cover design by Takashi Shimoyama (Red Rooster)

Printed in the United States of America.

www.kodanshacomics.com

9 8 7 6 5 4 3
Translation & Editing: Ben Applegate
Lettering: Steve Wands

STOP!

You are going the *wrong way!*

Manga is a *completely* different type of reading experience.

To start at the *BEGINNING,* go to the *END!*

That's right! Authentic manga is read the traditional Japanese way--from right to left, exactly the opposite of how American books are read. It's easy to follow: just go to the other end of the book, and read each page--and each panel--from the right side to the left side, starting at the top right. Now you're experiencing manga as it was meant to be.